Laurence Fleming is himself one of the 'last children of the Raj'. He is an artist, landscape designer and author of *The English Garden*, *Old English Villages*, *Roberto Burle Marx: A Portrait* and *The Entokil Man: The Life of Harold Maxwell-Lefroy* as well as several novels. He lives in St Leonard's-on-Sea, East Sussex.

Mark Tully is also a last child of the Raj, and returned to India as a journalist. He was the BBC's Indian Bureau Chief for over 20 years. He still lives in New Delhi, and was knighted in 2002.

Last Children of the Raj

To
All the Memsahibs
and to
Jean Fleming and Patience Tully
in particular

Last Children of the Raj

British Childhoods in India

VOLUME I: 1919–1939

Compiled by
Laurence Fleming

Introduction by
Mark Tully

Dexter Haven Publishing
LONDON

Paperback edition first published 2016 by
Dexter Haven Publishing
Curtain House
134–146 Curtain Road
London
EC2A 3AR

Original hardback edition first published 2004 by Radcliffe Press Ltd

ISBNs   Volume 1: 978-1-903660-20-1
         Volume 2: 978-1-903660-21-8

A full CIP record for this book is available from the British Library

Typeset in Caslon by Dexter Haven Associates Ltd, London
Printed and bound in Sweden by ScandBook

Contents

Acknowledgments

This book owes its existence to the generosity of:

Mrs Janet Axelrad, Miss Jessica Baker, Mr Philip Banham, Mrs Jane Barclay, Mr Marcus Barclay, Mrs Patricia Bartoszewicz, Mme Paul Beauvais, Mr James Benthall, Mr Patrick Berthoud, Professor John Blandy, Mr Bob Bragg, Captain Peter Broadbent, Mr Barry Bryson, Mrs Ernest Campbell, Mrs Sheila Carmichael, Mrs Noel Cash, Mrs Joan Carter, Mr Bill Charles, Mr Leonard Crosfield, Mrs Ann Davies, Miss Ruth Dear, Mrs Shirley Donald, Mrs Patrick Evans, Lady Egremont, Mr Dan Ferris, Mrs Philip Fielden, Mrs Marion Forward, Mrs William Fleming, Mr Adrian Frith, Mr Patrick Gibson, Mrs John Haddon, Mrs Valerie Harrison, Mrs Andrew Hastings, Mrs E.M. Hedley, Mr Robin Herbert, Mrs John Heyworth, Mrs Betty Higgins, Mrs Sonya Hilton, Miss Gloria Hollins, Mr and Mrs Thomas Inglis, Miss Elizabeth Ireland, Miss Lavender Jamieson, Mr John Judge, Dr Desmond Kelly, Mr and Mrs John Langley, Dr Jonathan Lawley, Mr Jeremy and Miss Jane Lemmon, Mrs Hugh Leslie, Mr John Lethbridge, Mrs Sheila Litt, Mrs Jane Lloyd, Mrs Dorothy Lowes, Mrs W.P.G. Maclachlan, Mr Robin Mallinson, Mr Robert Matthews, Mrs Betsy McCutcheon, Mrs Christopher McDowall, Mr Michael Muller, Mr Malcolm Murphy, Mrs Barbara Norton-Amor, Mme Maurice Nosley, Mr Ian O'Leary, Mr Tony Orchard, Mr John Pakenham-Walsh, Mr Blake Pinnell, Mrs Maeve Reid, Lady Rix, Mrs Lynette Sherwood, Mrs Russell Smallwood, Mr and Mrs John Smith, Mr Paddy Smith, Mr Graham Spencer, Mr Patrick Stevenage, Mr David Thom, Mrs Lorna Thomson, Mrs Yoma Ullman, Mr Francis Valentine, Mrs Janet Valentine, Miss Hilary Virgo, Mrs Ruth Walker, Mrs Margaret White, Mrs Auriol Young and two anonymous donors.

The extracts from *A Memoir of a Childhood in India* by Yoma Crosfield Ullman appear with her permission. Extracts from *The Way It Was* by John Langley appear with his permission. Extracts by Laurence Fleming from *Harrow on the Hooghly* by John Lethbridge appear with his permission. Extracts from *A Railway Family in India* by Patrick Hugh Stevenage appear with his permission. The extract by Zoe Wilkinson from her book *Boxwallahs* on pages 272–273 appears with the permission of her publisher, Michael Russell.

Our warmest thanks are due to Susan Lynn for all her valuable help in the early stages of this project.

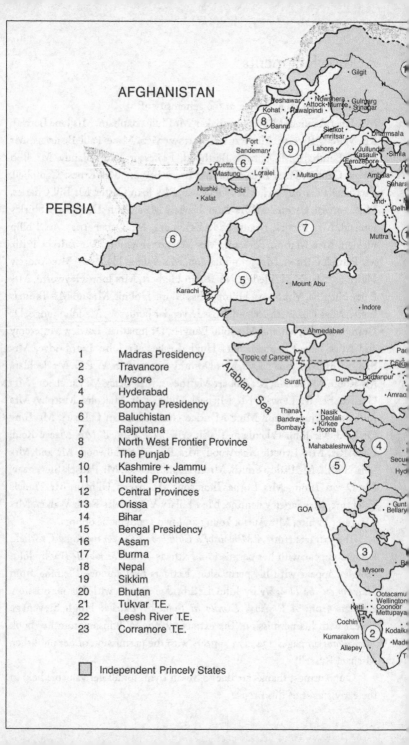

AFGHANISTAN

PERSIA

1	Madras Presidency
2	Travancore
3	Mysore
4	Hyderabad
5	Bombay Presidency
6	Baluchistan
7	Rajputana
8	North West Frontier Province
9	The Punjab
10	Kashmire + Jammu
11	United Provinces
12	Central Provinces
13	Orissa
14	Bihar
15	Bengal Presidency
16	Assam
17	Burma
18	Nepal
19	Sikkim
20	Bhutan
21	Tukvar T.E.
22	Leesh River T.E.
23	Corramore T.E.

Independent Princely States

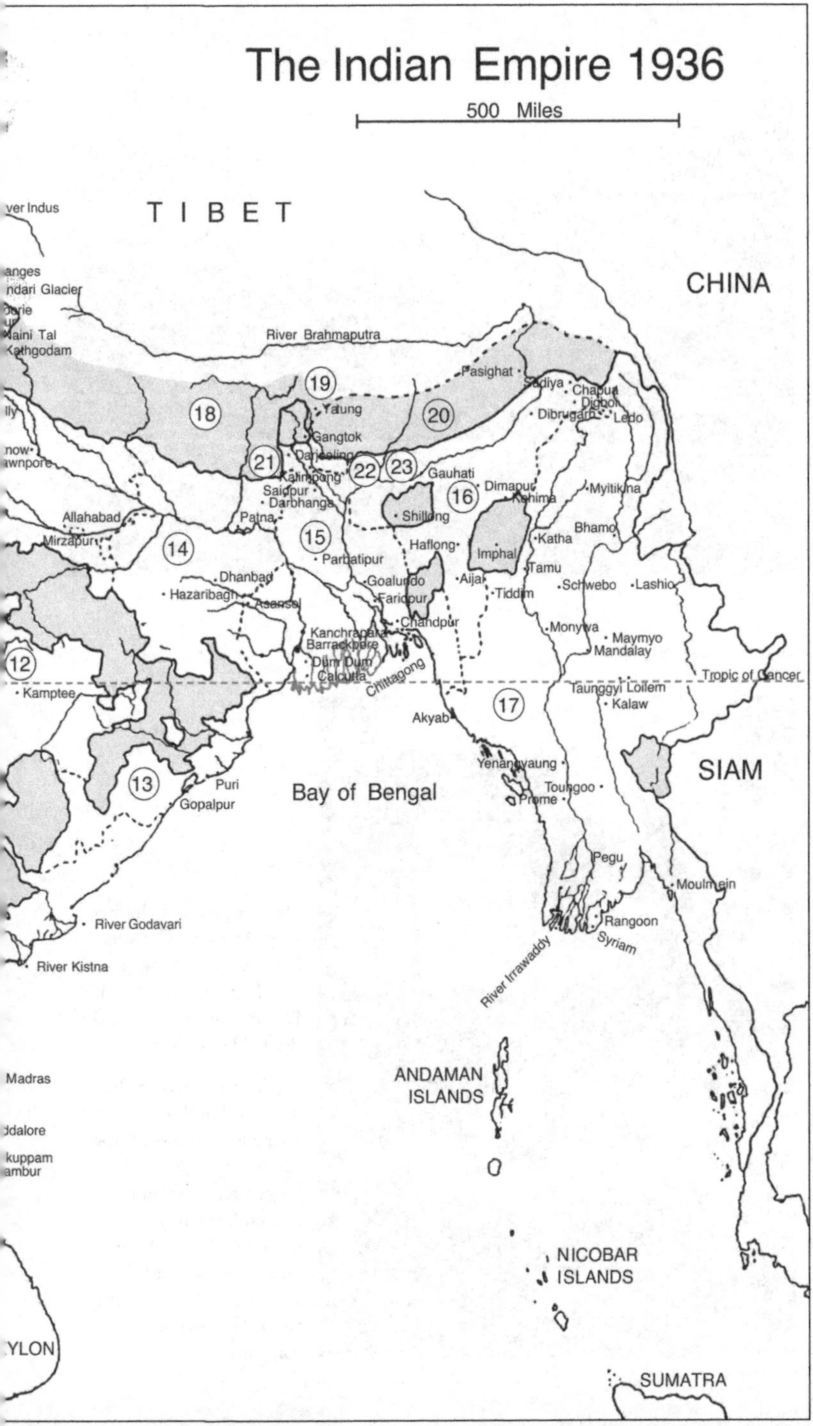

The Indian Empire 1936

500 Miles

TIBET

CHINA

River Brahmaputra

ver Indus

anges
ndari Glacier
oorie
up
Naini Tal
Kathgodam

lly

now
awnpore

Allahabad
Mirzapur

⑫
· Kamptee

⑭
· Dhanbad
· Hazaribagh
Asansol

⑬
Puri
Gopalpur

· River Godavari

· River Kistna

Madras

ddalore

kuppam
ambur

YLON

⑱
⑲
Yatung
· Gangtok
Darjeeling
⑳
Pasighat
Sadiya · Chapui
· Dibrugarh · Digboi
· Ledo
⑪
Kalimpong
⑫ ㉓ Gauhati
⑯ Dimapur
· Kohima · Myitkyina
Saidpur
· Darbhanga
Patna
· Shillong
· Bhamo
⑮
Parbatipur
Haflong
· Katha
Imphal
Goalundo
· Aijal
· Tamu
Faridpur
· Tiddim
· Schwebo · Lashio
Kanchrapara
Barrackpore
Chandpur
· Monywa
· Maymyo
Dum Dum
Calcutta
Chittagong
· Mandalay
Tropic of Cancer
Taunggyi Loilem
· Kalaw
Akyab

SIAM

Bay of Bengal

Yenangyaung ·
· Toungoo ·
Prome ·

· Pegu
· Moulmein

· Rangoon
Syriam

River Irrawaddy

ANDAMAN
ISLANDS

O

NICOBAR
ISLANDS

SUMATRA

above A group of children at St Andrew's Colonial Homes, Kalimpong, now Dr Graham's Homes, with Dr Graham himself on the right. About 1930.

left A small space in the midst of South Park Street Cemetery, into which the surviving plaques and broken tombs from the French Cemetery were moved on its closure in 1979. Carried out by BACSA with sponsorship from the Total petrol company.

The British Raj

Mark Tully

W hen looking back on our parents and the generations before them we must avoid judging them by the lights of our times. For the last children of the Empire this is a particular temptation. To most people now the idea of Empire seems preposterous, and much that our parents stood for at best simple-minded and at worst racialism. Yet a man as intelligent and humane as the former Indian Civil Service, or ICS, officer Philip Mason could write in his evocative history of the Raj, *The Men Who Ruled India*, 'If the British look back on their varied history, the long connection with India will be an achievement that can not be ignored...the achievement itself, whatever the future holds, is surely a matter of pride'. Mason judged himself and his predecessors who administered British India by standards which are eternal, not influenced by changed circumstances, new knowledge and under-standing, or indeed fleeting fashions which do so often affect our judgements. He judged a man 'not by his worst so much as by his best, and in the end not even by his best but by what he aimed at'. That was a principle Christianity taught Philip Mason; we who are tempted by post-imperial guilt to feel ashamed of our parents' achievements have a filial duty to follow that principle whether we are Christians or not.

If we accept our filial duty I think we will find much that is still of great value in the aims of the British in India, much that we can now see was mistaken too. We will find that there were men and women of great goodwill who served India, and those who only went to serve themselves and their vanity. Many Britons went out to the

ICS aiming to ensure equality for all before the law, to be the *mai bhap*, the mother and father of villagers, and to prepare India for independence. As far back as the early nineteenth century, the soldier, diplomat and administrator Mountstuart Elphinstone wrote, 'the most desirable death for us to die should be the improvement of the natives reaching such a pitch as would make it impossible for a foreign nation to retain the government'. At the other end of the Raj Penderel Moon, although awarded the ultimate Oxford accolade, a fellowship of All Souls, forswore the glittering prizes of academia to join the ICS in 1929 because he wanted 'to see the final accomplishment of England's mission in India – namely under her fostering guidance and care to bring India into the scale of free independent nations'. But there were also British administrators who believed 'the natives' would never be able to govern themselves. There were District Officers who ruled without affection for their subjects or care. Some ICS Officers followed the Punjab tradition: they were, according to the description of civil servant John Beames, 'Hard active men in boots and breeches who almost lived in the saddle, worked all day and nearly all night'. Others were little more than *babus*, or clerks, sitting in their offices ensuring that files remained in perpetual motion. There were brave and honourable police officers, but the service as a whole accepted practices unacceptable in Britain, such as torture, and some officers justified this on the basis that they were policing 'inferior' races. There were men who took commissions in the Indian Army to defend an Empire they believed in, and to win that loyalty of Indian soldiers which nurtured proud regimental traditions. There were officers in the same Army who were in India to play polo and stick pigs. There were British businessmen who tried to continue the pillage of the earliest traders in India, and there were businessmen who established and maintained the principles of accountancy, banking and law necessary for commerce and industry to be managed in a modern, equitable manner. There were missionaries who were religious bigots, despising India's ancient faiths, and clergy who studied those faiths with sympathy, striving to reconcile the exclusive claims of Christianity with the pluralism they discovered in Eastern philosophy.

What about their achievements? Again there were pluses and minuses. It could be said that the ultimate ambition of Elphinstone and Moon was achieved. For well over fifty years now India has not just governed itself, Indians have governed themselves. Except for the short eighteen months of Indira Gandhi's Emergency, Indians have retained the reins of power in their own hands. They have not allowed an ambitious general, or unscrupulous politician, to snatch them away. Much of the credit for this has to go to the apolitical tradition the British bequeathed to the Indian Army. But that tradition has not been upheld in Pakistan, nor did it prevent military interventions in the early days of Bangladesh.

Britain also succeeded in its ambition of uniting India, but ultimately it could not hold it together. Whatever can now be said about the pros and cons of Partition, no one can deny that India and Pakistan were hacked apart with a butcher's cleaver, rather than surgically separated. Before Partition, communal riots occurred more frequently in British India than in the states governed by the princes. During the dreadful carnage of 1947, only the Nawab of the small state of Malerkotla, situated in the heart of East Punjab, provided a safe haven for Muslims fleeing from murderous attacks by Sikhs and Hindus.

Partition was part of the price that the subcontinent has paid for the way democracy developed under British tutelage. The cynics would say that the creation of separate Muslim and Hindu electorates was a deliberate strategy to divide and rule. Others would argue it represented a democratic concern for the rights of a minority. Whoever is right, the Oxford Historian Tapan Raychauduri has no doubt that the steps the British Government took towards establishing democracy did divide Hindus and Muslims. He has written, 'the view that Hindus and Muslims are two distinct political communities with separate and compelling political aspirations that are the products of constitutional arrangements and executive policies of the colonial state is now widely accepted.' What is both ironic and tragic in today's India is that the very people who objected and still do object most strongly to the two-nation theory, the Hindu nationalists who yearn for the reunion of Mother India, are now reviving it. To fuel Hindu anger, they accuse Indian Muslims of being Pakistanis at heart.

The officers of the ICS and the Police believed they were establishing the principle of equality before the law among a people who had known no laws. But that was an oversimplification. There were laws and local judicial customs before we arrived, and the Police system set up by the British was not entirely dissimilar to the administration of law and order under the Moghuls. What's more, our legal system was far from foolproof. In his novel, *Strangers in India*, which was a disguised critique of the Raj, Penderel Moon described a young ICS officer surrounded by 'myriad' Indian magistrates who 'daily spent hours in their courts solemnly recording word for word the evidence of illiterate peasants, knowing full well that ninety percent of it was false'. False evidence is one of the less admirable legacies of the British Raj which survives to this day. I remember a Delhi magistrate complaining to the Police prosecutor, 'I know that you bring paid witnesses before me every day, but do you always have to bring the same ones?' It has been argued that it would have been better if the British had left villagers to try villagers in their traditional courts.

We provided an administration which managed to unite and hold together a vast and disparate subcontinent with remarkably little coercion. We brought order where often there had been anarchy. We formed a partnership with Indians without whom we could never have administered India. But the civil service was hierarchical and rule-bound, with everyone knowing the letter of the law and yet all too often, for a consideration, being prepared to bend it. Dishonesty was not a problem among the senior cadres of the civil service and the Police, but they were not able to stamp out corruption among their juniors. Moon also had a low opinion of the administrative systems, describing them as 'inferior replicas of unsuitable English institutions'.

Earlier, Lord Curzon, as Viceroy, had complained of the paper wasted by his administrators, saying, 'thousands of pages, occupying hundreds of hours of valuable time, are written year upon year, by score upon score of officers, to the obfuscation of their intellects, and the detriment of their official work.' This administrative system may not have been as bad as was made out. It did survive the disruption caused by Partition, law and order was restored, an unprecedented influx of refugees was accommodated, the princely states were persuaded that independence was not a workable option. But it has certainly not proved suitable for administering the construction of a new India. Files still go 'round and round like the diurnal revolutions of the earth', as Curzon also complained, tying India up in a straitjacket woven from red tape, and preventing Indians realising their full potential.

Historians argue over the impact of the Raj on India's economy, but it is beyond dispute that we governed India during the nineteenth-century industrial revolution, and we decided how that revolution would change India. What that meant to India is best illustrated by the railways. Those railways owe their existence to the vision of Lord Dalhousie. It was British engineers, and of course the Indians working for them, who laid tracks in hostile, mosquito-ridden jungles, bridged rivers never crossed before, climbed through mountains previously thought impassable, and constructed stations which were some of the greatest cathedrals of the railway age. Karl Marx had thought that 'the steam locomotive would power an industrial revolution in India', but it didn't, because the engines and most of the other requirements of the railways were always manufactured in Britain. The economic historian John Hurd wrote, 'India's loss from the purchase policies of the railways was not limited to her lack of progress in developing heavy industry. She also failed to reap the benefits of the spread effects to industry which would have occurred, instead the spread effects stimulated the British economy.' Marx rightly believed that Indians were quite capable of bringing about their own industrial revolution. He said, 'The great mass of the Indian people possesses a great industrial energy, is well fitted to accumulate capital, and remarkable for a mathematical clearness of head, and talent for figures and exact sciences'. The IT revolution which is taking place in India confirms Marx's judgement and leads me at least to wonder where India would be if Indians had been free to use their talents to industrialise on their own terms. Japan industrialised without having a Western colonial nanny, with results very different to the achievements of the British Raj.

But in the end surely we can be proud of the best of the Raj. There was nobility in that ambition which fired Elphinstone and Moon, no matter how condescending it might now seem. We did lay the foundations of the largest democracy the world has ever known. What's more we did that in partnership with Indians, which is perhaps why we left behind great goodwill. In more than thirty years of living in India it has always been an advantage to me, not a disadvantage, to have been born a child of the Raj. Teaching English did not just produce the army of clerks required by Macaulay. Men like Swami Vivekanand who brought Indian theology to the attention of the West, and the Nobel-prize-winning polymath – poet, writer, philosopher and artist – Rabindranath Tagore were both products of the remarkable nineteenth-century Bengali renaissance in which Western rationalism mingled with Eastern philosophy. Finally, if we are to judge the Raj by the imperialism of those times, Indians do have reason to be glad that they were not ruled by any of the other colonial powers.

Glossary

almira . . . . wardrobe
amah. . . . . Burmese nanny
anna . . . . Indian coin, 16 to a rupee
armsuth. . . . . dried mango pulp
ashram . . . . place of religious retreat
avatar . . . . incarnation
ayah . . . . Indian nanny
ayngyi, anghi. . . . . Burmese woman's blouse, jacket
babu . . . . Indian clerk
babul. . . . . a tree, *Acacia arabica*
bagh . . . . garden
baksheesh . . . . gratuity, tip
balloowallah . . . . owner of dancing bears
bandicoot . . . . kind of large rat
bandobast . . . . any kind of arrangement
baniyas . . . . traders or shopkeepers
barfi, burfi. . . . . kind of sweet
basha. . . . . hut of woven bamboo
basti, bustee . . . . village
begum. . . . . wife or mother of a Maharajah
bhil . . . . marsh
bhiljeewallah. . . . . electrician
bhindi. . . . . okra, ladies' fingers
bhisti. . . . . water-carrier
bhotiya . . . . Buddhist farmer, originally Tibetan
bhutta . . . . maize
bidi, biri . . . . small, pungent cigarette
bistra. . . . . bedding-roll
bobbachee, bovachee, bochi . cook
boda . . . . bullock calf, bait for tigers
boxwallah . . . . travelling tradesman; European in commerce
bulbul . . . . brightly coloured bird
bungi. . . . . labourers' yokes for carrying loads
burkha . . . . tent-like covering for Muslim women

burra . . . . senior, large

butties, hart butties . . . . hurricane lamps

cantonment . . . . urban area occupied only by military and Police

cha, gurram cha . . . . tea, hot tea

chapatti . . . . unleavened bread

chaprassi . . . . office messenger, peon

charpoy . . . . string bed on wooden frame

chatti . . . . earthenware water pot

chenar . . . . the Oriental Plane, *Platanus orientalis*

chibbutra, chabuttra . . . . raised platform in the garden

chikor . . . . small partridge

chini . . . . sugar

chinkara . . . . four-horned antelope

chokra . . . . boy or youngster

chota . . . . small

chota hazri . . . . early morning tea

chota peg . . . . small whisky

chowkidar . . . . night watchman

chuckla . . . . cobbler, shoemaker

chula . . . . kind of brazier

chula purdah . . . . Muslim seclusion for wives

chummery . . . . house shared by two or more bachelors

chunna . . . . kind of pea

coolie . . . . porter or workman, labourer

curriga, nay curriga . . . . can do, can not do

cutcha . . . . inferior

dah . . . . small sword, Burmese

dahl . . . . lentil sauce or soup

dak . . . . post

dandi . . . . litter carried on shoulders

deodar . . . . a tree, *Cedrus deodara*

dhirzi, durzi . . . . itinerant tailor

dhobi . . . . washerman, laundryman

dhooli, doli, doolie . . . . shoulder-borne litter; fly-proof cage

dhoti . . . . single-strip garment worn by Hindu men,
with one end pulled through the legs to
form 'trousers'

dhurrie, dhurry . . . . cotton rug

Diwali. . . . . Hindi Festival of Lights

doodwallah . . . . milkman

Durbar . . . . Jubilee, Coronation, Wedding celebration of Kings, Maharajahs

durwan . . . . night watchman, messenger

fakir . . . . Hindu holy man, ascetic

feringhees . . . . strangers, foreigners, 'from beyond the pale'

gharry . . . . horse-drawn carriage

ghat. . . . . step, as down to a river; also steep hillside, as in Eastern or Western Ghats

ghee . . . . clarified butter

ghur . . . . raw molasses syrup

ghusal-khana . . . . bathroom

godowns . . . . store rooms

gooli, goolie . . . . a ball

goolie dunda. . . . . a game, tip-cat

gulab jaman . . . . kind of pudding

gully-gully man. . . . . conjuror coming on board at Port Said

gunny . . . . jute

hajji. . . . . one who had made the pilgrimage to Mecca

havildar. . . . . NCO in Indian Army

hookahs . . . . Indian pipes

howdah. . . . . canopied seat on elephant's back

hulwa . . . . kind of sweet

jamadar, jemadar. . . . . sweeper; also NCO in Indian Army

jampani. . . . . 'dandi' carrier

jellabee . . . . kind of sweet

jheel, gheel . . . . reedy lakes, marshes

jutewallahs . . . . Europeans in the jute trade, frequently Scottish

kabaddi. . . . . a game, similar to Tom Tiddler's Ground

kalassi . . . . boatman

kansama, khansama . . . . cook

karezes . . . . underground wells, joined

kebabwallah . . . . seller of kebabs

khabari . . . . thief

khana, khanna. . . . . dinner, food in general; also a room
khitmagar . . . . butler
kukri. . . . . Gurkha fighting knife
kul-kul . . . . kind of sweet
langur . . . . kind of monkey
lascars . . . . Indian crew on India-bound liners
lathi . . . . long, heavy baton, metal-tipped
layhee . . . . flour-and-water paste
lotha . . . . clay water pot
ludoo . . . . kind of sweet
lungyi, longgyi . . . . long 'skirt' worn by Burmese men
machan. . . . . wooden observation platform at a tiger
                                        shoot
mahout. . . . . elephant rider
maidan . . . . park or large meadow, open space
maither. . . . . sweeper
makan. . . . . butter
mali. gardener
mangowallahs. . . . . seller, sometimes grower, of mangoes
marg . . . . garden
masalchi, malchi . . . . washer up
mehterani . . . . sweeper
mela . . . . festival, celebration, party
moochie . . . . leather worker, cobbler
moonshi, munshi . . . . clerk, writer, teacher, esp. of language
muleteers . . . . mule riders, owners
mullah. . . . . Islamic priest
murghi, moorghi. . . . . chicken
mynah. . . . . a bird that could be trained to speak
naan . . . . kind of bread
nappy, nappit . . . . barber
nawabs . . . . lords
neem. . . . . a tree, *Melia indica*
neilghai, nilgai . . . . kind of deer
ngapi. . . . . dried fish, Burmese
nimbu pani . . . . fresh lime juice and water
nullah . . . . ditch or stream

numdah . . . . small white Kashmiri rug

pan, pahn . . . . betel-leaves chewed as a stimulant

pandal. . . . . flower arch of welcome

pani. . . . . water

paniwallah . . . . water-carrier, washer-up

parata . . . . kind of bread

peon . . . . office messenger

pice. . . . . Indian coins, 4 to an anna

pinjamwallah . . . . one who renewed stuffing in pillows and
mattresses

poongyi. . . . . Burmese Buddhist priest, monk

popadams . . . . crisp pancakes

puggri, puggaree . . . . cloth bound turban

puja. . . . . Hindu festival

pukka . . . . superior

punkah . . . . ceiling fan

punkahwallah . . . . punkah operator

purdah . . . . lit. curtain, Muslim seclusion of women

pwe. . . . . Burmese celebration, festival, party

rajahs . . . . lords, titled landowners

roti . . . . bread

sadhu . . . . Hindu holy man

sahib-log. . . . . principally: the British in India

sari . . . . Indian woman's garment, one long strip
cunningly arranged

shamiyana, shamayana . . . . . very large tent

Sherpa . . . . race from high Himalayas, principally Nepal

shikar . . . . hunt, usually for tiger

shikara . . . . long, elegant Kashmiri boat

shola . . . . woodland, large copse

sirdar. . . . . in charge of porters, travel arrangements

subadhar . . . . NCO in Indian Army

suttee . . . . burning of Hindu widows

syce. . . . . groom

tamasha. . . . . any kind of party

tatti, chatti . . . . matting or slatted blinds against the sun

thaka, tikki, tikka, gharry . . . small horse-drawn carriage

thana. . . . . Police station
tonga. . . . . small horse-drawn carriages
tongawallah . . . . tonga driver
topee. . . . . pith helmet worn by all Europeans
towdu . . . . rice husks, rice chaff
tum tum . . . . horse-drawn trap
tussore. . . . . kind of silk
waler. . . . . kind of horse
wallum . . . . a boat
Yuvaraj . . . . heir to a Maharajah
zebus. . . . . Indian cattle

I

Madras

The Presidency of Madras was the southernmost of the three British Presidencies in India, and it was very large, extending from one side of the peninsula to the other. It was almost entirely agricultural, occupying 71 per cent of the population, and its principal products were rice, millet, sugar and coconuts; but cotton, coffee, rubber, tobacco and tea were also grown. Its industries were nearly all connected with these products, although there were also important railway works.

It had three great rivers, rising in the Western Ghats and flowing eastwards; the Godavari, the Kistna and the Cauvery, and there were huge irrigation projects associated with each one. It had no natural harbours but an artificial deep-water one was completed in 1927, at the city of Madras. The Madras and Southern Mahratta Railway was the most extensive, with the South Indian Railway servicing the extreme south; and a broad-gauge railway connected Madras and Calcutta.

The population was overwhelmingly Hindu – about 88 per cent – and the principal languages were Tamil and Telugu, with Malayalam and Kanarese a long way behind.

The city of Madras dates from 1640, with the foundation of Fort St George, and a chequered history was to follow, their chief antagonists being the Moghuls, the Mahratta and the French; but the British remained in control after 1762. It had an Anglican Cathedral, a university dating from 1857, and a great many schools and colleges of various kinds. St Thomas Apostle died there on St Thomas's Mount in AD 72.

ELIZABETH IRELAND

Along with his father and brother, my father worked 'in sugar', both in India and in South Africa. In 1915 he joined Parry & Co. (Managing Agents for East India Distilleries & Sugar Factories Ltd) as Confectionery Manager at their Nellikuppam, South Arcot, branch. Nellikuppam is 28 miles south of Madras on the mainline to Tuticorin. The station was probably built to meet the needs of the factory, and a spur line ran the half-mile or so to the actual sugar mill. Most of the rolling equipment came from Glasgow.

He worked from 7 until 9 a.m. and then had breakfast. Then again from 10 to 12, when he had 'tiffin'. Between 12.30 and 2 he would rest, along with everyone else at the factory. Then again from 2.15 until 4.30. It would be dark around six o'clock. My father took early retirement in 1937 due to ill health, and one of my greatest treasures is the farewell address given to him by the Indian Staff of the Confectionery Department when he left. It is printed in blue, on pink silk, by the Saraswati Press, Tirupapuliyur, and is dated 16 May 1937:

John Ireland Esquire

Nellikuppam
Sir,

We the members of the Indian staff attached to the Confectionery Department, E.I.D. & S.F. Ltd., Nellikuppam, wish to take this opportunity of approaching you with a few words of farewell on the eve of your departure from India. We are indeed deeply moved at the thought that you have to part from us after staying in our midst for such a long time.

In the early part of 1915 you entered the service as the Confectionery Manager when you endeared yourself to one and all by your kind disposition. This department was then about 50 strong. Ever since the reins of the administration of the Confectionery Department fell into your hands you have spared neither pains nor labour in the assiduous discharge of your duties. Among the many improvements you have made under your regime, we wish to single out a few, namely the installation of up to date machinery to increase the out turn to meet the heavy demands of the Confectionery on one side and with easy, quick and less fear in the manufacture by the labourers on the other. Though competition in the market is strong the new varieties produced by you have not only driven out competition but also increased the muster of employees which stands today at 326.

We feel nothing but admiration for the unbounded energy shown by you in all directions. The many qualities of head and heart which you possess made you the favourite of all and your chivalrous disposition has won for you immense popularity. To crown all, your patience, a rare virtue which is possessed by very few people, has earned for you golden opinions of all who came in contact with you.

Once again, we wish to give expression to our genuine feelings of regret that we have to part from you. But the regret is palliated by the knowledge that you are going back to your native land to repose your wearied limbs and enjoy happiness in the company of your beloved wife and daughter. May you, Mrs Ireland and your beloved daughter be long spared to enjoy health, happiness and prosperity. We request you to convey our best wishes to Mrs Ireland who left us a few years ago and hope you will ever remember us, amongst whom you have spent so large a portion of your life. We wish you a Bon Voyage.

The company provided Club facilities (for 13 Europeans) and if wives wanted to go out at night – say, for dinner – a *mali* became a *peon* and walked beside them carrying an oil lamp. There were billiards, cards, bar, UK periodicals. The company also provided two good tennis courts.

There was (in my day) a branch car, a Chevrolet, which could be used by staff (pecking order prevailed!), driver provided. The leather seats had loose covers of khaki drill, changed daily, to cope with perspiring passengers. Children could play in the gardens, around the steps/verandahs of the Club, but were not allowed inside.

We saw sugar cane planted, irrigated, cut and brought in bullock bandies for crushing in the sugar mill. A tour of the factory was an education, even for a small girl.

In Nellikuppam we ate curry and rice in some form every day – meat, vegetables, dahl (not popular), fish (seldom, as it could be tainted); chutney and poppadams were favoured side dishes. A pudding which remains memorable was malabar – a sago mould eaten with black treacle and coconut milk. Fresh fruit, paw paw, mango, pomegranate, passion fruit, tree tomatoes, limes (much used in drinks), oranges and plantains were regular fare. No fresh water was ever drunk. Soda was consumed in vast quantities.

Housing was provided by the company. Bungalows (all housing was so named) were spacious and, within the restraints of climate and materials, comfortable. There were no passageways, rooms led off one another. All floors were cement, red or grey – even the baths were brick-built, covered with cement. Always a wide verandah back and front (with bamboo *tattis*). Our bungalow was a semi-detached two-storey (somewhat palatial-looking) affair. True, it had only four main rooms, each opening on to a verandah, but this allowed Mother to walk for half an hour in the cool of each morning along the front verandah, through one bedroom, along the back verandah and through the second bedroom to the front again. She did this for exercise as there was no suitable place to go for walks, but at the same time did magnificent crochet work – the chart lay on the table beside one of the doors.

Sugar cane loaded on to bandies – all-wood two-wheeled carts. Occasionally the better-off managed a metal rim on the wheels. (Elizabeth Ireland)

top Sugar cane on train. (Elizabeth Ireland)

above The Confectionery Manufacturing Building, erected before 1920, with a very wide overhanging roof to deflect the monsoon rains. (Elizabeth Ireland)

right The Confectionery Manager's bungalow at Nellikuppam. The dark doors were made of louvred cedar-wood, and there were no internal doors at all. (Elizabeth Ireland)

Cooking quarters were 'down the garden'. We had electric light (via factory lines) but no fridges or electric fans. Light metal frames over the beds supported mosquito nets, and we made sure that these were well tucked in before going to sleep at night, *punkahs* were provided in public and bedrooms. A gardener (*mali*) sat outside the room when required and gently pulled a rope threaded through a hole in the wall. When arms grew tired it was not unknown for the man to make a loop at the end, attach it to his big toe and move his foot back and forth. True, this tended to make him sleepy, and the *punkahwallah* then had to be woken and revived.

One bungalow was set aside as 'bachelor headquarters' and this accommodated single men and married men whose wives for one reason or another were detained in the UK – as, for instance, my mother, on one occasion, with me in hospital. Necessary servants were on hand, but 'differences' were inevitable – the cook certainly had a hard time!

'Meat safes' – cupboards perhaps two feet square overall, composed of close wire-mesh walls (to allow air but not flies to enter) and standing two or three feet off the ground, were used for perishable foods – which lasted not more than two days. Butter came in tins, as did Cadbury's Chocolate, which, once opened, had to stand in water-filled containers. These safes, as well as wardrobes (*almiras*), linen chests and dressing tables, had the foot of the legs wrapped in strips of cloth wrung out in paraffin, and then stood in empty butter tins with an inch of water in them. Generally, this treatment deterred the ants, which could wreak havoc on clothing or materials of any kind. There were no insect sprays as we know them today, but each bungalow was provided with a syringe (similar to the one used for greenfly on roses) which could be filled with a potent killer and used if the room was badly infested with mosquitos. With Mother, I took an interest in caterpillar, chrysalis and butterfly development, watched the tiny transparent lizards on the white walls, which pounced on flies, and recognised the good and bad spiders – three to four inches across did not worry us. While all ants were a nuisance, the red ones did the biting. By placing a leaf in their pathway it was possible to divert a column of ants moving a piece of fruit across a garden path. Their persistence was remarkable and exemplified the proverb 'Go to the ant, thou sluggard; consider its ways and be wise.'

We had to be watchful for snakes and scorpions. The 12-inch-long krait was particularly feared, and our servants certainly had a superstitious dread of them. With scorpions, the automatic move before putting on shoes or mosquito boots was to turn them upside down and knock the heels together to see if anything fell out. A nipped toe could be very painful. But perhaps the most dangerous of all was the bandicoot – the great rat of India, which was known to bite unprotected sleeping children. It could carry frightening disease.

At dinner parties it was customary to put a clean pillow case on every lady's chair – she then put her feet and legs into the case to avoid mosquito bites. Men wore their boots until later in the evening.

We had a 'boy' – the superior one who acted as a butler, spoke good English and could act as an interpreter for other Tamil-speaking employees. The cook had enough English for his job. He went to the bazaar every morning, and sharp at 8 a.m. Mother took Cook's account (every item detailed by her in a book) and handed over cash for the next day's need. We were fortunate to have very honest staff, but to keep them up to scratch it was necessary to make sure some supplies were not bought too often.

There were two *malis*, who kept the flowers blooming and who watered the whole place every day in the 'cold weather'. We had crotons, zinnias, geraniums and 'bonnet-flowers', which I know only by that name. It was a profuse creeper, vine-like but with smaller leaves, with pink or white flowers, buds bell-shaped but small cup-shaped when open. Ours covered the big wire-mesh arch at the entrance to our garden.

The *malis* also carried water for the house, for cooking and baths, in large kerosene tins with wooden handles inserted. All water came from open wells – our men were fortunate because the well was not too far from our compound. There were three baths to be supplied each day, so water for these went straight to the kitchen, and when heated to the bathrooms.

We also had a sweeper (a woman) who worked for the adjoining bungalow too. It was her job to empty commodes twice daily. She carried these in baskets suspended from a long pole over her shoulder. The *dhobi* came once a week bringing immaculately laundered linen and my father's white drill or tussore suits. He carried one bundle over his shoulders and two were slung across his little donkey. The washing was done at a riverside (we never went to see it!) and the articles were beaten against large, flat stones. True, there was wear and tear, but the results were excellent.

In the bazaar there was a *chuckla* who repaired and, if he was a good one, made shoes. Sitting on his raised mud verandah would be the *dhirzi*, who could produce a new suit for Father in a few days. Singer (hand) machines were in universal use. These self-employed people gladly came to the bungalow for orders. Mother was something of a seamstress herself, so did not fall into the trap of other wives, who depended on mail order – via the Club's magazine – to London stores (there were no catalogues), and faced the embarrassment of two dresses exactly the same at the Branch Manager's dinner party – not more than ten women present!

In the bazaar, too, there were usually a few writers, alongside the *chucklas* and *dhirzis*. These men (invariably) would – for a fee – write letters for those with no education, either in Tamil or (if they were very good) in English. It was not unusual for an Indian applying for a job to describe himself as a 'failed BA'.

We had no radios. The *Madras Mail* was our daily paper. The *Times of India* was available in the Club. UK mail arrived at teatime on Sundays, bringing UK papers (all three weeks old). Wives did all family correspondence – my mother became a letter writer *par excellence* – their own and their husbands'.

Furniture, wherever possible – certainly all chairs – were wicker, for coolness. In the hot season, May to July, temperatures rose to

110 degrees between midday and half past two. Taking tea with per-spiration dripping from elbows was no cause for comment!

Two or three times a year the Salvation Army 'rep' visited Nellikuppam. We kept in touch with Mrs Richardson for many years. She travelled by train, third class, i.e. no windows, wooden seats, very crowded, and invariably spent a night with us. The wives all bought embroideries from her, and she would accept orders which were executed by the waifs rescued by the Salvation Army and brought up by them. What she valued most in our home was the luxury of a bath.

The company paid something towards the servants' wages but clothing for the boy, our butler, was our responsibility. Said boy lived in housing adjoining the kitchen with wife, two or three children and mother. They, and all the servants, regularly received extra *baksheesh* and other small perks. Some wives employed an *ayah* as nanny/lady's maid, but Mother was an independent type.

Our hospital was seven miles away at Cuddalore, run by a Roman Catholic mission. Dr Pereira, an Anglo-Indian, was renowned throughout the Madras Presidency for his skill with cataracts. Vellore Hospital, where Dr Ida Scudder was in control, though further away, was the preferred one, especially for wives. In the Cuddalore Hospital, relatives of patients could come in (at least one) and sleep on the floor below the bed. The natives, who normally slept on a six-foot high mud plinth around the edges of their godowns (store-houses), had a certain fear of beds – too high off the floor, might fall off. The relative concerned, in some cases, went away each day and brought in the patient's food.

There was no church anywhere near us. The Danish missionaries, from Tranquebar, were active in the district and their pastor, Dr Lange, used to conduct a service in English in his own drawing room at Easter and Christmas – his wife played a very wheezy harmonium. As his mother-tongue was Danish and he had learned Tamil for his work, preaching in English was a real task for him – and a real task for us to listen – especially if you were 12 years old!

We were 20 miles from Pondicherry, then capital of French India. A trip there was an event, and we would buy all sorts of things from 'Mademoiselle' – silk, perfume (Quelques Fleurs by Houbigant) and then chat up the Customs officials as we recrossed the border.

We were very 'colour-conscious'. St Hilda's in Ootacamund, where I first went in 1921, was the only school in south India which accepted European children only.

In Nellikuppam one of the chief engineers, a Londoner, had an Anglo-Indian wife, so his two daughters were 'touched by the tar brush'. One asked her mother one day, 'Why don't I have white skin and pink cheeks like Betty [me]?' but I do not remember her answer. There were some sticky situations at the Club, and consternation when it was decided to admit Mr Zachariah, who was from Tellicherry on the west coast of the Presidency and a graduate of Edinburgh University, but whose wife wore a sari!

Even as children we knew that Indians didn't have cemeteries. We were used to the sight of a flower-decked body carried at shoulder-height on an open bier. In my case at least, I was conscious of being engaged in an important conversation each time we drove past the burning *ghats*; but even if I couldn't see, I could still smell. We were also familiar with the small roadside shrines – niches between two very large stones, or spaces among the roots of a Banyan tree (one of which could grow into a small wood). The locals knew the significance of each site and would bring offerings of flower petals and wood ash.

There was really only one main road, which took us to Cuddalore. It was not surfaced, so we often got very dusty – the company Chevrolet was a 'tourer' and we kept the hood down. Returning home in the dark – say at 7.30 p.m. – it was not unknown for the driver to have to stop, go forward and waken the driver of a bullock bandy who would be asleep across the shafts. There were no street lights, but the reflection of the car's headlamps in the eyes of the bullocks alerted us to 'oncoming traffic'. The bandy driver just set the bullocks on the only road and let them get on with it!

If ever we needed ice, say for a dinner party, we ordered 28lb from Madras – it came, packed in a small sack, on the overnight train. What was left, after collection from the station, was available to at least chill the sweet course in the evening.

Mother once had dysentery; I once had a mild attack of malaria.

RUTH LUCAS

My grandfather Lucas went to India to set up a paper-making plant in Poona in 1888, and my mother had two brothers and two nieces all living in the Calcutta area for many years.

My father went out to India in 1911, after serving an engineering apprenticeship, to install ginning machinery in a cotton mill up country from Madras, and my mother went out to marry him at Colombo in 1913, as he had decided to stay and make his way in India.

He joined the Indian Army in the First World War and served in the Engineers in Mesopotamia (now Iraq) and was in charge of searchlights at the siege of Baghdad, and up on the borders of Russia when the revolution began and refugees were leaving Russia in great numbers.

My mother returned to live with her mother in 1916, shortly before I was born, and had a hair-raising sea passage through the Mediterranean, where many ships were being torpedoed. She carried all her money and papers in a cotton belt with pockets which she had made herself, and one of the engineers took it upon himself to promise that if they had to abandon ship she should take a stiff whisky and lie down on her bunk, and he would undertake to get her to the boats.

I went out to India at the end of 1919 when my father was demobbed from the Indian Army. I had Christmas and my third birthday on the ship and have a lovely Indian silver serviette ring which was a gift off the Christmas tree on the SS *Frederic August*, a German ship handed over after the War as part of the reparations.

My father met us at Bombay and we travelled by train to Madras, but the only recollections I have of this time are of crawling through a (bead?) curtain into a cabin where some men in shirt sleeves were playing cards, and being carried on my father's shoulder when he met us in Bombay.

My father was then working at Perambur, about 10 miles from Madras. The Buckingham and Carnatic Mills were cotton mills owned by Binney & Co. The khaki for the Indian Army was made in Carnatic Mill, also sheets and towels (both terry and honeycomb) and *deux soute* material, which made good cool shirts, being loosely woven. I think Buckingham Mill probably made more fancy goods, but I do not really know. The compounds were known as Buckingham Gardens and Carnatic Gardens. I still have two towels made in the mill which have withstood fifty years of wear – but now they are beginning to show it!

I am told that I refused to have an *ayah* and must have been rather a trial to my mother in the heat. I don't remember much of this first period in Perambur, but we came home on leave in 1922 when I was five years old. I had been told that I would not see any dark-skinned people in England, only to arrive in the heart of Lancashire's mining area by train just as the miners were coming off shift covered in coal dust from head to foot – no pit-head baths in those days.

After the leave we returned to our lovely large white house in Carnatic Gardens, with wide verandahs upstairs and down, shaded by heavy green *tattis*, which could be let down as required. Squirrels used to live in the rolled *tattis*, and letting them down entailed much noise and scurrying as they dispersed. The house was raised about 10 steps above ground level as protection from flood water and most of the houses boasted pots of flowers, ferns, pineapples etc. on these steps as the nearest to a flower garden that could be achieved.

The floors throughout were concrete and the doors like US saloon doors with gaps above and below to allow air to circulate. We had a large drawing room with father's study behind it, where he would sleep during the hottest part of the day, having got up very early to go to work in the cool of the day. On the other side of the hall was a large dining room with a kitchen behind, where my mother could prepare food, which was then taken away from the house via a covered way to a kitchen where the Indian cook cooked in his traditional way. The washing up was done outside the back door on the verandah, by the *chokra*. We had a 'boy' (butler) and a woman who cleaned in the house, a *mali* to do the garden and the *chokra*, who did the dirty jobs. I wasn't allowed in the kitchen where the cook worked and he was never in the house. There were godowns in the garden for the staff and I used to play with the 'boy's' son Ramasamee, who was my age.

Upstairs the house had two large bedrooms, each with its dressing room and bathroom. The bathrooms were rather primitive. There was a wash basin with one cold tap, a zinc bath for which the hot water had

'An aerial view of the houses, Club etc. for the workforce of the Buckingham and Carnatic Mills (quite separate, but adjacent). Our bungalow is the one nearest the bottom of the photo, and the enclosure to the left of it is the Indian housing for native staff.' (Ruth Lucas)

to be carried up from the kitchen via an outside staircase. There was a hole in the corner where the bathwater could be tipped to run out, and the loos were a series of enamel chamber-pots on metal frames of various heights.

In the hottest weather beds could be moved on to the verandah, where it might be just a little cooler. My bed always stood in tins of kerosene oil to prevent ants getting into bed for the crumbs I was apt to scatter. The mosquito nets were very fine netting over a large supporting frame, and it was necessary to learn how to sleep without getting up against the netting, as the mosquitos could bite through holes in the net.

As Chief Engineer at the mill, my father could only maintain and install machinery out of working hours, and this entailed his working unsocial hours, which irked my mother as he was seldom available for social events. He did his best to avoid them in any case. We had a two-seater car with a dickey seat and acetylene lamps and I can still smell the acetylene on occasions. Although my mother did learn to drive I never knew her to do so, and if we wanted to go to church or into Madras we used to hire a *gharry*. But the most exciting outings were always when father would take us to the Yacht Club in the harbour, where he kept his racing boat, and we could sit on the harbour wall watching the boats. Often the water was a solid mass of jellyfish.

The grass in the garden was kept short by women who used to come round at intervals and cut it with sickles, squatting to do this. There were six houses in our compounds, three in the next, all identical, and two or three smaller houses on a road at the back where some junior staff lived. There were compounds of identical houses for the Buckingham Mill staff. Each compound had a *peon* at the gate who was supposed to prevent just anyone coming through, but we would have regular visits from the *dhobi*, who called for the washing and brought it back after hammering it on the stones. My mother had some beautiful bed linen and drawn-thread work which she would not use because the *dhobi* ill-treated them. They

top An aerial view of the Carnbuck Club, with bachelors' quarters beyond. (Ruth Lucas)

middle 'The bungalow in which we lived at 8 Carnatic Gardens, Perambur, Madras (probably about 5–10 miles from Madras).' (Ruth Lucas)

bottom 'The same bungalow with tatties down – owner on home leave, at a guess.' (Ruth Lucas) exist to this day, having been carefully hoarded until their use could be sanctioned.

The compounds were separated by a three-storey bachelor quarters and a Social Club where we would all meet in the evenings. There were concrete tennis courts, a billiard room, lounge and bar, sand pit and swings for the children and a splendid 'rocking horse' made in the mill to a design of my father's. It could rock at least ten children at any one time, having five seats a side, one at the highest level on the rocking axis, two at a lower lever astride the rocking axis, and a further two seats at the lowest level.

One night I was got out of bed to 'go to a party' and dressed accordingly. There were riots in the area, and all the women and children were gathered together on the top floor of the bachelor quarters while the men patrolled the compounds carrying revolvers in case of trouble. This was the early days of the movement towards independence and Gandhi was held responsible for the unrest. I always thought of him as the bogeyman.

Going to church in Perambur was an infrequent event involving the hiring of a *gharry* to get us there and back in the heat of the day, but the vicar was a personal friend, having been in the Army with my father. The church had open arches all along one side and I was fascinated by the *punkahwallahs* who sat cross-legged, one to each archway, pulling ropes that operated the many *punkahs* inside the church. We had electric fans in the ceiling of all rooms at home, so *punkahwallahs* provided a novelty. Several times my mother and I stayed in a mission in Bangalore for short holidays; attendance at the church there was very stirring as all the music was provided by a military band.

Our doctor was the Army doctor from the Fort in Madras, and he would visit us when required. He would paint gollywogs on my arm prior to administering vaccinations.

When new shoes were needed one of the servants would be sent to summon the *chuckla*, who would come to the house and measure your feet with a piece of folded newspaper: one nick for the length of the foot, one for the distance round the thickest part and a final one round the ball of the foot. Armed with these three measurements he would produce a perfectly fitting pair of shoes, either with bar and button or to lace up. When I outgrew good shoes he would cut off the toes and add a toe-cap to accommodate growing feet. Since the leather was not waterproof the shoes were always exceptionally comfortable, as the leather was soft. When my grandmother came to stay with her second husband on their honeymoon, Grandad had a pair of shoes made by the *chuckla* and was so impressed that he was still sending out for replacements many years later.

I can't remember ever buying anything ready-made in Madras: new clothes were made by the *dhirzi*, who would arrive and set up his sewing machine on the verandah and sitting cross-legged on it; he would make anything from underclothes to dresses and men's suits, just so long as he had a garment to copy. We certainly bought materials in Madras and on the way we would pass through Vapery, where Mr Vencatechelliam kept a chemist's shop and spices could be bought – I think he was the Vencatechelliam of the curry-powder fame, and he often presented us with tin cups and trays advertising Player's Cigarettes or Colman's Mustard.

The panama suits that the *dhirzi* made for my father were later worn by my brother when he went out to Tanganyika as a surveyor in about 1949.

Hawkers would sometimes be allowed in the compound and would spread their wares on the verandah – beautiful Chinese silk which could be made into colourful dresses which, unfortunately, had a habit of rotting in the heat and sweat. And the convents would sometimes send round vendors with beautiful embroidered goods and children's frocks made of darned net suitable for party wear, and christening robes also. The nuns must have found their embroidery a useful source of income. Men selling live chickens and ducks in baskets on yokes would also visit and my mother would buy poultry to fatten up for the table.

Life amongst the women was a rather formal way of life. Each lady would have her 'at home' day, when anyone who wished could drop in and tea would be served. The old system of leaving cards was still in operation, and a brass tray was kept in the hall for the 'boy' to accept cards that visitors left. I have never understood the system of leaving cards and I don't suppose I ever shall now. Dinner parties were also held from time to time, and shortages of crockery or cutlery made up by borrowing from guests – the 'boy' would be sent round with a request. When a dinner party was held at our house the 'boy' would decorate the table very attractively with dyed rice grains fed through a paper funnel into intricate patterns which reminded me of patterns in paper doilies. I would always be allowed to say goodnight to the guests as they ate and was offered a port and lemon which, I must admit, I much enjoyed.

DOROTHY MARGARET BAKER

One legacy from India is a bit of social conscience. I put it no higher than a leaning to the left and a concern for fair play, which by the time I was an adolescent, I felt the Indians and even the Anglo-Indians were not getting.

At about five, having been nursed by lovely *ayahs* and played with the children of the *mali*, cook and 'boy', it was a rude awakening to be told, in response to my statement that there was a lady on the verandah selling oranges, that 'only women sell oranges'. I didn't at this stage think of colour differences and later, in the UK, I saw English women selling oranges. So was it class? Of course, Indian society, without any help from the Europeans, was class- (or caste-) ridden, and I soon realised that the cook didn't fraternise with the cleaner.

My family had a long association with India. My maternal great-grandfather joined the East India Company Artillery in 1844 (in Lancashire), going to Madras in 1845 and moving to the Royal Artillery in 1861. Four of his children were born before the Mutiny (he married in 1848 on St Thomas's Mount in Madras). He seems to have taken his discharge in India and to have had at least seven children, one of whom was to become State Governor. One was my maternal grandmother. How did they come to settle in south India; what was their association with the Nilgiri Hills? Those who could answer are long buried on those hills. One of my mother's uncles was, in the late 1940s, a Chelsea pensioner in the UK. One of her aunts married an Anglo-Indian doctor in Ootacamund (Ooty). I still recall my mother's concern to assure us that our branch of the family were English.

We think my grandfather had 10 children, two dying in infancy, and one being my mother. He had also gone to India with the Army, joining the Hampshire Regiment in 1882, and is known to have been in Secunderabad in 1886. He took his discharge in India to become a military clerk and then bursar (or something similar) at the Lawrence Memorial Royal Military School in Lovedale, on the outskirts of Ooty. I was born in Ooty, and Lovedale is my earliest recollection of 'home'.

Because my father (who also took his discharge from the Army after the First World War) had a post with Madras Customs, which provided for UK leave, we made trips back to England and my mother and sister and I stayed longer on each occasion, due to my sister's ill health. So, in addition to schools in India, I also attended schools in England and Wales.

At some point during my stay in India, I remember being taken away with my sister to meet my father's former in-laws. He had first married an Anglo-Indian girl, in Madras, and wife and child had died in childbirth. I can still recall the sinking feeling in the pit of my stomach when I realised that my father had not only been married before, but that his first wife had not been English. My father's honesty in telling us this also made me deeply ashamed of the notions of racial superiority that had by this time become part of my make-up.

My father was virtually self-educated, having had a very short secondary schooling. He was knowledgeable, kindly and I am sure (because he was promoted within the service) an able and efficient employee. By the time I was fully conscious of the nuances of social standing, he was Chief Inspector of Madras Customs. His superior, the Collector, and most of his colleagues were Indian or Anglo-Indian, and we mixed socially with the latter. We lived in a flat above the Customs House in Madras (long since gone) overlooking the harbour. I remember us driving into the compound at night and seeing huge bandicoots caught in the car lights, scuttling into the record sheds. These were the beasts that stole our dolls and ate their composition heads. At Christmas, Easter and other festivals, the contractors who were licensed to supply the ships in the harbour would bring presents of food and toys. These 'gifts' were allowed, but I remember my father saying he never took cash (though it was offered), as that would be a bribe. He meticulously saw to the despatch of confiscated contraband – no booze or perfume came our way.

Servants were treated very differently by my mother and father. My father was considerate and spoke kindly to them (first generation in India). My mother, with her long family association, was inclined

'Me and the mali, taken in Lovedale. He would have been local to Lovedale, or Ooty, and would have worked full-time to keep the garden to mirror an "English country garden". Again, he would have been a Tamil-speaking Hindu. I was great friends with all the servants and apparently spoke Tamil (no sign of it now!). Photograph taken by my mother.' (Dorothy Baker)

to shout at and bully them. My father often had to act as mediator and on occasion he explained to me that her attitude was partly due to her upbringing and partly to her 'time of life'. I hadn't a clue what he meant by that!

JESSICA MAY BAKER

Our father worked for the Customs and Excise Department in Madras, which he had joined on leaving the Army after the First World War. I am not sure why he did not return to England after the War, but I assume there was little work for someone of limited education in England at that time. In Madras, where he was in the choir of St Stephen's Church (I think that was the name) he met my mother, who had trained and was working as a nurse. In those days (the 1920s) it was very unusual for well-brought-up girls in India to work for their living, but both my mother and her elder sister had been allowed to go from Lovedale in the Nilgiri Hills (near Ooty) to train as nurses.

In 1933 my father had home leave, and we all travelled to England by ship and stayed with his brother in Mortlake, south west London. One of our cousins had boasted to his schoolfriends that his little black cousins were coming to stay, all the way from India. He was most disappointed to find two scrawny, very white children who were very timid and unwilling to be paraded before his friends. Our father returned to India at the end of his leave, but Mother (now pregnant) and we two girls stayed on in London so that the new baby could be born in England. In the event our mother was very ill, and the baby died soon after birth.

We returned to India in 1935 after my mother had regained her strength, and I started school in a convent in Madras (my sister had already started school while we were in England). I became ill with some sort of kidney infection and we were advised to return to the UK for health reasons in 1937. My mother took us back to England, where we remained until the start of the Second World War.

DONALD CATTO

There were five Lawrence Memorial Military Schools or Colleges in India in the 1930s. They were named after Sir Henry Lawrence, who died in Lucknow in 1857. Priority of attendance at these schools was given to children of serving servicemen and civil servants, followed by children of retired servicemen and civil servants, then European businessmen, European employees of the railways and the post and telegraph service. I do not recall any Indian children attending these schools.

The Lawrence Memorial Royal Military School, Lovedale, to give it its full title, was located at an altitude of about 6500 feet in the Nilgiri Hills, between Wellington and Ootacamund. I travelled to and from Lovedale by rail from Bangalore, where my parents lived. These journeys were in March and December from 1936 to 1938 inclusive.

About 30 miles from Ootacamund a cog in the train's engine engaged a third track running between the metal railtracks and hauled the train up a steep route, with beautiful mountain scenery, passing Lovedale Station *en route*.

Lovedale was a military-oriented boarding school for boys and had an adjacent girls' school about 500 yards away. The road connecting the two schools passed the principal's bungalow situated midway between them. The girls' school was out of bounds to the boys and vice versa. The girls had supervised walks around Lovedale and its beautiful surrounding countryside. Boys were allowed to walk alongside the girls and were permitted to talk to them while so doing. The staff supervisors ensured that none of the girls 'broke rank' with their boyfriends. I remember trespassing the strictly 'no go' barrier between the boys and girls late one evening on my last year at Lovedale. Accompanied by a friend, I visited the girls' school after dinner to chat to them. We were discovered doing just that by a member of staff doing her dormitory rounds prior to lights out. We were summoned to the principal's house the following morning. Fortunately, he accepted our explanation for this gross breach of rules, and believed that our motives were nothing more than curiosity and friendly socialising. We were dismissed with a warning not to transgress again.

Throughout the school year we wore uniforms. These military-style uniforms were khaki for weekdays and dark blue for formal parades and church parades. The blue uniforms had a white stripe running down the trouser legs. The prefects wore badges of rank of lieutenant or captain, depending on seniority, and the head boy wore a major's crown. These were changed to sergeant's and staff sergeant's stripes on the arm during my stay at Lovedale. I believe this was due to a protest by soldiers at Wellington when confronted with teenage officers in their area.

The school had its own Colours which, together with the Sovereign's Colour, were paraded on church parade and other formal parades. Church parades were held at intervals throughout the year and required the whole of the boys' school, led by the school band, to march to church. I was a colour bearer for part of my stay at Lovedale. The girls' school, also in uniform, marched to the same church under their own arrangements.

Boys over the age of 14 drilled with .303 Lee Enfield rifles, while those under 14 did so with carbines. We were taught how to fire .303 rifles fitted with a .22 barrel on the school's indoor rifle range, and had to qualify annually. A school team of marksmen entered the annual competition for the Earl Haig Trophy. The one year I qualified to shoot for the school for this competition, which was open to schools throughout the Empire, we produced a good result. We felt we would win, but the trophy that year was won by a girls' school in Canada.

We slept in dormitories and each boy had a locker by his bed. Each day the beds had to be stripped, the blankets and sheets folded and stacked at the head of the bed in a particular pattern and order. On Saturday morning the boys paraded by their beds while they and the dormitory were inspected for neatness, cleanliness and smartness. There was a specific way in which uniforms and other items had to be placed on the beds. For instance, trouser stripes and seams had to be dressed so that, when viewed down the length of the room, they formed a straight line.

I have clear memories of the need to have my trousers for Sunday parades properly ironed and with sharp creases. To achieve a passable standard I used to carefully dampen the trouser creases with water and place the folded trousers under the lower bedsheet at bedtime on the Saturday night. Provided I had a restful sleep they would be dry and have sharp creases on the Sunday morning. This obviated early Sunday morning or late Saturday night trouser ironing.

Our school sporting activities included hockey, football, cricket, boxing and tennis. We had a few good tennis courts and I found this to be my most successful sporting activity. On Founder's Day we competed with selected Old Lovedaleans, who challenged us each year. I played for the school. Once a year, the school boxing team competed, either in Lovedale or at Wellington Barracks, with the incumbent British regiment. Sometimes we won.

The school was organised by named houses, with their own housemaster and prefects. The prefects and all masters were authorised to cane the boys. Our weapon training, drill and physical training instructors were ex-Army NCOs, who ensured that we achieved the best they could obtain from us.

The school was also geared to the Oxford and Cambridge School Leaving Certificate of Education. Academic instruction was formal and, I believe, conformed to a British public-school pattern. The relationship between the staff and pupils was normal and the results were good.

Lovedale is surrounded by beautiful countryside and the climate during the school year was, I think, similar to the European Mediterranean area. Olive trees grew in the countryside, which had large rolling areas, ideal for hiking and camping. In Ootacamund some streets were lined with apricot trees which, during the summer, produced fruit which could be picked off the trees when we were lucky enough to go to Ooty.

Apart from the cane we were often punished by the prefects, who were authorised to allocate window-cleaning tasks to those they thought had earned such a reward. Cleaning had to be done on a Saturday afternoon during our free time. A specific number of window panes were allocated to defaulters and had to pass inspection by the prefect before we were dismissed. Meals were served in a large dining room three times a day. You were free to attend or not, and the standard of catering was quite good.

I think that my three years at Lovedale were a good training for a disciplined, physical and satisfying future, such as a career in the armed services.

ANONYMOUS

My parents first went to India in 1931 taking me, their only child, with them. My father was a civil engineer and had previously worked in the Victoria Street offices of Douglas Fox and Partners, which was then still a well-known firm of consulting engineers. They were the principal consulting engineers for the Sydney Harbour Bridge and with work on that project coming to an end, the younger engineers were told to find other jobs if they could, as civil engineering was badly hit by the Depression.

My father took a job with a firm of contracting and consulting engineers in Madras, south India. He was to be the senior engineer and only European in the firm. The head office of the company was in Bombay, but the Bombay side of the firm was not concerned with civil engineering, but with importing cotton-mill machinery. This led to considerable tension between the Madras and Bombay branches, as the capital requirements of the two businesses were completely different.

I was two when I first went to India but I returned to England and was left with an aunt and uncle (my mother's sister) on my parents' first leave two years later. I really have no memory of this first stay in India but my mother wrote copiously to her parents in this period and I have most of her letters. They are full of descriptions of places – she often went with my father on site visits all over southern India – but they say little as to the difficulties of adjustment to a new country, new way of life and a new climate. I certainly had an *ayah*, as she came to see me when I returned to India in 1940, but I had no memory of her at all. My mother did not keep her on as a personal maid when I was left in England as many of the English did.

The Madras which my mother described was the one which I found in 1940, and which I remember myself very clearly. It is a very spread-out city – almost American in that sense – the oldest part is the Fort (Fort St George), the original British trading post, with the old Indian town and bazaar next to it. Running south for miles from the old town is Mount Road, ending at St Thomas's Mount where Thomas the Apostle died in AD 72. Most of the important nineteenth-century buildings are on Mount Road.

There was a sort of town centre where the Madras Club, Spencer's, the largest and longest-established department store, and an old hotel formed a group on Mount Road. The newer hotel, the Connemara, was nearby but not actually on Mount Road.

Further from the centre was the Anglican Cathedral, again on Mount Road, and beyond that my parents' house, Teynampet House, and further still the district of Adyar. Even further was the airfield (not yet an airport) and Guindy, which had a golf course (my father's favourite) and the racecourse. The cathedral area of Madras had many fine old nineteenth-century houses (my mother liked to think that Teynampet House was eighteenth century, but I do not believe it was); they were all placed in large compounds with large old deciduous trees.

Teynampet House had two storeys, the upper somewhat smaller than the ground floor, and was divided into two; my parents and I lived on the ground floor and another British couple lived on the first floor, which they reached via their own front door and a staircase at the side of the house. The two lots of tenants did not get on and never saw anything of each other.

The front of the house had a *porte-cochère* from which a short flight of steps led up to the double front doors leading into a wide hall. Two archways led into a dark sitting room and from there two further archways into a much lighter dining room. From this three archways opened on to the back verandah, which is where life was lived. From the back verandah a longer and wider flight of steps led down into the garden; beyond the garden was a coconut-palm plantation.

Behind and to the left of the house proper was the godown, a single-storey building built round a square, half of which was used by my parents' servants and the other half by the other tenants' servants. It was in the godown that my mother's cook had his kitchen and cooked all our meals. She, and sometimes I with her, would inspect the kitchen frequently and make the comments and criticisms that would be expected.

Servants to English people in the south of India were expected to, and did, speak English. My mother and father certainly knew a few words of Tamil but would only use them when absolutely necessary. As far as I can judge my parents had seven or eight servants, two or three indoor male servants who served the meals and one of whom acted as valet to my father, the cook and his mate, the gardener and his mate, and the sweeper (a woman), who emptied the thunder-boxes and cleaned 'our' rooms in the godown. My father also had a driver (chauffeur) but I believe he was paid for by my father's company.

The suite of rooms already described, hall, sitting room, dining room and back verandah, ran in a line from the front to the back of the house; they were all openly interconnected by the archways and unless the monsoon rain was very hard the outside doors (to the hall and between the dining room and the back verandah) would be open throughout the day so that a breeze could blow through the house. All the rooms had *punkahs* (electric fans) and very high ceilings (15 feet?). The bedrooms, dressing rooms and bathrooms were off to the left and right of the main axis. I had a bedroom suite off to the left of the hall, on the right was a similar suite for visitors, and a bedroom, a dressing room and two bathrooms for my parents. There was no glass in any of the windows. The windows were closed by shutters with adjustable wooden louvres in them. If the sun was shining on the wall of the room you were occupying the shutter would be closed and the louvre would be more or less open, depending on how much draught you wanted.

We had electric light and, indeed, a ring main for power sockets, an enormous American fridge in the service room off the dining room, and piped cold water to the bathrooms. But no hot water – that was brought to the bathrooms, all of which had doors to the outside, in cans by one of the servants – and no flushing toilets.

As a tenant my father had made numerous improvements to the house at his own expense since they had first moved in in 1932, but he jibbed at the substantial cost of flushing toilets and had been unable to persuade his Indian landlord to meet or even share the expense.

MALCOLM MURPHY

To go on an exciting adventure is every boy's dream. To grow up in India in the 1920s and 1930s is to have it served to you on a platter.

We lived in a railway environment in Southern India. The suburb of Perambur, outside Madras, was where the Madras and Southern Maharatta Railway had chosen to locate its broad-gauge workshops, turning what was a sleepy backwater into a bustling town, with a sprawling railway colony and Institute (Club) to match. The M&SM Railway Rifles Regimental Band played on the lawn on Saturdays. The Regiment itself was part of India's Auxiliary Force, the AF(I), a territorial second line of defence which stemmed from the original Indian Defence Force (IDF) and was open to Europeans and Anglo-Indians only. Whilst every or most of the great railway companies in India had their own units, there were other AF(I) regiments as well. As far as Madras was concerned, for instance, there were the Madras Guards, the Madras Coastal Battery and, among the élite, the crack Southern Provinces Mounted Rifles (SPMR). Evidence of military activity, albeit part-time, gave Perambur the air of an Army town or cantonment. My journey to school meant passing the Adjutant's Office and the Armoury. When the men left for their annual camp to Bellary less than five hundred miles away in the 'camp special' every year, you'd think they were off to the Front, judging from the damp-eyed, handkerchief-waving send-off they got at the Railway Station.

As a family, we were prone to setting off on an excursion or trip into the country at a moment's notice. My father owned a vintage Alvis which held the whole family, plus two servants at a pinch. We'd stay at a PWD Inspection Bungalow in the mosfussil or, on occasion, in a Forestry Department bungalow at Sholavaram on the margins of a fairly dense forest or in the Nagri Hills. Dad – with his gun bearer, Palayam – and I, would go in search of small game and jungle

The Murphy family 'off on a picnic and shoot in Dad's Alvis, his gun-bearer Palayam (posing), Dad at the wheel of his beloved car. The building in the background is an outhouse of the Forestry Department Bungalow at Sholavaram near Madras.' 1935. (Malcolm Murphy)

fowl, with the chance of an occasional wild boar if we were lucky. Back in the bungalow with mother and the servants, we retired well bolted-in at nights and fell asleep (or not) to the sounds of wolves nearby, or distant drums, or some unidentifiable wail from, perhaps, one of India's myriad spirits, which made me long for the break of dawn. The magic of these excursions was undeniable. But like all good things they would come to an end, and we would return to our everyday homelife near the Parade Ground and the Workshops and the forbidden enchantment of the bazaar.

You could be sure that every Anglo-Indian family had relatives 'up-country', and it was an understood thing that periodic visits would be made to Guntakal, Rajhamundry, Pakala, or even the Khurda Road ('Wasn't Uncle Jack in the BNR?'). My father was entitled to five free passes (four 'home' and one 'foreign line') a year, which gave us a wide sweep of India by rail. First Class travel in those days was sheer luxury. All the major trains, like the Grand Trunk Express, the Frontier Mail and the Deccan Queen, to mention a few, had luxurious dining cars attached, and most of the Railway Stations had well-equipped refreshment rooms. The caterers were British companies. Spencer's served the Madras and Southern Mahratta Railway and the North Western Railway; Kellner's the East Indian Railway and Brandon's the Great Indian Peninsular and the Bombay, Baroda and Central India. Only the BNR, the Bengal Nagpur Railway, did its own catering.

BILL CHARLES

Journeys were a great excitement. Those of us who attended boarding school were lucky to have to travel by train and road. An Indian train journey is something apart, especially for a teenager – your own bunk in a four- or six-berth carriage with its own washroom and loo. 'Bag the top bunk' was always the first call!

We travelled from Bangalore to Ootacamund by the night train. Great excitement! We would stop at Erode for dinner. All would leave the train carriage and make our way to the dining room on the station. The caterers were Spencer & Co. There would be an hour's halt before moving on. No one would sleep. At midnight we would be at Jularpet, the main railway junction for the south of India. We would be shunted off to a siding to await the arrival of the Madras Express on to which we would then be hitched to continue our journey to Mettupalayam. Here we would change from the broad-gauge Madras Express (steam, of course!) on to the narrow-gauge cog mountain railway train, known as the Blue Mountain (Nilgiri Hills) Express. Having rushed to 'bag' our seats in the front observation car, we would fall into Spencer's above the station platform for breakfast.

There is nothing like an Indian railway station. When the train pulls in the whole world comes alive and the station takes on the atmosphere of a market. Everything is on offer to the weary traveller.

At 7 a.m., in just 15 minutes, if on time, we would be off up the *ghats* to Ooty. There were two engines puffing away, one pulling and the other pushing! We would stop halfway at Runnymead, when the engines would take on water, and then off up again to Ootacamund via Coonoor and Ketti. The railway track between Mettupalayam and Coonoor was cog, the incline being so steep. This slow climb allowed us schoolchildren to throw our *topees* out of the window, jump off the train and retrieve them!

At other times we would travel by car when travelling as a family. My father would load the car up to the brim, even placing holdalls between the spare wheel and the body of the car. We would stop at a *dak* bungalow (resthouse) *en route*, where resident servants would be happy to provide a meal for a small charge. The road between Mysore and Ootacamund was through forest where deer, elephant and jungle fowl were always to be seen. Some elephants lived in the wild, while others would be at work hauling timber. The main hazard was the bullock carts which would, for some unknown reason, always cross over to the other side of the road just as you were approaching!

The Blue Mountain (Nilgiri Hills) Railway which ran from Mettupalayam to Ootacamund, calling at Runnymead to take on water and then on to Ooty, queen of the hill stations, stopping at Coonoor, Aravankadu, Ketti and Fernhill. This train carried scores of children of the Raj to their boarding schools situated in the cool of the Nilgiri Hills and away from the heat of the plains. Between Mettupalayam and Coonoor the railway (narrow gauge) is equipped with a cog to help the engine negotiate the steep climb. On the downhill run, the engine reversed, leading the way down, thereby preventing a 'runaway train'. (*above* Gloria Hollins; *below* Bill Charles)

Travel was just a part of life's adventure, but other adventures were self-motivated. Thinking of myself as a budding motor engineer I, together with a school buddy, designed free-wheeling trolleys (go-karts). All very serious – from drawing board to finished product. The trollies were made of timber and metal, mounted on pram and lawn-mower wheels. The steering was by foot and rope – as were the brakes! We would make tracks through the woods, down the hillside, on which to travel. During the holidays the servants' children would join in the fun.

On one occasion, while on holiday in Ketti, the elder of my two brothers and I set off for Coonoor: eight miles down the *ghat*. We were bound for Nonsuch Tea Estate, where my 'engineer' partner was staying at the time, his father being manager of the estate. We took to the main road and, being downhill, had no problem with propulsion. Needless to say, we were hooted at by every passing bus, lorry and car. However, our goal was reached. The return journey was by bus with the trolley being carried on its roof! It was not only people that travelled on the bus, but goats, chickens and dogs – thankfully, in cages up on the roof!

Snakes seemed to be quite common. One could not go out into the woods or on to the downs without, at some point, seeing a snake. Not all of them were poisonous. At one stage we had a nest of cobras in our compound. My mother kept guinea fowl. Great snake detectors! They would screech when one was near.

My only real encounter with a snake was in my bedroom. This was in Bangalore – a bungalow in a residential area. On this particular night I was alone in the bungalow. My mother and two brothers were in England. Having gone to bed I felt uneasy and could not get to sleep. I had the feeling that all was not well. Switching on the light I saw, to my horror, a long, green snake appear from under the dressing table, move across the floor and make for the verandah. I was up like a shot, grabbed a hockey stick, went on to the verandah and did battle, killing (I now regret) the snake. I did not sleep easy that night, expecting its mate to come looking for it. That, I'm glad to say, never happened.

My father, on the other hand, had many an encounter with snakes. They would find their way on to the verandah of his farm bungalow, where grain was stored. The dogs (of which we had many) would find them, and let my father know in no uncertain terms. They would all then be shot – the snakes, that is!

ELIZABETH IRELAND

In June 1920 I went to Mrs Scotland's Prep School in Coonoor, which served as a 'feeder' to the Hebron High School. There were not more than 20 pupils at Mrs Scotland's. One girl's surname was Wales, two had just left called English – so with my surname we made a very British little group. Beds here (and later at St Hilda's) had a woven webbing base attached to a wooden frame. We children had to go to sleep lying back to back with the girl in the next bed – to stop us talking! There was no plumbing, and we used oil lamps. Brightly striped blankets. Lessons were spelling (lots), reading, writing (copying a line from top to bottom of a page) and learning tables. I have no recollection of games or food.

In January 1921 I moved on to St Hilda's, Ootacamund, run by Church of England nuns (Sisters Iris and Muriel). I recollect that their order was founded at St Hilda's, Whitby. They added CSC after their names in my autograph album. A chapel was attached to the school, and although we didn't have to leave the building, we had to wear panama hats a.m. and p.m. Teachers came from New Zealand, Scotland, Germany (from Miss Knope I learned 'Lord Ullin's Daughter', a Scots historical saga). The local Church of England minister gave us extra 'religious education' on Saturday mornings. We went in 'crocodile' to St Stephen's Church on Sunday mornings, one mile plus. Again, no plumbing! How did we escape illnesses? Lamps here, too.

The teaching was thorough and we had to work hard. A separate schoolroom block was opened by Lady Goschen (wife of the Governor of the Madras Presidency. Ooty was their summer residence). Splendid bamboo arch filled with wisteria and arum lilies for her visit. School colours were navy and trimmed gold. Motto 'Beati Nundo Corde' – 'Blessed are the Pure in Heart'. I still have my hatband and badge.

Even at 8000 feet we wore *topees* in hot weather and got chilblains in the cold. Apart from the 'big girls' (13–14 years old) we all slept at ground level, staff rooms interspersed with dormitories (of six beds). The total roll was approximately 40 – there were a few day-boys (sons of the rector). There were good tennis courts and a garden on three levels – a house at the high end of the road. (Snooker was invented at Ooty Club in 1875.) Very few cars. Some private rickshaws pulled by gardeners (in uniform!).

There was a small community of Todas, an aboriginal tribe – believed to be the last existing. We went for walks in the woods – eucalyptus – and on Broom Hill (truly named) – we used to collect ladybirds and hairy caterpillars in small boxes and tried to

St Hilda's Prize Giving, Ootacamund. Guides and Bluebirds. Note the arum lilies (which grew wild) in floral arch. Some guests are wearing their garlands, but others have removed them from their necks to avoid risk of 'poochies' going down their backs or into their hair. The central figure is Lady Goschen, wife of the Governor of Madras. About 1926. (Elizabeth Ireland)

feed them. They usually died. Being mainly female, we played endless games with dolls.

As a church school we observed all the festivals – silence all day on Good Friday – Easter breakfast on the lawn. Every girl had to give up something for Lent. As a Scot I didn't take sugar on my porridge so was directed to give up sugar in my tea (I have never had it since). At the end of Lent the school (boarding) gave each child a sum of money (eight annas, perhaps £1.30 in today's money) equal to her self-denial (this proved the school wasn't making anything out of our self-sacrifice). The sum of money was transferred to the other hand and put in the missionary box. The lesson was obvious.

Tables continued. There were 12 pies to the anna, four pice to the anna, 16 annas to the rupee. As we learned pounds, shillings and pence, 'If you've learned the 12 and 16 times table, you can learn 13, 14, and 15 times as well.' We had Girl Guides and Bluebirds (not Brownies). Food was generally good, but a few dishes were unpopular, e.g. spinach on toast with a poached egg on top (ugh!), tapioca pudding. On bad days we put pepper and salt on bread and butter. On public holidays we took picnics to Pykara Falls or a Maharajah's grounds.

Each year we put on a show in the local Assembly Rooms (used for concerts, plays, cinema etc.) – I was part of the crowd in *Chu Chin Chow* – after spending hours making pink tissue-paper cherry blossom. Another year I was the jellyfish in *Pearl, the Fisher Maiden*. Costumes for that were very inventive. I wore a pale green gauze umbrella on my head trimmed with varying lengths of spangles.

The south-west monsoon hit Ooty each year, usually about the end of May. These fierce rains cause landslides on the *ghat* railway. One year we had to go to Mettupalayam by bus – a real adventure. The red clay soil eroded at the roadsides, and the gutters became red rivers. The beautiful mimosa bloomed at the same time, and quickly revived in a brief spell of sunshine.

Journeys to school usually involved a night's stay in Spencer's Hotel, Madras – a rare treat – they even had fans. Mother would take the opportunity to buy two or three books – perhaps costing five rupees each. Friends thought this extravagant, but she pointed out that theatre seats would have cost the same and several people could read her books.

I left India for the second time in 1927, to complete my education in the UK. I went to a school near Shrewsbury, where two former pupils from St Hilda's already were. We became 'separated children'. Fortunately, the parents of the three of us were all to have home leave at different times, and as we had all met in India (mostly at weepy farewells on Madras station platforms) we gladly shared our parents with each other at home.

LAVENDER JAMIESON

We went annually to Coonoor in the Nilgiri Hills for the hot weather, travelling in great luxury in our own saloon – two carriages, one the day and sleeping carriage and the second for the kitchen, luggage and servants. It was connected to whatever train we wanted to travel by. It had armchairs riveted to the floor in the living saloon. I can't remember what they were covered with. But there were straw chicks (blinds) on the windows, kept doused with water to keep cool, as well as fans. We had to change into a very small rack-rail train at Mettupalayam to climb up the *ghats* to Coonoor, and I was always scared that we would fall off the line. There was one link in the line where the train passed the down train, and we would wave to each other.

Coonoor was lovely. We went annually to the same boarding house, Clovelly, run by two old spinsters. It was high up on a hill overlooking the Club and very near a large park, Sim's Park, where we'd go with Ayah and play on swings etc.

Coonoor was infested with fleas and I hated going to bed – as everyone put eucalyptus leaves under the sheet – and I did not enjoy lying on them, fleas or no fleas.

We returned to Britain in 1924, when I was nine, and I didn't go back until 1935. I was desperately disappointed to find that the Red Sea was not red. I loved the Suez Canal but was rather disappointed by the *gully-gully* men – who made chickens come out of your ears – at Port Said. The night before I was to be left at home to go to school we went to see 'Rose Marie' and I remember being very miserable, as I knew Ma and Pa were away the next day, and would be for two or two-and-a-half years.

BILL CHARLES

All my school days were spent in India. Hebron High School for Girls, in Coonoor, was the first of the two schools I attended. I was all of four-and-a-half years old! Hebron accommodated boys up to the age of seven. I can remember my first day very clearly – wailing as my parents left me. I seem to remember my mother crying too.

Hebron was a mission school, run by Plymouth Brethren. It was very strict in its outlook on life.

I cannot remember much of my early days, but I do remember being woken up at what, to me, were the early hours, by music students who had drawn the short straw for their piano practice! That was before the rising bell, which rang at 6.30a.m.

The sick room also comes to mind, and being nursed by the senior girls when we were down with chickenpox or measles, and I recall a young lady, all of seven years old, endeavouring to hold my hand each time she passed me.

Age seven approached, and I found myself attending Breeks Memorial School, Ootacamund. I was to remain at Breeks, as a boarder, for the rest of my school days, which included the war years, 1939–45.

Breeks was a co-educational school, with both sexes being taught together but each having their own boarding homes, quite apart. The boys' boarding house was situated between Government House and the Todas and overlooked the Botanical Gardens. The Todas are a warrior-like hill tribe – then only 600 in number but now numbering some 3000. Their origins are said to be in Syria, many hundreds of years ago.

Breeks was very different from Hebron, where all the teachers had been female. Now I was confronted by masters, both at the school and at the boarding house. The school masters had all come from university – some Cambridge and others Oxford. I found myself in awe of their gowns and mortar boards. They commanded great respect, yet at no time did we ever fell threatened – rather, in fact, protected.

Among the teaching staff were four Indian nationals, one of whom was the maths master. He was a brilliant teacher treated with great respect by all his pupils, not only because of his ability to teach, but also his presence. At the time of my leaving he was Deputy Head.

Speech Day was the day in the eyes of the school. The school choir would sing, the school orchestra would give their recital and Shakespeare would be performed. Prizes would be given. Speech Day was always attended by the Governor of Madras. Very important! Our neighbour when he was resident at Ooty.

Scouting was a great activity at Breeks. It was well known that the school had the finest Scout troop and Wolf Cub pack in the whole of the country. Known as the 1st Nilgiris Scout Troop, later on – while I was there – to acquire the title Governor of Madras' Own.

'Picnic in the tea bushes. With my younger brothers Ernest and Noel. Prospect Tea Estate, Ootacamund, Nilgiris, South India, 1938.' (Bill Charles)

The Scout troop performed many duties, among them collecting for Flanders Day and guard duty at the Ootacamund Flower and Fruit Show – a yearly event held in the superb Botanical Gardens. We would hope to be placed on guard at one of the fruit stalls, as we would, at the end of the day, be rewarded with a basket of fruit by the stallholder, especially if he had won first prize!

I remember one sad occasion, when the troop mounted a guard of honour at the graveside of my first headmaster's wife, the patrol leaders serving as pallbearers.

Some holidays were spent in Ketti, where my parents had property. My father would awake me at 4 a.m. and we would steal away to fish for trout in the Pykara River beyond the Ooty Downs. My mother and brothers would follow, with servants, at midday, bringing lunch with them. Any fish caught would be taken home for supper.

The dormitories at Breeks all had doors and windows that opened on to a verandah. One night, as I recall, one boy who slept by the window (which on that night was open), awoke with a shriek, calling out that he was being attacked by a wild animal. The whole dormitory leapt to its feet to discover that a buffalo had found its way on to the verandah and, having placed its head into the window alongside the boy in question, was breathing down his neck!

Once a month was barber day, for each dormitory in turn. 'Bag first hair cut' – 'second' – 'third' – 'fourth' would be called out. The occupants of the dormitory in question would then file out into the open quad to be shorn, one after the other! All this at 6.30 a.m.

Birthdays, I remember, were important days in one's school year. The birthday boy was allowed to take a few friends out to tea (parents having provided the funds) to an approved cafe. My tea party always included birthday cake!

While at Breeks I was caned twice, receiving four strokes, two on each palm, on the first occasion. The second was for swearing while acting as scorer during an inter-house cricket match. That time I received six of the best on my seat. Another occasion saw me 'gated' for three weeks. This was for being caught at hiring a cycle and making my way down to Coonoor to see my then girlfriend (a Hebron girl who is now my wife!). Not only was I gated but I also had to spend every spare moment copying out Bacon's essays. How I came to hate that man! However, the foregoing could not have done much harm, as I ended up my schooldays as being the school's senior prefect and head boy.

So many memories come flooding back: collecting and feasting on hill guavas (a guava the size of a large garden pea); roaming the Ooty Downs (famous for the Ooty Hunt) in search of the Toda Cathedral (holy shrine); climbing Doddabetta by foot and pony – the highest peak in the Nilgiri Hills at 8500 feet; playing the scout game Relievo, where one patrol had a half-hour headstart, leaving tracks and signs for the following patrol, who tried to catch them up before they returned to base; being taken to the Gymkhana races by my father to see his horse win!

Spending a school holiday on a tea estate where the planter was also a pig breeder, and being introduced to his prize boar, Horace. Also being shown the large litter of piglets for which Horace had been responsible!

While at Hebron, in Coonoor, being taken for a walk at dusk in order to observe the thousands of glow-worms and fireflies that clustered in the roadside banks at that time of day.

Keeping baby lizards as pets and feeding them on flies caught sitting on the dining-room table; taking them to class tucked under our blazer lapels.

At remote railway stops, having to keep doors and windows closed in order to prevent the carriage being invaded by monkeys, which would abscond with fruit or any other goodies on view.

The oil lamps that lit our way after dark – which would go out if one went over a large bump or pot-hole – necessitating the carrying of a box of matches; they would smoke if the wicks were not kept trimmed.

My mother, looking into and under the beds before we got into them so as to be sure that there were no snakes or scorpions hiding there; sleeping under mosquito nets.

One could not have wished for a happier and freer childhood than to have grown up in such privileged circumstances and while history was in the making. There could not be many others blessed with a like experience. I am glad that I was one.

BETSY VICKERS

My introduction to school was horrendous. Just before my sixth birthday my mother decided that she would take me to Hebron High School, Coonoor, in the Nilgiris, herself, as this was my first time away from home. Usually one parent from each area of India would take a party of children up to school. We had to change at Madras and had most of the day there as the Blue Mountains Express did not leave until the evening. Shortly before boarding my mother had a massive heart attack in the ladies' waiting room, so I was escorted on to the train by another mother, leaving mine all alone. Today an ambulance would be called, but not then. Fortunately a very kind English lady, who was a nurse, heard what was happening and took my mother to her own home and nursed her there. For days I heard nothing. My father received a telegram from the school. 'Betsy has arrived. We do not know where your wife is.' Not a very auspicious start.

Hebron, approached by a Chinese Moon Gate, catered for children from the age of four. Some poor little mites of that age came from as far away as Assam, way up in north-east India. One or two children came from Ceylon, another from Singapore, and we were very mixed by nationality, all white, which in those days was quite normal. Most of the teachers came from Australia or New Zealand. When I first arrived the principals were two very harsh sisters, but then Miss Shirtcliffe, who came from Nelson, New Zealand, arrived back from furlough. Tall and stately, she really was a welcome change.

She created and maintained a large and beautiful garden and I kept in touch with her long after I left Hebron and she had returned to New Zealand, from where she sent me seeds to plant in our garden in Liverpool.

Scattered throughout the grounds were the dormitories and the classrooms. Hebron was surrounded by tea bushes, all beautifully laid out in neat rows shaded by occasional trees. A patch of jungle by the Moon Gate was infrequently host to a troop of monkeys. During the War this jungle was to be our shelter if the Japanese should decide to bomb the Nilgiris. Apart from the night before April Fools' Day doors, and often windows, were never shut! We were never pampered. Our beds were made of wooden frames with wooden laths across to support the mattress. It was wise at April Fool to check that someone had not removed the laths as a joke, otherwise one landed, with a bump, on the floor. Twice a week we were each supplied with two buckets of lukewarm water, which we poured into a tin tub for our baths. If we wanted to wash our hair, as

The girls of Mount Hebron School, Coonoor, at their Chinese Moon Gate, 1936. (Gloria Hollins)

girls do, we had to creep into the woodshed where the boiler was and quickly get some water before the water man arrived, or we would be in trouble.

When I arrived I was put into Bogie Dorm run by a strict Scot of that name. Thank heavens for my teddy bear, for without Pooh I would never have survived. I do not think that any of the teachers or matrons understood what a shock it was for such young pupils, from the back of beyond, suddenly to find themselves in a totally white environment. I had never even played with white children, but towards the end of 1937 my mother was very ill and we had to return to England.

RUTH LUCAS

At the age of six I was sent away to school at St Hilda's, Ootacamund. By this time my mother had taught me my letters and I could write a basic letter home. She also taught me to read music and play simple tunes, but I later discovered that I had to re-learn the fingering, as I had learned old English fingering and had to change to the (then) more modern continental fingering. I was encouraged to use the sewing machine to make simple dolls' 'magyars' and to iron handkerchiefs after the iron was switched off; yes, it was electric, but we had no refrigerator and a large wooden box was kept in the house and kept supplied with ice from the mill to provide cool storage. Boiled water was always kept available in the ice-box in square Johnny Walker whisky bottles.

Going away to school cannot have been very traumatic. Several other children from the mills went to the same school and I am still in touch with two of them as we also went to the same school in England. The journey to school was quite an adventure, as we always met at about 8 p.m. in the dark on the railway station in Madras, where we boarded the train, having an eight-bunk compartment. There would be about six to eight children with an adult in charge and the bunks were four up and four down, lying fore and aft of the train. The boys were expected to take the upper bunks, so I would unfold my bed roll on a lower bunk and settle in.

As we travelled across the Deccan in the night I was fascinated by the huge moon, which shed its light on miles and miles of nothingness. We seemed to have a lot of fun but must have settled for the night at some time, having enjoyed a drink with little legs hanging over the sides of the bunks and I suspect much tickling of feet. By morning we had reached the foot of the mountains and left the train at Mettupalayam, where we had breakfast in the railway dining room before boarding the ratchet railway which climbed the Nilgiri Hills. The journey was slow and steep and entailed crossing several trestle bridges over deep gorges. From inside the train you could not see the bridge beneath you and it was scary.

The seats were smooth wooden slats and children travelling backwards had difficulty in keeping their seats – little legs could not reach the floor and the train was often at quite a steep angle as it struggled from one cog to the next. One time when we were returning to school there had been a landslide on this railway and we had to get down from one train, climb over the rubble, and get into a train on the other side of the slip.

Christmas was the only holiday when we would get home, as the line was often washed out by monsoon rains when our summer holiday was due, though I remember one time when a carload of us came down the hills through the forest when a rogue elephant had been reported in the area. I don't suppose there was any danger really but I am sure we children preferred to think there was.

During the hottest weather tigers were often seen in the forest behind the school and guards would be employed to patrol the premises at night. I used to make sure my arms were well under the bedclothes in case of tigers! Our dormitory was at the end of the building with doors to the outside, but the only contact with others in the place was a 12-inch hatchway through to the under-matron's bedroom, and she would not have been able to get us if the route out of doors was impeded in any way – a horrible thought.

The school was run by Church of England nuns in those days, though a lay headmistress had taken over before I left. Life was great fun for most of us, though I suspect that the older girls, who were much fewer in number, did not get so much out of school as we did. There were no older boys, but I grew up well amongst all the boys and apparently had a reputation of being able to keep them in their place. I was always short of girls to play with at home, and at the age of seven my brother was born when I was home on Christmas holiday. I was very fed up at getting a brother when I really wanted a sister.

One year the monsoon broke while Mother and I were visiting neighbours. The 'boy' came for us with an umbrella to help us get home, he carrying me and my mother wading in water a foot deep. When the floods were up my father would make me a boat out of a cigarette tin hammered into shape and powered by a piece of bent tubing under which a small piece of solid fuel could be burned. The water was sucked in one end of the tube and jetted out into the other, and the boat puttered away with great gusto.

I never wear a straw hat without remembering the joy of being able to dispense with a *topee* in cooler weather, even if you had to put a cabbage leaf inside it to protect you from the sun – Christmas and Easter were the time for panama hats if possible, when Father Christmas came to the Club and we had a roundabout and lots of fun and one of the bachelors sweltering in a red outfit and fluffy whiskers.

There was great excitement on the occasions when ice cream was made by hand at the Club. Constant stirring of the mixture in its containers inside a box of ice was worth seeing, though I imagine the Indian doing the stirring was not quite so excited as we children. The constant cry was 'Is it ready yet?'

I left India at the age of eight to begin a serious education over here. My brother left at the same time, he two and me nine. It was heart-rending for me, but I think I made a better recovery than my brother, who still resents being a deprived child.

JOHN LETHBRIDGE

My mother's father, an Australian, Lieutenant Colonel J.B. Christian, whose grandfather was one of the pioneer sheep-station owners, qualified at St George's Hospital in London and joined the Indian Medical Service in 1900. Until just before the First World War he served as a medical officer in Indian Army regiments stationed in North West India. In 1903 he was in Fort Sandeman, seven miles from the border with Afghanistan, and the only British officer in the regiment to be accompanied by his wife. She was about to be sent down to Quetta to give birth to my mother when the tribe rose and the fort was virtually under siege. My mother always believed that she was the only European baby to be born in Fort Sandeman.

In 1913 my grandfather had leave to England to study for the Fellowship of the Royal College of Surgeons. This was interrupted by the First World War, during which he was employed as a surgeon in the Indian Military Hospital at Brighton, where wounded Indian soldiers were sent back for treatment from France. He was later posted to Darjeeling as Civil Surgeon, and it was part of my grandfather's duties to examine the porters for the Everest Expedition of 1924.

My father was the son of a colonial civil servant who was invalided back to England from Hong Kong with a tropical disease and who spent the rest of his career as a prison governor in England. After reading Greats at Oxford my father took the competitive

John Lethbridge's grandfather's house in Coonoor. 'I am in the picture aged about four. The house is an odd shape because my grandparents added a room whenever my mother had another baby.' The car was a DeSoto, much prized for its performance at 6000 feet. (John Lethbridge)

examination and became an Indian Civil Service probationer, staying on at university for another year, where he studied Sanskrit, among other subjects, and had to pass a stiff riding test at a local cavalry depot. He went out to India in 1911 and was posted as a subdivisional officer to a district in Bengal to do general administrative duties. Later, on reaching the appropriate level of seniority, he chose to follow the judicial side of the Indian Civil Service rather than the administrative. Among other posts, he was the District Judge of Burdwan, Legal Remembrancer to the Government of Assam, acting High Court Judge in Calcutta, District Judge of 24 Parganas on the outskirts of Calcutta, District Judge of Darjeeling and finally President of a tribunal dealing with cases of bribery and corruption by civilian contractors to the armed forces. He had also been sent to England to study the Workman's Compensation Act, and then back to India to draft equivalent legislation suitable for the subcontinent. Like other members of the ICS, on several occasions he was seconded from his district to work on flood or famine relief. He retired shortly before Indian Independence but came back in 1950 as a legal adviser to the British High Commissioner dealing with the British Nationality Act.

Once, when screening applicants for British nationality whose families had lived in India for generations and who had to show one grandparent with significant links to Britain, my father was confronted by an old lady whose only link was her grandmother's recipe for haggis. She got in.

My earliest memories of living in India were in 1930 when I was four years old and my mother had taken my brother and me away from the heat of the plains to stay with her parents in Coonoor in the Nilgiri Hills of south India, where my grandfather was once more the Civil Surgeon. A civil surgeon, I should explain, was an officer – a major or lieutenant colonel – in the Indian Medical Service. He had certain official duties with a district and these included inspecting hospitals, public health and medical responsibility for measures to ameliorate epidemics. He was allowed to have a private practice but

I seem to remember that he had to treat Government officials for no fee as part of his duties.

My grandparents' bungalow, named Kenilworth, was situated about a mile outside the town on a hillside with a forest below and a tea garden above. The view was heavenly with blue mountains in the distance and treetops in the foreground, many of them pale blue-green eucalyptus. As children we had a blissful time running wild in the forest climbing trees and playing hide and seek. We were about 5500 feet above sea level so the climate was very pleasant – although there was quite a lot of rain it was mainly concentrated in the monsoon.

Gardening was a delight – anything would grow. Domestically, conditions were primitive: we had no supplies of water or electricity and of course no mains drainage. I cannot remember how we got our water; we used oil lamps for lighting and the Indian cook used an oven made of baked clay. The sweeper emptied the thunder-boxes and put the content into a giant cesspool. At table we were waited on by a Goanese butler.

Milk was delivered to the house every day. There was a time when it gradually became more and more watery, so my grandfather checked its specific gravity with a hydrometer. It had of course been watered, and he demonstrated the proof to the milkman. After that it returned to normal for a while. Then it began to taste a little odd, and my grandfather found that it had been watered again, but powdered chalk had been added to restore the specific gravity to the right level. This time he took stronger measures; the cow was brought round and milked in front of us. Although it was possible to buy good-quality New Zealand butter, my grandmother did not like it and got him to make fresh butter by shaking milk in a bottle continuously. They also kept chickens and turkeys, for which he periodically acted as a vet. Sometimes the garden was invaded by wild pigs, which my grandfather used to drive off with a golf club, exercising considerable care as a boar could easily disembowel a man. We never ate wild pork.

A succession of governesses and nannies came to look after us children. The former did not often stay long, either because they found a husband or because they could not stand our riotous behaviour. One Anglo-Indian nanny used to take me out for an early morning walk before breakfast, and at the same time meet her boyfriend, who was a British soldier. Possibly because I described what I had seen when I got home, they decided I should sleep during their meetings, so the soldier was instructed to buy raw opium in the bazaar and this was put under my fingernail and I was given my finger to suck. All went well for them until one day I fell asleep over my porridge and could not be roused. My grandfather opened my eyelids to look at my pupils and said, 'This child is in an opium coma!' whereupon I was fed innumerable cups of black coffee and marched around the room until I recovered my senses. The nanny, of course, was dismissed, but was most upset at not being given a reference.

We spent several years, on and off, staying in Coonoor in the hot weather while my father sweated in the plains. Each time my mother had a child my grandparents would add another room to the bungalow, so after three it became quite elongated and there were problems with the roof. There was a verandah that ran partly along the front of the house, and under this were the usual long easy chairs with leg rests. I have a vivid memory of arriving in bright sunshine down the dusty drive to find my grandfather reclining there in the shade doing the crossword.

In 1932, at the age of five, I was sent to a school named Hebron in Coonoor. It was run like an American high school by American Baptist missionaries and had a junior department for both sexes but girls only from the age of eleven upwards. The kindergarten, where I started as a day-boy, as far as I can remember had about 20 pupils and was taught by an American woman. Some of our work was done on slates, but we also had copybooks.

The teaching staff at Hebron were mostly ardent Baptists. At home, at that time, we had a nanny who was a Roman Catholic.

When my form mistress heard of her faith, I was taken on one side and urged to convert her to Protestantism in order to save the poor girl from going to hell. At the age of seven I felt this was beyond my powers, and besides I did not feel that she would be damned. I also had doubts about the efficacy of praying for the victory of our team before a sports meeting, especially as all the other teams were sending up similar prayers. Their attitude to sin, even by animals, was extreme. One day the whole school was formed up in a hollow square on the sports field. The school dog was then led out by a person, who I believe was the principal, who was carrying a chewed-up *topee* in her other hand; she was followed by a teacher carrying a bundle of sticks. The poor dog was then beaten until all the sticks were broken.

The next year, 1935, my grandmother's health had improved, my parents were able to go home to England on a year's leave. My brother Alan, aged six, and I were sent to Hebron as boarders. This was to prove a most unpleasant experience. It was our first separation from our mother, although this was partly ameliorated by our being able to see our grandparents most weekends. It was the matron who made our lives a misery. She would cane us severely on our hands for the slightest misdemeanour, although at that age we often did not know what was against the rules. During the day I was fortunate in having a form mistress who was kindly though a firm disciplinarian and who made the lessons interesting. Our purgatory was ended when the matron went a step too far. One of the boys, probably aged about seven, was an habitual bed-wetter. Losing patience with him the matron lined us all up to watch, stripped the boy naked and caned him on his bottom. When my grandparents heard about this they took us back to live with them, even though my grandmother was not at all well. My grandfather was the school doctor, so I imagine the matron was disciplined in her turn.

My brother and I continued to attend Hebron as day-boys. As well as being taught the three 'R's I remember geography lessons illustrated by models which we made of Eskimos round an igloo, Red Indians round a wigwam and various other subjects. In nature study we were introduced to the pistils and stamens of flowers and shown some of the wonderful examples of the natural world that abounded in the Nilgiri Hills, such as the nest of the weaver bird. We had one period a week for handicrafts in which we made raffia-work baskets. In English literature, not surprisingly, we read *The Pilgrim's Progress*. In 1936 we left Hebron, Coonoor and India to go home to England and prep school.

BEATRICE BAKER

My family owned a property in Kodaikanal, a beautiful hill station in the Palni Hills and it was here I spent one or two 'hot weathers' on my return to India aged 18. My aunt, Dora Baker, had also been to school in the UK but returned and stayed on after the First World War, and made her home in Kodaikanal at the bungalow there and it is there I was born. Staying with Aunt Dora was not an ideal arrangement for Mother or myself, but she was a very generous lady, and I had a very good time in Kodai at the English Club, the Golf Club and the Missionary Club. People used to say Kodai was divided, you either belonged to 'Kodai Carnal' or 'Kodai Spiritual'. The Missionary 'Spiritual' and the English 'Carnal' Clubs did not mix much except for tennis matches and amateur dramatics – but we were all on very good terms, and used each other's libraries. The Missionary Club was rather better equipped than the English, I remember. The English Club was in a superb position at the top of the *ghat* overlooking Kodai Lake where there was boating, some residents owning boats rowed from one side of the lake to the other to reach the Club and bazaar. Kodai had quite a cosmopolitan feel about it. There were several schools in Kodai for English, European and Indian pupils. The Presentation College was run by Irish nuns, my elder brother and I attended the convent until he was seven and I was five, when we went 'home'. There was a very flourishing American school called Highclere, still in existence today, but international.

There were a number of young people brought to Kodai from Madras for the 'season'. A number of young men from Madras on leave, some for health reasons, nothing very serious. Tennis was played a lot, and golf. Kodai golf course is quite exceptional for India, green and lush with a variety of trees, many firs amongst them, there was a real feeling of Scotland. The snag was that it was approximately 10 miles from the centre of Kodai. However, my aunt owned a car, an Opel (the first car in Kodai, I believe) and a driver. She was very generous with her car, so I was well placed for going to the course. Funnily enough this was mostly with girl friends. The young men in Kodai were never there for long. Missionaries appeared to make a longer stay, and there was a memorable occasion when I took the part of Kate in *Taming of the Shrew*. It was a combined effort between the two Clubs. It was a great success. The part of Petruchio was taken by a handsome young missionary and the producer/director was a highly educated American scholar missionary called Hess. Costumes were hired from Madras and the performances were on the stage of the English Club, large and well equipped. We had glowing notices in the *Madras Mail*; everything was done professionally, even to the extent of my receiving a bouquet of flowers at curtain call!

My Mother and I spent one or two 'hot weathers' in Ooty. So much has been written about Ooty, my account of course is very personal. We stayed as paying guests with retired American missionaries, the John X. Millers, who had a lovely bungalow nearer Coonoor than Ooty itself. Club life was again the order of the day. I can remember little or nothing of the Ooty Club except for going to the Ooty races and perhaps going there for tea or whatever. My life was at the Wellington Club, mostly frequented by the Army. In my time the King's Dragoon Guards (KDG) were stationed there. I was overwhelmed by one of the officers in KDGs who spoke of his polo ponies, his country house at 'home' and his membership of 'posh' golf clubs in the UK. Mother and I had our own car (an

Overland) in Ooty and he and I would go to the cinema in it, and to a restaurant called Davis's. The proprietors were English I presume, but never appeared. Davis's had a private dining room which one could book, and I had one or two dinners there with my KDG friend (Lieutenant Colonel Weatherley) and an ADC to Lord Erskine (Rex Madoc) and his 'girlfriend', a married Irish lady whose husband was a *boxwallah*, sweating away in Madras. I didn't enjoy these occasions very much; the other participants were far too worldly and sophisticated for me.

Both these gentlemen married heiresses, one English and one Australian. I think they must have thought I was one; little did they know that our estates were part-owned by my Father's sisters, Aunt Dora in Kodai and Aunt Clara in Olesha (Kottayam). Although we were rich in India it was the 1930s recession and there was no money in the UK. However I enjoyed being invited to functions at Government House in Ooty, when at one dance Colonel Weatherley put his name beside all the dances on my programme.

A friendship I had with the Yuvaraj of Chitral in Ooty was not approved of by my mother. He was tall, good looking, charming, spoke perfect English and had the most beautiful manners, but of course he was Indian, and in those days mixed marriages were frowned upon, and so that was 'the end of the affair'.

In Kodai we had a cousin out to stay and she became enamoured of an Indian Army officer who, I believe, eventually became Colonel-in-Chief of the Indian Army. My aunt sent poor Yvonne 'down the *ghat*', as the saying was in those days.

Ooty was surrounded by coffee plantations, many were owned by English families. I was often invited for weekend parties. My mother would never allow me to accept these invitations, I think she had visions of drunken orgies. Perhaps she was right; I shall never know. Coonoor, another hill station adjacent to Ooty, had a much more modest, but very pleasant, pretty Club. I played a lot of tennis there and table tennis and still have two cups presented by an Indian rajah. There was a small number of Indian members at Coonoor and at Kodai. I don't remember any Indians at the Wellington; I'm sure there would have been at the Ooty Club.

While in Ooty, my Mother arranged for me to stay with *boxwallah* friends in Madras. They were a charming couple with three small girls. I imagine Mr Reid was head of a company he represented in Madras. I travelled by train to Madras with my own personal servant, one of our trusted *Malayalees*; my father insisted on this. I think the journey must have been made on the Madras Mail, a famous express train. It must have been fast as I remember little about it, except that I had a carriage to myself.

I had a wonderful time with the Reids, who lived formally. For dinner on my first evening I wore a short, what was called in those days, 'afternoon dress', only to find Mr Reid in a dinner jacket and Mrs Reid in a long evening gown. I remedied this on future occasions. I had brought several long frocks with me, all 'sent out' by Bourne & Hollingsworth, but quickly had one made in the bazaar for 100 rupees (worth about £4). It was far smarter than the B&H dresses, and I felt really good in it, particularly at Gymkhana dances!

There was a ritual observed by the Reid household of spending Sunday mornings on the cathedral beach, with the three small girls and the Anglo-Indian nanny. There were always other groups on the beach, all eyeing each other, but not joining up. The beach was clean, the sea too, and I really enjoyed those Sunday mornings. I don't remember attending the cathedral. Tennis again was my preoccupation in Madras, mainly at the Gymkhana Club. There were floodlights so it was mostly played in the evenings by young men after work. One 'regular' four I had was with three young men. There cannot have been many girls who were keen players at that time. I do not remember playing with any. Dances at the Gymkhana and Adyar Clubs were enormous fun. I remember particularly the Adyar dances. The Club was by the river in beautiful grounds where one strolled in the intervals – kissed and cuddled perhaps. The Adyar had an excellent band comprised of very talented

Anglo-Indian musicians; they played the latest Fred Astaire and Ginger Rogers 'hits'.

I had many 'proposals', some of my more ardent suitors following me to my home (Kumerakom), where they were welcomed by my parents. My father could never understand my refusing these young men, mostly *boxwallahs* in good positions. Whilst staying with the Reids I was invited to Government House for various functions. One particular 'highlight' was a very formal dinner, where I wore long gloves and was taken by an ADC to be introduced to the Governor and his wife, Lord and Lady Erskine, on their podium. Lady Erskine asked me what my father did. She looked completely mystified when I said he was a coconut planter! Not much later, a relative of ours chaperoned the Erskines' boys to spend their summer school holidays with their parents. We never made contact. A special boyfriend I had in Madras was a prominent member of the Madras Hunt, with which I had no part, but we met on the cathedral beach, and of course at dances. He'd ask me to dinner '*à deux*' at the Madras Club, which I remember as a very sombre place, all leather and mahogany, wonderful food and service and an excellent swimming pool with high diving boards. I enjoyed the Gymkhana and Adyar Clubs much more.

LYNETTE SMITH

My parents were second cousins, both being descended from Richard Middlecoat Cuxton, who was born in Secunderabad of British parents in 1826. His mother died before his first birthday, his father three years later and his mother's brother, his guardian, when he was seven. He was placed in the Upper Military Orphanage in Madras, on the recommendation of his godfather and, at the age of sixteen, he entered the Police Academy, from which he graduated as a non-covenanted officer in 1845.

On one of his circuit riding Police tours he saw a young, high-caste Hindu girl and fell in love with her. She was a virgin widow, having been given in marriage at the age of five and been widowed soon after. She had been spared the rite of *suttee* because Lord Bentinck had outlawed this practice in British India in 1829. She was treated by her own family as a non-person, and made to work like a slave, so it is not surprising that she eloped with Richard Middlecoat Cuxton. Her brothers, however, filed kidnap charges against him and he was either dismissed or forced to resign from the Police Force.

However, because she had been baptised and given the Christian name of Emily when Richard married her, the law was on his side, and he was able to come to some agreement with her family whereby she was given certain paddy lands around the village of Samianellur. Richard was unemployed for a few years but they managed to survive on the produce from these lands.

In 1857, he volunteered for service with the Madras Fusiliers and saw service in the vicious fighting before Cawnpore and in the relief of Lucknow. On his return to Madura, where he had lived with his wife, he was rewarded, in 1861, with a lease of land for 99 years. This consisted of a large block on the edge of what had once been the moat – filled in in 1845 – that was the second line of defence for the ancient city of Madura; and on this he built a secure, bungalow-type house for his family.

All the windows were barred and the doors provided with massive bolts. The walls were of brick and plaster and the roof thatched. There were three very large rooms and smaller ones at both ends. It was flanked on two sides by a spacious verandah with a stone parapet and pillars with split bamboo trelliswork in between. Much of the stone, ready dressed, had been excavated when the foundations were being dug. It is very likely that a large building, bordering the moat, had been destroyed in the past when Madura had been invaded. I remember two matching granite cubes with floral motifs that had been unearthed which stood at the entrance to the porch. This dwelling came to be known as the Big House and it was here that I was born in 1931.

The chatelaine of the Big House was at the time my Aunt Margaret. She was my mother's sister and a widow. Her husband had died as a consequence of a serious railway accident. He had been an engine-driver on the South Indian Railway. Due to some fault in signalling his train met head on with another approaching from the opposite direction. This happened on the railway bridge spanning the River Vaigai. He was not killed outright but was thrown into a workman's alcove where he lay, seriously injured himself, helplessly listening to the agonised crying of his fireman, who was caught between the two engines, one having mounted the other through the force of the impact. The boiler had burst and the poor man was slowly scalded to death. My uncle never recovered from the trauma of this experience and he died within the year. Margaret was paid some compensation by the railway and it was used to clear certain outstanding Cuxton debts. For this reason my grandfather Charlie Cuxton willed that Margaret should be allowed to live in the Big House for the rest of her days.

The verandahs at the Big House could be partitioned to serve as extra bedrooms. The need for this arose often enough because over a hundred years all family weddings, christenings, Christmas celebrations etc. saw a gathering of the Cuxtons under its roof.

At the back was a large dining area, pantry and a storeroom which, when I was a child, was filled with ancient items to excite my imagination. Richard's saddle hung on the wall, with an assortment of bridles, harnesses and old riding boots piled in a corner. A penny-farthing leaned against a perambulator. There were empty bird cages and rusting tools. There was a mangy-looking leopard skin said to be a trophy from Richard's policing days. A village on his circuit had been terrorised by this animal and it was part of Richard's duties as a Police officer to shoot it.

The central room was used as a sitting room. My Uncle Reginald, who was rather artistic, had painted the walls cream and hung up framed prints of the Royal Family together with his own floral paintings which were remarkably good. He also painted a Scottish scene using a postcard he had been given as a child by the Rev. Cameron, the minister of St George's. It depicted cows grazing by a stream, orange cows that caused me some amusement. It would be with a pang that, years later, I would come face to face with Highland cattle and realise what my uncle had captured. Strange indeed because the cows at the Big House were zebus!

There were plenty of built-in bookshelves filled with old books as all the Cuxtons were great readers. Some of the names bestowed on the Cuxton children were obviously plucked straight out of literature. There were a whole lot of Dick Turpin paperbacks and boys' annuals, and a fine first edition of Jack London's *Call of the Wild*, which to my regret went missing later on. Westerns mingled with Dickens, Kipling, Jane Austen and the Brontë sisters.

There were children's tales, both European and Indian. In a niche in the wall there was a strange musical instrument: it had a keyboard and could be played resting on the ground, and operated like a squeezebox. I was told that it was called a *bulbultara*, but have no idea to whom it once belonged.

There were two bathrooms but no running water. Two deep wells had been dug at opposite ends of the property and supplied fresh, sweet water to meet all the household needs. I have never known them to run dry, even when the monsoon failed. I was particularly fascinated by the woman servant who drew water from these wells and filled massive brass urns, part of my great-grandmother's dowry, for bathing and cooking. She was from the Kalar caste, a reformed tribe of bandits, as the word *kalar* itself means 'robber' in Tamil. Her grandfather had been arrested by Richard Cuxton for petty theft and had been released into his custody on parole. He became Richard's most trusted servant. It seemed so natural that his granddaughter should be working and living at the Big House. She was very dark-skinned and had earlobes that stretched down to her shoulders, due to the heavy earrings she wore. She added weight to them whenever her meagre earnings allowed her to buy a new jewel. She wore no blouse under her sari because her caste forbade this.

She also cared for the garden, which contained several fruit trees and was ablaze with colour all year round with bougainvillea, hibiscus, jasmine and oleander.

By the 1930s my great-grandfather's stables, where he kept his horses, served to house Aunt Margaret's two cows. Richard had been a fine horseman and loved his horses. Before the railway reached Madura he did all his cotton purchasing on horseback and would ride away with two grooms leading spare mounts and disappear for months on end. When he died in 1909, at the age of 84, only one horse remained, an ancient mare called Sundrie that he had been very fond of. The descendants of his grooms still lived in a hut on the estate and cared for the cows. They also ran a blacksmith's business in a small way, under a large tamarind tree behind the timberyard. So from an early age I was aware of the caste system and the restrictions it imposed on how people lived and worked.

The unoccupied part of the property had been cleared and sublet to a family of timber merchants from the west coast. Enormous teak logs and other hardwoods would arrive from their holdings on the Western Ghats by railway and, transferred to bullock-drawn wagons, would be hauled to the timberyard. These bullocks wore iron shoes just like horses and were the main customers at the makeshift smithy. A giant Indian fig grew in the middle of the timber-yard and had been used as a support when part of the yard was roofed over. When the figs were ripe, scores of monkeys would descend on the tree. Their coming and going, chattering and fighting, went on all day, and they were not above raiding our kitchen and making off with anything they could find.

The Big House had by then seen many changes. The thatched roof was replaced with red Quilon tiles, the oil lamps which I remember dimly gave way to electricity. Another momentous im-provement was the installation of Turkish-style toilets to replace the insanitary latrines of an earlier age. The house was about this time given the name of Hazeldean but to us it was always the Big House.

It remained an oasis of rural serenity in the middle of a bustling city. There were always chickens, ducks and geese, and the cooing of pigeons mingled with the chattering of squirrels. Aunt Margaret had a dog called Rolly and my Uncle Reginald's cat, a lovely white one with oddly matched eyes – one blue and one green – was of course called Beauty.

A great many people lived at the Big House. Young cousins who had recently started working on the railway, old retainers and widowed aunts. Richard had set aside one-third of his property for his widowed daughters. There were two widowed aunts and their spinster sister when I was a child. Their side of the house always smelt of sandalwood, jasmine and roses, and there were large wooden chests filled with beautiful silk saris which may have belonged to my great-grandmother.

There was, lastly, a very old lady whose story is worth recounting. Infanticide had been widely practised in India, where girl babies were starved to death or abandoned in isolated spots to fall prey to jackals and stray dogs. This was because poor families were unable to provide dowries for girl children. Infanticide had been outlawed by the British but continued unpunished because the law could not be enforced.

One night as my great-grandfather was returning home from a cotton-purchasing trip with his grooms, tired and longing to get home, he heard a cry and reined in his horse. It sounded like a hungry infant. He went to investigate and found a large earthenware pot of the kind still used to store rice or lentils. Inside was a newborn baby girl, wrapped in a piece of cloth. The grooms tried to persuade Richard to leave the child where she was but he picked her up and carried her home to the Big House. They called her Patchie and she grew up with the Cuxton children.

She was given in marriage to an Indian Christian man and on his death she returned to the Big House to join the other widows. She was a small woman, light skinned and with a mass of curly grey hair. She wore large, gold, barrel-shaped earrings with big red stones that formed a flower in the centre, a very traditional Tamil pattern. She was blind in one eye. She had lost her eye because of her devotion to the Cuxton family. One day the whole family had set off on a railway journey, the line having reached Madura by 1880. One of Richard's grandchildren fell out of a window of the moving train and without hesitation, Patchie jumped out after the child. The baby was recovered unhurt but Patchie had fallen in a thornbush and lost an eye in consequence. She could have been almost a hundred years old when she died in the 1950s.

The widow's portion of the Big House had its own compound with separate entrance. There were three cottages at their end, occupied by various rent-paying tenants. One was a nurse whose children made lively playmates. The second was an Indian Christian gentleman who worked as a clerk in the A&F Harvey Mills. These mills had been set up by two Scottish brothers, Andrew Craig and Frank, to produce cotton yarns for export. The clerk was called Master Christian. He played the organ and owned the first typewriter I had ever seen. It was an ancient Imperial, on which my mother, Hilda Cuxton, had learned to type. My mother, before her marriage, had also worked for the mills in the administrative offices as personal typist to one of the Harvey family. The last cottage was rented by the postmistress, a delicate little spinster called Rosie Sawyer. We loved visiting her cottage as it was quaintly constructed around a *neem* tree. She gave us fresh lime juice on hot Sunday afternoons.

LORNA BRADBURY

In the latter half of the nineteenth century my grandfather, William Henry Bradbury, was Superintendent of the jail in Bellary. All his children, two daughters and eight sons, were born there, the boys being educated in the Roman Catholic school, which was the only English-speaking school. This, in spite of the fact the family was Church of England with Methodist leanings. The girls were educated privately.

The small town of Bellary was clustered at the foot of a rocky hill on which Tippu Sultan had built a fort. It was reached by about 300 steps, wide enough for elephants to climb. The fort was never captured, but was abandoned after the defeat of Tippu. A large area at the foot of the hill was enclosed by rampart walls and a moat, and within this area lived the Anglo-Indian community. The 'city', where the Indian inhabitants lived, was outside the fort walls and was reached through two fort gates and a drawbridge. During the years before the First World War barracks were built within the walls and British troops were stationed there.

My memories of Bellary are of holidays we spent in the family home, Katie Lodge, in the 1930s. My grandfather died in 1922, and his elder daughter Katie and her husband lived there now. There were four other houses near each other owned by members of the family, Flora Lodge, Grace Villa, Bonnie Nestie and Rose Cottage. Every three or four years my father would take his annual leave, and we would spend these three or four months in Bellary. This happened in 1928, 1932 and 1935. My memories are of the last two visits.

Much of the enjoyment arose from planning these holidays, which were timed to overlap the two months school holidays during the summer, so that I would not lose too much schooling. This meant that other members of the family would also be visiting Bellary. The train journey from the Central Provinces took about 36 hours, and there was always much discussion about the best route, as at least two changes of train were necessary. Presents had to be bought for all the family who would be there, dress lengths for aunts, shirt or suit lengths for the uncles. My father usually expected to be transferred at the end of his leave, so suitable arrangements had to be made about the rented home and the servants.

My happiest memories are of these train journeys. My father would reserve a six-berth carriage for us. During the day a large block of ice would be deposited on the floor with a fan directed on it. At night we would sleep with the louvred shutters down. I can still remember the feel of the grit from the coal dust settling on the bedding, and the smell of anthracite. I would wake at some junction to the flash of arc lights through the shutters, the shouts and cries of the vendors on the platform and the jolt as the engine was recoupled after taking on coal and water. The final departure would be announced by the blowing of whistles and shouting.

There were about four stops on the last part of the journey after changing at Guntakal. How tedious this was! The slow progress of the train over the wide sandy expanse of the Tungabundra River, the welcome sight of the Rock Fort and Bellary, at last! Two of the uncles had livery stables, so we were met by two carriages. As the female members of the family were accommodated in the carriages, I anxiously hoped there would be no room for me and I would be allowed to sit on top with the coachman. All the men in the welcoming party walked back to Katie Lodge. The luggage was transported on a hand cart pulled and pushed by two men.

The first glimpse of Katie Lodge, after passing through the fort gate, was exciting, with its flight of eight steps leading to a pillared verandah furnished with cane chairs and two armchairs. Life at Bellary was so different from our everyday home. Only breakfast was eaten in Katie Lodge, all the families ate lunch and dinner together in Grace Villa. There was no one else near my age in the family, my father married late in life and my cousins were much older than I was. I was made much of by aunts and uncles and teased by my older boy cousins. There was no piped water within the fort, but every morning the water cart arrived and the man used a large, round, metal pot to fill the earthen containers in the bathrooms and kitchen. It was my privilege to count the number of pots each morning. Did an adult supervise, I wonder? The bath water was caught in barrels for watering the flower beds and pot plants. I can still recall the faint soapy smell as I 'helped' in this job.

Then there was the ritual of preparing the lamps. None of the houses had electricity, so the oil lamps had to be prepared every day. A cloth would be spread on the dining table and the servants would assemble the lamps there. Uncle Sam would then attend to them.

For the drawing and dining rooms there were large table lamps with fancy tall glass chimneys. Smaller oil lamps were for the bedrooms and verandahs, but for the children's bedrooms we used hurricane lanterns. Glass chimneys had to be cleaned, wicks trimmed and oil filled. I don't remember many candles being used. To go from one house to another, a servant always accompanied us with a hurricane lantern which cast daddy-long-legs shadows as he walked. The darkness frightened me, thinking of tales of panthers told to me by my older cousins – true or exaggerated? I do recall that though it was summer and we slept outside at night, the dogs were locked indoors.

In the years just before 1939 the Anglo-British troops had been withdrawn and the barracks were abandoned. The 'ball-alley', a sort of open-air squash court, was cracked, with grass growing in the cracks. The families in the fort made their own amusements. My mother was considered to be an expert at fancy needlework. The younger cousins would spend mornings with her embroidering underlinen and house linen for their 'bottom drawers'. For the older aunts she would re-trim their hats and even remodel the shape. In the evenings there was visiting when we younger ones were expected to perform our party pieces, singing, reciting or playing the piano. This often developed into a sing-song round the piano.

There were no English cinemas in Bellary, but occasionally an English-speaking film was advertised to be shown in the city. The screen was in the open air with a fence surrounding the theatre area. The chief seats were a row of deckchairs arranged in the front for this occasion, the normal seating being rows of wooden benches. Audiences were attracted to the show by a small group of musicians playing pipes and drums in the street outside. At that time all the films were silent, without the benefit of a pianist to set the mood. But the unofficial audience, peeping through the fence, added comment and applause quite spontaneously.

By one last visit, in 1935, there was a change in the air. There was little employment in Bellary for the younger members of the family, they were working in other parts of India and Bellary was just a holiday place. The older generation felt the need to move from the large houses and so, in the next few years, they sold up and moved to smaller but more comfortable homes in Bangalore.

LYNETTE SMITH

I have many happy memories of the Big House. Elephants being taken from the temple down to the river to be bathed, passing along the road behind the Big House and stopping to reach over the wall with their trunks to collect bunches of succulent leaves from our drumstick tree (*moringa oleifera*). Paddy being brought from my great-grandmother's dowry lands in Samianellur in bullock carts and stored in a large wooden silo in the back yard. Mice going frantic over this sudden appearance of largesse, and Beauty the cat washing her face and biding her time. Village women would arrive to dehusk the paddy, using the age-old method of pestle and mortar and then winnowing gracefully by sieve. The rice would then be parboiled and dried before it could be sold or used to feed the household.

There would be tamarind, widely used in Tamil cooking instead of vinegar, brought in gunny-bags when in season. Coconuts and bananas also came from my great-grandmother's marriage portion. I was sorry that she died long before I was born but I remember an old sepia photograph of her, in an oval frame, which hung over the door to the main bedroom. It was a portrait-sized one, formally posed for in a studio, a bust and not a full-length photograph, so I cannot say how she was dressed. It appeared as if she were wearing a rather high-necked gown instead of a sari. She had a beautiful, fine-boned face with large, dark eyes and luxuriant hair drawn into a heavy knot on her neck. I recall a straight nose and a full-lipped, slightly smiling mouth. The photograph, together with my Uncle Reginald's paintings, disappeared at the time the Big House was sold.

Mixed with personal memories there are stories told and retold that may have gained somewhat in the retelling but nevertheless retained the element of truth, some funny, others exciting or tragic. One such incident was my favourite because I had played a small part in the adventure. The year I was born, for some reason, most of the Big House was empty. I was three months old and still woke up at night for a bottle which my mother prepared for me. One night she was about to perform this task when she noticed a light in the room furthest away from where we were sleeping. The room was used to store clothing and belongings of cousins who visited the Big House frequently. A display cabinet held silver trophies won by some members who were outstanding athletes. One cousin held the snooker championship for the railways, and his silver cups were much prized.

My mother woke my father, who was far from pleased at being disturbed but he soon realised that there was an intruder in the house. There was always a dog in the Big House, but strangely enough it had not barked. My father moved towards the light as noiselessly as he could. What he saw must have come as an unpleasant surprise. He did not stop to think or he may have lost his nerve. My father was in his late twenties at that time, a well-built man who played football for the South Indian Railway, but the intruder was very large, very dark and glistening with oil from head to foot. This was a common practice among professional thieves in India, who covered themselves in this manner so that anyone trying to apprehend them would find it almost impossible to gain a hold. His long hair was done in a knot on the top of his head and he wore only a loincloth. A knife was held between his teeth so both hands were free and were busy transferring the contents of the cabinet on to a bedsheet spread on the floor. He had lit a candle to help him in his unlawful activity. My father quickly entered the room and caught him from behind, locking his arms as tightly as he could given the slippery surface of the man's skin. In the struggle the knife fell to the floor and my father kicked it out of reach. In the meantime my mother's cries roused the young men sleeping in the timberyard and they rushed to help. The intruder was overpowered and secured. It turned out that he was a wanted criminal and there was a reward offered for his arrest. My father shared the reward money with the timber workers. The family dog had not barked because the thief had broken his neck.

FRANCES WINDRAM

I went to India from Singapore in 1938, when the regiment that my father was in was posted to Wellington, a military station in the Nilgiris. We landed in Madras and went from there to Mettupalayam at the foot of the Nilgiri Hills, and then up the *ghat* in the 'toy train' to Coonoor Station, which as a young child, I had thought a wonderful experience. We had three different homes in Wellington, all bungalows with lovely gardens. One garden had a large circular lawn surrounded by jacaranda trees, and another had a beautiful tiered layout running down to the golf course. There were snakes in these tiers, and I remember one day, when we were looking for a golf ball, our dog found a snake that had just swallowed a live rat, a sight I've never forgotten; I think it was responsible for my hatred of snakes from then on. We kept rabbits in a hutch in this particular bungalow, and on one morning we woke to find an entire litter had been killed by a hyena, a very upsetting sight. We had seven servants, which of course was quite normal even for the smallest bungalow – the bearer and the number two boy, the cook and the cook's mate, the *ayah*, the *mali* and the sweeper. Most of these lived in the godown not far from the bungalow. I remember our bearer, David, very well. He was a Christian and brought his two well-dressed little boys to visit us most Sundays.

On our arrival in Wellington I went as a day girl to Hebron School in Coonoor, which was near and which I enjoyed very much, making good friends, some of whom I still see. Hebron was set amongst the tea bushes, and we often went to Lambs Rock for picnics, which we ate off banana leaves while gazing at the plains miles below. Holidays were spent with my family down on the west coast at Quilon and Cannanore, which I remember as being extremely happy times.

2

Southern Princely States

our of the largest Princely States in the south of India were Hyderabad, Mysore, Cochin and Travancore.

The Nizam of Hyderabad was a Muslim presiding over a state largely populated by Hindus. He was one of the richest men in the world, having a blue safe for his sapphires, a green one for his emeralds and a red one for his rubies. Golconda, five miles west of Hyderabad City, was well known for its diamonds.

The state occupied a large portion of the eastern plateau of the Deccan, had in general a good climate and, while some land remained untouched by agriculture, there were no deserts. It had coal, copper, iron, diamonds and gold, but its principal exports were cotton and cotton clothing, oil-seeds, grain, timber and hides. Tobacco, fruit and various kinds of garden produce were also grown, but principally for internal consumption.

The Hindu Maharajahs of Mysore were restored to their throne by the British, who defeated the usurping Tippu Sahib at Seringapatam in 1799. They made over a small tract of land at Bangalore to the British, to form a 'civil and military station', and their relations with British India were always particularly good. Mysore was a very prosperous state, with silk and gold among its exports. It was well irrigated, and its monsoon rarely failed.

The Maharajah of Cochin lived at Tripunthora, not at Ernakulam, which was the capital. The town of Cochin seems to have been largely European in origin, the Dutch and Portuguese having preceded the British. Cochin principally exported coconuts. Together with Travancore and some smaller states it was included, in 1923, in what was called the Madras States, in direct relation with the Government of India. The Maharajah, however, still rated a salute of 17 guns, the Nizam and the Maharajah of Mysore both receiving 21. He was a Hindu but had many Christians, mostly Roman Catholic, and Syrians among his subjects. Most interesting of all were the so-called White Jews of Cochin, the precise date of whose arrival was unknown, but whose Synagogue was one of the oldest in the world.

Travancore lay south of Cochin, a beautiful country whose staple crop was rice, but pepper, tapioca, coconuts and cardamoms were also grown, with tea, coffee and rubber in the hills. The Periyar irrigation project took water back through those hills to irrigate the district of Madura in Madras. The Maharajah, who rated a salute of 19 guns, was Hindu and about a quarter of the population was Christian.

STAR STAUNTON

My father, Colonel Staunton of Skinner's Horse (as he was when he was killed in North Africa), was of Irish extraction, his father a sea captain of sufficient distinction, so I was told, to have held command of the *Lusitania*, though not on her last fateful voyage. He was tall and slim with a shock of dark curls. I often catch a fleeting glimpse of him in my own mirror. He was a man's man, physically very active, a fine polo player and a devoted hunter of big game. But most of all he was a linguist. It was his love of language that made his career and largely determined the nature of my own early upbringing.

Having done a year at Sandhurst, he was attached to the London School of Oriental Studies to learn Urdu and Hindi with a view to service in India, and was already fluent in these languages when he first landed at Bombay in 1920, a commissioned officer in the Bengal Lancers.

He had another gift that must have been just as outstanding. He was a natural actor with histrionic gifts that enabled him to sink himself effortlessly into the camaraderie of any group in which he found himself, a Muslim among Muslims, a Brahmin among Brahmins, a Sikh among Sikhs, a gentleman among gentlemen, and a dutiful, if undemonstrative and unaffectionate, father, when called upon by circumstances to play the part of a parent. I wonder, meditating on my early life, what kind of a man he was when he was just being himself; but that is a question to which I shall never know the answer.

His extraordinary linguistic and diplomatic gifts would have been wasted had he followed a conventional Army career, and his superiors, recognising this, had him seconded to the Indian Civil Service, in which he was to play so successfully the part of a trouble-shooter.

The British Raj was still intact but was already shaken by the groundswell of Indian nationalism. During the First World War Gandhi had taken hold of the hitherto loyal Indian National Congress and turned it into a revolutionary weapon. I was only three years old when it came out officially for complete independence. It had its uniform – white homespun and the Gandhi cap – its flag, its national holiday – Independence Day – and its unarmed but well-disciplined paramilitary organisation. Tension was strong and continually growing stronger throughout British India, as the ruling nation sought to sedate its restive subjects with liberal reforms tentatively aimed in the direction of democracy and minimal self-government.

I suppose my father's duties brought him into contact with active members of Congress. Indeed, I am told that I once sat on Gandhi's knee (Gandhi – our honoured guest), though I have no memory of that occurrence. But, fortunately for me as it turned out, his main field of action lay in what was called Princely India, the India of those 562 princely or native states which remained nominally independent all through the days of the British Raj and only came to an end with the complete triumph of Congress.

Princely India covered about two-fifths of the territory of all-India and included rather less than a quarter of its total population. Here, except in a few cases, there was no truck with ideas about democracy or human rights. The Maharajahs, like their predecessors from time immemorial, were autocrats. They ruled their islands of despotism in ancient anachronistic splendour, keeping the reins of Government in their own hands, treating the state treasury as their own property, combining in their own persons the functions of legislature, executive and judicature. Some of them were immensely rich. A few represented one aspect or another of the ancient and varied culture of the subcontinent, keeping their dignity as best they might, preserving the odd lineage and native tradition more or less intact, while others might be odd, vulgar, sadistic, mongrelised through generations of breeding out of nondescript foreign concubines, unpleasant in a variety of ways.

The British Raj was not concerned with such matters as these. So long as they did not shock the conscience of their contemporaries with too gross an exhibition of waywardness or cruelty, and so long as they always sided with the paramount power, the princes could behave more or less as they wished. British forces were stationed at strategic points alongside their territories, in case any trouble arose, and most states had a British Resident or Agent General to keep an eye on them on behalf of the Delhi Government. Trouble was unlikely because, as time was to show, the British Raj was the bulwark of Princely India against the liberalisers of the Congress. When the British a few years later withdrew their soldiers, the Princely States disappeared like snow in summer.

In my childhood years, however, Princely India still hung on and my father's business was to help it do so. I have the impression that his speciality was what might be called 'princely relations'. With his gift of languages and his social poise he was just the man to smooth over difficulties, convey warnings, ask delicate questions, arrange for the extradition of wanted agitators, discourage the spread of Congress influence, and generally serve as lubricant at those points where Central Government and princely ruler came most sensitively into contact with one another. He could play the aristocrat among the aristocrats and on a tiger shoot or a polo match whisper a word in the Maharajah's ear that would be beyond the finesse of the run-of-the-mill Resident. He was evidently well thought of by the rulers, whose guest he became from time to time, and felt very much at home in palaces that were often luxurious beyond belief, and run with the formal protocol of rulers highly sensitive in the matter of their royal status.

Perhaps it was a sign of the regard in which he was held that he took the liberty of arriving on his duty visits accompanied from time to time by his small, demure, dark-haired, motherless daughter. For accompany him I did on a number of occasions, and when he was introduced into the royal presence, went in with him and followed his formal greeting with my own. Hands together in front of the lower part of the face. 'Maharajah' (bow), 'Maharajah' (deeper bow), 'Maharajah' (very low and reverent-seeming bow). At least, being European, I did not have to go down on my hands and knees. 'Maharani', 'Maharani', 'Maharani', with the same bows, though not quite so profound. Then I would be led away to the palace nursery to prattle there in Urdu, Hindi or Punjabi with princesses of my own age, exercising that strange ability which little children have to override language barriers when they are at play.

In that conservative milieu the primitive tradition was still that divided very sharply between the two sexes, making one inferior to the other, and I saw more of the girls than of the boys. The young princes confidently, though without obtrusive disdain, put themselves on a different plane of being from ours, and did not give us the pleasure of their company.

Of course, I was always on my best behaviour on these occasions, on pain of not being allowed to come again. I have no idea how I managed to conform so simply and naturally as I know I did. My training in the social graces from birth onwards had been odd to say the least. Perhaps I had inherited some of my father's histrionic ability and quickly learned from his own example. One way or another I seemed to have passed muster! Most of my father's friends found me charmingly quaint and beautifully mannered.

LAVENDER JAMIESON

My great-grandfather, Dr James Bryce, DD, was the first Scottish minister in Calcutta in 1814. He took six months to get there in a sailing boat. The Church of England church was nearby, and the story is that each wanted to have the highest spire. The Church of Scotland won by putting a cock weather-vane on theirs! I have some china of his that was presented to him, made in China and sent back to India in 1830. The Duke of Wellington, the Iron Duke, had exactly the same china, which is now on show at Stratfield Saye – but ours had a 'B' on each piece.

I was born in Edinburgh but was taken out to India at the age of 15 weeks, passing through the Suez Canal during the Battle of El Cantara, but this I do not remember. My father was chief auditor for the Great Indian Peninsular Railway (GIPR) at that time, stationed in Bombay. My earliest recollection of a house in India was Father's flat in Peddar Road. I used to stand on the verandah with my *ayah* and watch the sun set, cheering when it disappeared into the sea.

Father was still with the GIPR when we moved to Secunderabad, near Hyderabad on the Deccan, but he later took a post as agent of the Nizam's Guaranteed State Railway, and a very nice bungalow went with this job. I remember being very frightened when a small friend, who was playing with me, fell into the fish pond. I was convinced he was going to drown, but the *peon* – who, I suppose, was keeping an eye on us anyway – stepped straight in up to his shins and pulled him out. The friend was called Mike. I remember too a time when our parents, his and mine, had gone up to Simla to the railway

top The Viceroy's train coming into Hyderabad station. (Lavender Jamieson)

above The Viceroy (hidden) and Lady Irwin arriving at the British Residency in Hyderabad, about 1926. (Lavender Jamieson)

left The Viceroy, Lord Irwin – later Lord Halifax – leaving the Residency after lunch. (Lavender Jamieson) conference and I was staying in his house with his rather fierce English nanny. I said, 'What will we do, Mike, while our parents are away?' And he replied, 'You know, Lavender, I think it would pay us to be good.'

The daily routine was a walk with *ayah* and the *syce* in the donkey trap. Then lessons on the verandah. I had an Anglo-Indian governess and there was another small girl. She is still in touch with me and she came to my eightieth birthday party! We had a snooze after lunch and then either there would be a party of kids to tea with me – birthday parties usually had a camel or an elephant to provide rides – or we were taken to the Club with our parents. There was a lovely kids' playground and the parents would play bridge, with drinks on the lawn, which were forbidden to us! The pipers of the Royal Scots would play some evenings at the Club; we kids would walk up and down with them and must have been a menace. Then back home to supper on the verandah.

BETSY VICKERS

Home for me, until I was ten, was a remote Wesleyan Methodist mission station in the small town of Jagtial in His Exalted Highness (HEH) the Nizam's dominions, probably better known as Hyderabad Deccan. Being what was then called a native state we had our own currency and postage stamps for internal state use only, but if we wrote to an address outside the dominion we used British Indian stamps. Monetary transactions were quoted as being in HS or BG (Hali Sikar or British Government). The British King was represented by the Resident.

My father went to India as an ordained minister in 1913. In 1914 my mother arrived as a highly qualified nurse; they married in Medak in 1918. My father travelled many miles on horseback, and my mother even rode to one surgery on a camel. On their marriage they moved to Jagtial, where they lived for 20 years. In 1927 I arrived, so our little family was complete.

I loved Jagtial, though it was very isolated. The nearest railway station was 80 miles away, five days' journey by bullock cart. There was no electricity, radio, television and no telephones. It was rumoured that HEH did not approve of telephones.

Our compound covered 80 acres and contained a small prayer house, as the church was not yet built. The congregation sat on the floor, the men and women sitting on separate sides. The singing was accompanied by cymbals. Of course, the whole service was in Telugu. Newly arrived missionaries were required to learn Telugu to the standard of editing a newspaper and were provided with a *munshi* to teach them. There were also a boys' boarding school, a girls' boarding school and a small hospital, as well as a bungalow for the two lady missionaries, one medical, the other educational, and our bungalow. As we had no electricity, we had two Petromax lamps and an assortment of hurricane lamps, all our water came from a well, either to be stored in the large earthenware 'ali baba' pots in the bathrooms or to be boiled as drinking water, which was then kept in earthenware jugs, so the water always had a strange taste. Hot bath water arrived in old kerosene tins. All our floors were of stone. We bathed in tin tubs and then emptied the water on to the floor where it emptied through a hole in the wall, where a piece of wire netting kept out the rats and snakes. A low wall round the bathing area kept the water from covering the floor. Even so, my mother had an alarming experience when a cobra positioned itself between the bath and her towel. Jagtial was a very 'snakey' place, and I was taught from an early age never to scream unless I was in danger.

Our nearest white neighbours were 35 miles away in Karim Nagar and shopping was done once a year by my father in the city of Secunderabad.

Between Jagtial and Karim Nagar there was a magnificent tree known as the thieves' banyan. Weary travellers, not knowing its reputation, would thankfully camp under this tree, for its shade was widespread and the ground beneath flat. Either they would be joined by a cheerful stranger offering them a drink, whereupon they fell into a drugged sleep, or they fell into a deep sleep through tiredness. It mattered not, for whilst they slept they were robbed of everything, bulls, carts and possessions.

Such a life was heaven for me. There were always animals to play with. A Parsee friend gave me a pair of rabbits when I was six and I had their progeny until I was 19. We had chickens, pigeons, ducks, guinea fowl and a small herd of water buffalo for milk. Some people used the milk for making very rich white butter, but ours came in tins from Poulsons in Bombay and always tasted slightly rancid. Bread was made in our kitchen, using toddy as leaven. A wide range of vegetables came from our own garden, watered nightly by the *mali*. Our bathwater watered papaya trees. Not the puny fruit seen in shops here, but the lush orange-fleshed rugby balls bristling with black seeds inside, which are so good for the digestion. Meat can be tenderised wrapped in its leaves. We never touched beef or pig, beef because it offended the Hindus and nearly all the Christians were originally Hindus. Also, an animal was seldom killed unless it was diseased. Pigs, being scavengers, specially of the gutters which at night are used as latrines – the contents more euphemistically called 'night soil' – were definitely taboo. Each night as I had my supper on the verandah our bulls, Redskin and Paleface, were brought round so that we could watch them being fed their oil cake. The bulls pulled the cart used by my father when on tour as we had very few roads, only cart tracks.

One of my great joys when small was when our car got stuck in a river bed, there being few bridges; then I could paddle and chase small silvery fish whilst palm leaves were being cut down to put under the wheels so the car could be pulled out. Cars were such a curiosity that bulls would shy and would have to be unyoked before we could pass, in case they took fright and plunged down the built-up sides of the road. I too was a curiosity, being the first white child that many of the villagers had seen.

By 6 a.m., as the first crows winged across the morning sky, we were up and having *chota hazri*. Soon sunbirds would visit the cannas seeking nectar, little grey squirrels with three brown stripes down their backs where they had been stroked by an Indian god would run up and down and in and out the banyan trees, and my mother would go to the storeroom to give out the day's provisions. Nargayah, our cook, was a fearsome yet kindly man. If I visited our kitchen I would soon be chased out as he snatched up a lighted brand from the fire, yet he took trouble to teach me animal pug marks all indented in the *towdu*, the powdered husks of rice which were fed to the buffaloes and the chickens, after being mixed with water: this is the footprint of a goat, a camel, a dog, a deer, and so on.

I delighted in visiting the Muslim officials with my father, especially when we went to the old fort where piles of cannonballs were neatly stacked. Indians love children and I was always welcome. The smell of cardamoms today whisks me back to those days, for we were always were offered this spice. When the officials' wives visited us every window was shut, every curtain drawn and every male servant banished, for *purdah* was strict. I dreaded those visits as the ladies would always pinch my cheeks in true Muslim fashion, but compensation was to hand as very sweet Indian sweetmeats would be served and small pink iced cakes and lashings of lime juice. My father had an excellent vegetable garden in which grew a very productive lime tree.

When I was at play I was on my swing under a huge tamarind tree. When I visited Jagtial with my husband in 1964, the metal hoops of the swing were still in place on one of the branches. I had little Indian friends and we played Indian games, very simple ones. Hiding a small stick in a sausage of sand and trying to pinpoint it. My first friend, Prema, and I are still in touch.

I loved to be out on the road in the car. One never knew what one was going to see. My favourite people were the sellers of glass bangles. Walking from village to village, a pedlar would have hundreds of glass bangles strung over his shoulder, a riot of colour all glinting in the sun. I loved the Lombardies, the Indian gypsies, colourfully clad in multi-coloured skirts, bodices with small bits of mirror sewn in, heavy anklets and earrings and many bracelets. I was fluent in our local language of Telugu and would talk to the shy Lombardi women. They called at our kitchen selling tomatoes and firewood and would stop and chat about my white rabbits.

We had our own carpenter's shed. I spent many an hour watching the curls spill from the planes or watching the bulls going round and round grinding limestone for making mortar for use in building. People tend to think that missionaries are busy on Sundays only and do nothing but preach the gospel. In fact they had to be skilled builders, able to sink wells (we found out later that my father could water divine and never bored a dry well).

My mother at first ran a dispensary from one of the bathrooms, giving over 3000 treatments until my father built the hospital, and some of my first memories are of me playing in the dispensary whilst my mother weighed the ingredients for medicines. She had to act as a doctor as well, once sewing on a man's nose after it had been kicked off by a bull. Often patients were shepherds who had been clawed by leopards whilst guarding their flocks by night. The shepherds wore a rough, dark blanket sewn across the top forming a cape which they wore over their heads and they always carried a stout stick. The blanket gave them protection from the chill of the night but when a leopard was around they wrapped the blanket over one arm, ready to thrust it into the springing leopard's mouth whilst they killed it with their stick. Some youths had been playing with gunpowder they had found in the fort. Unfortunately they left a trickle as they stole away, so when they lit a match a loud explosion occurred. Most of the fingers were ripped off one lad's hands. His thumb was hanging by a thread. He begged my mother to fix his thumb so that he could hold a tool, otherwise he would have no livelihood, and she did. My father was also one of her patients when he got cholera whilst touring. He and a servant arrived back very ill. My mother offered to nurse the servant alongside my father but he replied, 'You have your hands full with the Dorra,' and he died five hours later. News reached Karim Nagar that my father was ill. Such was the death rate then from cholera that, instead of sending a doctor to help him recover, a minister was sent to bury him. My mother nursed him better, which was a triumph then.

Such a blissful life could not last and, when almost six, I was sent to Hebron High School in Coonoor in the Nilgiri Hills, where I finished my education at 17. After a break in England, because of my mother's ill health, we lived in Medak, a sizeable town and mission headquarters. We now had electricity, for the compound had its own powerhouse and many more fellow missionaries, but water still came from the well, but we now had septic tanks instead of the twice-daily visits from the sweeper. We were only 60 miles from Secunderabad and had a railway station only 14 miles away. Telegrams were sent to the station and then came to Medak on the bus.

Though India was agitating for Independence I was never threatened, nor was anyone ever rude to me. Whilst still a schoolgirl I travelled unescorted on local buses in the Nilgiris to spend weekends with my mother in Kotagiri, where she lived for the sake of her health for six months of the year. I would go down to the shandy, the bazaar, to catch a toast-rack bus (no sides, just seats the width of the bus), and I was always treated well.

BILL CHARLES

My father's estate was vast. Given over to fruit and dairy farming, it was situated just outside Bangalore at a place called Gunjur. My father had brought his Sikh estate overseer, complete with family, with him from the Central Provinces. His young son, Jaga Singh, was my only friend. We were both about four years old.

My parents soon established themselves; the dairy, having expanded, moved into Bangalore. My father was to introduce the first pasteurisation plant into southern India.

The compound in which the dairy was situated was, again, vast and walled all the way round. There were two sets of large gates. Within the compound were bananas, among papaya and 'flame' trees.

The bungalow had, at one time, been the Royal Engineers Officers' Mess. It had a large porch, front and rear, under which cars parked, steps to verandahs, six bedrooms, each with dressing room and bathroom, a walk-in pantry (*koli*), living and dining room. The kitchen, with its own verandah and washroom, was situated some distance away. Servants' quarters were situated just inside the compound wall.

Apart from their wages they each received a daily allowance of rice and sugar, though these had to be rationed during the war years.

Apart from Bangalore, my parents fell in love with the Nilgiri Hills in southern India (where the best tea comes from!) and acquired a property in Ketti, situated between Ootacamund and Coonoor. There were two bungalows on this property, and, in all, 10 acres of ground, which my father put down to blue gum and fruit.

Once again, oil lamps for lighting and wood fires for warmth. It can be quite chilly at 6500 feet above sea level!

Water was channelled from a natural stream which ran through the property, and piped to the bungalows.

The Dawn Estate, Ketti, Nilgiris, South India, 1937. Blue gum (for eucalyptus oil), fruit and potatoes. 'Where I and my younger brothers spent many happy days when not away at boarding school.' (Bill Charles)

Many a happy time was spent here by my family and friends, during which time I acquired two younger brothers.

Sadly, my father was to die suddenly, at the age of 43, from a massive heart attack, while my mother was in England and my two brothers and I away at boarding school (July 1939, just before the War broke out). My mother returned post-haste to India to be with us. She continued to run my father's establishments with the help of the managers, all of whom had been employed and trained by him.

PATRICIA McCOY

My father's family were from County Monaghan, Northern Ireland, but both my parents were born on the Isle of Wight, so were entitled to call themselves 'Corkheads'. In 1904, my father joined the Royal Engineers, serving in China, the Middle East and in France during the First World War. In 1920 he was posted to India. My mother sailed out in 1923, and was married on arrival at St Thomas's Cathedral, Bombay, by special licence. They then travelled to Bangalore, where my father was stationed, in Queen Victoria's Own Madras Sappers and Miners.

Their first child was stillborn, and I was born in the British Military Hospital, Agrum, in 1928. I was a sickly child in the early years, but my health improved considerably after the age of ten. We lived in various bungalows in Bangalore. The main shopping streets were South Parade and Commercial Street. The garrison church of Holy Trinity was at one end of South Parade, and St Mark's Church was at the other. There was also St Andrew's Scotch Kirk, St Patrick's Roman Catholic and many others. Most families had cars, but there were also rickshaws and horse-drawn carriages called *gharries*. The majority of the population used the buses. There were several cinemas and Clubs, the most important being the British United Services – known as the BUS Club – and at the Bowring Institute, one could take dancing lessons, ballet and tap.

Our bungalows were large, usually surrounded by large verandahs. The gardens had a very colourful array of flowers, bushes and large trees, mangoes, papayas, bananas, guavas, limes, jackfruit and jasmine, flame of the forest and many more. We had a tennis and badminton court, servant quarters and garages. A lot of people still had stables. Several of our servants, my *ayah*, for instance, had started to work for my mother around 1924. Her husband was a cook – all her children were born during her service, and they were well-educated. The eldest son worked for the post office, the daughter became a nun and a teacher, while the youngest son worked for the Imperial Tobacco Company. Our servants were also allowed to build a small temple in the grounds, at which they could hold their rituals, placing milk and food for their gods.

Mother led a leisurely life, meeting friends for tea or coffee mornings, afternoon tea and shopping. They would often look at the wares a 'Johnny Chinaman' carried around with him on the back of his bike. A tailor (*dhirzi*) would travel around with a sewing machine on his bike. One would employ him to make up all sorts of garments – in fact, one could buy a piece of material in the morning, and a dress was complete in a couple of hours. One could also get shoes made to measure, either by Indians or Chinamen, in a couple of days.

I first went to Bishop Cotton Girl's School in 1934, starting in the Kindergarten. Bishop Cotton, George Edward Lynch, was Metropolitan of Calcutta in 1860. From his wide experience of missionary activities in India, he proposed a scheme for the establishment of boarding schools in the hills, and day schools at several stations in the plains. These schools were to provide a British type of education, for the children of Europeans and Eurasians, supported by Government grants and by the parents of the pupils. The Bishop himself drowned in an accident in 1863, while touring Assam in the Governor's yacht on the River Gorai. Schools with his name had already been established at Simla and Nagpur, and his name was also given to houses at Rugby and Marlborough in England.

His school in Bangalore opened, for both boys and girls, on 19 April 1865, with Mr G. Reynolds, from St Augustine's, Canterbury, as headmaster. It functioned originally from a bungalow in High Grounds called Westward Ho, but the early years were difficult, mainly due to lack of funds. But in 1870 a site of 14 acres was acquired by the school, for Rs 47,000, to be paid over the next ten years to the owner, a Mr Putnam. In 1871 the school moved to its present premises, and Dr G.U. Pope became headmaster. He had a simple formula for running the school: 'Good food, good teaching, and a good thrashing'. He left in 1894 to become a Reader in Tamil at Oxford University. The Girl's School was in St Peter's Building with its own principal.

Things continued to be difficult, however, so much so that in 1907 the British Resident of Mysore, Mr S.M. Fraser, appealed to the Bishop of Madras to take measures to save the school. As a result, the Society for Propagating the Gospel (SPG) took over the running of the school, in particular the Reverend Herbert Pakenham-Walsh, who had just finished his work in Trichinopoly, becoming chaplain. By the time he left, in 1913, Cotton's was in a solid position and the future looked bright. The school's motto was chosen by the Reverend George Uglow Pope, and is *Nec Dextrosum – Nec Sinistrosum*, meaning 'Neither to the Right nor the Left', and comes from the book of Joshua. The first verse of our school song is worth remembering:

On Straight on, on Cottonian on.
Muster on the side of right.
March like warriors to the fight,
Mark the foe and strike with might.
Nec Dextrosum, Nec Sinistrosum.

Our kindergarten was in the junior school block, which had six class-rooms, and we were there till the age of ten or eleven. One could either go home for lunch, if living close by, or your lunch could be sent in by more distant parents and eaten at tables in the junior hall. We sat for Junior and Senior Cambridge Examinations, and our papers were sent to Britain for marking. Sports day was usually held in September, but the highlight of the Senior School was the St Peter's Social, which was held every June at the boy's school. A boarding school was part of the school, as many pupils came from outside the area, and our uniform was a navy skirt, white blouse and socks, black shoes and navy tie.

During my summer holidays, we used to drive up to the Nilgiris, and stay in a cottage at Ketti, which was owned by friends of my parents. This so reminded me of England, as it was cooler. On my father's long leaves from the Army, we visited England – the very first time for me – in 1933 and 1938. In 1933, we toured most of the south coast of England, and I was fascinated with the bed and breakfast accommodation, my parents preferring to stay in farm houses rather than hotels. In 1938, we spent most of the time in the Isle of Wight, as my father purchased a house for his retirement from the Army in 1942. Due to the War, however, he only retired in 1944, when we returned to England, and sadly he died in 1949.

Having been born in Bangalore, a large Garrison city, I look upon it as my second home. When I returned to England I really missed the hot, sunny weather and the carefree time I had spent there. Two of our servants worked for my parents from 1923 to 1944. They married and had their family, and to this day I am friends with their younger son and their daughter, who became a nun. I have the fondest memories to look back on, and would not have missed this part of my life for all the world, although I had a very quiet life in India, with a very strict father. Many children here today just do not appreciate the freedom they have. When I talk with my grandchildren, they hardly believe what life was like with my parents!

NETTIE LAMONT

My father, Donald Lamont, was an engineer, and, in particular, a dredging specialist, who worked for a Scottish company called Simon's, on Clydeside. They built a dredger, the *Lord Willingdon* –

I think he was Governor of Madras, but he later became Viceroy – for the Indian Government, and my father brought this dredger out to India in 1926. It was to break the sandbank across Cochin Harbour and dredge it to make it suitable for large vessels.

The size of the sandbank across the harbour made it necessary to have a powerful dredger. The *Lord Willingdon* had a cutting instrument at one end, which was lowered into the sand to be cut. This passed through a pipeline, to be disposed of where required and, in this case, all this material was used to make Willingdon Island.

The *Lord Willingdon* was a sea-going dredger which had to be kept outside Cochin in the open sea for many weeks in the year; but the *Lady Willingdon*, who lived within the harbour, was a small

above The Lord Willingdon, the sea-going dredger on which Nettie Lamont's father sailed out to India in 1926. (Nettie Lamont)

below The Lady Willingdon, a bucket dredger which lived within the harbour at Cochin. (Nettie Lamont)

bucket dredger, and the material from her buckets was collected in barges.

My father actually travelled out from Glasgow on the *Lord Willingdon*. I should think there must have been a ship's master for the voyage, as I do not know if my father ever had such a certificate. He certainly had a great many for engineering. Originally, there were mainly British engineers on the project, but local engineers were trained there and many of the British ones returned home.

My mother and I came to India in 1927. I think we sailed to Colombo, where my father met us, and we went by train and backwater to Cochin. We lived in a large bungalow with a large verandah, and I know we had a pleasant life but unfortunately I cannot remember it! My two sisters were both born there, Lisbeth in 1928 and Margaret in 1930. We each had our own *ayah* when we were small, but when we were older there was just one.

We had an uncle who was a tea planter in Munaar and we spent many happy holidays with him and Aunt Marie. The estate was called Panniar and it was quite a few miles from Munaar, in the High Ranges. Everything there happened in the early morning to avoid the heat. We were allowed to watch the tea pickers, who work so fast, and to go to the tea factory on the estate. There were many elephants, but they did little damage unless they turned rogue. We were there once when this happened, and it damaged lots of houses, including the assistant's, but no one was hurt. Deep moats were built around the houses to keep the elephant away, but in the end it became so dangerous that the men had to go and shoot it. One of the things we hated were the leeches, which were everywhere in the bushes and hard to get off.

My mother was a schoolteacher, so she taught us at home until 1933, when we returned to Scotland, intending to stay. But as my father was again asked to remain in Cochin, we went back in 1936, with war clouds developing. This time we had a house on Willingdon Island, a completely false island which had been made from the material dredged up to deepen the harbour.

When we were there, we usually rose early and went to the Malabar Hotel for a swim and then home for breakfast. Then we would have friends in, or we went to see them, and sometimes we went fishing from a small boat. There were no bridges to Ernakulam or Cochin at that time, so we all had to have jetties and launches to take us around, although these were still used after the bridges were built. My father was responsible for them, too.

We were often taken to festivals up the backwaters by launch which were fascinating, although one that happened every year, and was magical, was when all the islands in Cochin Harbour, and there were many, were lit on this special festival, half coconut shells with oil and wicks. It really was beautiful.

Cochin was a fairly small town when we were young. Besides having rides in rickshaws, which we thought great fun, we liked to go to the beach, and further along to watch the fishermen using huge nets which were reputed to be Dutch. The Dutch had been in Cochin before the British, as had the Portuguese. The first tomb of Vasco da Gama was in the church.

Cochin runs into Mattancheri, where there were settlements of both black and white Jews. When we were older, we sometimes

Ann Marindin on holiday in Cochin about 1938, with her minders and her father, in bathing costume and topee, behind. (Ann Marindin)

went to the Jewish synagogue, which was near the old palace of the Maharajah of Cochin. He lived in a new one outside Ernakulam. And the Cochin Club, as in many small places, was where people collected to play tennis and meet friends.

Willingdon Island originally had houses for port staff, plus the Malabar Hotel and administrative officer's house, responsible for the pilots who took the ships in and out. Then came our house and then three other houses, all built to the same design. Downstairs was an entrance leading to the lounge – which had a door to the garden – and the dining room. To the left were the pantry, storeroom and kitchen, with the servants' quarters beyond. Upstairs were the bedrooms and bathrooms. We went to boarding school, Hebron at Coonoor in the Nilgiri Hills. When we first got there we had Scottish accents, and wore kilts while our school uniform was made. We got a lot of teasing, which I can still remember, but I enjoyed that school very much, the learning, sport, which I was not very good at, and the general enjoyment of friends and walks.

ROBERT BAKER

My great-grandfather, Henry Baker, was born in Essex in 1793. Soon after ordination, in 1817, he sailed for India under the aegis of the Church Missionary Society, working originally in Tanjore. Here he met and married Amelie Dorothea Kohlhoff, a descendant of the greatly respected Reverend John Balthasar Kohlhoff, a native of Pomerania and one of the first Protestant missionaries to venture, in 1737, to south India. Henry and Amelie were sent to the recently established mission centre at Kottayam in the kingdom of Travancore.

For the next 48 years they devoted themselves to missionary work in the region – called Kerala today – and it is no exaggeration to say that its pre-eminence in literacy is in no small way due to the pioneering efforts of Henry and Amelia. They had 11 children, who all lived, and who were all educated in England.

My grandfather, their third son George, returned to India, but not as a missionary. It was he who was able to realise a long-held scheme to create a coconut plantation on the shores of the Vembenaad Lake, at that time a mangrove swamp. The lake today is in fact a great backwater, or lagoon, which stretches some 70 miles from Cochin to Alleppey and beyond, and at Kumarakom, where my grandfather built his house, it is about five miles wide.

He dredged mud out of the water and created 'bunds', banks along which the coconuts were planted, producing at the same time a system of canals, bringing a large new area into productive life and creating a place of great beauty.

His house was originally a single storey, but a second was added in 1891. It was thatched every year with 'olas', the plaited fronds of coconut palms dried in the sun, split up the middle and plaited by women. Even when I left, in 1962, there was no running water. It was brought daily by *wallum*, a local boat, in large barrels, the drinking water in large clay pots – *gouchas* – from Olasha, a village some six miles away where there was a good well in the compound of my Aunt Dora, my father's sister. There was no sanitation and all access was by river.

My grandfather died in 1899, when my father was 20. He carried on the administration of what was by now a considerable estate, with the help of his mother. He married in England in 1912 and I was born in the following year. I lived in India until leaving for the first time in 1921, and all my memories of that time are very happy ones. I remember spending early mornings at Kumarakom with Kunyapanikkan, a coolie boy slightly older than myself. Together we went poling in *wallums* and fishing; there was also an *ayah*, who did little for me. Also an old man, Govinda Pillai, who slept on the floor beside my cot and told me stories, some of which I remember to this day. But the other lasting memory is of our annual stay in the hills in the hot weather. In our case the hill station was Kodaikanal, 7000 feet above sea level.

It was my mother who took us – my sister Beatrice and my brother David – up to the hills. My father always stayed down at Kumarakom until after the paddy harvest was over, and the monsoon had broken, which was always on 1 June or within a day or two of that date.

In Kodaikanal we stayed with my grandmother and Aunt Dora, who lived permanently in Shoebury, a bungalow named after the village from where my grandmother came – which had four bedrooms each with a bathroom en-suite, but of course no running water or sanitation. Shoebury had a compound extending to nine acres, with many eucalyptus trees of all sizes – some giants more than 200 feet tall.

In Kodai I went to school at the Presentation Convent run by Irish nuns. The convent opened only in 1916 when I was three years old. I don't believe I attended that convent before I was six, so spent only two short hot-weather terms there at most. My memories of the convent are not particularly happy, perhaps because for the first time I experienced the very rudiments of discipline.

There was a boy at the convent I remember, who pulled hair from his head until there was a bald patch as large as a rupee. Perhaps he too was unhappy at school. But I had happy memories of Kodai, of riding a grey pony, and of its bolting with me once, and I did not fall off, before finally the pony came to a halt at the steps leading down from the dining room at Shoebury, to the covered passageway to the kitchen.

Quite exceptionally we had a bullock so docile that the saddle used for the pony was girthed to the bullock which I rode as if it were a pony. The bullock also pulled a small cart specially made for the purpose in which Beatrice and I could ride side by side.

The journey up to Kodai from Kumarakom took four days. First lap to Quilon – the nearest railhead – 70 miles by *wallum*, taking 24 hours (from 1920 by motorboat, taking eight hours). The second lap was by train a further 24 hours from Quilon to Amaanaikkanur (now renamed Kodai Road Station). Third lap was a 20-mile bullock-cart journey from Kodai Road to Krishnaikan Tope (Krishnaikan's Garden). At Krishnaikan Tope the road ran out, and here there was a travellers' bungalow – a *dak* bungalow – and some rests on beds for a few hours available before a dawn start on the last lap, up the *ghat*.

Ghat literally means 'step', hence the bathing *ghats* of Benares, and by extension the *ghats* referred to the hill ranges running parallel to the east and west coasts of India which rise as huge 'steps' off the coastal plain. From the Tope to Kodai is a rise from 1000 feet to 7000 feet. This last lap took all day for we were carried up by *dhooli* – a form of sagging stretcher with a coolie at each corner. We rose 500 feet in each mile, and as a consequence there were frequent halts.

At a point some 5000 feet above sea level, reached in early afternoon, travellers and their retinue were customarily met by servants from Kodai, bringing what was something very like an English tea – bread, butter, cakes large and small. All this was spread on white tablecloths on the ground. The servants and the tea were supplied by an Anglo-Indian gentleman by the name of Tapp, who lived on the side of the lake at a point known subsequently as Tapp's Corner.

Tapp had a bakery and provided bread to all Kodai. All Europeans in India yearned for bread, and Anglo-Indians who aped Europeans in all possible ways also laid great emphasis on bread as an essential part of their diet.

I vividly recollect arriving by *dhooli* in the dark, with the lights of Kodai twinkling ahead. I also remember waiting at the top of the *ghat* with my mother, for the arrival of my father by bus from Kodai Road Station.

The *ghat* is still known as Law's Ghat, after the chief engineer of the district at that time. My father said Law was most frequently to be found in the Club in Kodai and it was his assistant who was responsible for the supervisory work. The assistant's name now no one knows – probably not even then. Still, the world is ever thus.

In 1921, with my mother, sister, brother and English nurse, we set out for England. My father accompanied us to Bombay, which of course we reached by train from Quilon. I wore a white shirt and shorts and occupied the top bunk for all the journey. I became filthy black with a mixture of soot from the engine and dust from the Deccan Plain, and revelled in it.

A strange mystery that worried me on that journey was the railway catering staff that served our meals in our carriages as we travelled. I worried as to how they would get back to the point where they came aboard the train.

When at last we reached Bombay my father accompanied us to the dock where the SS *Morea* was berthed, and I looked down at him standing on the quay. My father said he would go back to the hotel and get a bath, and return once more to us, to say a final goodbye. But that was the last we saw of him for three years. What must it have been like for my father on his lone journey home, I wonder?

Of the journey home by sea, I remember the surprise of seeing white people (stewards and stewardesses) doing menial jobs; my mother enthusing about the Australian fruit available on the ship; and finally having pointed out to me some faintly rising land just above the horizon which my mother told me was England. I believe now it must have been the Isle of Sheppey.

Finally we came alongside at Tilbury, and there on the dockside was my Grandma Baker and Aunt Dora, who had gone ahead of us in 1920, also by the SS *Morea*.

I stayed at schools in England until August 1932. My passage was booked for me by an uncle and it was aboard the P&O *Baradine*, built specifically for the emigration trade to Australia. I played a great deal of tennis before leaving and, not wishing to have my tennis spoiled by a sore arm, I delayed having all routine inoculations until the last minute. Two or three days before leaving I started to have them, and actually took on board with me the last two phials for the ship's doctor to administer.

Our voyage took 21 days from Tilbury.

The *Baradine* anchored some way off the quay at Colombo and we were taken ashore by motorboat. Standing at the stern outside the awning, smoking a cheroot and wearing a tussore silk suit, I recognised my father. He was always larger than life and he certainly looked that to me on that day. He was very sun-tanned and wearing a large white pith helmet or *topee*. His shoes were bazaar-made, brown leather, square-toed and very shiny. We shared a bedroom at the Grand Oriental Hotel for two or three nights, and on one occasion went to the races.

At this time, three years after the great Wall Street crash of 1929, there was no money anywhere; no one had two coins to rub together. Tea was fetching sixpence a pound at Mincing Lane, and rubber had fallen to twopence a pound. Most estates were on a 'care and maintenance' basis, a euphemism for 'not being tapped'.

The ferry from Talaimannar to Dhanishkodi – the Adam's Bridge of the atlases, not quite joining Ceylon to the Indian mainland – took about an hour as I remember. At Talaimannar we boarded a train that took us more or less all day to get to Madura.

Aunt Dora met us at Madura, having come down the *ghat* in her own car. It was called an Overland. Having her own car put Dora in a different category to other Kodai residents. Few, if any, had their own car. My father had no car. Dora was put up at the railway waiting room. By the standards of the day the room was very comfortable. No English baths but running water, English sanitation, and beds with mosquito nets.

It poured in the night and the next day we went for a drive round the town in Dora's car. There was no question of going round the temple, which was sacrosanct to the Hindus until 1936, I think. The roads in Madura town were not at that time of tarmac, but of laterite. Everywhere there stood vast puddles, or more accurately, stretches of water. I remember my amazement at this standing water in the main roads.

We reached Quilon in the afternoon of the following day, the nearest railhead to Kumarakom, and my mother met us on the platform. After that we travelled the rest of the way in our private motorboat, and a vast company of *wallums* escorted us. I stood on a little bit of decking at the prow of the boat and, as instructed, 'salaamed' everyone who 'salaamed' me from the banks of the rivers and canals we passed along. At the bungalow landing-stage there was an elaborate *pandal* under which we all passed. There were speeches of welcome from local big-wigs and from lesser wigs. I was profusely garlanded. The scent of jasmine was all-pervading. Finally, after a large meal, we all went to bed.

My mother, father and I were alone at Kumarakom. My father would go to work himself at about eight each morning, certainly not an early start for work on the land. We then had breakfast with porridge, toast, eggs and bacon. After breakfast there was a cursory visit to the office and then my father set off on a tour of inspection of where his coolies were working. I was always in attendance and by listening intently (and perhaps because I had been fluent in Malayalam as a child) I gradually learned Malayalam all over again. I heard English spoken only by my mother, otherwise it was Malayalam all the way for weeks, months and two years and two months.

Then, on 30 October 1934, I left home and joined the Central Travancore Rubber Company as an assistant on Rs 250 per month plus Rs 24, the allowance for two coolies.

BEATRICE BAKER

In 1932–34 I was a member of the Fishing Fleet, an expression used to describe the daughters of British families stationed in India who went out to join their parents, uncles, aunts and friends with the idea of finding a husband. I understand there was a Fishing Fleet from Australia whose 'venue' was mostly in Calcutta; my stamping ground was predominantly the Madras Presidency, as it was then called.

In my case finding a husband was not a specific idea as my family (the Bakers) were a long-established family in India. My great-grand-father, Henry Baker, having gone out to India in 1819 as a Church Missionary Society missionary, one of the first in south India. It was always presumed that on leaving school, Malvern Girls College, I would return to India where I was born to enjoy the wonderful life on our family estate Kumarakom. This property was recently bought by the Taj Hotels, and is now known as the Taj Garden Retreat, which will give you some idea of the beauty of the place.

My mother and I set sail from Tilbury docks in the SS *Orsova* for Colombo on a dank and dreary winter's day in January 1934. We were seen off by two of my boyfriends, who made me promise not to get hooked up in India (which of course I never did!).

Life on SS *Orsova* was a simple affair by present-day standards, but I thoroughly enjoyed all that it had to offer and was a foretaste of the social life I was to lead in India. The swimming pool was made of canvas, deep and fairly large, but not big enough for diving or racing. All the same it was great fun. I took full advantage of all the deck games provided; there was nothing organised; after all, the *Orsova* was not a cruise ship (I'm not sure there were any at that time). I cannot remember much about the other passengers, except that my mother spent most of her time with Mr and Mrs Jacobs. Mr Jacobs was PWD (a member of the Public Works Department, a Government job) and stationed in Quilon, which we often visited. I spent time with officers on board and with two very attractive and very well-behaved girls on their way to meet and marry their fiancés in Colombo. I think I was the only unattached girl on board, and consequently enjoyed a great deal of attention from the *Orsova* officers, being invited to the captain's table on gala nights, when there was dancing to an excellent band, probably members of the ship's crew. It was all very exciting, having been brought up on the Tennis Club and my brothers' public-school events.

Simon Artz in Port Said was a magical store with its wealth of Eastern wares. It was here that my mother bought me a 'double *terai*'. It was made of two felt hats, one on top of the other, quite an attractive garden-party shape, but soon to be discarded by me for the much smarter *topee*, but I did wear the *terai* to meet my father in Colombo.

My enduring memory of arriving in Colombo is looking through the porthole of our cabin and in the very early morning mist seeing the breathtaking beauty of the harbour. When we docked, Mother and I went to the rails of the ship and there was my father, all six feet of him, standing on the quayside looking magnificent in a tussore silk suit, highly polished brogue shoes and *topee*, always worn at a rakish angle. There appeared to be few folk around and he shouted and waved at us. What excitement! It was five or six years since we'd seen each other. I don't know how long we stayed in Colombo, a day or two perhaps, but it was at the Galleface Hotel (Mount Lavinia), which I thought was the height of luxury. I was somewhat disillusioned when my father warned me not to walk barefoot about the hotel in case I caught hookworm. All the hotel servants in those days were barefooted.

Now the long journey by train and ferry to mainland India. As was the custom in those days we had a carriage to ourselves, which contained in different compartments, sleeping, washing and kitchen quarters and it was bright and airy. The desert-like scenery seen through large windows was fascinating. I thoroughly enjoyed it all – the shops at the stations, full of noise and bustle; the insistent sellers of oranges, plantains, sweetmeats, mangoes, paw paws, cold and hot drinks, tea and coffee. My mother would only eat fruit which had a skin on it and never touched any of the other food unless thoroughly cooked!

The final stages of the journey to Kumarakom were by *wallum* through the canals with banks rich with flowers and foliage, women doing their washing, children playing, and occasionally a 'temple' elephant being bathed. A typical rural sight in Kerala. Our arrival at Kumarakom was celebrated by the usual *tamasha*, an archway of flowers, garlands galore and greetings from all the staff. Particularly for me from Cheeran, a privileged 'indoor servant', in fact a sweeper, who had known me from birth and who I remembered as a young woman, pale skin, small featured, slim and sweet smelling. She was old now, few teeth, and still without a top (camisole), and the lobes of her ears stretched from wearing heavy gold earrings. Still, there was beauty there, and she gave me a fond embrace, her arms tight about my waist.

My first evening at Kumarakom is a never to be forgotten memory. After dinner (always delicious food, I think I would describe it as Anglo-Indian) I walked with my parents to watch the sunset over the Vembinad Lake. The walk is through the garden in front of the house and on a recent visit I see it is still a ritual observed by the tourists. I was overcome by the loveliness of it all and near to tears.

One of my father's top priorities was to introduce me to the Maharani of Travancore. Travancore was a native state with a large Christian community. There have been many books about how this came about. The ruling family, however, were Hindu. Their palace in Trivandrum, the capital, was completely unpretentious; large grounds, meticulously laid out flower beds and tennis court, where later I was invited to play with the young Maharajah, his sister and her husband. We were invited to tea and my outfit for this presentation was typically English garden party of that era: floral silk dress, large Ascot-style hat, gloves, silk stockings and high-heeled court shoes. I envied the Maharani and her daughter their diaphanous saris, gold sandals and bare feet, their luxuriant long hair decorated with flowers. My father was also in this 'Sunday best' – tussore suit, collar and tie and his shiny brogues. The Maharani was a widow, and she and my father were old friends. She was a highly intelligent, vivacious lady, who had paid visits to the UK and became a friend of Queen Elizabeth, the late Queen Mother. She and my father carried on a mildly flirtatious, animated conversation. I enjoyed the experience but, apart from being invited to play tennis, had no more contact with the royal family of Travancore.

In south India the Madras Presidency could be termed the 'catchment area' for the Fishing Fleet, I imagine. Alleppey, Cochin and Quilon were all situated on the west coast and all within easy access from Kumerakom. They were trading posts with comparatively large European communities – all members of the English Clubs which had dance-floors, dining rooms, bars and a snooker/billiards room, no swimming pools and no Indian members. Alleppey was my father's favourite. He was born in the mission bungalow there, and it was there that he traded. Alleppey Club was small but in a lovely position near the sea. Alleppey was dominated by William Goodacres, a firm which dealt in mats and matting and had a policy of only employing married men – a sparse fishery for the Fleet! However, I enjoyed weekends staying in the large mission bungalow with the Haydons, great friends of my parents, playing tennis, sailing and outboard surfing around the small harbour, which boasted a lighthouse on a small island.

Cochin was a very different kettle of fish, with its large, attractive and extremely busy harbour, with visiting navies, the Royal Navy and the Royal Indian Navy among them, and Willingdon Island on which was built the Malabar Hotel, which had a very adequate swimming pool. The only one along the west coast, I would guess.

Cochin's English Club was also in a scenic position near the beach overlooking the now-famous Chinese fishing nets. Cochin boasted a very popular Yacht Club. My particular boyfriend was an excellent yachtsman who one weekend sailed all the way from Cochin to Kumerakom, finding the inlet opening from the Vembinad Lake to the estate at the appointed time. It meant studying maps and other aids to find his way. My father was very impressed. The firms in Cochin had no rules as to marriage; there was a plentiful supply of bachelors; needless to say it was one of my favourite 'watering' places!

Quilon was the headquarters of Harrison and Crossfield, agents for that area. This firm had no restrictions as to marriage and employed a rather, dare I say it, superior public-school type of staff. We spent some time in Quilon, as the family had a small property there with a bungalow in a spectacular position on a rocky peninsular overlooking the sea. The bungalow was let most of the time, until those renting it became nervous of it falling into the sea. My father had no such qualms and, as my mother and I loved the place, he had boulders hurled on to the rocks already there, to stem the encroaching of the sea. We were very proud of Tangaseri, as it was called, since it was deemed part of British India, having been an East India Company Trading Post; it had a lighthouse just behind the bungalow. We spent many happy times there, especially when my parents gave a party on my twenty-first birthday.

Life in between these 'sorties' to the west coast was – in the hot weather – spent at Kumerakom. We had visitors almost every weekend, if we were not away ourselves. Kumerakom was generally described by those who knew and enjoyed what it had to offer as similar to an English farm, an imposing bungalow with a back farmyard with chickens (my mother was particularly proud of the Rhode Island Reds), duck, turkeys and guinea fowl, and in the stable a 16-hand horse. Beside the farm animals my father was very fond of his dogs, about half a dozen smooth-haired fox terriers, who accompanied us all on walks around the estate. They loved their swims in the Vembinad Lake where we threw sticks for them to retrieve. My father had been a keen horseman in his youth, but in fact there was little opportunity of riding at Kumerakom as it was reclaimed land with coconuts and later rubber trees growing on the bunds. My father and brother fished and shot teal and snipe on the lake. We had, too, a small sailing dinghy, but what I and my friends enjoyed most was the laterite tennis court my father had made. He'd also trained some of the servants to ballboy!

As a legacy from my family's missionary days we were teetotal. However everyone knew this, and would bring their own supply of alcohol, consumed in the privacy of their bedrooms, and appeared at dinner in an excellent mood. As a family (at that time) we did not need the stimulus. The food we had was I think excellent, fresh fish and poultry, teal and snipe when in season, pineapples, mangoes, paw paws, and plantains (small and sweet), all estate produce. My mother disliked curry; my father loved it and it would be specially prepared for him. The cook, trained by my mother in English ways, would make us a mild curry, and with the most delicious accoutrements, fresh from the garden.

My mother and I eventually set sail for the UK from Cochin in one of P&O's latest ships (very different from the SS *Orsova*). No adventures on board. Arriving back in the UK I auditioned for RADA, just missing a scholarship, but enjoyed a term or two there; a fellow student was Richard Attenborough. It was just before the Second World War and many of us left RADA when war was declared to join up. The atmosphere was such that one felt one had to do something. After training I was accepted as a 'plotter' and posted to Northolt during the Battle of Britain. When that was over I became an officer and ended up as an instructor at WAAF officers' school. I met my husband in the RAF.

RONALD RULE

The Rule family commenced its Indian saga with the birth of a boy in Scotland, to John and Elizabeth (née Fergusson) in June 1824, and baptised in Glasgow that year. His name was William – one to occur again and again in later family names.

This William joined the Army, the Heavy Artillery, and married a widow, Mary Ann Gray, in Bangalore, one of the military cantonments established by the British, and home to several families of domiciled Europeans who had retired there. William number two, who was to become my paternal grandfather, became an overseer in the Public Works Department in Bangalore, and retired with the rank of captain. However, by this time he had married a Letitia Pritchard and raised a large family. His home was named Craiglin, and stood at number 4 Tannery Road at the top of St John's Hill, Bangalore. My father Malcolm was the eldest son – born on 12 April 1889. His brother was another William, who worked in the Customs and Excise (Salt) Department, also fathering a large family of four girls and two boys. They lived in a cottage in the grounds of Craiglin. Dennis, the youngest son, went to Malaya as a rubber planter and remained a bachelor for most of his life.

Just before his 21st birthday, my father was engaged by the Eastern Extension Telegraph Company (later Cable & Wireless) as an operator for service in Madras. He was shortly afterwards posted to Batavia in the Dutch East Indies and again, in 1914, to Singapore.

At the other end in Bangalore, my maternal great-grandfather Charles Kirkpatrick had built his retirement home in Langford Town – another settlement for domiciled Europeans. Charles Kirkpatrick had worked in the administrative centre of north and central India (believed in the education service). He had married a lady called Annis Corrigan, who bore him three daughters – Maisie, Doris and Edie. Maisie married a Daniel Fitzpatrick and she herself had three girls – Margaret, Eleanor and Doreen. This family also gravitated towards Bangalore and settled in at Kirkville, Norris Road, Langford Town. This was inscribed on a marble shield on one of the front gates! These girls attended Baldwin's Girls' School and obviously socialised with the Rule family through tennis, dances and other events. Margaret, probably sent for, married my father in Singapore, at St Andrew's Cathedral, in January 1918. I was born in November 1918, a few days after the armistice was signed to end the Great War.

The aftermath of that war influenced my early upbringing in terms of king and country, the empire and the military. I remember an Indian barber in Penang asking my parents if he was to give me a Prince of Wales-style haircut! My mother was ambitious, and I think I had an inkling that she had devised some plan to map out my life, education and so forth. When I was about 10 years old I was taken to India and Bangalore, to live at Kirkville, under the guardianship of my grandmother Maisie Fitzpatrick.

This fearsomely Edwardian lady was a stern disciplinarian and I owe her much – not that I was appreciative at the time. She had just returned from a voyage aboard a troopship as a volunteer, and claimed to have been the only woman present in the middle of the Gallipoli campaign. (An article about this was published in a Bangalore newspaper.)

As a male grandchild in a family of several females, I was honoured and disciplined in equal measure. The house was large and comfortable. The floors were of stone (and cool) under rugs. My grandmother, her daughter Doreen and I slept in a wing with bathroom – a zinc bath which was filled though a side door by the *mali* with hot water and a set of noisome commodes which were emptied after dark by the 'nsc' (night soil cart) – often referred to as the 'queen of the night' in polite society, after a sweet-smelling jasmine creeper.

My great-grandfather had his own bedroom and bathroom into which he disappeared after meals to engage on fretwork, samples of his labours – shelves, letter-racks, picture frames etc. – being much in evidence around the house. He was a taciturn man, and meals were eaten mostly in silence – broken only by a certain clicking sound. This was caused – and I was told never to mention it again – by a loose denture!

My great-grandma Annis never came out of her room for meals. She had her own *ayah* and lived a life on her own. My grandma, Aunt Doreen and I were taken to her room every evening around 6 p.m. to visit her and have some conversation. She was nearly always dressed in black, propped up in a large armchair with very white skin and very white hair. She used to have a tot of some drink or other, probably arrack.

Tea was probably my favourite meal. The circular dining table had a large 'lazy daisy' with ample plates of bread and butter, and a similar number of dainty cakes, curry puffs and other goodies by courtesy of Baclava's – a well-known patisserie on South Parade in town. There was one simple rule. Bread and butter first. Knowing my proclivity for selecting mentally my preferences from the cake plate, my aunt would often distract my attention and heap her plate with my favourites. And so it went on – always passed on as a lesson in restraint and good behaviour.

Breakfasts were mainly of 'hoppers', a sort of pancake, and tea and biscuits. Other meals were often spiced cutlets or devilled this or that, and fresh fruit – mangoes, papayas, guavas etc. – guava jam, guava 'cheese' and even guava 'leather' were always popular in season, which of course was most of the time. We were indulged with sweet-meats from the bazaars, rich with honey and *ghee* and delicious – there was no such word as cholesterol in the Indian language, thank goodness! (Although I was to remember these excesses with a gall-bladder removal in Singapore Hospital half a century later.) Bazaar sweetmeats were supplemented by home-made fudge in Kirkville and *kul-kuls* in Craiglin.

In this context I found that my grandma seemed to be engaged in a curious 'agency' to receive bulk supplies of fresh butter (white, and possibly buffalo), parcel these into rectangular blocks, wrapped in thick greaseproof paper, and despatch these by hand to various local homes, who sent their servants to collect them.

I was sent to Bishop Cotton's School, and walked through Richmond Park there and back. I don't remember a good deal about the class work, but more about the school chapel. I think I must have been in the choir and used to enjoy packing up the vestments and other articles employed during a service. The War was never far from us, and we were constantly reminded of it as Mr Lanyon, the organist and choirmaster, always gave a dry cough before he came into the chapel…he was gassed in the War. Other reminders were a plaque to the memory of Flight Lieutenant Leefe Robinson, who had been to the school and had brought down the first enemy airship to be shot down over England, winning the VC for it.

Bishop Cotton's School was founded in 1865 in memory of a Metropolitan Bishop of Calcutta, who had seen the need to establish schools in the hills for the education of Anglo-Indians, or 'settled' families who were unable, for one reason or another, to send their children to schools in England. This was certainly valid in my case. My father had joined the Eastern Extension Telegraph Company in Madras but worked in Batavia, Singapore and Penang. He was only able to receive benefits and leaves not beyond India.

I recall being sent to the school sanatorium during a bout of mumps, and my grandma and Aunt Doreen speaking to me through an open window (no doubt to avoid direct confrontation of germs) and to tell me that my great-grandfather had died. I learned later, when I returned to Kirkville, that his mosquito net had caught fire and led to his demise.

On other occasions when I was ill with fever, I was put to bed and wrapped in blankets (Indian temperatures notwithstanding) to sweat it out, and dosed with castor oil (in orange juice) and CAQ – the horrible cinnamon ammoniated quinine.

My Aunt Doreen, who was my recognised 'keeper', was a secretary to a large jeweller's firm on South Parade. She would take off on her bicycle and perhaps, in the evenings, a couple of soldiers from the resident military in Bangalore would call and take her, and sometimes my visiting Aunt Letitia, to the Bowring Institute for a dance. The costumes of Spain were in fashion and I was allowed to watch the aunts don their black net dresses, a mantilla with lace and red roses pinned at the shoulder and waist. Make-up was endless, with 'beauty spots' and hair black and glossy which had been waved by tongs heated on a small stove fuelled by methylated spirits and cleaned by crimping some Bromo toilet paper before applying to the hair. More roses or other jewellery followed suit. I was unhappily involved in dancing. Tangos were all the rage, and the wind-up gramophone blared out 'La Composita' and 'O Sole Mio'. My aunts tried to make me dance the steps by gripping my ankles and twisting them towards the footwork. This hurt.

The soldiers, who smelled of sweat and hot serge of their uniforms, were keen to please, and I was very demanding – especially to get hold of the coloured 'hackles' they wore in their caps. I could see that they exchanged glances when these were handed over. Having come to realise the strictures of the quartermaster's stores in later days, I can well imagine what they may have had to go through when getting replacement from their units! I used them to grace my own *topees*, or the DIY uniforms for my private army of boys of my age from neighbouring houses. These were *de rigueur* for parades on the tennis court on 11 November, when we stood to attention for the two minutes' silence on Armistice Day.

ROBERT BAKER

I met some chaps in India who were very, very heavy drinkers, but few who were victims of delirium tremens. There was, however, the case of one Ross-Clark, whom I met on my first visit to Kodai in 1933. He had been an employee of Madurai Mills and had chosen to retire, with his charming, tall, auburn-haired wife, to Kodai. In the Club, Ross-Clark drank only grapefruit juice. I learned that this was because he had been a victim of delirium tremens and could not trust himself to have even one small alcoholic drink. In due course, although they were childless, Mrs Ross-Clark booked a passage home to visit her relations in Scotland. It is said that Ross-Clark had his first drink before his wife had time to reach the bottom of the *ghat*. He was dead within a week.

RONALD RULE

As part of the plan to get me away from India, I was sent to Breeks Memorial School at Ootacamund, Southern India – more than likely to get used to a boarding-school life, and also to experience a colder climate – at about 8000 feet above sea level in the Nilgiris Hills. The so-called plan was obviously to prepare me for a job in Britain with all the benefits which were to be had, and which my father had not experienced as a 'local' engagement. My friends, too, in Bangalore were more likely than not to be Eurasian boys and girls who lived around us at Kirkville, prompting habit-forming attachment to the dreaded 'chi-chi' accent. Otherwise, I had many young friends to play tennis and climb trees with. Flying kites was rampant, and long duels were fought to bring down your opponent's kite. This was achieved by making a mixture of boiled rice and crushed glass in a paste which was applied to the strings of the kites. Once in the air, one fought against another by rubbing the 'armed' strings together!

We were kind to our servants. There was a boy (man about the house and server) in his newly starched uniform. The cook was generally invisible in his quarters next to the house, plus his wife and snotty offspring. We had a *mali* for the garden and as general dogsbody for tasks such as filling the tin baths with hot water. Local travel was by bicycle, and any distance by horse-drawn coaches and *gharry* and driver. The driver would drive into town to shop for cloth and rich sweetmeats. There were very few exchange visits with other local residents. At Kirkville there was a small *chokra* boy who would always whistle when he passed our garden wall. This enraged my grandma, who would fly out of the house with a cane and have words with him in her best Hindustani. She always maintained this was 'impertinent'.

After a couple of years at Breeks, I returned to Penang to spend my Christmas holidays there. One day a telegram arrived for my father announcing that I had passed my Junior Cambridge Exam in India. Subsequently, things had to move, following, as I understood, a conversation between a friend of his, the Harbour Master of Penang, who was known to have a son at school in England. This turned out to be Deal School, in Kent, which specialised in boarding youngsters whose parents worked and lived overseas.

In the days of no aeroplanes, contacts between parents and offspring were remote, and the school looked after pupils in the holidays and so on. Therefore, round about January 1935 (I was about 16 years old then), I took passage on the P&O SS *Cormorin* for England. I was put in the charge of a friend of my parents who, whenever I called to see him in his cabin, appeared to hurriedly disengage himself from another lady passenger. He spent very little time with me!

On our arrival at Tilbury, we caught the boat train to Waterloo, and I was met there by my aunt, Doris (aunt to my mother), who was going to give me a home at her house in Kingston-on-Thames. On the train journey down I got very excited stopping at Wimbledon, as

I was very keen on tennis. Otherwise, the only 'English' affectation I had was, on a visit to London with my cousins, marching around the Cenotaph several times, lifting my hat as I passed by.

My aunt took me down to Deal in time for the summer term, and I met boys from South Africa, South America, The Persian Gulf, and a Parsee boy from Bombay. Settling in was not difficult. Christmas holidays were spent with my cousins in Kingston (Father was in the Malayan Civil Service), and in two successive summers, the Headmaster rented a vicarage at Abingdon. The following year at Felixstowe, we took our bicycles with us and spent time in that way, and at Felixstowe I also entered a local tennis championship and won the Junior Competition for singles!

Lavender Jamieson outside the Char Minar Mosque in Hyderabad. (Lavender Jamieson)

3

Bombay

The Presidency of Bombay was enormous, bounded on the north by Baluchistan, the Punjab and Rajputana; on the east by Indore, the Central Provinces and Hyderabad; and on the south by Madras and Mysore. To the west it presented some 500 miles to the Arabian Sea, with very few harbours. The Western Ghats, a range of rocky hills, ran along it, sometimes plunging into the sea, but more often leaving an irregular plain, five or fifty miles wide, between them. The province of Sind, far in the north and with Karachi as its principal city, was also a part of the Presidency.

The Governor of Bombay was appointed directly by the India Office. As the climate varied considerably, and was nowhere considered healthy, he spent only December to March in Government House, Malabar Hill, in the city of Bombay. April and May were spent in Mahableshwar, 4500 feet high, the Monsoon in Poona, 1905 feet high, and October and November in Mahableshwar again. Then he returned to Bombay.

The island on which the city of Bombay is built was originally sacred to the goddess Mumba, an incarnation of Parvati, consort of Shiva. It has had a long and chequered history, being frequently fought over on account of its excellent harbour, known to the English as Back Bay. It came into British hands in the dowry of Catherine of

Bragança, a Portuguese Princess, on her marriage to King Charles II in 1662, although they were unable to occupy it until 1665. The word Bombay is a simple anglicisation of Bom Bahia, Portuguese for 'good bay'.

Development of the deep-water port, on the other side of the island, began in 1750, but it was the arrival of the railway, in 1853, and the opening of the Suez Canal, in 1869, that brought its enormous prosperity to the city. It has been known as the Gateway of India since 1911.

In addition to being the principal deep-water port in India, it was, in particular, a centre of the cotton and textile trades. The Great Indian Peninsular Railway and the Bombay, Baroda and Central India Railway both used the great Victoria Terminus, a magnificent example of Indo-Gothic architecture, from which one could travel to Delhi, Calcutta and Madras without changing trains. Bombay University dates from 1857.

The East India Company first established itself at Surat, 167 miles north of Bombay on the coast, in 1610.

PAMELA ALBERT

My parents met at the Royal Bombay Turf Club. She was 18 years of age, he was 30 and on leave from his regiment. It was a glamorous setting – ladies in long flowing dresses and big hats, coloured tents, regimental bands playing; bearers scurrying around doing all that would bring pleasure to the Raj.

The Army officers in their very colourful uniforms, buttons shining, shoes polished till one's face shone in them! It was no wonder that a young girl fell in love with a reddish-blond young lieutenant in his striking uniform of the 11th Bengal Lancers!

They had only ten days to spend together, as he was due to return to the North West Frontier and the famed Khyber Pass, but they corresponded and thereafter saw one another when possible. Marriage was not permitted until he was a captain and at least 30 years old, so the wedding actually took place in October 1926 at St George's Cathedral, Bombay. My father had accumulated one year's leave so they spent their honeymoon in Egypt, the Continent and England, where I was born nearly one year later. (One year's leave every three years was part of the contract with the Indian Army.)

In those days, it took 21 days' sailing from England to India. The passage began in the Atlantic Ocean, then into the Mediterranean Sea calling at Gibraltar, Malta and Port Said. From there, the ship entered the Suez Canal, calling at Port Sudan in the Red Sea, and thence into the Indian Ocean. Army officers and family travelled first class, and even with a six-week-old baby, they had lots of time to enjoy the many facilities on board. There were Captain's dinners, cocktail parties and such like – and always the grateful assistance of ships' stewardesses. The last night aboard ship was usually a night of partying, and a fancy-dress ball was usually held. As a result, most of the revellers were still asleep when the ship moved into Bombay Harbour. The ship docked at 2 p.m. and my grandparents were on the pier waiting to greet us and anxious to see their first grandchild. Whilst my father was supervising the luggage, I was delighting my happy grandparents with my flaming red hair and bright blue eyes. It was agreed I looked like my father! I was immediately handed over to Ayah, who was to be my surrogate mother, friend, keeper and confidante for many years to come.

A devout Roman Catholic from Madras, Fat Mary (as we all called her) was hired by my grandmother to care for all my needs. She was with us through thick and thin for 18 years. Almost as wide as she was tall, she had long black hair done in a bun, sometimes with jasmine flowers wound into the shining bun. She always wore a crisp white sari, with white blouse and brown sandals. Whenever I smell the scent of jasmine, I am reminded of Fat Mary. At this time, Mary would possibly have been in her mid-twenties, but it is hard to tell the age of Indians as they seem always to look young for so long, and then they seem to age all of a sudden. She was very dark skinned, lovingly fat, and had black eyes. She had a gold stud in her nose and in each ear, with flawless ebony skin. She was a gentle soul who was much loved and who would take care of my mother and me.

One taxi carried us away from the docks with a second close behind with our huge pile of luggage. The remainder of our baggage would be sent on by the agents via rail to Rawalpindi where the regiment was stationed.

We arrived at my grandparents' home in Mazagon. My mother's father, Thomas C. Ross Perry, was a captain in the Merchant Service of P&O and the British India Company. His family had been seafaring men in the East India Shipping Company. Their family home was in Sunderland. When my grandfather began to lose his eyesight, the company gave him a land position in charge of ships' supplies, stationed in Mazagon Docks, Bombay.

This was a community owned by the P&O British India Lines, where the compound seemed to stretch for at least 20 miles. It included dry docks, ships' stores, storehouses – godowns, as they were called. Then there was an area about a mile from the business district that was set aside for residents who worked for the shipping lines. The living area comprised of homes, tennis courts, a swimming pool, squash courts and parks with swings and see-saws for the children plus a huge sandbox.

Around the perimeter were sited the living quarters with a variety of homes, bachelor flats and larger houses for families. There was a huge Club house where most of the entertainment was held – musicals, parties, dances, plays and every type of special occasion. My grandfather's home was a large one: you walked up to an open verandah to the front door, and this opened into a downstairs reception room. Beyond that was the dining room and behind this was located a separate cookhouse, with servants' quarters.

From the dining room, you climbed a staircase to a second-floor landing. At the head of the stairs was the formal sitting room with doors leading off to a verandah. Off to the right of the landing was my grandparents' huge bedroom and bath. It was a room with large windows and a window seat area where grandfather used to have his *chota hazri* ('small breakfast'), and watch the train go by at 5 a.m. There were two further bedrooms and bathrooms on that floor, and on their third floor it followed the same pattern but without the verandah. This house was to be a stability to all the family, and many times housed the whole family and guests. No matter where any one of us was in India, Ceylon or in Singapore, this was home, for in joy or in sorrow everyone headed home to Mazagon.

CAROLINE BURDER

My grandfather, H.C. Burder, a London solicitor practising in Bombay, was retained to defend a Mr Jacob, an Armenian jeweller from Delhi, in a case brought against him by the Nizam of Hyderabad about the purchase of a diamond.

The Imperial Diamond, as it was then called, although it is now known as the Jacob Diamond, was believed to be South African. It was of perfect colour, rather larger than the Koh-i-noor, and believed to be the third largest in the world. It was thought to have been stolen and had certainly fallen into the hands of a syndicate, who offered it to Mr Jacob for £75,000. He paid them half the cost on account and then offered it to the Nizam for £300,000, an astronomical sum in those days.

The Nizam agreed to this, also paying half the amount down, the rest to be paid on delivery. But, at the time of purchase, 1894, the state of Hyderabad was suffering from severe famine and the Indian Government considered it inappropriate for the Nizam to be indulging in such an extravagance at such a time. The British Resident in Hyderabad was therefore instructed to stop the purchase. The chosen method was to persuade the Nizam to institute proceedings against Mr Jacob, on the grounds that he had obtained the advance payment fraudulently, this being a criminal charge, and that is what actually happened.

It was here that my grandfather came in. On his first visit to the Nizam, in Hyderabad itself, he was shown into a large dark room lit only by candles. When everyone was assembled and ready to talk, all the candles suddenly flickered and went out, whereupon the Nizam's advisers said this was a very bad omen and that 'nothing would take place'. So my grandfather had to go all the way back to Bombay, and I believe that happened several times!

In the upshot there was no valid case for the charge, but the Nizam, in spite of his rank as a ruling sovereign, was obliged to appear in person as the prosecutor. He proved to be an absolutely hopeless witness and was caught out, more than once, quite simply telling bare-faced lies. In the end, my grandfather and his leading counsel were able to prove conclusively that the whole case had been trumped up by the Government and that it had no foundation at all in fact. The judge accepted the evidence and Jacob was duly acquitted.

But the Government was not satisfied. They tried to persuade the Nizam to bring a civil suit against Jacob for the recovery of the down payment, but this the Nizam refused to do. He was sick of the whole affair and so was Jacob. He asked my grandfather to hand over the diamond to the Nizam and take whatever the Nizam was prepared to pay for it. This he did. The Nizam finally paid only the balance of Jacob's original purchase price, £75,000, and there the matter ended. There was no profit for Jacob, of course, just vast legal expenses, but he also gave my grandfather a bronze group of two figures, Chinese or Japanese. The man is standing upright with sword and bow, while the woman bows to him and offers him some food. It is about 11 inches high, on a stand, and one of my favourite possessions.

My grandfather remained in India and my father was born there in 1900. My grandparents' social life in Bombay seems to have centred around pig-sticking and horse shows. My grandmother, Kate Wilson, a daughter of Wilson's Breweries in Cheshire, was a very successful horsewoman. She won many prizes on a native 'cat', a grey waler, and a local paper is on record as having said, 'It's a pity some of the gentlemen don't ride as well as Mrs Burder'.

In the photograph albums, the horses are always named, but the people are usually not! There is one splendid photograph, taken in 1895, entitled 'Jodhpur Pigsticking Meet' – '54 pigs killed before breakfast'. The pigs are all laid out in rows, though one can only count 40. And there are only two pig-stickers, though there must have been more. Perhaps they were all having breakfast!

PHILIP BANHAM

At the very outbreak of World War I my father was sent with his battalion to India to serve on the North West Frontier. He finally finished up as a Warrant Officer, in charge of the Army Records Office in Poona. By 1920 he had come to love India. He wasn't too keen to returning to his bakery job in Paignton. Knowing this, his Commanding Officer had a word with the Deputy Inspector General, and my father was offered a post in the Bombay District Police Force. So he opted for demob in India, and began as a Sergeant in Charge of Traffic in Poona. Of course there was a disadvantage: he would not be entitled to the allowances and paid holidays home that he might have got had he come to this occupation from England. It meant that he would never be able to afford to send us, his children, to be educated in boarding school in Britain, and that we would have to grow up entirely in India and go to schools there.

I was proud of my father. He started in a little elementary school in Teignmouth, started work at thirteen, and would have worked, perhaps, in that Paignton bakery for the rest of his life. The Great War took him to India – Karachi, Quetta, Multan, the North West Frontier, Lahore and Poona. Having started as a Police Sergeant in 1920, by 1938 he had become a full-blown Superintendent. He always thought of his sepoys wherever he went. He checked that they were getting all possible allowances, rewards and medals. He was respected and loved. And when he had to arrange for and per-sonally arrest the Mahatma and a couple of Congress leaders, he did it in a very gentle, considerate way.

And I was proud of my mother. Her family were already living in India before 1914 because her father had gone out to India to work in the Bombay Government Secretariat. She brought up four of us in very difficult circumstances, especially in view of my father's low salary. As he had been demobbed in India, he didn't qualify for any of the allowances that went with 'covenanted service'. So money was always in short supply.

I was born in the Sassoon Hospital in Poona in 1922, and I was followed by Patricia in 1923, Patrick in 1924 and Peter in 1927. Aged four I went into a ten-day coma with enteric fever and was not expected to live. But they fed me through the nose and I did. We lived in a flat above the Police Station, known as Bowli Chowki, situated on the side of a vast roundabout. A War Memorial stood in the middle and there were Remembrance Services there with military bands, troops, guns and armoured cars. The railway station and Sassoon Hospital were not far from here and, of course, this was the cantonment.

I was six when I went to my first school. It was a Roman Catholic convent in the heart of the city of Ahmedabad which took boys for a few years at the start of their schooling. Ahmedabad was a large industrial town with many cotton mills just along a branch line from Karaghoda, where salt was panned. This became the object of Gandhi's protests against Government control of salt production.

Dad was now a railway Police inspector. His job entailed a lot of days and nights away 'on line', so he was hardly ever at home, and because my mother was scared of the various epidemics (smallpox, cholera, typhoid) that kept sweeping through the city and because there was so much communal strife between Muslims and Hindus, I hardly ever went to that convent. Life was an almost endless holiday, spent in bare feet with nothing more to wear each day than a pair of shorts. I spent my time dodging pariah dogs, avoiding snakes and scorpions and watching the antics of monkeys.

We looked forward to the visits from the snake charmers, the *mango-wallahs*, the sweetmeatwallahs, tumblers and gymnasts, the festival dancers and the man with the dancing bears. There was also a wandering Chinaman with a box of silks! We survived enteric fever, malaria, diphtheria, boils, ringworm, prickly heat, dysentery and mid-summer temperatures of 130 degrees Fahrenheit in the shade!

My second school was called St Joseph's and was in a northern suburb of Bombay called Bandra where my dad was the Home Inspector. But before long he was transferred to Thana, and since there was no suitable school there I was sent at nine and a half as a chorister to the Cathedral High School in the heart of Bombay, and put into Standard 3. This was too ambitious and bewildering a beginning for me. I had had so little schooling that I could hardly read, write or spell anything except my name. As for the simplest sums, they were beyond

St Mary's Church, Poona. 'My grandfather and grandmother attended this church with my mother and her sister and two brothers. Grandmother sang in the choir, and when my father and mother, two brothers and sister went to Poona we also went to this church. There was a school and college attached. My sister went to the college before she joined the Army nursing service at the beginning of the 1939 War.' (Philip Banham)

my comprehension. Here every 35 minutes a bell would ring and, unlike the convent where I had had the comforting presence of a nun all day, a master would enter, and quite a different one from the one before. You had to stand up each time he entered or left, and had to say 'Sir' when you spoke to him and raise your cap to him outside the classroom. Here you had subjects! Whatever were they, I wondered? Subjects with strange names like geography, history, algebra, geometry, scripture and Latin. What did it all mean? I was given a desk full of textbooks (textbooks?) and exercise books (what, no slates?). When the master said, 'We'll have scripture, get ready to read from chapter three,' I whispered to the boy at the next desk, 'What's scripture?' 'Don't you know?' 'No, what book is it?' So he foraged around in my desk and took out a thick black book. As I was a new boy, the master soon called my name (always by surname in this school) and I stood up, stared at the open book, stammered and stuttered until he said, 'Sit down, Banham, you fool!'

Every three weeks the form positions were put on the class notice board. I was regularly 39th, bottom of the class for all to see. This meant that I had to spend another year in Standard 3.

Fortunately I was also in the cathedral choir. This was taken very seriously, half an hour's practice every day with services on Saints' days and Sundays. When the choirmaster realised my reading disability he put me next to the head chorister, who used to run his forefinger under each line like a cursor! It helped me to learn to read very rapidly because as I looked at each word I was able to hear what it sounded like. It was the same throughout all the services, and he extended his help to cover even the prayers and Bible reading.

By 1939 I had obtained my School Certificate with exemption from London Matric, while rising through the standards at the same school. The headmaster, Colonel Hammond, said that after the War England would need teachers. I wanted to join the Army at once, since I saw it as my duty, but I took his advice and went to the Chelmsford Teacher Training College at Ghora Ghali in the far north west – set

8000 feet up in the Himalayan pinebelt. There I saw for this first time houses with fireplaces, roofs hanging with icicles, thick snow everywhere, frost, ice and distant mountain ranges gleaming white in the tropical sunshine.

PATRICIA BANHAM

My earliest recollection was when I stood at the balcony of our flat above Poona Cantonment Police Station. I was about three. My father, who was the sergeant-in-charge, had his office downstairs. As I stood at the balcony of the verandah, I remember what seemed a vast roundabout where three roads joined, with a War Memorial in the middle. It must have been 11 November 1926, because my father was there on parade smartly dressed in his Sam Brown belt, khaki pith helmet, shining boots and leggings, and ceremonial sword. Proudly like all the serving ex-servicemen that day, he wore his First World War medals. Bands were playing and contingents of the Indian Army, British Army and Indian Police were marching along those three roads, converging on the memorial for prayers and hymns and the laying of wreaths. It was all wonderful to us, but I couldn't really understand when Mother tried to explain about the sacrifice that the Indian soldiers and British Commonwealth soldiers had made, laying down their lives to fight in a 'war to end all wars'.

My first school was in Bandra, a suburb of Bombay. It was a Roman Catholic convent school, and I spent a couple of months there as a boarder. The dormitory seemed ever so large, and each bed had a blue curtain all round so we couldn't look at each other at night! As for the bathroom, it was very strange: as large as a gymnasium, with taps jutting out of the walls and a small paved enclosure allotted to each tap. We went in about 10 at a time, each one to a tap. What struck me as odd, even at that tender, innocent age, was that we had to bath and soap ourselves still wearing our bloomers! As young as we were, we were not allowed to remove all our clothing.

Another memory, a candle-lit one, was the Feast of Mount St Mary. We were dressed in white and carried little baskets of confetti and flowers which we strewed at little grottoes of saints around the convent grounds. Then came the procession to the Virgin's shrine on the promontory by the sea. How can I forget the sight of hundreds of candles wending their way up to the holy place on the mount?

Thinking back, I just wonder where all those devout Christians came from in a land that was so predominantly Hindu and Muslim. It was amazing what the early Portuguese missionaries had managed to achieve.

My boarding school days there came to an end and I continued as a day scholar. But mother, who was a Methodist, became alarmed when she found me placing some lighted candles in front of a picture in the sitting room. It was a large picture depicting the boy Jesus preaching to the elders in the temple. When my father came home she said, 'Patsy's burning candles in front of the boy Jesus'. But my father was not perturbed. He said, simply, 'Take no notice. She'll grow out of it.' I never saw that picture anywhere else – not in any house, book, magazine, shop or art gallery. But 20 years ago, when I came to England to see my father before he died, it was still with him. He gave it to me to take back to South Africa. It's been here with me ever since. It's a constant reminder of my fond memories of early childhood, where British, Anglo-Indian and Indian children grew up together: we learned to be natural with each other, oblivious to ethnic origins, treating each other happily as equals. We made great friends among ourselves; we did not know what racial prejudice was. I was grateful for that experience, that upbringing, particularly when, after serving in the Second World War as an Army nurse, I married and came to live in Johannesburg.

The next school I remember was the Taylor High School in Poona. Father had been transferred to a place in Thana where there was no school for us. My grandfather had to give up work as he was going blind. I remember he was always cheerful, kind, never lost his temper. Though blind, he used to keep everything neatly in his chest of drawers. He used to say, 'A place for everything and everything in its place' and 'Cleanliness is next to godliness.' He was deeply religious, spending an hour or two every afternoon on his knees praying in his bedroom. He also loved my reading to him; news items from the *Times of India*, the poems of Kipling and others.

It was in this school, the Taylor High, that the teacher made me use my right hand when I preferred to write with my left hand. It made me cry and I didn't want to go to school. So, an unusual thing for those days, my mother asked my teacher to make an exception in my case. I was happy then, and made good progress. I also learned to play netball and badminton. There was play-acting too, and at one concert I was a doll-bride. The doll-groom was in a top hat and tails. I wore a long white dress and had my mother's wedding veil with an orange blossom circlet. We had our two small fingers tied together with white ribbon and in the end we had to walk to the edge of the stage and sing a song.

ANONYMOUS

In the middle of 1926 my father, who was an Army surgeon, was transferred from Barrackpore to the British Military Hospital in Poona. So in December of that year I had a train journey of 1500 miles, two nights and three days. The price of the railway ticket was halved because another schoolfriend had two sisters and we all travelled together as a party of four: a party of four travelled half price.

How well I remember those long train journeys, with Aloysius and Ena and Freda. We formed a party of four for the Christmas holidays from 1926 to 1929 and became lifelong friends. Aloysius rose to be a brigadier during the War and Ena and Freda both married.

The Bengal Nagpur Railway (BNR) ran the train from Calcutta to Nagpur, where the Great Indian Peninsular Railway (GIPR) took over the mail for Bombay. We changed at Kalyan for Poona. We visited one another often while we were there. Their father was a Commissioner of Customs – pretty high up – and he owned an Armstrong Siddeley, very rare and expensive. My father, as an assistant Army surgeon, had a Chevrolet which suited his more modest means.

Second-class railway travel in India was very clean and comfortable. There was a restaurant car on mail trains. The guard would come round enquiring who wanted morning tea, lunch or dinner and at the next station (there were no corridors on those trains) we went to the restaurant car for our lunch and dinner. We benefited from the intense competition between the BNR and the GIPR. The food and service was ever so good. It puzzled me, at 13, which knives and forks to use out of the array before us. 'Start from the outside and work inwards,' Ena told me. So we got it right.

I was still at school at North Point, in Darjeeling, so this journey was performed once a year until I was 16, in 1929. The most coveted Government posts for civilians were in the Indian Civil Service (ICS), the Indian Police (IP), the Indian Educational Service (IES), the Indian Medical Service (IMS), the Indian Forestry Service (IFS) and the Public Works Department (PWD). The Jesuits at North Point had brought me up a good Catholic man, healthy and fit, and ready to face the world and I decided to join the Indian Police, well paid, physically demanding and an independent job, running a district Police force.

So I applied to the Deccan College in Poona and went there in 1930, staying until 1935. In retrospect these were the happiest days of my life. The Deccan College was originally built for the sons of local princes and landholders only. The main building, containing the library, assembly hall and administration offices, was in the high gothic style (1864), as were the PWD Secretariat in Bombay, the Bombay University Hall, Elphinstone College, the clock tower and the General Post Office, which was built by Frederick William Stevens between 1878 and 1887. So the main building had a tower and the windows and ceilings were Victorian Gothic.

I think it catered for 50 resident students and about 200 day students. I cycled about three miles each way from the Poona cantonment, over Bund Garden Bridge, past the Aga Khan's palace (where Gandhi was later imprisoned and fasted to death – almost) and on to the road to Kirkee. The Deccan College had huge grounds in a vast open space.

Entry to the college was entirely dependent on an interview with the Principal, a fresh-faced, cheerful individual called Hugh George Rawlinson. Years later I discovered that he had written some 17 books in Indian subjects. He taught us English and History. The Vice-principal was E.A. Wodehouse, elder brother of the more famous P.G. Wodehouse, and he taught us English literature.

The Mutha and Mula rivers joined just above Poona and so the river flowing through it was called the Mutha-Mula. We had a boat club, single skiffs and fours, and a crew of four; an Australian was stroke; a Goan was behind him, with another Goan behind him. I was No. 1 in the bow. A Parsee was our enthusiastic cox. We had one year's practice before our first regatta and we worked like slaves. On the great day itself, we broke the college record for the distance.

The father of our Australian stroke was a horse trainer. The Royal Western India Turf Club held 12 meetings in Poona between June and October, and 22 meetings at Mahalaxmi, Bombay, between November and March. I heard about part-time jobs at the Turf Club in Poona, so I applied and was taken on as a 'non-starter runner'. I had to have my own bicycle. I was supplied with an armband to wear on my upper left arm and I had to be present at the starting point of each race. The starter was a very smart Englishman in breeches and polished riding boots and, in case a horse refused to start, it was up to him to phone the totalisator manager, who removed all bets on it. If the phone was out of order, it was my job to cycle with a written note, before the race, to get there first and deliver this important piece of information. I attended 12 meetings of 6 races each, and not once were my services required! But I was paid 12 times eight rupees, that is to say 96 rupees, for doing nothing. And I was taken on again when the Bombay races began, this time at 15 rupees per day, for 22 meetings.

We travelled from Poona to Bombay's Mahalaxmi Race Course by train, the Race Special. It ran non-stop for 120 miles to arrive in good time for the punters to have had lunch on the train. That train was always full – first, second, intermediate and third class – all rich before, few still rich on the return journey. The camaraderie amongst us part-timers was terrific and it was all great fun.

There was a platoon of the University Training Corps (UTC) at the Deccan College, 32 students in all. Two of the schools in Darjeeling, St Joseph's, where I was, and St Paul's, had foot platoons of about 30 cadets in the Northern Bengal Mounted Rifles (NBMR). I joined at 15 in 1928. We fired an annual musketry course, 10 rounds .303 at 100 yards and another 10 at 200 yards. All of us finished up with very sore right shoulders. We did squad drill weekly. The NBMR was made up mostly of tea-planters, who were all mounted, riding their horses up and down their tea estates.

So when I joined the UTC at the Deccan College I was made a corporal in my first year as a result of my cadet training at school, and a sergeant for the next two years. We paraded weekly and I became good at drill. I learned to shoot partridge and quail and snipe with a 12-bore shotgun.

Let me confess that the Deccan College was for me both a culture shock and an eye-opener. To start with, there were six women students in our class. Then, I had not met Indians as equals before. I discovered that, among my fellow students, who were Hindus, Muslims, Parsees and Jains, there were young men as good as, and even better than, me. For instance, Appa Sahib Pant, heir to the chieftainship of the Ismail of Aundh, south of Poona, was to become Indian ambassador to London in the 1960s; and Sikandar Khan Dehlavi became Pakistan's ambassador to London, also in the 1960s.

So the time finally came for me to try for entrance to the Police. One had to be a British subject, aged 21 on 1 September, graduate of a recognised college, and one then had to pass a medical and go for an interview. The snag for me was that my birthday is in October and so, in the end, had to twiddle my thumbs for one-and-a-half years.

One applied in writing, with supporting documents, to the Public Service Commission, and when I did so, there were 200 applicants for one vacancy. Of these only 50 passed the medical, and of those only 16 were called for interview at the Council Hall in Poona. We had to do our written examination in Bombay and, of the remaining 16, only one could come top, and that, I am happy and proud to say, was me.

I completed my Police training in 1937, at Nasik, 107 miles north east of Bombay, and two years later married a wonderful girl whom I had known since I was at the Deccan College. We found ourselves in a very tight class system. The Indians had a rigid caste system, into which one was born and could not get out of. The Europeans' system was based entirely on the husband's job and this determined one's social position. The Civil Service, the Police, the Education Service, the Medical Service, the Forest Service and the PWD formed a social clique that excluded the others. It was far more rigid than any class system in England.

There was, in fact, a book called *The Warrant of Precedence*. It laid down one's place for functions at Government House, for instance, and though it was not meant to be funny it was. Superintendents of Police, I need hardly say, came very low down the list. But woe betide any hostess who placed a lady at table one place lower than her husband's rank dictated. I shall remember forever the headaches this caused us whenever we entertained.

PHILIP BANHAM

By the time I was six we had moved to Ahmedabad. Here was a city which suffered continuously from malaria and, periodically, from dysentery, diphtheria, cholera, typhoid and smallpox. There may have been preventatives for all of them in existence at that time but I can only remember vaccination for smallpox and teaspoon-doses of sugar-sweetened quinine for malaria. It was there, in Ahmedabad, that we first learned what it was to have prickly heat – and boils.

I still have several small scars showing where the doctor's knife cut open my blind boils to let out the blood and pus. Mother had certain remedies for some common problems: for cuts and sore throats there was iodine; for constipation, Eno's, castor oil or enemas; for phlegm on the chest, mustard plaster.

When I was about six-and-a-half, and my father was 'on line', Mother woke me at three one morning. 'Philip, I'm very ill. You must get help,' she pleaded. 'Look out for snakes and pariah dogs. Go to Mr Armstrong.'

More than anything else I was worried about his two huge Alsatians, but I had to set off through the darkness to walk the four hundred or so yards relying on the paltry light of a kerosene lantern. I'd hardly reached his little garden gate when the barking began. I was too petrified to go any further. 'Please don't let them loose,' I thought. Lights went on in the bungalow. 'Who's there?' he called, opening the front door slightly. 'It's only me, Philip,' I stuttered. 'Who...?' 'It's only me, Philip,' more loudly. He could see the lantern, but not me. He came out, and then was obviously incredulous that I stood there, scared, all on my own, so far from home. As he led me indoors I explained. Leaving his wife to ring for a doctor and comfort me, he rushed off to my mother. An hour later he returned with my brother and sister. 'Winnie's been taken to hospital,' he said to his wife. 'Diphtheria.'

While she tucked us up in bed in her spare room, he got on the phone to the duty *havildar* at the railway Police station. 'Get a message to Banham Sahib. Tell him the Memsahib is in hospital and the children are with me.' At that time Dad was in Baroda. He caught the first available train home to Ahmedabad.

When I went home on holiday from boarding school, my father was usually 'on tour'. This meant moving from place to place, staying in a *dak* bungalow or under canvas. There would be a village or town nearby and fields of cotton or rice or millet. But beyond there was always open country – jungle or sparse scrub, or some of each. It was this open country that made these holidays so memorable:

it was there to wander, to explore; it was full of the opportunity for adventure.

After a breakfast of sago, bacon, eggs and tea, my brother Patrick and I would set off armed with our catapults, a Scout knife and a haversack containing a flask of water, slices of bread and butter and half a dozen mangoes. What was so fascinating about these expeditions was the abundance of 'wildlife'. One only had to look behind a pile of stones or peer into a bush to discover, sheltering from the sweltering sun, a huge lizard (we called them 'bloodsuckers'), or a black scorpion exhibiting his frightening stinging tail or a colony of large red ants who, given half a chance, would swarm all over you and nearly bite you to insanity. As for deadly snakes, there was no shortage of them at all. There might be one up in a tree, down in the hollow between two rocks, or curled up in a thick tuft of dead grass. Very often there would be one moving slowly, zig-zagging through the dust just in front of you, the bright sun glinting off his icy skin.

On one of our walks we saw what we thought was a quail go around a bush. We got out our catapults and moved around to get a good view and a shot at what we thought would be a nice titbit for supper. But to our surprise it was a mongoose confronting a cobra. It was like a scene straight out of Kipling. The mongoose moved in, tempting the cobra to strike. When it did the mongoose dodged, and before the snake cold raise his head, the mongoose sank his teeth into the back of the snake's neck, then let it go. The striking, dodging and biting was repeated about half a dozen times. When Rikki became aware of our presence he grabbed this Kala Nag in his teeth and hauled him away down a *nullah*.

Often we would go bathing in a river and be pestered by scores of trout-sized fish 'nibbling' at our limbs. It must have been our salty sweat that made it worth their while! And when we noticed them swim rapidly away we'd get out of the water pretty quick because there were crocodiles about.

Back at the camp in the evening, sitting out having supper, we'd be visited by monkeys, ready to snatch food from the table, and in the night, lying out under the stars, there was the crying of jackals not far away. And overhead the silhouettes of flying foxes going in search of fruit trees. If there was a jungle nearby we'd sit up at night in a *machan* over a pool and watch out for nila or panther, wild boar or black bear.

Once, returning at daybreak, the surprising sight of a mother bear walking upright with a baby bear walking beside her. It was 'holding' Mother's 'hand'! Oh, if only one could have afforded to own a camera!

Apropos of cameras, we grew up in an age when, in our family, they were never thought of. Photography was too expensive a hobby so I have very few snaps and the few in existence are of family or school groups.

We all had to go to a boarding school eventually, and that's where I went at nine years old – to the Cathedral High School in the very heart of Bombay, as a day-scholar, because Father had been moved from Bandra to Thana. I stayed in Bombay and went to live with a man called Frank Preece. He showed me how to get to school on the fast (that is, non-stop) train to Church Gate, the terminus. He took me to the school and handed me over to the Secretary, a middle-aged Parsee gentleman who always wore a black brimless hat. Eventually I was led to the Headmaster's Office. He had ginger hair, narrow, steely-blue eyes and a very severe, thin-lipped mouth.

'Name?'

'Philip John Banham.'

'Say SIR when you speak to me.'

'Philip Banham, Sir.'

'Age?'

'Nine-and-a-half.'

'What did I just tell you?'

'Nine-and-a-half, Sir.'

Frank Preece accompanied me to school for a few days and then gave me my season ticket, leaving me to travel daily on my own, getting off the train, setting off on foot to the school, crossing wide

The 'toy' train that goes from the Bombay–Poona mainline railway up to Matheran. It moves at about 7–8mph. Little local boys and girls trot alongside holding pretty posies of flowers high up in their hands asking for *baksheesh*. The length of the line was about 18 miles. At weekends our scout master, Arty Lunn, used to take a small party of boarders to stay there, so we travelled on that train. *below* Turning into 'one-kiss tunnel'. (Philip Banham)

roads packed with trams, taxis, cars, ox-carts, double-decker buses, rickshaws, bicycles and also, of course, cows and pariah dogs and beggars and lepers. Thinking back, this was some achievement for a nine-year old who had never yet been in a city such as this before – who was a 'country kid' used to quiet streets or a tonga or two.

About Major Bruce, standing in for the regular Headmaster who was on leave in England. No boy aged eight to sixteen dared trifle with him. He looked fierce and he wielded the cane on the backsides of miscreants with 'you'll never come back again' force. I soon learnt that he had survived four solid years of trench warfare on the Western Front. He was the Chemistry specialist, MA Cambridge.

Within a couple of months I came to like him, and when, much later, I was prefect on duty at the end of school one day, I cradled a girl (from our equivalent Girls' School around the corner) in my arms as she lay dying, bleeding excessively from an accident in a school bus. He was so helpful, so shocked. 'Banham,' he said, 'I've been through years of war, four years in the trenches, but I've never seen so much blood spilled.' I washed out her books, and her satchel, to give to her parents when they arrived. The bitterness of her blood, so thick, so fresh, still lingers in my dreadful memory. She was bleeding through her mouth, from a fractured main blood vessel.

LAURENCE FLEMING

My mother was married 'off the ship' in Bombay in 1928. Chaperoned by an old family friend, she had sailed from Genoa by Lloyd Triestino, her ship the *Genova*. This was the shortest sea journey to India at that time, though it was preceded by a train journey of 24 hours. They called only at Naples and Port Said, and their ship came alongside at Bombay very early in the morning. While they waited for visitors to come aboard, they had breakfast.

At eight o'clock my father, in full defiance of superstition, came aboard to meet them. Her luggage was taken off by a clerk, probably from Burmah–Shell, so that she herself did not have to go through

Customs. They went straight to the house of some friends of my father's, where they had another breakfast.

My father had travelled some two thousand miles by train in order to be there. He was not quite a stranger in Bombay, having landed there himself once or twice before; but on the voyage at the end of his last leave, the year before, he had made friends with his present hosts, a solicitor working in Bombay and his wife. They had invited him to use their house when he came to Bombay to be married.

There was no requirement for residence on the part of the bride. Indeed, it is quite possible that the requirement was for the marriage to take place within 24 hours, and for this reason there were a great many churches in Bombay. There was an Anglican and a Roman Catholic cathedral. There were two Anglican churches, All Saints, Malabar Hill and the less fashionable St John's, the Afghan Church, at Colaba. There were two Catholic churches, both with Portuguese names, a Scots kirk, a Baptist church and a Methodist church, to mention only some.

One reason for this was that the authorities very much disliked unattached European women. They were in India as someone's mother, wife, daughter, sister, aunt or niece, and the man to whom they were

All Saint's Church, on Malabar Hill, Bombay, where the parents of Hazel and Kristen Squire and John Langley, among many others, were married. (John Langley)

related was entirely responsible for them. Women doctors, school-teachers, governesses and missionaries would be there under contract and their employers were responsible for them.

After a morning spent at the hairdresser's, and buying a new pair of shoes – her silver kid shoes having been ruined on board ship – their party was entertained to lunch at the Yacht Club. As my father worked for the Assam and Burmah Oil Companies, the chances are that their host was the agent of Burmah–Shell, the company which sold their products. He was called Mr Cook.

After lunch they went back to the solicitor's house, changed into their wedding clothes and were married at the Church of Scotland, Waudby Road. The family friend stood best man to my father and the bride was given away by their host in Bombay. A small reception was held afterwards at his house. At five o'clock the newly married couple moved into the Taj Mahal Hotel, where they gave a dinner in the evening for everyone who had entertained them during the day.

The menu from this occasion has survived, written entirely in French; and they danced to the music of Cherpino's Broadway Follies, who were there for a two-week special engagement, under the baton of Maestro Joe Cherpino. There was a complete change of programme each Monday and Thursday.

They set off on their honeymoon the following night. An over-night train journey took them to Pachmarhi, a charming and peaceful hill station in the Deccan, summer seat of the Governor of the Central Provinces. At some point during this time, they must have remembered that they had had no photographs taken in Bombay, to 'send home'. This had to be remedied when they reached Calcutta, a 24-hour journey away.

My father's bearer went off to the bazaar, where he procured, to my mother's amazement, a handsome bouquet of mixed flowers and asparagus fern. They then reassumed their wedding clothes and were photographed by Bourne & Shepherd, the only evidence of this hasty unpacking being a huge crease across my father's left sleeve, which was recorded, of course, for ever.

They were by no means at the end of their journey. Two trains, a river crossing, another train, possibly two, the whole taking about 36 hours, lay ahead of them. Digboi, their goal, was a small oilfield in the extreme north-east corner of Assam. Perhaps the refinery and the oil derricks were the only ugly things in the whole of that beautiful state, but they brought their compensations. The roads were metalled; there was electricity, and running water, throughout the station. There were pull-plugs in the company houses. They were surrounded by superbly maintained tea gardens and by natural forest, home to the hulock monkeys that were unique to Assam; and the cold-weather climate was one of the best in India.

Their wedding presents were all received at home, and a tea party was held to view them. They were then crated and shipped, from Grangemouth to Chittagong, arriving in Digboi about four months later, to civilise the rather spartan furnishings supplied by the Assam Oil Company.

ADRIAN FRITH

My parents were married in Karachi, in the Trinity Church in Victoria Road, in November 1926. My father's regiment, the Baluch, was stationed at Coonoor in south India, so it was a long journey for him. My mother, however, had an even longer one, from Montreal. She was married from the house of her sister, Constance, whose husband, Frank Hawkes, was someone very senior in the North Western Railway, and a magnificent account of the wedding has survived, in the form of a letter from Constance to their mother. My mother is the Erica of the letter, and my father John.

Dearest Mother,

The wedding is over and all is well. Erica was splendid, far better than my greatest hopes. I was rather nervous, as she had not been able to sleep well for the last day or two. She was really splendid and I have never in all my life seen her look so well. Her dress was perfectly lovely (Spanish lace of a deep cream colour, train cream, satin embroidered with wild roses. Long plain almost tight sleeves. She was to wear a seed pearl necklace, one of her presents). The veil and the white heather wreath were beautifully arranged.

We had arranged beforehand that Gwen and a couple of others were to come in the morning and help put out presents and one of the two others to help arrange furniture in the garden. An old Parsee friend of mine lent most of the furniture from his shop. I had got all the glasses and tables for the tea and drinkables the night before. In the morning we were hard at it and about 10.30 when all the furniture was being brought up by motor lorry, and dumped in the garden, and we were arranging it all in a nice group, came our first set-back! A plague of locusts! Was ever anything so unfortunately timed? It is the first plague we have had for about five years.

They came in clouds, as only locusts can come. Enormous grasshoppers as big as young sparrows. I was taking the children in the car to a friend's house for the morning when they started. It was like live hail. Hundreds hit the front glass, blew in to the car and covered the road in swarms. By the time I got back, every tree in our compound had a dozen locusts on every top twig. They covered the trees and the plants, and in half an hour the garden with all its chairs and tables set out for a hundred people was absolutely uninhabitable! Then we did not know what to do. Would they go away or not? They go as quickly as they come when they have eaten all there is to eat. We lit half a dozen smoke fires, we got *chokras* to beat tins and shake the trees with very little effect. Twelve o'clock, one o'clock, and they were worse than ever – coming in millions.

Meanwhile all the presents were arranged in the dining room and verandah. The drawing-room was filled with flowers, with a space left for John and Erica to stand and receive. The flowers were glorious. The head *mali* from Government House had been told to bring over a basket. He brought the most enormous one I have ever seen, about a yard across, filled with lilies and roses and bougainvillea. Mrs Barker sent more and our great trouble was to provide pots for them. We had tall crotons all along the verandah and huge brass and pottery bowls everywhere possible. It looked wonderful!

The presents were more than wonderful. Everybody was breathless with delight over them. The number ran up to about 220 I think, and lovely, lovely things.

Then those beastly locusts – threatening to spoil everything! At one o'clock I sent Erica lunch and got Mollie Essame to stay and talk to her while she ate it, and she did eat it, wonderful to relate. She had also stayed in bed, all morning, sewing at something or other, quite unnecessary, as all the really necessary things were done!

Frank and I had a little lunch upstairs, in the children's nursery. I had arranged for them to be out! At 1.45, we decided the garden was hopeless, and went downstairs to alter everything again. We put a rug on the verandah, and arranged a spot for Erica and John to receive there. Chairs and tables were cleaned and brought in from the garden. Every chair and every table had, of course, to be brushed and dusted and cleaned from the damage of the locusts. We had mercifully lots of help. We had Coolies and Trolley men and Gov. House Chuprassis and several old helpers who appeared from the back 'compound' – relations of my servants – They all worked – We arranged table for about thirty in the drawing room and for about 25 or so in the verandah. The rest would have to stand!

All the presents were taken into the dining room and crowded there – the caterer's tables were put along the far end of the verandah, and the

The wedding of Adrian and Virginia Frith's parents at Trinity Church, Victoria Road, Karachi, November 1926.
(Adrian Frith)

drinkables, soda water and lemonade etc. had to be stuffed in by the stairs. There was no other room. At 2.15 it was slightly better but still hopeless outside.

But then, at 2.45, the locusts all suddenly got up and left leaving bare tops to every tree; but they left, and left entirely!

In five minutes we were taking all the furniture out again, and rearranging it in tidied garden! By 3.10 it was ready (quick work!)

Erica was ready absolutely to time. I left the house just after 4, and she arrived exactly to the minute. The hymns went beautifully, led by the choir boys, who are not much use and the voluntary choir, who all turned up most nobly. I am especially grateful to the Organist, who had a temperature of 102 but came and played and went back to bed.

Erica and Frank walked slowly up the aisle and everyone agreed that they had never seen her look so well. Erica had a sheaf of tall lilies – the only creamy coloured flowers we could get – with long trails of fern hanging down.

John spoke up very well, I could hear him perfectly. Erica began well, but couldn't get her words out by the end, however, the Padre took them as said! Then we all went into the tiny vestry, and kissed everyone all round. A kind of relieved feeling that the main part was over! Then back down the aisle, and down a beautiful arch of swords at the church door, with a pause at the end for the photographer. I do hope the photos will be good enough for you to see how nice she looked. Then away to the house. We had the Commissioner's car for Erica (by kind order), all tied up with white ribbons, and a taxi for me, so that I should not have to drive our own – just as well, as one of our tyres went flat at the last minute.

The cake was cut with John's sword, and the Colonel-Commandant, as chief guest, proposed the first toast and everyone sat down to enjoy their tea, while the bride and groom were rushed over the wall (over steps!) to the Sleigh's Compound, where the photographer was waiting for them in peace and quiet, without all the guests looking on. I am glad we arranged that. It was much better.

I meant to write this on copying paper, so that I could send the copy to everyone at once, but the book was packed and I could find nothing thin enough. Will you read this and send it on to them all as I can't write more today. I did mean to send a copy to Mrs Frith but they have gone off without giving me her address.

*   *   *

My sister and I were both born in the Wellington Military Hospital in Coonoor. This usually closed at the end of the monsoon, when the regiment returned to the plains, but on this occasion it had to remain open until my own birth was safely accomplished. Did the whole regiment wait for this important event, I wonder, before beginning its journey, or was it only the hospital staff who had to wait behind?

My father's military career ended with the surrender of Singapore in 1942. After four years in Changi Jail he resigned his commission and entered the church.

ELSPET GRAY

My father, James MacGregor-Gray, a Scot from Peebles, went to India to work for Cox & Co. – later Lloyds Bank – in 1922–23. My mother, Elspet Eleanor Morrison, from Aberlour and Elgin in Morayshire, went out to Bombay to marry him in 1925.

In 1929 my mother was sent back to Elgin for the birth of their first child – my father wanted his son to be born in Scotland. He never said he was disappointed when I was born in April!

My father was then posted to Delhi and my mother and I, with a young Scottish girl as nanny, joined him when I was a few months old. My sister, Rhoda, was born in Simla in 1930.

My first memory of India was our bungalow – Bank Bungalow, of course – in Karachi and the excitement of a white bullock running wild in the street with no one able or willing to catch it. Despite the explanation that, to the Hindus, the cow was a sacred animal and free to roam at will, I remember the fear that it would charge into the compound and kill us all.

In 1935 my father was posted to Calcutta and my sister and I were shipped back 'home' to begin our education.

From today's perspective it seems barbaric for two small girls – six and five years respectively – to be sent so far away from their parents, but then it was accepted that children would be sent back to the UK for their education, and anyway, the idea that children had needs and feelings was unheard of in those days; so back we went. My father had 'home' – UK – leave once every three years and 'country' – India – leave once a year, and as there were no phone calls – that I can remember – and no quick plane journeys, which we now take for granted, it was to be a long separation.

I have only rationalised this later on in my life and come to realise how painful an arrangement this must have been for my parents – and I doubt that it did much to convince Rhoda and I that the world was a happy, secure place.

We travelled by sea, through the Suez Canal, mostly on the large P&O liners and our first port of call – as I remember – was Aden, where scores of little boats appeared as soon as we docked and swarms of traders clambered all over the ship determined to sell us their exotic-looking wares.

The sea voyages were magical and exciting. The glamour of the ship, salt-water swimming pools, games of every sort, particularly deck quoits and gymnastics. Being wrapped up in deckchairs – when chilly – on the boat deck and served hot Bovril, mid-morning, by the steward.

For the adults the 'one-upmanship' began on the Captain's table – essential! – dressing for dinner, parties every night – gaiety and excitement and fun was the overriding impression.

Back 'home' we were to go to a Montessori school, in those days very progressive and, I'm sure, chosen with great care, attached to a large co-educational school, St George's, Harpenden. There must have been other memories, for we were there for between three and four years, but the things that stick in my mind are: one vegetarian day a week – lots of nuts and raisins. Nobody allowed to blow their nose at the table – you had to go into the corridor! First lessons in horticulture, growing cress in the airing cupboard and learning to ride – both horses and bicycles.

I can still picture the scene when my mother finally left us there. Rhoda and I waving and sobbing through the bay window of the headmistress's study while my mother, also sobbing, was led down the drive.

Both my parents came back after a year, on a home leave, and we spent Christmas in Winchester in thick snow. I remember freezing in the rented Hillman Minx, eating dark Cadbury's chocolate – my mother's favourite – singing 'Daisy, Daisy, give me your answer – do!' to keep the cold out!

We always went to Scotland when my mother was home. To our grandparents in Elgin – where Grandpa Morrison allowed us to pick

above 'P&O SS *Ranchi* at Port Said in October 1932, with self, a few months old, on board. *Ranchi* was typical of the Indian Service P&O ships of the time. Stately, snobby, slow but comfortable ships in a seaway.' (Paddy Smith)

below The SS *Viceroy of India* stuck across the Suez Canal in 1937 with Ann Mitchell and her mother on board. (Ann Mitchell)

and eat as many of his beloved raspberries as we wanted – or to Aunt Daisy and her husband Jim, who was a baker in Ardrossan, where Rhoda and I were allowed to sleep in the bakery in the marvellous, dark, comfy bed in the wall.

My memory for dates is a bit hazy but in I think in 1938 Rhoda and I were moved to St Margaret's School in Hastings, so clearly the Montessori was no longer considered to be up to scratch.

My mother came back to England before the War was declared in 1939 and we were evacuated – with the school to Sutton Courtenay, early 1940.

STAR STAUNTON

I had just had my twelfth birthday when I was given notice of two important decisions, first, that Papa was about to remarry, and secondly, that I was to be sent to school in England. Papa had had to go into hospital earlier that year with an acute attack of malaria and had been nursed by Mary Alice Burns, a Queen Alexandra's Military Nursing Sister. The professional relationship had blossomed into a hospital romance that was soon to lead them to the registry office.

My stepmother-to-be would not want a girl of my age under her feet, and in any case it was time that an attempt should be made to stop some of the appalling gaps in my formal education, so I must be packed off to a boarding school.

Our series of Christmas expeditions à deux would now be brought to an end, so Papa planned an especially exciting one as a culmination. We were to go to Ethiopia, whither, I suspect, my father was being sent on some kind of business as we were to be received in court by the Emperor Haile Selassie. After that we were to spend some days with an old Army friend from Sandhurst Days, who was now Emir of Lahej, near Aden. We flew from Bombay to Djibouti and thence by a rickety old plane to Addis Ababa where, on 20 December we attended a Christmas party at the palace. This was the Christmas of 1934 and, not long afterwards, I found myself at a convent in Belgium.

During the first summer I returned to India, where my parents were temporarily living in a flat in Bombay. Bombay was hot and humid and my stepmother treated me like a guest, her constant solicitude about my health, my needs, my wishes, becoming an irritation. But in the midsummer of 1937, when my parents' long leave came to an end, the three of us together boarded the boat for Bombay.

For me, this voyage back to the East had always been a pleasant experience, the little girl all on her own, everyone kind and considerate and inclined to spoil her and to comment on her beautiful manners, the pleasant prospect lying ahead of meeting our servants at Lahore, and then going on to stay with the Jinds. But this year was all different. I was not in the charge of the captain, but of my stepmother, just an ordinary member of an ordinary party, and even so, my stepmother gave me no support, for to my disdain she spent most of the time in her cabin prostrate with seasickness.

And what a change when we berthed in Bombay! The dull routine of the voyage was suddenly transformed into pure opera, and I found myself, for the first time in my life, appreciating India as a land violently different from Europe, gay, colourful, friendly, a land where I was not just a more-or-less anonymous schoolgirl, at the beck and call of my teachers, but Missy Sahib, my father's daughter, a person of consequence, in his right if not yet in my own. Boats of all types laden with garlands and excited people nudged our ship as she approached her berth, and as we stood by the rails waiting to disembark we suddenly found ourselves surrounded by our servants, led by Khitmagar, Moonshi, and our bearer, who bore garlands of frangipani, jasmine, roses, lilies and marigolds to drape round our necks. As each man delivered his fragrant burden, he intoned the customary vow of love and loyalty. Amidst the scent of these flowers, so redolent of India, and amidst all the hubbub, I could almost consciously feel the sense of loneliness and love despised dissipating in my innards to be replaced by grateful joy. This was India, and I was back where I belonged.

Off we went, to be welcomed by friends as guests for a week – or two weeks, it didn't seem to matter – no one discussed the length of a stay. With so many servants, guests were no burden. An invitation was awaiting us to attend a party in Government House on Malabar Hill to be given by the Governor of the province, Lord Brabourne, and his beautiful wife. Thither in due course, suitably attired as a young lady, Miss Star Staunton, accompanied her father and stepmother, very much on her dignity – though, I hope, with a twinkle in her eye. It was fun to be grown up.

To my great satisfaction I was invited by Lady Brabourne to attend the birthday party to be given for her son John later in the week. This party is one of the outstandingly blissful events in my treasure store. We were taken in the Governor's yacht across Bombay harbour to the tiny island of Elephanta, so named from its shape, which recalls that of an elephant. There, we swam across lagoons, explored caves, played catch-as-catch-can games in the woods, supervised by one tutor and two governesses – for there was to be no impropriety – and then at dusk, oil lamps were lit, and we danced on the smooth sands to tinny music from a portable gramophone. There was no romance, so far as I was concerned, to disturb the friendly tranquillity. We were just a set of juveniles, fancy-free and happy in the open air.

I now noticed India as I had never done before. Coming back to it now, older and to some superficial extent Europeanised, I could perceive that I was a foreigner to the Indians and they were foreigners to me.

To give an impression of this changed perspective, I will set myself the task of describing the visit to the bazaar to which I set off with my parents the day before the party at Elephanta Island, all very fine and uppity in a Victoria.

Bazaars in India are places of magic that had at that time, I believe, changed little in a thousand years. They are a microcosm of

India, where you may meet every caste, class, dress, colour, occupation, animal, bird, fruit, and foodstuff, all concentrated in a labyrinth of streets enclosed within a stout surrounding wall reminiscent of the wall of some medieval city. The wall is pierced at intervals by gates, and in between the gates, both outside and inside, dwelling places – mostly hovels, housing a teeming population – crowd up against the walls. Apart from these, the whole area is occupied by shops and stalls.

We entered the street of the sweetmeat shops, where they sold delicious concoctions of honey and clarified butter, maize, sugar, coconut, raisins, dates and rose-leaf jam. Then the cloth merchants, displaying brilliant saris in silks and cottons, woven cloth from the villages, veils, brocades, finery too varied to attempt to enumerate it. Next, the medicine men, dentists, doctors, opticians and chemists, these last selling for the most part every-day cures for malaria, plague, dysentery, snakebite and such common ailments, but also specialities that I noticed in particular, like thinly beaten silver to cure impotence, or ivory compounded with fat as a hair-restorer.

Our destination was the next lane, that of the metal-workers, where the air was hot from the ovens and the Bunsen burners, and noisy with scores of different hammerings. We made our way to the silversmiths and pored over delicate silver brooches, necklaces, rings for the nose, toes, ears and fingers, heavy silver anklets of attractive design and wonderful craftsmanship, but looking as though they might discourage locomotion. Nothing there suitable to take with me as a birthday present at John Brabourne's party. But further on, I found just what I wanted, a set of Rajput toy soldiers, moulded in silver, their uniforms picked out in bright enamels.

Indian railway stations are as typically Indian as bazaars and just as theatrical, especially at night, and night-time it was, two hours before midnight, when we began our journey. All seems chaos. Around naked flames brown men and women are squatting in groups of various sizes. Some people are eating, some gambling. Luggage stands around in huge piles. Goats are bleating, sheep baa-ing, chicken crates are giving forth one multitudinous chirrup. Through the mass of movement stalks a brahmini cow looking debauched, her garlands bedraggled, vegetation dribbling from her chomping lips, and no one gives it a smack on the rump to drive it off, for to the Hindus the cow is sacred. Adding to the cacophony, a wedding party arrives heralded by a band of musicians, dancers, and riders on horseback, heavily garlanded, who jink and jingle their way through the throng to the edge of the platform, where firecrackers are let off. Young boys swing incense-burners. Gorgeously gowned young women scatter flowers around, giggling self-consciously and walking along in front of and around the bride who, incongruously, is sobbing, but only in make-believe – for custom requires her to bewail the approaching sacrifice of her virginity. The lady has a towering crown atop her head and seems bowed down by the weight of it, not to mention the jewels that bedeck her bosom, the rings on her fingers, toes, ears, nose and the anklets on her legs. Behind her come matronly women pretending to overcome her feigned reluctance with pokes and shoves, accompanied by lewd gestures.

The train arrives. The Indians, including the bride and bridegroom, make a concerted rush for places, but we lordly British have no need to do so, for an entire carriage has been booked for our use, consisting of two long compartments, each furnished with two bunks, two arm-chairs, a table, a wardrobe and an adjoining bathroom closet. The compartments are linked by a communicating door. Each of them has a huge block of ice placed centrally underneath the fan, our primitive air-conditioning.

This was to be our home for three nights and two days. It contained no cooking facilities. For breakfast, bearers brought us trays of food which were collected empty at the next stopping place. Luncheon and dinner were usually served in the dining room of a main station, the time-table being arranged in such a way as to permit us this convenience.

The train seemed always festooned with non-paying passengers travelling precariously on foot-boards, roofs, or between carriages.

They disappeared on arrival at stations and mysteriously re-attached themselves in time for departure. Presumably the accident rate was high, but no one seemed to mind, unless it was the victims themselves. Life was cheap in India – I mean the lives of the natives. I do not remember feeling greedy as we lolled in our roomy family compartments. I should have been a remarkably sensitive young lady if in those days my newly awakened apprehension of India had extended so far as that.

We arrived home in a great excitement of people and animals. I had been away for nearly three years, and my parents for more than seven months, during none of which, I believe, had any wages been paid, but everyone was delighted to see us. Ayah was astounded by my height, and Cook and his numerous family, which included four married daughters, brought babies to be admired. The *bhisti* had freshly watered the bamboo curtain around the verandahs. My old friend the *durzi* was looking distinctly older.

One item of our homecoming made it feel very different from earlier occasions of a similar sort. It was now my stepmother who took charge and gave the servants their instructions.

4

North West Frontier Province and Baluchistan

The North West Frontier Province was one of the smaller provinces to have a British Governor. It was constituted in 1901 by the amalgamation of various districts of the Punjab, but it did not become a Governor's Province until 1932. It bordered Afghanistan on its western side, and was separated from Soviet Russia by the Pamirs and the great mountains of the Hindu Kush.

The British presence was a small one, mostly confined to members of the Indian Civil and the Indian Political Services, the Army, both the Indian and the British, and to the employees of the North-Western Railway, one of the more remarkable of the always remarkable Indian railways.

The principal city was Peshawar, 11 miles from the foot of the Khyber Pass. It was served by that railway and was a centre of a caravan trade coming through the pass from Central Asia. The inhabitants were principally Pathans, who were Muslim, and whose languages were Pushtu and Western Punjabi. It had two periods of rainfall. The regular south-west monsoon in the summer was followed by winter storms coming chiefly from the west, both of which were known to fail completely, with disastrous results.

Baluchistan, consisting largely of mountains and sandy deserts, was very thinly populated. It had a Chief Commissioner rather than a Governor. Its chief city was Quetta, 5500 feet high, and a headquarters of the North Western Railway, which by now extended as far as the border with Persia. It was almost entirely destroyed by an earthquake on 31 May 1935, the death toll being estimated at 40,000. Among the British casualties were an officer and 50 men of the Royal Air Force, suggesting the existence of at least an airstrip. The city was entirely sealed for at least a year afterwards, on medical grounds.

DESMOND PAILTHORPE

In 1925 Dad was posted to a place called Bannu, somewhere near the frontier of India with Afghanistan, close to the North West tribal territories. He had been promoted to the rank of Conductor and had been transferred on a regular basis from the British Army to the Indian Army Service Corps. He had been third in command of the 4th Mule Company whose duty it was to supply mule carts for the Dehra Dun Brigade when they went on manoeuvres. There were very few motor lorries available at that time.

Like many frontier towns, the military cantonments at Bannu were completely surrounded by several rows of barbed wire and were constantly patrolled to keep out marauding tribesmen from the nearby hills, Afridis, Mahsoods and Pathans, all armed with home-made weapons, plus any Lee Enfield rifles they had managed to steal.

In tandem with the majority of British households in India, my parents employed, what seemed to me at the time, a whole host of servants. Number one in the hierarchy was John the Goanese cook, an educated man who performed wonders with Indian, European and French cuisines. He was paid 75 rupees per month. (One hundred rupees was the equivalent of about £7 sterling.)

To assist him, John had a *masalchi* at 25 rupees, a *khitmagar* or bearer named Mohammed Khan who received 50 rupees. To assist him a houseman was paid 25 rupees, my *ayah* got 30 rupees and the *mali* 25 rupees. Last in line was one of the 'untouchables', the sweeper or *maither*, who was paid 22 rupees per month, but, when the family had finished lunch and dinner, remains of the food would be handed down to the sweeper. All these servants lived in 'outhouses' located about 50 yards from the main house, tiny rooms and candlelit; in some cases the inhabitants were provided with hurricane lanterns and the necessary paraffin. Most servants had families and I was always aware of Indian children, we called them *chokras*, ready and willing to play with me.

The bearer and houseman wore a uniform whilst serving at table. This consisted of a long white cotton coat fastened with a waist sash (cummerbund) and a turban band. In my father's case the colours were of the Indian Army Service Corps, navy blue, gold and white.

The first of January 1932 heralded the New Year's Day military parades throughout British India, it was a chance to show the local tribesmen on the frontier the might of the Raj. We were up early that morning – I think it was a Friday – and I was glad to be off school; anyway, I was coming to the last few months at Mrs Birch's school, my parents had enrolled me at one of India's top public schools, Bishop Cotton in Simla, where I would be a boarder from March 1933. Today, however, I proudly marched alongside my father, resplendent in his uniform with his medals jingling, spurs jangling and a sword dangling from his Sam Brown belt. My parents and I had tickets for a special enclosure for Army warrant officers to watch the march-past of the Peshawar Brigade.

The annual parade was held on the Royal Air Force Aerodrome just outside the cantonment perimeter, a vast level piece of ground with runways for the military planes, I believe they were mainly Bristol Bulldogs and some Hawker Siddeley bombers. The main event would be the parade of infantry, cavalry and newly arrived armoured cars of the Tank Corps … the transport sections and gunners would also follow the infantry and cavalry.

It was about half past nine when we seated ourselves under the large canvas *shamiyana* and although it was so early in the year, the day was going to be quite hot. Far across the field the foothills of the

Himalayas shimmered in the early morning haze, further afield, snow-capped peaks could just be seen. The Peshawar Brigade were already assembled; facing us on our left were the Seaforth Highlanders, their kilts shifting slightly in the light breeze, their white spats gleaming in the sunshine; to their left was a battalion of the 1st Punjab Regiment. I was to learn that they were the oldest of the Indian Infantry regiments, originally raised in Bengal by the East India Company, but now consisting of Sikhs, Punjabi Mussulmans, Hazaras and Rajputs. Next in line was a battalion of Gharwal Rifles to complete the infantry line-up. Further across the field were the beautifully groomed horses of an Indian Lancer Regiment; to their rear I could make out the Indian Mountain Battery, mule carts, a small detachment of the Camel Corps and in the distance the heavy guns, probably 25 pounders of the Royal Artillery.

To our left were other tents where civil-service families were housed, further to their left were the open spaces for the natives from the bazaar, servants from the cantonment and many tribesmen; the latter had been ordered to leave their rifles and other weapons at home. Mingling with the natives were detachments of red- and blue-turbanned Police constables armed with *lathis* (long staves) and Father told me that there were plain-clothes Police among the large crowd to ensure that any tittle-tattle was relayed back to the young Police inspector who was marshalling the crowd. The young man was an Anglo-Indian named Hibbert, olive skinned but very conscious of the fact that he was NOT Indian!

Many Indian traders were present; they would hire coolies to carry baskets of fruit, sweetmeats, curries, chapattis etc. and they would expect to do a roaring trade amongst the various onlookers. Cries from some of the vendors could be heard above the general hubbub: 'Pan Beeri!' (this from a seller of Indian-type cigarettes and betelnut wrapped in leaves), Hindu 'pani' or Mussulman 'pani', each caste being very careful to drink water from his or her religion. I recognised some of the *baniyas* from the Saddur bazaar flogging their sweetmeats, and my mouth watered at the thought of sampling some of their wares

– unfortunately I was now a *chota sahib* representing the Raj and I must not stoop to such lowly things!

I was partially comforted by the sight of Mohammed Khan carrying a hamper, which he deposited behind mother's chair; this would no doubt contain many delicacies prepared by Cook!

There was a buzz of excitement and peering round I spotted the ceremonial coach containing the Governor of the Province with his lady turning into the main gate, preceded by a detachment of Lancers, red and white pennants fluttering from their lances, a second detachment followed the carriage which moved towards a special tent bedecked with flowers and several important civil servants in plumed helmets stepped forward to help the lady alight. The massed bands played the National Anthem and the ceremony commenced with the Governor inspecting the parade followed by the march-past. With several thousand soldiers on duty, it was almost noon before the final detachment of armoured cars drove past.

SHEILA WRIGHT-NEVILLE

My father was an officer in the 5th-2nd Punjab Regiment of the Indian Army and attained the rank of Lieutenant Colonel before his death in 1944. My grandfather was in the Indian Civil Service and my father was the eldest son of his third marriage. Grandfather died when my father was a child and we saw very little of my grandmother, who died when I was seven.

The practice in the Indian Army after the First World War was to allow British officers six months' home leave every three years so that, for health reasons, they could spend some time in a cooler climate. And whenever possible, parents wanted their children to be born in England. I was born during one such home leave in 1927; then, when I was a month old, my parents and I returned to India.

My earliest recollections concern life in an Army cantonment in Bannu, on the North West Frontier. I was then four years old. My father's regiment was housed in a well-fortified compound, because marauding North West Frontier tribesmen were hostile to the Army and anyone, especially a white woman, would have made an excellent hostage. Our quarters had high ceilings, plenty of space, and a jumble of assorted pets. My fondest memory is of Robin, our golden cocker spaniel. The plumbing was non-existent and a sweeper or *maither* removed and cleaned the thunder-boxes (toilets). We had running water: a cold tap poured into a tin bath. Water for baths was heated in the cookhouse and carried into the bathroom in copper jugs by the *bhisti*.

The house had no kitchen but it did have a pantry. Meals were cooked in the cookhouse (separate from the main house) and brought to the pantry to be kept hot on a brazier before being served in the dining room by the *khitmagar* and the bearer. The latter also served as a personal valet to my father and was considered senior among the staff. The pantry also held an ice-box for cold drinks and perishable dairy foods. A clearly defined ranking order among the servants determined each individuals' responsibilities. Good cooks were always hard to find. Extreme tact was required in checking their accounts. The cook shopped for provisions, and my mother then checked the prices in his book. Inevitably, the cook padded his accounts and, while my mother knew this – and he knew that she knew – a fine and unspoken line was drawn between the acceptable and the unacceptable. The wise *memsahib* crossed this line at her peril. Other *memsahibs* were not above bribery in order to steal a good cook from a friend.

Jai Singh, one of my father's orderlies, a tall, bearded Sikh with impeccable manners, courage and loyalty, always walked beside me when I rode my donkey and whenever my mother and I were out together. I first learned to read and write at the cantonment's small nursery school, run by the Army wives, and still have my first effort, a somewhat derivative fairy story about wicked witches.

I had an *ayah* to take care of me, wash and iron my clothes, sit with me whenever my mother wasn't around and who, with good grace and humour, would allow herself to be bossed about by a small child. She even taught me little nursery songs in Hindustani, some of which I still remember. She would also look after my mother's clothes and see they were laundered and put away. The laundry was done by the *dhobi* in a river if there was one, or other body of water. He would beat the clothes on stones and then iron them with a charcoal-filled iron. Those *dhobis* did a superb job under the most primitive conditions – wash-and-wear fabrics had yet to be invented – but everything was always perfectly done, and daily, too. Another frequent visitor to the house was the *dhirzi*, who sat cross-legged on the verandah, with his sewing machine in front of him, copying dresses etc. from magazine pictures for my mother and me. Few suitable ready-made clothes were available at the local bazaar, and clothes bought on the last leave never survived to the next one, so the *dhirzi* was a real necessity. He even made shirts for my father. Father usually wore khaki shorts and knee-length khaki socks with short-sleeved uniform jackets, but he needed other civilian clothes too. Father always owned horses or polo ponies and was a great rider, winning trophies at point-to-points and polo matches. He taught me to ride almost before I could walk. He also played grass hockey for his regiment but omitted to pass that talent to me.

Fancy-dress children's parties were held at the local Club in Bannu. Several British civilian families lived in the surrounding area, hence the existence of the Club. My oldest photograph album shows pictures of adult fancy dress parties too, and other events. The Club was

Sheila Wright-Neville with her mother, father and the family car, Bannu, 1934. (Sheila Wright-Neville)

the centre of social life for English families, with a bar, dining room, dance-floor and swimming pool.

During that time I had a brush with one of the most feared diseases in India: rabies. Someone's dog had puppies and several of us children went to play with them. The mother dog was later diagnosed with the disease and had to be destroyed. I visited the hospital every day for two weeks for 14 injections in my stomach. Although I don't remember being either hurt or frightened, I know my parents were worried.

HAZEL SQUIRE

My first coherent memories of India start when my father was posted to Baluchistan when I was four-and-a-half and my sister two years old. We lived in remote places – Mastung, Nushki, Sibi, Ziarat – and our family life seemed idyllic, and in retrospect, self-contained.

My father entered the Indian Civil Service in 1920, having studied Persian at Oxford after serving in the First World War. He was posted to the Central Provinces. This being one of the directly governed provinces of India was under the domain of the ICS, a body of approximately 1200 officers, of whom by 1939 40 percent were Indian. The Indian Political Service, to which my father was transferred in 1924, to Hyderabad, was, however, a much smaller force of around 150 men recruited two-thirds from the Indian Army and one-third from the ICS. The Viceroy himself was head of this body, which was concerned with the large area of the subcontinent composed of states with their own Indian rulers, tribal areas such as Baluchistan and the North West Frontier Province, and some areas beyond India such as Aden, the Gulf and Afghanistan. The roles of administrator, resident adviser or diplomat might all be required at various times by the IPS officer.

In Hyderabad my father met my mother, who was teaching at the Mahbubia Girls School, a school for Muslim girls. She was one of quite a few women who had come out to India to teach there.

They were married in Bombay in 1926, early in the morning, my mother just having disembarked from the boat from England.

Back to Baluchistan – rugged, barren and mountainous with deep ravines and gorges, an area about the size of the British Isles. It had extremes of temperature and was fresh and bracing. My mother, who loved the fresh air, would arrange for us to have breakfast in the garden as soon as she felt the days growing warm enough. In protest my father used to appear in his enormous *poshteen* and hat. I say 'enormous', as he was over six feet tall and his *poshteen* was a full-length lambskin coat – of the kind quite fashionable now in the West – with black lamb's fleece on the inside and embroidered on the outside. His hat, though, was very English!

We were surrounded by animals – ponies, a dog, ducks, hens, rabbits, guinea-pigs. We had a habit of collecting tortoises when we went out for picnics. At one point we had 11 of them. We tried to contain them in a walled plot, but they always escaped by climbing over or burrowing under. So we hit upon a scheme of putting holes through the tail-end of their shells and tying them with long lengths of string to different trees. Unfortunately, the trees were not far enough apart and in the morning we found they had criss-crossed each other's strings, tying themselves in terrible knots. We found one of them dangling over a wall.

Hazel Squire's father, in *poshteen* and hat, chatting with some local inhabitants, Mastung, Baluchistan, 1934. (Hazel Squire)

Our rabbits wouldn't breed, which was a problem. One day one of the servants let them out in the garage which had a mud floor. We found that they had burrowed. They were finally caught and properly housed again. But that seemed to have done the trick, and in due course they produced a litter.

We endlessly sat on batches of eggs. The gardener offered to sit a very scrawny hen on 16 duck eggs at his place. We were very envious when all 16 hatched out, and we wondered how he had done it. We discovered he had placed the nest behind his cooking stove inside his house.

We had a governess, though that scarcely seems a correct description. She was a young girl of 19 whom my mother had brought out with us when we returned after one of my father's leaves. The pattern seemed to be a three-year stint in a post, then nine months' home leave in Britain. So changes like this had to coincide with this routine. Dinah was a wonderfully resourceful person and had brought out books with her on how to make almost anything under the sun. We made all our Christmas presents for each other, and even our own crib set. I remember having to sit on a packet of pins for half an hour to 'hatch' them into a packet of needles to put into a needle-case I had made for a long-suffering parent. To this day I attribute my resourcefulness in making things to that early training.

Although the countryside was very dry we often had lovely gardens. One such was Mastung, where we lived when my father was Political Officer to Kalat. There were 16 acres of lawns, flowers and fruit trees.

A railway line crossed Baluchistan from the Indus at Sukkur to Chaman. There was a branch line to Nushki, which continued on to the Persian border. I think it must have been in Nushki that the railway line ran along the bottom of our garden. The great event was when the one train of the day passed and we would run down to see it. It was something of a law unto itself and came when it felt like it, never arriving at its scheduled time. The story goes that one day it did arrive on time. A delighted official congratulated the stationmaster. The surprised reply was, 'Oh, but this is yesterday's train.'

We had a Humber Snipe car. Luggage was tied on to a grid which let down at the back, and bedding rolls were frequently tied on to the mudguards at the side. The roads were unmetalled, and there were often signs saying 'This is a fair-weather road'. I have memories in the rainy season of seeing a river in spate rushing towards us as we stood on a river bank, the water two to three feet high. The river beds were very wide and the water not deep, so we often tried to drive through them, hoping the engine wouldn't stall. When it did, people had to be enlisted to push the car through to the other side.

On the other hand, I have a vivid memory of a dust storm. Sometimes we could see them coming towards us. We would shut ourselves in the house. I can remember the strange yellowish-green light as it gradually got darker and darker. It would sometimes last for quite a few hours.

We had wonderful picnics and excursions, mostly on horseback but occasionally on camels. Especially I remember the ones from the summer hill station, Ziarat. Unlike the other places we had been, Ziarat was wooded and with plenty of water which ran down from the hills, filling the various swimming pools in the gardens of the bungalows. By this time I had been given a baby goat as a birthday

The Squire family on an excursion from Mastung, 1934. *left* Hazel (left) and Kristin mounting the camel. (Hazel Squire)

present. She was as devoted as any dog could have been, and used to bleat pitiably if we left her behind. So she always came with us, insisting on leaping along the hillside just above the path we were riding on, sending down showers of stones. Her favourite hobby was chewing the leather chin-straps of our *topees* if we had inadvertently left them on the ground. One time, returning from a long day out we had to cross the racecourse. This was too big a temptation for my pony and she bolted. I clung round her neck for dear life, and arrived home long before anyone else.

There was one occasion when my father set off with quite a big party to climb Khalifat, 11,434 feet, the highest mountain in some of the grandest peaks in Baluchistan. The camp was a wonderful affair, with camp-beds, tables and chairs. The party seemed to consist mainly of his Indian staff, though in the photos there is another British couple whom I cannot identify. Naturally we children were left behind when the grown-ups made the final ascent. The staff spoiled us, giving us wonderful meals while the others were away. The mountain was stony with sparse conifer trees, but no snow. We had reached the camp on horseback, so I am left to wonder how all the equipment got there.

On other occasions when we were out riding we often came across *karezes*. These were part of a wonderful irrigation system, quite unique in the world. The wells were dug sometimes as deep as 100 feet, to where the water was caught by an impervious stratum of rock or clay. Underground water tunnels were then dug for miles linking further wells and punctuated by chimneys that had been sunk at intervals for the removal of the soil. Often we would find a man down in the well, keeping channels unblocked. This provided an irrigation system with little seasonal variation in quantity.

Dinah had a holiday from us and went to stay with a doctor's family in Quetta. Sadly she was there when the terrible earthquake struck. We felt the strong tremors of it 50 miles away. Mastung was also flattened. She helped in the rescue work, and shared in the grief of those who lost members of their families. She came back to us not long before the family was due to return to England. She developed shingles from the shock. One by one we caught chickenpox from it, and there was a series of cancelling and rebooking our passages home on a later ship.

This leave was to be one on which I was to be left at home to go to boarding school. My younger sister would join me three years later. I went to the school that was selected, for the summer term as a daygirl. Then during the autumn term, when the time came for my parents to leave, I was taken one evening to the school. An older girl took me by the hand and led me into the gym where all the girls were playing. There were no tears, just a terrible numbness.

So it was good-bye for three years. I was by this time eight-and-a-half. My parents went out to Iran. Luckily for me, they decided it would not matter too much, two years later, if I skipped the summer term and went out to join them. They would help me to keep up my studies. Dinah was still with the family. So I set off with my guardian (an old schoolfriend of my mother's) on a wonderfully romantic journey. We crossed Europe on the Orient Express, taking three days. I kept a diary and drew pictures of what I saw. Arriving in Istanbul, we crossed by boat to Hydarpasa. A further day on the Taurus Express took us to the border north of Iraq. At one point we were chugging up a narrow mountain gorge at an incredibly low speed. Finally, in a clearing we passed a bewildered-looking wild camel. It turned out the camel had got caught in the gorge ahead of the train and was setting the pace. We crossed Iraq in a superb American motor coach, with an iced-water container and paper cups at the back, stopping overnight at Mosul. Looking out, we could see the ruins of Nineveh. A night on the train from Kirkuk to Khanikin brought us to the rendezvous with my father in the early hours of the morning. From thence it was six days across Iran by car to Meshed, stopping at caravanserais or in a British home in Teheran. I can still see in my mind's eye the first view of Meshed. As we came over the rim of the hills surrounding the plateau where the city stood, three gleaming domes shone in the sun in contrast to the dry, baked earth around us – one turquoise, one green and one gold.

The summer months were a happy resumption of family life, with lessons every morning. I cannot remember a single thing about the return journey by the same route. At least I was returning to a life that was a little more known than on the previous parting. The only difficulty was that the school authorities, in their wisdom, decided to keep me back a year as I had missed the summer term. So all my friends moved on and I had to start again.

This time the separation was only for a year, which probably made it more bearable. The next September the family were all set to leave for home, and all their luggage had been sent in advance by sea, when war broke out and all leave was cancelled. My indefatigable guardian collected the trunks at Tilbury, repacked them with larger sizes of clothing for my two sisters, and sent them all back again.

BARBARA ANN JARDINE

My family had roots in India for four generations, one of whom built the main road from Lahore to Peshawar, including the Attock Bridge and then was the brain behind the recapture by the British of the Red Fort, Delhi during the Mutiny. One grandfather was a High Court judge in Bombay. All my father's brothers worked in different capacities, such as the Army, banking, missionary work, or as oil company geologist in India.

My main home was in Peshawar where my father was District Commissioner and Revenue Commissioner. Our house was two storeys with a huge garden, tennis court, stables, servants' quarters. I recently went back and found the house, although all the garden is built over and servants' quarters and stables are now Police HQ.

In the summer months we went up to the hills – Nathia Gali – to a bungalow with five bedrooms – and our father would join us later (the bungalow is still in existence). I remember mainly our *ayah* who looked after my sister and myself and sang me to sleep with a song, 'Nini baba nini – Roti makan chini – Roti makan hogia – Chota baba sogia'. Also my pony, on whom I learned to ride. When I was only a baby my mother left a biscuit in my cot and a rat came and bit me on the head. The mark is there to this day. From then on I was put to sleep in a meat safe. My father told me that sometimes the frontier tribes came raiding down to Peshawar and he had to rush us as a family into the Fort where the British Army was, to protect us.

In 1932 Father had the normal leave that came every four years so my sister and I travelled with our parents to England and stayed with our grandparents in Surrey. When our parents returned to India my sister and I were settled into boarding school. We were extremely miserable, being so young, but that was what many children of parents working overseas had to experience. One reason was lack of modern medicines and another that we had to be thoroughly British in our culture. I remember that table manners were very important in my schools. In 1938 my mother came back to England and a brother was added to our family.

BARRY BRYSON

I was born in Weymouth, Dorset in 1929, my mother having to manage a guesthouse after my father Andrew Bryson spent or wasted most of the inheritance he received from the sale of a family flour mill in Glasgow. He died when I was about two years of age.

Reginald Thom, whose first wife was from Weymouth and who had died in India in childbirth, came to Weymouth on one of his periods of leave and within a few months he had married my mother and taken us all back to India. We naturally adopted his surname. Reginald was a kind and gentle man. My brother and I carried the name Thom throughout our childhood, each independently for different reasons reverting to our birth name, Bryson, well into adulthood – in my case it was because my future wife Mary, when given the choice, preferred it.

We sailed from Tilbury on the P&O *Maloja* in September 1936, after watching Father's new car, a Morris 12, loaded on to the ship destined for Bombay. I can remember all the coloured paper streamers used by passenger and well-wishers as the ship sailed. We travelled 'tourist class', but it was an excellent holiday for us all, lasting about 21 days, and I recall being denied access to the upper deck, reserved only for First Class. The food was excellent and we had many deck games and the use of a small pool. We had also taken a portable hand-wound gramophone with us with about a dozen records (78s) which we endlessly played. I can remember the smell of Port Said, and the bustle of 'bum boats' coming up to the ship to sell tourist gifts to the passengers through baskets pulled up by ropes to the decks. Father had organised a car and driver so we disembarked and drove along the canal to Port Suez, where we re-embarked. On the way we stopped at the Pyramids, and my brother and I can remember climbing up part of one side of one as they were not smooth sided and the blocks of granite were capable of being climbed. (Later when I was in the Army doing National Service, stationed near Ismailia, I could see ships appearing to sail through the desert and was reminded of our trip along the canal by road, years before. I swam across the canal on one occasion, nearly being put on a charge for it.)

Quetta suffered a massive earthquake in 1935 and there was hardly a building standing when we arrived in October 1936. We had to live in tents and for some years after lived in a small bungalow made out of railway sleepers and mud – it was very warm and comfortable however, but had no drainage. David, our new young brother, was born in 1938, but of course we only got to see him in the long school holidays. Gradually our new bungalow was erected with earthquake-proof, reinforced pillars to take the roof with the walls being constructed later. This one had full drainage with 'squat down' flushed lavatories, which I always preferred. We had a large compound close to other railway domestic compounds. We had a cook, bearer, two gardeners and a general man who cleaned the portable toilets, prepared the car with hot water in very cold winters (no antifreeze), polished everything from shoes to car etc. And of course an *ayah* when younger brother David arrived. Our cook, Devi Dal, was a lovely gentle guy who spoke reasonable English and whom my mother trusted implicitly and was never disappointed. He was with us the whole of our period of stay at what we now know were very low rates of pay. As the servants could not read or write they signed for their wages with a thumbprint on an inked pad and then to a record book – the receipt never had to be used as proof. Most *memsahibs* went around jangling a huge bunch of keys with absolutely everything locked up – we did not. Cook had a wife and two sons

above Hazel Squire 'abandoned' on the Quetta–Mastung road, 1934. (Hazel Squire)

left Barry and Peter Bryson, with their mother 'and our own transport', 1938. (Barry Bryson)

living in the compound in one of a few servants' quarters of two rooms each. Mother used to encourage my younger brother David to speak Urdu, but the cook told his children to speak English when they all played together.

Quetta was a military garrison town and had a Staff College. It was a trade, road and rail centre. One of the North Western Railway's major workshops was sited there and I believe they did all the routine services and maintenance of all steam engines and carriages for the area. Father was responsible for this and could recognise engines by the sounds they made. Our home was within a short distance of the station and he would sometimes say, 'That's 135', or some number which identified the engine. Quetta was strategically important for the military garrison and the railway played a useful part in movement of the Army. The military and the railway people were quite separate and didn't socialise much. As father was a Freemason he had contacts outside just the railway fraternity, which increased our circle of friends. The father of one of our schoolfriends was the manager of the Army's model farm which provided cows' milk to the garrison but we drank buffaloes' milk at home. During our three months at home in Quetta we did no schooling and, surprisingly, no homework, so we enjoyed ourselves. However, not normally living there, we did not make many friends. We had bikes and could

Peter and Barry Bryson with their mother in the railway yards at Quetta in the winter of 1938–39. (Barry Bryson)

go where we liked and there seemed to be no restrictions; we felt completely safe. Our parents never warned us of any dangers – they didn't think there were any. Our memory of the indigenous population was that they were friendly and peaceful although their backgrounds were tribal, Afghan, Pushtu, Baluchi and Pathan. We would wander around the *khabari* market (believed full of thieves) where one could possibly find anything stolen from one's house. Our winter evenings were spent in front of an open fire, lying on the floor, eating our home-grown almonds, reading Arthur Mee's *Children's Encyclopedia* and other books and listening to the BBC – especially a regular programme *In Town Tonight*, where celebrities in London at that weekend were interviewed. As a treat we sometimes went to a suitable flick (film).

Occasionally, one or both of us would accompany Father on one of his 'on line' trips. He had his own large carriage and would add it to the back of any train so that he could inspect the various areas of his responsibility. The carriage had a comfortable living/sleeping area with two pairs of bunks, a dining table and chairs, two armchairs, and a wardrobe. It had a solid-fuel stove for winter journeys and fans for the summer. It also had a bathroom, a kitchen and bunks for any servants, and each window had three separate screens – a glass one to keep out the dust, always present, a fine mesh against insects and a wooden louvred one for night time and privacy. It also had a large verandah where we could sit and watch the countryside. The carriage had various dials so Father could monitor the train's and the engine's performance and he would frequently ride on the engine. At certain stops we would hear a man going along the train tapping the wheels, listening for cracked ones. We would go off for a week at a time, right up to the stations bordering Afghanistan.

Occasionally travellers from China visited us on bicycles with huge bundles of quality handmade linens and silks. These would be un-wrapped and laid out and the bargaining would start. Similarly, we had travellers from Persia (Iran) with beautiful rugs, some of which we still have.

Almost all our long holidays were spent in Quetta. We had Father's brother's family in Lahore and we visited them occasionally. One Christmas we stayed with Army friends in Bangalore. We swam in an open-air pool on Christmas Day. Midges were a problem in the evenings. Milk was delivered by buffalo to each house gate. When the animal and its owner arrived, we went outside with a suitable container and the buffalo was milked appropriately, under supervision and the milk paid for. Then the animal and owner moved on to next door for a similar milking.

Quetta was the dry countryside one imagines and which has recently been seen in the media following hostilities in Afghanistan (2001). Our garden was very productive – we grew apples, pears, figs, peaches, grapes and nuts and Quetta had many fruit farms growing fruit for Baluchistan. We were fortunate in that we rarely experienced the intense heat associated with the plains of India. Our Quetta home was 5000 feet up near the mountains on the Afghan border and school was 7000 feet up in the Himalayas. Quetta had snow in most winters, when we were there, and little rain in the summers, which were hot. There were large reservoirs at the bases of the mountains which held melted snow and water from these was channelled to farms and gardens at regular intervals during the summer. Our gardens had water twice a week.

At Christmas time all the family would travel on 'Father's coach' to visit all the stations he had responsibility for and the station staff would arrange entertainment and feasts for us in each station institute. We travelled from 5000 feet above sea level from Quetta's snow to places like Sibi, below sea level, one of the hottest places in India. We once saw an egg fry on the pavement there and Mother would have to remove bracelets and other jewellery which would be too hot to wear.

NANETTE BOYCE

My father's permanent commission in the Indian Army was gazetted in October 1918 and his first regiment was the 11th Mahars. This was a regiment raised for war service and it was disbanded in 1922. He then joined the 2nd Battalion of the 14th Punjab Regiment, Duke of Cambridge's Own (Brownlow's).

His first station was in Jubbulpore, in the Central Provinces, but this was brief. Within a very short period of time the regiment was moved to the Zhob, a river valley in the north east of Baluchistan.

He met my mother in Jubbulpore, when she was 16, and they married in Bombay in 1926. Her family had records of service to the Raj going back to a Lieutenant Patrick Baxter, who survived the Siege of Lucknow in 1857.

After six months home leave he joined the regiment, by now in Bannu on the North West Frontier. I was born in 1928 in Mussoorie, in the United Provinces. But when I was three my father was transferred to Peshawar and so all my earliest memories are of the North West Frontier.

My father, an examiner in Pushtu (the language of the Pathans) was then serving in Kohat with his regiment (2nd Battalion, 14th Punjab regiment, Duke of Cambridge's Own [Brownlow's]). The battalion had been raised in 1857, at the time of the Indian Mutiny by Lieutenant Charles Brownlow (later Field Marshal) and had in fact stationed in Kohat in 1878. The raids had changed little in 30 years.

In one of these raids on Kohat they had kidnapped a woman and her daughter and, before ransom could be arranged, had killed the woman. The garrison had then been surrounded by a barbed-wire fence. Gates closed at 4 p.m. and only opened at dawn. Bungalows had security lights on all four corners, and when an Army officer was away on reconnaissance patrols regimental guards were posted around his house. I suppose the only effect this cloistered life had as a child was an awareness: an awareness of uniforms, medals, bugle calls. I had my own regiment, the Royal Buglers – a regiment which I gather was usually to be seen in full flight pursued by a brigade of geese! On one occasion the commandant of the Royal Buglers, for reasons unknown, spread glue liberally on her father's chair. A chair on which he sat wearing his mess trousers. Not a good mixture; the formality of the navy trousers with their broad red stripe. The commandant was treated to a ride in a car (out of mother's sight and hearing) and collected a lifelong dictionary of swear words.

Schooling was usually in small groups with a governess. In retrospect, I think my family must have run a matrimonial agency for governesses. Each home leave seemed to procure a new governess. I remember one, French, I think, who was singularly unimpressed with my rendering of 'They're Hanging Danny Deever in the Morning'. She didn't think much of my 'Dictionary of Swear Words' either.

Children's parties were usually entertained by camel rides or snake charmers. On one occasion we were given rides in a cavalry brake (coach).

Nanette Boyce, with her father Captain T.W. Boyce MC, MM and the hockey team from No 2 T.C. Company, 10/14 Punjab Regiment, winners of the Ferozopore Brigade Area Inter Company Hockey Tournament. Peshawar, 1934–35. (Nanette Boyce)

I suppose this awareness for me was highlighted in a drive back from Nowshera, where we had been to a wedding. My father's orders were, as with all serving officers, that if a sniper fired at your car tyre, you were to carry on. As we drove along the long hot dusty road a tyre was punctured and we apparently couldn't make sufficient speed to get us inside the gates by four. After fruitless attempts to get the jack in position it was decided that the last possible solution was to push the smallest member of the wedding party under the car. In all this I remember a tremendous sense of urgency, the heat and the smell of dust, but never a sense of fear.

What else do I really remember from my early childhood in the North West Frontier Province, Waziristan and Baluchistan, I wonder? The dust devils blowing across barren plains like genies from Aladdin's lamp, leaping and swaying and spiralling; the silk caravans with their camels coming down the Old Trunk Road from Fort Jamud at the entrance to the Khyber Pass; the smells, of the hookahs, of the *kebab-wallahs* burning braziers, of the freshly made *naan* bread; those are very clear. I remember a garden as a patch of sand with the occasional thorn tree and a struggling canna plant. There were archways leading into dark rooms with *punkahs*. The nights were lit with 'hurricane butties', nights that were spent on *charpoys*, wooden-framed beds with webbing. Scrawny *murghi* or chicken for supper. We travelled with our own mosquito nets which gave a feeling of security, not against mosquitos or marauding tribesmen, but snakes! On one occasion my governess threw a ball of paper into a coal scuttle. There was a scuffling sound as a deadly krait made known his resentment at being disturbed.

My father, a fluent Pushtu speaker, has been posted to Peshawar as a general staff officer (Intelligence), but after home leave in 1937 he was loaned to the Intelligence Bureau of the Government of India, and we returned from England to Quetta, still recovering from the disastrous earthquake of 1935. There was a ravine, the Habeeb Nullah, which ran through the town and which had broken the quake. The houses were left standing on one side of it, but were reduced to rubble on the other.

My father's brief was, I learned later, to watch Pathans for any assistance they might give to Italians or Germans crossing the passes from Afghanistan. He regularly visited Kabul and Kandahar, his Chevrolet saloon rattling across dry river beds, rock-strewn mountain roads and sand tracks. In school holidays he would often take me with him. I remember Kalat particularly well. The Khan lived in a palace within a citadel built on a high rise, the grandeur of the citadel somewhat diminished by its surroundings of flat-roofed mud houses. However, perhaps etched in my memory most is the Fakir of Ipi, who believed he was a holy man credited with supernatural powers! In 1937 30,000 troops had been deployed against him, to no avail! He was known to entertain Italian agents and I believe that, after Partition, unchanged in attitude, he refused allegiance to Pakistan, wishing to have his own Pathan state.

In our garden, well away from the house, stood a small hut. During the summer months we slept in the garden. I would be aware, not only of the sound of jackals hunting in the town's rubbish dumps, but of shadowy figures coming and going from the hut. Years later I was to learn that these were the 'contacts' coming in from the surrounding Suliman Hills.

But in 1940 this unforgettable chapter came to an end. My father was recalled to his regiment and this had been posted to Hong Kong.

IAN O'LEARY

Our family had quite a long connection with India. A great-grandfather and a great-great-grandfather, both called Hutchinson, were in the East India Company, and one of them saw active service in 1857. My mother's brother was Brigadier Gordon Osmastou MC, of the Survey of India, and her father was Bertram Beresford Osmaston CIE, Chief Conservator of Forests in the Central Provinces. He was a great hunter, and had been a man of many adventures in the subcontinent during a working lifetime in the Imperial

Indian Forestry Service. He was known to many of his contemporaries as 'B.B.', and it was in his house in Oxford that I was born in 1927.

In the same year, I sailed to India with my mother on the SS *Elysia* (Anchor Line) to join my father, who was an officer in the 2nd Punjab Regiment. In that year I travelled to Secunderbad, Amballa and Multan.

I now quote from my mother's diary:

April 14 1928. Left Multan with Ian whose temperature was 112 – sick unto death.

April 15. Arrived Rawalpindi, and proceeded at once by car to Srinagar (Kashmir). Stopped night at Chinari Dak Bungalow. Ian nearly died, but his life was saved by Dr Caldwell.

April 16. Arrived Srinagar (Nedou's Hotel).

June 25. Proceeded to Gulmarg by lorry, and thence sitting Ian in front of my saddle rode up to Hotel (Nedou's).

September 1. Left Gulmarg in a *dooly* carried by two Kashmiris— torrential rain all the way to Tanunarag. On by car to Srinagar, a hair-raising journey with colossal floods and bridges under water – flood water rose 25' 6" – highest on record. Back to Multan via *gharry*, Rawalpindi and Lahore.

In March 1929, Mother sailed back to England with me on the SS *City of London*. Again, I quote from Mother's diary:

Oxford. Ian fell head first into the river – completely submerged, luckily a passing man pulled him out by his leg.

10 October 1931. Sailed for India with Ian on the *City of Paris* from Liverpool. Nov 2nd arrived at Bombay, transhipped to S.S. *Vita* and arrived in Karachi on Nov 4th.

At this period we travelled extensively, visiting Kohat, Kalka, Dagshai, Lahore and Rawalpindi, where Captain Rossel gave me a glass of neat gin, thinking it was water (I still don't like the taste of gin!). Then on to Barisal. In Barisal I took to wearing a khaki uniform. I would go out to the parade ground with my bearer when I knew my father's battalion was returning from a route march, and stand beside the dirty road at attention, with a miniature swagger-stick tucked under my arm. It was a source of great pleasure if a passing *subadar* with a smile on his face would order his men to 'eyes right' and cut a big salute himself. Of course, I always raised my right hand to my *puggri*, returning the salute in the correct military manner. When Father heard of this escapade, he was not amused. He said to me, 'Who do you think you are? Some general reviewing your troops? Don't ever do that again.' I left his presence feeling a bit downhearted, but my bearer taught me 'Gooli Danda' to cheer me up. It's an Indian game played with a stick about two or three feet long (which is the bat), and a small stick about three inches long. The batsman hits the pointed little stick gently to make it jump into the air, and then with a terrific clout hits the little stick as far as it will go. What fun! I quickly rounded up *malis*, orderlies, *syces* and the *masalchi* to be fieldsmen.

We all rode in India, and I started at a young age on my father's charger – no baby's pony for me, and no leading rein. The time sped by, with children's parties, birthday parties – they always made a wreath of intertwined flowers for my big day.

Ian O'Leary 'helping the mali', Multan, 1929. (Ian O'Leary)

In March 1933 we left India, sailing on the *City of Lahore* and on the voyage home landed at Port Sudan, Port Said (where the *gully-gully* man came on board and performed wondrous conjuring tricks, making dozens of little chicks appear by magic and run around the deck). The Captain even found a little seaman's cap for me.

In September 1933 Mother left for India. I will never forget the taxi leaving with her from our house in Oxford. She had given me a box of toy soldiers, and a little toy car which I pressed against the window of the taxi as it pulled away. I waved sadly until it was finally out of sight. Grandpa hugged me and said, 'It's all right to cry, even if you are six now'. I walked up the stairs to my bedroom and closed the door. The light seemed to have gone out of the world.

Ian O'Leary on his father's charger, Bannu, 1932, on his bicycle in front of the family bungalow, Bannu, 1933, and with his father, an officer in the 2nd Punjab Regiment, Bannu, 1931. (Ian O'Leary)

In May 1934 Mother and Father returned from India. What rejoicing. But of course they were off again to India that year, and I found a letter I had written to Mother in November 1934: 'Today we played football, I got six goals. Grandpa and I have been boxing and rowing, but I am very desolate without you.' I used to get some comfort from dressing up in my tribal clothes.

My mother wrote to me every week during the long years of her absence in India, and Father did sometimes. They were a godsend during my years at some of the more brutal British prep schools I attended – something to hold on to. Finally, at Wellbury Park, I met my life-long friend Mike Bruce, whose parents were also in India. We were to meet again in India in the 1940s at a school up in the Himalayan Mountains. In 1938 I see from Mother's diary that she was back in England, and she notes:

> Ian seems to miss having no real home very badly and always feels the thought of my return to India, without him, hanging over him like a sword. Every time he kisses me good night I feel like he is saying a long farewell... he seems to hate the beatings at school, poor soul, and even the food is often nauseating.

She had heard that the Headmaster had me chained and padlocked to my bed in the dormitory each night to prevent my sleepwalking. Joy of Joys! In 1939 I was given permission by my family to return to India if I wished. I could stay in England with my grandparents if I preferred to continue my education there. What a wonderful choice: India, India, India here I come...

My mother, sister Merula and I left England on 9 January 1940 from Glasgow sailing via Gibraltar, the Red Sea and on to India.

5

Kashmir

The Princely State of Jammu and Kashmir was one of the largest, its Maharajah rating a salute of 21 guns on ceremonial occasions. There was a British Resident, who lived in a handsome house in Srinagar. The Maharajah was Hindu, but the majority of his subjects were Muslim. The Hindus were mostly of the highest caste, and were known as Pundits, living principally in the south of the state, Jammu. They had their own language, Kashmiri, not unlike Punjabi.

The Vale of Kashmir was one of the most beautiful, as well as one of the most fruitful, areas in the world. The river Jhelum and its tributaries, fed by the melting snows, watered it, and this was a source of water which never failed. The rainfall was irregular, heaviest in the spring months. The staple crop was rice, but all the temperate fruits – pears, apples, peaches, cherries, and apricots – some of them indigenous, grew there, and all the European vegetables.

A pass was required by British visitors to enter Kashmir, and originally only 200 were issued each year. Tourists were accommodated in houseboats moored on the Dal Lakes of Srinagar, and there were several European-style schools. Those who found the summer heat of Srinagar, at just over 5000 feet high, intolerable, could migrate to Gulmarg, the Meadow of Flowers, 8500 feet high, where in the winter they could go skiing. There was a Nedou's Hotel in both places.

PAMELA ALBERT

Peshawar was the stepping-off point to Kashmir, our holiday haven in summer. We always looked forward to our holidays there with great anticipation, for a houseboat would usually be hired for the month of July from the Skinners' agency. The houseboat would be moored on the Dal Lake. We would spend one week at Gulmarg first and the rest of the time on the houseboat. To me, Kashmir has been my own little bit of heaven. It pains me greatly to see it torn apart by its political and religious strife. How senseless it all seems that people should fight over, and ruin, what nature took so long to make perfect.

In the distance were the snow-covered mountains, the beautiful Dal Lake with its sparkling rivers, the green hills around, and the grand Trunk Road lined on both sides with poplar trees. All this made for a memorable holiday in a setting that would never be forgotten.

There were, too, the Shalimar Gardens, the Moghul emperor Shah Jahan's concept of heaven. Our houseboat was berthed on the Dal Lake and its accommodation consisted of two bedrooms, drawing/dining room, small sitting deck in front, and a larger one on the roof. Behind was the cook's boat, and this was towed behind us each time we moved from one spot to another on the lake.

Kashmir, in my opinion one of God's most blessed spots on earth, never changed and you knew what to expect every time you went there. The last occasion I was in God's country, August 1945, the same beauty was there – the snow-capped mountains in the distance, blue skies, fresh air and the calm Dal Lake – I would sit on the small deck of the houseboat in the early morning and watch the smaller craft laden with fruit, vegetables and flowers for sale, sliding by. Oh, those flowers! There were so many that you could not see the boat, it was like a floating garden.

I would like to tell you about the floating gardens of Kashmir. The locals that lived on the water would drag their gardens behind them on the surface of the water. These consisted of reeds wound tightly together with soil placed on them, and on these beds the people would plant their vegetables. What a sight! I could not believe my eyes the first time I saw it. It was a wonderful time to be alive and to see these things and I do not believe it will ever be the same again.

LAVENDER TODD

My father joined the Indian Police in 1913 and was posted to the Arakan in Burma. In 1915 he was transferred to Government House as ADC to the Governor, Sir Harcourt Butler. After some months in that post, at his own request, he was released to join Probyns Horse and went with them to Mesopotamia; he served with them until the end of that war in Baghdad. Thereafter he was selected for the Indian Political Service which provided the link between the Viceroy and the rulers of the Indian states and also with the people of the frontier areas. He saw service in Quetta, Gilgit, Sibi and Rajastan until his final appointment as Resident, Eastern States, some 30 in number, with his headquarters in Calcutta. He was fluent in nine Eastern languages. He was knighted on retirement in 1946, and he and my mother both died in the 1980s.

I was born in Quetta in 1926, but my earliest recollection of India is trekking in the north west through Kashmir over the Burzel Pass to Gilgit. My sister and I travelled in *doolies*, a form of palanquin, and our parents rode on horseback or yak. We stayed with the Maharajah of Kashmir in his capital, Srinagar, and in Government resthouses *en route*. Our father was taking up the posting of political agent in Gilgit, Hunza and Nagar. There were five European families resident in Gilgit, and I have memories of shooting camps at Christmas and rafting down rivers on fishing expeditions on rafts made up of poles strapped across blown-up sheepskins with tarpaulins and rugs to sit on. There was always the fear that we small children might fall through into the fast-flowing river beneath – we didn't!

Our father was a very fine polo player and Gilgit was said to be the place where the game had started many years ago. Play was with sticks of a sort, and a sheep's head served as a ball. We had trips to Nagar Hunza of the delicious apricots, and we played with other British children in the colourful gardens – to name two of our companions, there were Raleigh and John Trevelyan, whose father commanded the small military unit which was stationed at Gilgit. Raleigh is an author of note and he has written an excellent book entitled *The Golden Oriel* about his youth in India.

Communication with the outside world was of course very slow and letters took weeks and sometimes months to arrive. Stores had to

Heather Todd, Lavender's elder sister, on her way to Gilgit via the Burzel Pass, in 1924. (Lavender Todd)

be ordered from the UK as much as a year ahead to arrive via ship to Bombay, rail to Rawalpindi and thence by mule over the passes to Gilgit.

I remember the arrival of the first small plane in Gilgit. It brought the Hart Expedition, which was concerned with an exploratory project, and the members staying with us sleeping in tents in our garden. Amongst their number was one Yakoflev, a wonderful artist who had travelled with the expedition from Africa. Needless to say, the arrival of the first plane was greeted with enormous interest by the populace, who flocked to see it.

We returned to the UK in 1931, and when our parents had to go back to India my sister and I were left with our grandmother at Blackheath. For the next three years we were so well looked after by her and her cook/housemaid, from whom we had great affection. We began our education at the local high school and later went to a boarding school in Hampshire, and this was followed by Godolphin School in Salisbury. Our parents returned every two-and-a-half or three years.

ROBIN MALLINSON

My father was in the 17th Dogra Regiment of the Indian Army and their base was at Jullundur in the Punjab. We lived in a cantonment, which was a few miles outside Jullundur City. This was a military town, spaciously laid out with large bungalows and gardens for the officers and barracks for the troops. There was a Club for the officers with tennis and squash courts and a cricket ground. There was also a polo ground. Jullundur City, where we occasionally went for shopping, was completely different – very crowded, dirty, narrow streets, but buzzing with activity.

The Dogras were Hindus from the Kangra Valley and other places such as Jammu in the lower reaches of the Himalayas. There was only one regiment of Dogras, the 17th, and in peacetime only a few battalions, but in wartime this number was greatly increased. They were, like the Gurkhas, small in stature but like other hill people tough and redoubtable soldiers.

When the regiment was at the base in winter the families of the officers would be there too, but not in summer when the families 'went to the hills'. In our case this was Kashmir and if the regiment was not at Jullundur in the winter we also stayed in Kashmir. As Kashmir was an autonomous state with a Maharajah, the British were not allowed to own property. However, Srinagar, the capital of Kashmir, was surrounded by lakes and the British could own a boat and in particular a houseboat, so a number of British families actually lived on houseboats.

Srinagar is some 5000 feet above sea level, but it is situated on a plain surrounded by high mountains, the highest being Nanga Parbat at over 26,000 feet. In the spring when the snow melts the lakes and rivers frequently flood, sometimes with loss of life and homes. Winters were cold with snow and ice, but the houseboats were made very cosy with wood-burning stoves. I was born on one of these houseboats in 1928.

In the summer, we would move to Gulmarg (altitude about 9000 feet) where for many years we rented on a semi-permanent basis a wooden chalet which had magnificent views. On one side we looked across the '*marg*' or meadow towards where most of the other chalets were and, above them, to a 14,000 foot mountain which dominated the area. On the other side we looked across the Vale of Kashmir to Nanga Parbat, 90 miles away. No cars, trucks or motorbikes were allowed in Gulmarg – one rode, walked or, if old or sick was carried by four men in a *doolie*, like an elongated sedan chair on two poles. Nearly everyone rode the local ponies, each of which had a *syce* to look after it. I remember that, after one winter in Jullundur, my mother hired a truck with driver, which took her, three children and our pony and *syce* over the high pass into Kashmir, a journey of several days.

We had an aunt in Kashmir, Miss Muriel Mallinson, later to be awarded the MBE. She went out to Kashmir with the Church

Missionary Society soon after the Great War and spent the next 40 years as headmistress of the first girls school in Kashmir. She started with one small, mud-floored room and finished with hundreds of pupils. A few years after her retirement to England the school sent her a return ticket so that she could be present at a ceremony when the school was renamed after her. Educating girls was not popular in the 1920s and she had great problems, but her faith, optimism and sense of humour overcame everything. She became a well-known figure in Kashmir and, in particular, was a friend of Sheikh Abdullah, who became Chief Minister after India's independence. When I went back in 1987 I was surprised, and very pleased, to find her still remembered for all she had done for the women of Kashmir.

In 1933 we joined my father in Burma, where we lived in the Army cantonment of Mingaladon, or the hill station of Kalaw. I remember little of this period except for the snakes – I once saw 12 before breakfast – and the large pagoda in Rangoon, the Shwe Dagon, where shoes had to be taken off before entering the dark, crowded and mysterious interior.

ORIOLE MALLINSON

'Geography lesson on your doorstep,' declared my father waving at the view – Nanga Parbat and K2, amongst several other peaks over 20,000 feet high. We were in Gulmarg, Kashmir, for the summer months, perfect for us children. The garden had red and yellow raspberries, potatoes, chickens, daphne bushes and other flowers and shrubs, and also the stables for my hill pony, or *tat*, called Doc, and my sister's pony Judy, who was more dainty. I used to feed them local coarse brown sugar, called *ghur*. The Kashmiri *syces* were wonderful – very patient and good riders. Judy came up with us from Jullundur (in the Punjab) in the back of the lorry, and munched hay which found its way down my back and tickled for ages. She initially refused to enter the lorry in spite of *syces* pulling, pushing and urging her on with titbits. However, after everyone had given up in despair, she just walked in up the ramp. My mother was relieved and amazed. The luggage and bedding rolls were piled round Judy and my bicycle was loaded on top of the lorry – going through the Bannihal tunnel its handlebars were bent, having caught the roof of the tunnel.

above Sheila Wright-Neville on her pony in the bazaar at Gulmarg, 1932. (Sheila Wright-Neville)

right A distant view of Gulmarg. (Sheila Wright-Neville)

below The houseboat 'Rolls Royce' moored on the Dal Lake, Srinagar, 1932. (Sheila Wright-Neville)

In Gulmarg we rode our ponies and went on picnics to the Ferozapore Nullah and to Kilanmarg through pine woods and across rickety wooden bridges over rushing mountain streams in single file. If a hole was spotted in the bridge the word of warning went from one to another. Gulmarg had a bazaar, a church, Nedou's Hotel, a Club and several golf courses – one was for children. We had various governesses who gave us lessons, and my mother also taught me and another girl. Our hut was built of pine with wooden shingles on the roof. One year we went up before the season opened. There was a lot of deep snow and we enjoyed tobogganing. The favourite toboggan had tin runners and was much faster then the plain wooden ones and with two up we could make it go much faster. Although it was cold we did not seem to feel it, and had a marvellous time playing in the snow. Soon the spring came and the *marg* was covered in daisies and buttercups and in the valley the almond trees were in blossom.

The road to Srinagar was edged with poplar trees and the flat fields on either side were bright with mustard flowers. I was born on a houseboat like my brother. We loved Srinagar, sometimes going on the Dal (lake) in a *shikara* (a long, narrow gondola-type boat) which had embroidered cushions and felt very luxurious. They had fanciful names in English like 'Lotus Lily', 'Queen of the Lake', 'Love in the Mist' etc. The boatmen were very skilful at handling the *shikaras* with their heart-shaped paddles. We loved the bazaars where everything was embroideries, materials, woollen scarves, slippers and *papier-mâché* boxes and bowls – also walnut-wood carvings, furniture, rugs and carpets. The river was lined with houseboats. We lived in one called Brunehilde. She had a narrow gang plank and the cookhouse was a separate smaller boat. The bund was built high as a precaution against flooding, but one year the water from the river rose right over the bund and there were marks on the chenar trees to record the highest level. We loved going on *tonga* rides in Srinagar: wheeled vehicles were not allowed in Gulmarg at that time, only ponies, or litters carried by porters.

SHEILA WRIGHT-NEVILLE

Holidays were often spent in Kashmir on a houseboat, usually on Nagim Bagh (the biggest lake). We took with us the cocker spaniel, Robin, and I also had a large white rabbit and a hired pony. I recall one occasion when the rabbit fell into the lake and had to be rescued by one of the servants, much to his disgust. These houseboats are still there today largely unchanged. Ours was beautifully panelled and furnished, with a canopied roof for sunbathing. A following boat housed the kitchen and servants' quarters. We would take our personal servants (bearers, *ayah*) on these holidays, but the other servants would be hired locally. A bathing boat was moored in the middle of the lake; we would row out to it and swim from there as the edges of the lake, where the houseboats were moored, were weedy and dangerous for swimming. The bathing boat had changing rooms and a bar, and one local entrepreneur had a motorboat which towed behind it a board with a rope handle. Although I could only dog-paddle at the time – I was then six – I can remember standing on this board and whizzing round the lake with a rubber tyre round my waist. That particular lake claimed several lives because people would party on the bathing boat and exchange dares as to who could swim to the shore. It wasn't the distance but the combination of alcohol, weeds and floating waterlilies that drowned them.

We sometimes went on picnics by boat to the Shalimar Gardens. My father was artistic and did some beautiful drawings in crayon of the gardens. These pictures were framed and hung in our other homes in India. And then there were the hordes of peddlers who came to the houseboat in *shikaras* with wonderful things to sell: exquisitely embroidered linens and clothing, brassware, *papier-mâché* and intricately carved furniture. One particular furniture-maker was called Suffering Moses, and I still have two small walnut tables with his label on them. Since one of my tables must now be well over 150 years old, I suspect the original Suffering Moses was already dead by this time, but he had become so famous that his descendants continued to trade on his name.

Occasionally there were trips to the mountain village of Gulmarg in the Kashmir hills, deeply snow-covered in winter where people went to ski, and beautiful in the summer. We travelled the last part of the journey up the mountain on ponies and stayed in a hotel in a village. We picnicked on the mountain meadows and paddled in shallow, cold mountain streams.

Sheila Wright-Neville and her friend Richard Finzel rowing on a weedy part of the lake, 1933; with her father and mother and their cocker spaniel Robin on board the houseboat 'Laughing Water', 1933; with her pony in front of their houseboat, 1934; with her father and his *shikari* and the giant mahseer they had caught in the lake that day, 1934. (Sheila Wright-Neville)

6

The Punjab

The Punjab takes its name from the five rivers which descend from the Himalayas and cross a huge plain, joining together to form the Indus. A vast system of irrigation canals, begun in Moghul times, was already in place, and it was still being extended, transforming a sandy desert into rich agricultural land producing wheat, millet, barley, maize, cotton and sugar, to name only a few of their crops.

The monsoon here was also unreliable, arriving in June and ending in September, but there was a second period of rainfall in the winter. The hottest time of the year was June, just before the monsoon, with temperatures up to 120 degrees, and frosts were frequent in January.

The capital city, Lahore, with cotton mills, flour mills and an ice factory, had also an important railway works. Particularly beautiful carpets were made there, in the gaol. It was known to be one of the hottest places in India. The population was principally Muslim, about 50 per cent, the rest being Hindu or Sikh. Sikhism derives from Brahminism, in a more puritan form, and the Golden Temple of the Sikhs was in their sacred city of Amritsar. While Sikhs were to be found all over India, the Punjab must be regarded as their home territory.

The North Western was still the principal railway, but there was also the Southern Punjab Railway, and there was a small oilfield at Attock.

The chief language was Punjabi, but Hindustani was the language both of the Law Courts and of the administration. Hindustani was originally an actual living dialect of Western Hindi, but by now there were two forms; Urdu, with many Persian words, was the language

above Robert Bragg, in white turban, and his younger brother Ed, dressed as Jat sepoys, with two Indian friends at Jhelum, 1935. The *dhobi*, with his huge bundle, is in the left background. (Robert Bragg)

left Ed Bragg inspects a sepoy of his father's Regiment, the 3rd Battalion of the 9th Jats, Jhelum, 1935. (Robert Bragg) of educated Muslims, while Hindi, with many Sanskrit words, was spoken by educated Hindus.

Murree, at 7000 feet, was the most favoured hill station in the Punjab. There was a famous brewery there, and the road to it began at Rawalpindi and continued on into Kashmir.

Simla, technically situated among the Simla Hill States, was the summer seat of both the Viceroy – at Viceregal Lodge – and the Punjab Government. Built at heights between 6600 and 8000 feet, the earliest European house dated from 1819, and it had long been the site of European-style schools.

ERNEST CAMPBELL

We were four American children who grew up in the Punjab between 1912 and 1919. Our parents were Presbyterian missionaries in a small, old provincial town in Sialkot District. We camped much of the winter and could see the snow peaks of the Pir Panja Himalayas on the northern horizon.

We grew up in a fairyland 'compound' of some four acres surrounded by a fence. We lived in an old brick and mud 'bungalow' with 25-foot ceilings, six major rooms and a wide verandah surrounding the house. Parts of this verandah had been bricked in to make bathrooms, dressing rooms, pantries etc. We children slept on the north, back verandah, and we had daily 'tea' on the west verandah, which faced a seemingly endless vista of mustard fields.

These were two Persian wheels in the compound, a guava orchard, a rose garden, a tennis court and a servants' courtyard, which also included the buffaloes' shed, the chicken coop, the tent godown, a garage and the cookhouse.

We were so isolated from the English speakers that we children all learned to be fluent in Punjabi, and later in Urdu. We, and some of our children, are still fluent in these languages. We are quite an oddity, as Europeans no longer live in India long enough to really learn the language.

My parents came to India in 1909. My grandchildren, some of them, are still in India. Our son works as a forestry specialist with the Ford Foundation in New Delhi; the other visits India, Nepal and Tibet a number of times each year on 'consultancies' for the World Bank and other foundations. He is an anthropologist.

I have vivid memories of British India. As a boy, I watched with fascination the polo games played in the Sialkot cantonment. We occasionally met British soldiers or 'tommies' – but had more to do with the Civil Service. Deputy Commissioner Brain and Sir Malcolm Dorling were very concerned with the welfare of villagers and shared a community of interest with the 'district missionaries'.

All my companions were Indians. I had a sort of guardian who was a giant (or so he seemed to me). He had a kind of arrested development and must have had a mental age of 12 or so. He taught me how to make and fly and fight kites, how to make bird lime and

left The Persian water wheel in the Campbells' garden, to irrigate it and provide water for the house in buckets made of old tins. A local boy drives the cows. (Ernest Campbell)

below 'All aboard for camp. The trucks piled with all the gear. I drove this one at a very early age!' 1932–36. (Ernest Campbell)

catch bulbuls and train them. We played a game similar to hockey with sticks cut from *babul* trees, a kind of acacia. These primitive hockey sticks were called '*kundi*'. The ball was wrapped cotton thread enclosed in a cotton net. We preferred dirt roadways or empty canals. Since we were barefoot we were safe there from ground thorns and cockle burns. We also of course played *goolie dunda* (tipcat?) and had variations where the loser had to carry the winner on their backs. We played *kabaddi* in a disorganised sort of a way. We made slingshots and bows and arrows. Our special enemies were the flying foxes and parrots that ate our fruit.

I was in India (excluding three 'furloughs' in the US) from my birth until I was 18 years old, that is to say, from 1917 to 1935. I then did four years in college in America, three years of being a parish minister and two years of postgraduate study in sociology. Then I returned to India.

DONALD CATTO

I was born in Quetta in 1921, when my father, a member of the Indian Army, was serving in that station. I was the youngest of four sons. My earliest recollection of schooling in India was when, at the age of six in 1927, I was admitted as a non-Catholic boarder to the Catholic Convent in Murree. I think this school was chosen because of its location in the foothills of the Himalayas at an altitude of about 7000 feet and within 40 miles of Rawalpindi, where my father was serving at the time.

The most indelible memories I have of the convent, which I left in 1928 after an almost terminal attack of double pneumonia, necessitating hospital admission and a long period of convalescence etc. are these.

A sister called for volunteers for the choir and for Urdu classes. In my enthusiasm for games and other diverting activities, I volunteered for both – I thought that Urdu was a board game. My association with the choir lasted about 20 minutes, before the sister finally located the boy who was singing so badly that he had to be removed before she could continue with the practice. I have never attempted to sing since then. My brush with Urdu developed more favourably and, in 1940, it enabled me to pass the University of Punjab BA Intermediate Examination, with Urdu as a second language.

Meals at the convent were supervised by sisters on duty. Children were required to eat everything served to them. Anything not eaten at a meal would be served again at the next meal that day. Thus, I found it necessary to covertly slip turnips and other vegetables which I did not and could not eat into my pocket, for disposal later in a nearby open incinerator fire. I cannot remember ever being asked to explain the gravy-encrusted pocket interiors to any of the sisters. Physical discipline was, I think, restricted to a slap with the end of the leather thongs worn round their waists by the sisters.

One of my fellow schoolmates had an irrepressible appetite for eating candle wax. What better place to find unaccounted-for and freely available wax than the chapel? He satisfied his craving by volunteering to become a chapel helper and cleaner, which accounted for his many trips to the chapel to clean the candlesticks and holders: childhood ingenuity which enhanced his reputation with the sisters!

After the convent I attended a Bishop Cotton day school in Rawalpindi for about a year, but I have no specific memories of it.

Before revealing what my father's job was and recounting memories of exotic or exciting journeys with him in India and beyond, I will get out of the way the annual voyage to Europe that occupied three months of my every year from five years old till ten. These interludes were so different from the Indian norm that they seem to belong to another life.

Not surprising in view of the circumstances of my entrance into the world, I was accounted a delicate child, and soon after my fifth birthday I developed what was diagnosed as a 'heart murmur'. The doctor advised I should be sent to Europe for three months of the hot season, and that is how it happened.

The following June my father took me to Bombay and handed me over into the charge of the captain of the *Victoria*, Triestino Line, bound for Genoa. The captain delivered me to the chief stewardess, and so I set out on a sea voyage, the first of many, a parcel sent recorded delivery, to be returned along the same route three months later.

My eventual destination was the Ursuline nunnery in Paris where my mother had received her education. It was perhaps the one place in Europe which my father knew of where a small, delicate child could be boarded and receive the special care he was deemed to need.

PAMELA ALBERT

Rawalpindi was our next destination, as my father's regiment was stationed there.

It was the task of the Indian Army to protect, supervise, sometimes judge local situations, such as shooting man-eating tigers. These people were Rajputs. All the *subadhars* and the *subadhar* majors were Indian. I did hear that once long ago the sergeants used to be British, but I never saw any.

It was at about this time that my father decided to start my riding lessons. I was all of 19 months old and had to be taught to

The Special Loco kept in Rawalpindi for VIP trains. (David Thom)

sit up straight, learn patience, and above all get a really good seat for riding well. A ring saddle was ordered and a donkey was purchased from a local *dhobi*. The donkey was stabled with my parents' mounts and looked after by the *syce*.

On my first ride, I joined my parents before their ride and we all just walked the animals around the compound. They then departed for their ride and I was left with the *syce*, who held on to the reins while I held on for dear life to the ring saddle with my feet in perfect position in the stirrups. My time in the saddle was increased each week until I was able to sit straight and was comfortable with the animal. I would ride daily in the morning after breakfast and again at four in the early evening. This was really the beginning of my complete love of horses and in fact with animals in general. I can remember when I was 12 years old my mother saying to me, 'One day, Pamela, I hope I will be able to put my arms around you and not have you smelling like a horse!' It never happened.

Rawalpindi, nicknamed "Pindi' by all who went there, was a good-sized city with a large British population who enjoyed their Clubs, Gymkhanas, restaurants etc. according to their lifestyle. We lived about 10 miles out of the city at what was known as a cantonment area set aside for the regiments that were assigned to Rawalpindi. On duty at this time was the 7th Rajput Regiment, our regiment. The parade ground was the centre of an area of about 10 square miles with quarters for the single officers, bungalows for married officers, Club House, quarters for the men, plus stables. Sometimes these areas were walled, sometimes not. The smaller the city, the smaller the cantonment. My parents and I, with my father's company, were sent, when I was four years old, to Fathegarh, a village in the middle of nowhere. It was a lonely place after 'Pindi. The three of us, plus my *ayah*, settled in to a pretty little house called a *dak* bungalow ('*dak*' means mail).

It appeared that because bandits were causing trouble, killing the local cattle and running off with the women of the village; 'A' Company of the 7th Rajputs were being sent to the area.

Our home had no electricity or running water! As in most of these *dak* bungalows, water was drawn from a large well at the back of the garden. When a small amount only was required, it was drawn by a leather bucket on a rope. For watering the garden, two bullocks were tied to a yoke attached by rope to a huge wheel. On each spoke of the wheel were elongated leather containers, and as the bullock walked away from the wheel, water would be drawn up and deposited in a ditch. These ditches were ploughed in a line to water the plants. When sufficient water was fed into one ditch, the *mali* would block off that row with mud, and open the next ditch to let the water in.

All baths were taken in tin tubs placed on a little raised platform about eight inches off the floor, then a small wall around the platform kept the water from running on to the floor. At one end there was a hole to dump the water out when the bath was finished, this water being diverted directly into the garden. Chicken wire was placed over the hole, as invariably snakes would find their way in. This task was done by the *bhisti*, so, if you wanted a bath, you had to let him know in plenty of time. Then there were the thunder-boxes! These looked like heavy wooden chairs with lids on the seats. When you lifted the lid, you saw a potty recessed in the hole of the seat. If you were lucky, you might get a thunder-box with arms! There was a special design for men wearing spurs. Each house came with a full complement of servants, so, other than my father's personal batman and *ayah*, we had no need to bring any. My father's batman was assigned to him from the Army to take care of his uniform, boots and all his belongings.

My grandmother spent Christmas one year with us in Fathegarh, and I recall she had little white gauze bags made to protect the fruit on the guava and custard apple trees from the hungry birds. Isn't it strange – the funny things you remember?

The oil lamps that took the place of electricity in the bush were really beautiful to see as they had Tiffany glass shades over the tall funnels. They cast the most beautiful light, and I can still smell the scented oils of those lamps.

My most vivid memories of those years of *dak* bungalow living were my lying on my bed and hearing the high-pitched call of a peacock or a jackal, and the unforgettable sound of the regimental bugler sounding the Last Post or the Muslim *mullahs* calling the faithful to prayer.

My father's next period of one year's leave was in 1930. I was then three years of age, and it was decided that we go to Singapore and Java before sailing on to the Continent and home, spending a week in Malta and Gibraltar. The choice of Singapore was because my mother's brother Claude and his wife Gladys and child were there. It was decided to call there first as my uncle was working for the Wakefield Oil Company.

FRANK HIPPMAN

I was born on 29 April 1923 in the Princess Marie Louise Hospital in Aldershot. My father was a serjeant (the correct spelling at that time) in the Royal Fusiliers, and in 1929 he was posted to India. We boarded the troopship *Neuralia* but my younger brother got chickenpox and we were turfed off. The *Neuralia* sailed on, taking all our possessions with it. After an isolation period in Hounslow we embarked on the *City of Hong Kong*. The change didn't mean much to me, but my parents were thankful for it after the bleakness of the troopship.

We joined the First Battalion in Ambala in the Punjab (where we caught up with our baggage, somewhat damaged by Customs treatment) and I encountered the first series of married quarters, mostly identical in pattern. My brother (aged two) and I accepted the new situation, with an *ayah* and bearer, as if we'd been born to it.

I'd been to school in England and started again in Ambala, but I can't remember it at all. The school in Kasauli seemed to be a general one but that in Kamptee was a regimental one with, at first, a major in charge and then a Miss Brought. She married a Sergeant Brewer and we met them again back in England. The Deolali school was another general one. My detailed memories of school started with the Lawrence School at Mount Abu, which I first went to in 1931.

The uniform was khaki shirt and shorts with black woollen stockings and boots. The cap was a 'havelock', that is a leather kepi covered with khaki drill, with a neck flap, as worn by the old French Foreign Legion. The girls wore khaki dresses (not a Dior design). In the winter we had navy-blue jackets. For church parades we wore blue suits in winter and white suits in summer, with red and blue ties. The men teachers wore khaki without any badges of rank.

The headmaster was a major in the AEC (Army Education Corps), while the rest of the men teachers were sergeants from various regiments. (After the War the teachers were civilian graduates.) Discipline at Abu was largely in the hands of corporals, usually from a regiment stationed locally. Three women teachers taught the very youngest children.

The school term started at the beginning of March and finished at the end of November. Three-month Christmas holiday sounds fine, but nine months without seeing one's parents was, I think, not good for children as young as five. A few children had visits if their parents happened to be nearby, but the visits tended to be rather strained affairs.

Abu made little acknowledgement of the fact that we were in India; what we did learn of its culture etc. came about more by accident than by design.

One thing which probably surprised all children raised in India, with its blistering heat in the dry season and refreshing, if rather violent, rain in the monsoon, was the attitude in the UK to thunderstorms. We exulted in the rain, and failed to understand the apparent dread which many British people had of what seemed to us to be rather mild outbreaks of poor weather.

Another common attribute was knowledge of the 16 times table, which we had to learn, there being (in those days) 16 annas to the rupee, a gift which I still find handy on occasion.

The food was generally poor and monotonous (although I've yet to meet a boarding-school pupil who thought the food at school was good). Rajputana was a state where the eating of beef was forbidden so we had nine months of mutton, with the occasional chicken. Dahl and rice at breakfast were relieved by an egg at Easter, and there was pink salmon for tea on the King-Emperor's birthdays. There seemed to be an obsession with eating one's cabbage. If there was mince, I often used it to cover my cabbage, there apparently being no rules about mince.

Inoculations were frequent, and once a week we had quinine, against malaria, and Epsom salts, against constipation. To make sure that we had swallowed the dose, which was administered by the head-master's wife, we had to say 'Thank you, Madam.'

In the monsoon there were many indoor activities such as Housey Housey. One was a game called in the UK Hi, cock-a-lorum. There were two teams, one of which formed a line of boys in the leap-frog position each hanging on to the rump of the boy in front, the front boy being supported by an upright anchor man. The other team leap-frogged on to the line trying to concentrate as many bodies as possible at one point in the hope of making the line collapse under the weight. Our version of the game was bound about with esoteric and pointless rules such as a requirement to keep one's fists clenched and to say 'Heaps' without showing one's teeth.

There were also concerts etc. given by the Army units, and occasion-ally visits to see silent films. Rin Tin Tin and Charlie Chaplin were the favourite one-reelers but there were sometimes multi-reelers such as Jules Verne's *Mysterious Island*. A characteristic of watching the films was that, as they were silent, the audience noise created little distraction, and there was a compulsion to read aloud the subtitle in English to disguise the fact that the players could be speaking anything but. German and French films, for instance, were occasionally on the menu.

In the hot season, Reveille was earlier, we had a *chota hazri* ('little breakfast'), had two periods of lessons, then a *burra hazri*, followed by more lessons until dinner. After dinner we were supposed to have a sleep but I can't remember anyone doing so.

Once a fortnight a barber called, but he didn't bring his own cape. Each boy had to use his towel, which meant that the hairs stuck in them came out on to our bodies after we'd had a bath.

Parades, as may be expected, were required for every occasion: church, lessons, meals, or just for the fun of it. We took part in the King's Birthday Parade with Army units, and on one occasion, a parade for the presentation of the North West Frontier Medal to one of our teachers. Girls paraded separately from the boys, but lessons were co-educational.

The most popular parade was, of course, the weekly pay parade, when we got our pocket money. This varied according to the affluence of one's parents. My father, being a CQMS, was comparatively rich, and I got four annas (about 4d), most of which was squandered immediately at the tuckshop.

Church services at the other three Lawrence schools were held daily and twice on Sundays. Abu's children were apparently not so evil, and made do with just the two services on Sundays.

Punishments were applied with Victorian enthusiasm for any slackness or failures at lessons, the cane being used with monotonous frequency, the only variation being in the part of the body where it was applied. The girls' punishments were as bad, but not as barbaric as those meted out at the convent schools.

There was no electricity (in 1934, when I left Mount Abu), illumination being provided by pressure and ordinary oil lamps. Nor was there any piped water. Water for washing came from a well, while drinking water was brought up on the backs of mules fortnightly, to replenish the drinking water tank.

I was naturally shy, and on my return to UK the Indian experience gave me a standing with my school fellows and later, my fellow apprentices, which helped me to offset the effects of this shyness. The experience also helped me to look at things in a cosmopolitan light and has provided me with a fund of anecdotes for use on social occasions.

VALERIE THURLEY

My father arrived in India in 1932. He had hoped to enter the Indian Civil Service, but the Mahatma launched one of his civil-disobedience campaigns, which caused recruitment of Englishmen to the ICS to be suspended for five years. So instead he was recruited to teach Latin and English at the Lawrence College, Ghora Gali, near the hill resort of Murree. He and my mother (also a school teacher) stayed until 1952 – my father by this time having been appointed principal of the college.

Ghora Gali was the only 'home' we children knew. There were five of us – three brothers, my sister and myself. It was an idyllic place to grow up in, and I think with great nostalgia about the small house on the edge of the forest, and the lovely garden my mother and the *mali* together created for us. Larkspur and hollyhocks, dahlias and phlox, and the beautiful scented tea roses which covered the trellis at the end of our garden.

We grew up without any sense of fear. When we were very young our *ayahs* made sure we did not fall into any of the deep *nullahs* which criss-crossed various parts of the estate, and showed us how to cross the small streams without falling in. But by the age of eight or so we were allowed to roam about on our own, and that freedom allowed us to know every nook and cranny of the place, from the clearings in the forest to the various boundaries which marked the estate. We knew every servant, every woodcutter, and the various pedlars who came down the winding road from Murree, bringing tin boxes packed with treasures: cakes from the bakery, gorgeous Indian sweets, ludoos, pearers, *jellabees* and stickjaw toffee. Or the little man whose tin box was crammed with haberdashery, rick-rack and bias binding, buttons, silks for embroidery, needles and cotton, hooks and eyes, and some Butterick patterns.

In mid-November the school closed down and the boarders returned to the plains. Our family stayed on, braving the deep snows and isolation. Quite often we were entirely cut off from Murree (two miles up the mountain), and isolated from Rawalpindi in the plains. I remember in particular two really heavy snowfalls when we could not get out of the house for the better part of a week and had to live on what was in the storeroom. This was always kept well stocked against such an emergency. A side of salted beef hung on a hook, and there were gunny sacks of dried fruit, tins of condensed milk, as well as all the more usual provisions.

From November until early March, when the school was re-opened, the entire estate belonged to us, and to the few other members of staff who had chosen to stay on for the winter. Snow covered the hills, weighting the trees down. The jackals became bolder and the panther came to carry off goats from the butchery *khanna*. We kids were in seventh heaven. I can still remember how exhilarating it felt to come hurtling down in our home-made toboggan.

Winter was always hard on the servants. My mother used to worry about the servants' children in particular, and our *ayah*'s children spent the worst days in our kitchen. There were four of them and the eldest, Alice, was only a few years older than me and not nearly as precocious. It was from the servants – and particularly from the children – that I learned to speak Urdu fluently, picking up from them their bad grammar, and learning to swear robustly. We used to play jackstones and spillikins and marbles, and although the friendship was never very deep, I still remember how horrified I was when I heard that Alice was to be given in marriage to a man old enough to be her father.

Besides our house servants were the servants who were employed primarily by the school but who we also called on when necessary. The carpenter, the *bhijleewallah*, who dealt with the electricity, and the *pinjamwallah*, who arrived every winter to tease the cotton stuffing in the school mattresses and pillows, taking up his position in one of the back yards, and plucking the old cotton wool with his bow to do the job.

There were only two shops on the estate. One sold general goods, and the other sold sweets. I don't think there were any toy shops in

Murree, though there may have been. In any event, our toys were very basic. For instance, we devised a hand-cart made out of an old tea-chest and some wooden wheels scrounged from the carpenter, and we would play with this for hours. Walking on stilts was another great game, and so was skipping and various games which involved the use of a ball. Another favourite game was called witchy-witchy. This was another game of chase, but with the added hazard of having to walk on upended flower-pots (*gumlas*). Anyone who fell off was captured by the witch and tortured. In the winter a big Sears, Roebuck catalogue somehow found its way into the house, and after the adults had finished with it, we kids were allowed to take scissors to it, and we would 'furnish' whole houses with things we never knew existed: electric kettles and toasters, swivel chairs and hoovers. Cutting these items from the catalogue and sticking them into our 'homes' page of a scrapbook.

Christmas decorations and cards were always home-made. The cook used to mix up a great bowl of *layhee* (flour and water paste) and we would cut crepe paper into lengths and make our chains and bells. We ended up with glue on our hands, on the coir matting covering in the small 'study' room, and on the poor cat. Just before Christmas we used to trail after my father into the forest and select our own Christmas tree and help him decorate it with 'real' bought glass baubles which came from England, and had to be stored away in layers of cotton wool. On Christmas morning we would find such exciting things in our stockings: nuts, an orange, a small bar of chocolate, pencils and crayons. Under the tree would be our 'big' gift. A book perhaps, or a doll's tea-set made of tin and garishly painted. My brothers would get wooden toys like an engine or a boat. My mother would get a bottle of perfume. And every year my grandmother would send us wonderful rag dolls she had made and dressed. Always a pair – a girl and a boy doll. Sir Percy and Lady Blakeney one year, Uncle Tom and Chloe the next, or a boy and girl gypsy doll.

The cake and pudding were made by our cook. Sometime about mid-November we children had to pick over the sultanas and currants, wash them and dry them in the sun, and try not to guzzle too much. Cooking arrangements were very primitive. Most of our food was cooked on a raised clay affair with several hollows, under which was a fire fed with coke and coal. There was a *chula* too, used mostly for boiling things. The 'oven' was a large empty kerosene tin which was carefully balanced over the fire. The Christmas cake was placed in this, and the 'oven' sealed. More charcoal or coke was heaped on the top of the kerosene tin, and somehow, with great skill and constant vigilance, our old cook turned out the most perfect cakes, soufflés, bread and the most wonderful Christmas cake I have ever tasted.

STAR STAUNTON

One of the palaces in which we spent a good deal of time on and off was a replica of the palace of Fontainebleau. I remember it as a beautiful and most luxurious place, but somehow un-Indian. There was an English butler, an English valet, both a French and an Italian chef and Italian waiters. It was like living in a luxury hotel in Europe. And there were so many Maharanis, all Europeans, some relics of the late Maharajah, the rest the wives of the current holder of the title. Strict protocol was *de rigueur*, or how could the peace have been kept? The tribe of pallid Eurasian children seemed overburdened by their mixed blood, never really knowing what they were or to whom they belonged. To me that was a sad household.

Far different was the atmosphere and manner of life that prevailed in the family of my dear friends and benefactors the Maharajah and Maharani of Jind.

Jind was a small state to the north west of Delhi, its ruler the sort of person with whom my father was most at ease, a hunter, a polo-player, cultivated and easy in manner whether the company was British or Indian, true to his breed and culture and proud of the purity of his own stock, but liberally minded for his station and determined that his children should enjoy some of the Western freedoms and standards of value.

The Maharani was the daughter of a rich Punjabi merchant brought up in the Indian tradition and happy in it. She had no foreign training and spoke only Punjabi. But she was a woman of lively intelligence and took pleasure in her daughters' emancipation from the restrictions placed upon women by Hinduism.

The two of them and their large family maintained a luxurious standard of living that was in a different league altogether from our suburban affluence at Lahore. They were royals and in a genial way well aware of that fact. As in our own case, their servants and, indeed, those vastly worse-off multitudes whose labours paid for their luxuries, might well have detested them as bloodsuckers and sympathised with the Congress agitators and their vision of a fairer and more egalitarian society. In fact, I think they did not do so to any great extent, being to the manner born and finding security in an ancient and secure leadership that gave shape to their society and provided them with a sense of glory as it were by proxy.

Probably I first met the Jind children as I met so many others in my father's company. I would be taken to pay my respects and then be despatched down the long corridors of the palace state rooms to the domestic quarters where the family had smaller but still extensive personal suites. There I would meet the children, all of the same mother, and especially the three girls nearest my own age, Princess Rose, two years my senior, Princess Buttercup, the same as I, and Princess Pansy, who was two years younger. They had other names in their own language, which was Punjabi, and all were the names of flowers. Like myself, they could move easily from language to language.

We liked one another at once, and it was not long before I had become a regular guest in their home. They befriended my loneliness and gave me the sense of belonging to a family which I had always lacked. At an early stage we made ourselves sisters according to the understanding of Princess Rose, and at her lively instigation we bravely stuck a needle into our fingers and smeared blood on one another, gravely intoning in Punjabi and English the vows of everlasting sisterhood.

From all that I can remember, Rose culled the idea from one of the books by Arthur Ransome that we read together with avidity. She was our natural leader, the oldest of the four and bright as a button, full of fun and with an appetite for adventure. Buttercup was slower and gentler, Pansy just as quick and active, taking into account her lack of years.

Sometimes I would go to stay at the palace for days on end and be swallowed into its normal rhythm. I would join in the family schooling, run by two more or less omnicompetent tutors, with proper classroom routine in French and English and involving serious study with homework to do in the evening. Under this regular discipline the princes and princesses were all better scholars than I, who had at that time to rely almost entirely on the sporadic attentions of my *moonshi*.

Schoolroom was for the morning. The afternoon went on games, often performed under professional tuition with the usual prodigal expense of manpower. Tutors for basketball, cricket, swimming, riding. It was intended that the royal offspring should be competent in those activities to which they would be likely to set their hands in later in life. Again, I lagged far behind.

But when our homework had been done we were free to play our own games ad lib, the four of us together as a group, and here I felt less at a disadvantage, though I could never keep up with Rose. The palace, of course, stood in its own extensive grounds. We never lacked for space in which to go on adventures, do our feats of competitive daring pursued by a tearful and terrified Miss Smith and Mme Vignolle, our two governesses. The most blissful memories of my childhood congregate at that beloved spot in that innocent and gracious company that made of me Princess Tara and satisfied, if only sporadically and as occasion offered, the part of me that longed to be accepted, that longed to belong.

DONALD CATTO

I attended the Lawrence Memorial School at Ghora Gali in the Punjab between 1931 and 1935, with a year off when my father was on leave in the UK and I went to a day school in Plumstead SE18. I returned to Ghora Gali in 1939/40 to study for the University of Punjab Intermediate BA Examination, followed by a teachers' training course. At this time my parents lived in Bangalore and my brother Frank, who is a year older, and I had to travel by train to Rawalpindi and thence by car to Ghora Gali. This journey, of about 1900 miles, took four days and five nights (or five days and four nights, depending on the starting time) including a 12-hour stop at Bombay. It was a steam train with carriages providing self-contained compartments of two or four berths with adjoining toilet facilities. I would be 17 years old at this time.

Ghora Gali School was located about four-and-a-half miles from Murree, at an altitude of about 6500 feet and was accessible only by road running from Rawalpindi via Murree to Kashmir.

I remember years when deep snow lay on the ground until May and the risk of falling into deep drifts was always present. During such protracted winter periods one also had to be aware of the long, heavy icicles which hung from the eaves of buildings with more than one floor; they sometimes became detached and fell to the ground.

The school maintained strict discipline, exercised primarily through prefects. Caning by masters was authorised and freely administered to those who needed to be activated educationally, or to inhibit bad behaviour. I remember a chemistry master who always caned on the palm of the hand during cold weather, either to satisfy a sadistic instinct or to doubly impress the student with what he was being taught. Serious offences warranted a public caning before the whole school in the assembly hall.

Hockey, football and boxing were the main sports practised. At the beginning of the school year one had to be careful and aware that the rarefied air at that altitude quickly produced breathlessness after physical exertion. It could take up to three weeks for the system to adjust to the thinner air. Once a year we had a competitive road race of about six miles in the Murree Hills, terminating at the school. This 'marathon' was restricted to school pupils and was keenly contested by those who enjoyed long-distance running.

Heating could be a problem in early spring and late autumn. To supplement the ration of firewood and coal, the students had to organise pine-cone-collecting parties in their free time.

Meals were served three times a day in a large dining room and were adequate, though not brilliant. How much you ate was your decision. Topping-up could be done at the tuck shop. Those with a liking for Indian sweets such as *jellabees, burfis, hulwa, gulab-jaman* etc. could satisfy their needs from the regular visits of itinerant *sweetwallahs*. All purchases were for cash from one's pocket money. The sweet salesman usually had a large double-tiered cabin trunk type of container, carried by a coolie. On opening the trunk one was given a visual display of two trays of sweets and could make a choice.

There was no military-style school uniform and as far as I remember no military-style drills or parades took place except for those over 16 who joined the Auxiliary Force India. Those under 16 joined the Boy Scouts. The masters were all white. Competitiveness was encouraged and the ethos was that of a normal British public school. Senior students were allowed to visit Murree over the weekends, to go to the cinema, cafes etc. but they had to be back at school on the same day.

ROY DE VANDRÉ

Dad was a driver on the North Western Railway, though he finished up as loco-foreman. But for most of the time we're talking about he was chief engine-driver. If there was a special train journey they'd ask Dad to do it. My childhood and teenage years were spent in Baluchistan, Surkha, Peshawar, Quetta, Rawalpindi, Saharanpur and Lahore. My main memories are of Saharanpur and Lahore.

We were always in railway colonies. They had quarters for Indian employees, Institute for Indian Railway Workers, and European Institute and European quarters, and their own Police lines. The bungalows were standard. I am not sure if they were of one or two storeys, but they had three bedrooms, dining room, lounge, two bathrooms and at the back the servants' quarters. The servants lived in a long terrace, cooking in the front and sleeping at the back. On one end was the kitchen, the cook and family lived next to that, next the bearer, next the sweeper, at the end the *mali*. There was no sanitation, the night cart would come at night with a bell on it, consisting of two bullock carts with bloody great tanks on them, and lanterns and a bell hanging on the shafts. You would whiff it if you were sleeping out on the *chibbutra* – a raised platform in the garden. You could catch a bit of breeze in hot weather. Dad grew roses, and kept cows in the godown and geese, ducks and chickens. The *mali* was a damn good gardener and used to double jobs by taking Dad's *khana* box – *khana* was food. In the bottom part would be Dad's clothes. The next layer was food, tea, sugar, biscuits, on top were his tools: a long stick with a hammer

Damage to the North Western Railway caused by the Dharamsala earthquake, Punjab, 1934. (Brian Haskins)

for tapping the wheels, black hat with brass badge and a handful of jute.

Everybody working on the footplate always carried jute whatever their work, the reason being that, as you will appreciate, the engines were coal-fired, steam-driven, therefore, notwithstanding the heat of the climate, and that everything on the footplate was metal, and the heat from the firebox, everything on the footplate, especially the controls which were on and around the firebox, were extremely hot to touch with the naked hand. Hence the jute. Also people, especially the firemen and greaser, usually had a towel hung round their necks to wipe away the sweat. Dad carried two lots of jute, one for handling the controls and the second for personal use.

We lived 100 yards from the Shalimar Bridge in Lahore and we'd get a call from the cook every time Dad came back from a trip and then we'd rush like hell to stand on the bridge and he'd lean out waving his handful of jute. Then he would blow the engine's whistle with a sound like cock-a-doodle-doo twice. This was to let us know that within an hour he'd be in the local shed and the *mali* could be sent to collect his *khana* box, together with anything else, e.g. bundles of sugar cane for us children, or a sack of Indian corn – *bhutta* – or, which was more often than not, flowers in pots, cuttings of ferns and rose bushes for the garden. Then he'd arrive – black as coal.

Grandad was loco-foreman and his brother was a permanent inspector. For my uncle's wedding Grandad had six red and green coaches for free at Saharanpur. His house was next to the railway line and he had the carriages detached from the train and shunted off into a siding. We slept in them.

BEULAH BETTY STIDSTON

Life in India began for me on 29 September 1933, in the Lady Willingdon Hospital for Women in Lahore – a very grand establishment, according to a newspaper picture at the front of my baby photo album! My father was Dr Dudley Dayre Stidston, then working at the railway workshops, Moghalpura, Lahore. Dudley was born in Rangoon in 1896, the second son and third child of James Wakeham Stidston of Plymouth. His schooling was at the St Andrew's Homes and the Bourdillon School, Kalimpong. He had served with a field ambulance in Mesopotamia between 1917 and 1919 and then completed his medical degree in Calcutta in 1920. He obtained surgical qualifications at St Mary's Hospital, Paddington, in 1926–27. He was with the Indian Army on the North West Frontier during the Third Afghan War and, at various times between 1920 and 1925, was based in either Landi Kotal or Peshawar, the North Western Indian Railway between 1929 and 1938, and then went back to the Army from 1938 until 1948, retiring with the rank of major.

My mother was Elizabeth Violet Brown-James of Ballinger, Buckinghamshire. I was their only child. My parents were married in Calcutta in 1930 and spent the first couple of years of marriage in Khanewal and the Kalabagh on the Indus River. Tribesmen from the tribal settlement across the river used to amuse themselves at night by shooting out the lights on my parents' side of the river. Initially, their residence had armed guards at night – until one of the guards shot another guard! Mum panicked one night, thinking lions were roaring outside – apart from her doubtful knowledge of the distribution of lions, I am always amazed that she had apparently never heard donkeys braying while growing up in rural Buckinghamshire!

Lahore was our home until I was three, when Dad was transferred to Delhi. The high points of each year were the annual pilgrimage of wives and children to the hill stations (as they were called) to avoid the heat of the plains: Kasauli for my second birthday, back in Lahore for my third birthday and then Mussoorie for my fourth birthday, where Oakgrove School (for some reason which I do not know) let me have my party. Then it was back to Delhi until 1938, when Dad returned to the Army after his spell with the railways and was transferred to Kohat. That summer was spent in Priory Cottage in Murree, while the summer of 1939 was spent in Kasauli again.

My memories of this period (and indeed for most of my life) centre around animals. Memories of family pets are common to many children, but, living where I did, some of my memories are different. Monkeys were common in some hill stations, particularly langurs and rhesus monkeys. I vividly remember the young rhesus monkey which electrocuted itself on the power line strung across the valley in front of our holiday home, and the way in which the older monkeys investigated the situation, taking care not to touch the wire near the unfortunate baby. I also remember meeting a langur on a narrow path one day and taking the brave decision to walk carefully past it. We used to put a bucket of water out in the garden for the monkeys and then watch them come to drink from it.

One of the hill stations had an animal-research establishment, involved, I think, with the manufacture of vaccines. Probably because my father was a doctor, I was somehow invited on a tour of inspection with the director, and was most disapproving when we came to a pen full of guinea pigs. I'm sure the poor director had anticipated I'd be delighted with them, instead of which I told him off for docking their tails! Everyone tried to explain to me that guinea pigs don't have tails, but my reasoning was that guinea pigs are animals and animals have tails.

Then there was a time when a leopard was said to be in the vicinity of the hill station guesthouse, and all of us went trooping around the grounds looking fearfully at the tangle of creeper and brush where it was thought to have lain up – hardly a sensible activity if it really had been there. Perhaps that incident, together with reading Jim Corbett's *Man-Eaters of Kumaon*, was the basis for my later occasional nightmares about tigers.

By five I was in Kohat, living in a unit in a block of flats with their own gardens stretching down to a stream with a watermill. I caught my first fish with my bare hands, a little tiddler stranded in a small puddle in a diversion channel. I took it proudly to show Mum, and was mortified to be told off in no uncertain terms (because of the danger that the water might suddenly be rediverted), and made to put it back. I got into other strife that children everywhere might: a stone-throwing battle with another girl against a horrid boy – poor kid, it was entirely our fault – and I was often in trouble with the gardener for pinching peas. During my time in Kohat there were various security alarms, most seriously when a woman missionary was abducted and held to ransom by tribesmen in the hills.

I remember, too, the itinerant traders who used to come around selling door to door. The fruit vendor was a regular with his Nagpur oranges, bananas and other fruit in season. Also a regular was the *nappy*, or barber, coming around to cut my father's hair and often rendering neck adjustments similar to those of chiropractors today. At longer intervals came the *boxwallah*, usually Chinese, who came by bicycle with tin boxes of haberdashery. I still possess some of the little embroidered handkerchiefs with rolled edges which used to be given to the children of the house as gifts by *boxwallahs*. Another occasional tradesman to call was the man who rejuvenated the cotton in pillows. He used a very large stringed tool slightly like a big bow, with which he fluffed up compacted cotton – no doubt at great damage to his own lungs. Unfortunately, no one thought of that in those days.

STAR STAUNTON

Mary Alice, now my stepmother, had been a working Sister in the hospital where my father was sent to recover from a bad bout of malaria. I emphasise the word 'working' because apart from nuns and postulants and the brief contacts I had had with family life in Italy and Jamaica, I had never lived at close quarters with a white woman who had ever earned her living either as a professional person or housewife. Mine had been a world in which all the hard work was done by numerous and specialised servants. White people only gave orders. Whereas my stepmother, no doubt, at least during her training as a nurse, had emptied bed-pans and sputum-mugs, assisted at childbirth, bandaged wounds, laid out the dead, accepted the responsibilities of authority. She was, or had been, a working woman.

How she enjoyed being my father's wife she naturally never confided to me, but now that the long honeymoon period was over, and she could anticipate a settled existence at Lahore, she set up a clinic, first for our own servants and their families, and then for a wider clientele. There was a large room in the servants' quarters fit to house her activities, and thither she caused to be transported gallon drums of lysol, iodine, castor oil, cartons of aspirins, quinine, sodium bicarbonate, Epsom salts, surgical needles, scissors, forceps, thermometers, gut, dental tools. She must have had a wonderful time making out her lists and storing the items when they arrived. She also brought a library of up-to-date medical literature and subscribed to appropriate journals. Now she had the means of keeping herself significantly employed, and so she did.

She was British India in person. The natives had to do as she told them, but it was for their own good. She was a natural healer if ever there was one. Where her neighbours would be engaged in playing bridge or canasta or chatting at the Club, she would be occupied in 'playing' doctors, whipping out teeth or babies, advising on personal hygiene both male and female, inspecting toes and fingernails, ears and hair, seeing that everyone was regularly deloused, inspecting the living quarters and providing for liberal coats of lime-wash, splashing around the lysol. And the natives seemed to like it, at any rate the healing part: whether they enjoyed being made so aseptically clean, I cannot say.

The servants told their friends and custom grew. Free medicine was something they were unaccustomed to. Nor was there any doubt about the effectiveness of the treatment. Where any form of medicine is a rarity it is wonderful what a dose of castor oil will do, but my stepmother's healing went a long way beyond simplicities of that kind. She never lost a patient, even in childbirth. The babies she helped into the world seemed to fare well, and their mothers, sometimes children themselves, recovered under her hands from their ordeal. I shall never forget our *malchi* arriving at the clinic with a severed finger in one hand and a bleeding stump on the other. Undaunted, Mary Alice clamped the two together with gut beautifully stitched, and set the finger in splints, well bandaged. Six weeks later the *malchi* was working with four whole fingers and a thumb on each hand.

My stepmother had found her vocation and fulfilled it with energy and skill that amounted to genius.

In fact, I needed something to do that had the semblance of preparing me for a career.

But what career?

Apart from my very flimsy general education I had my languages, spoken not written, my singing voice, such as it was, and the small skill in art which I had picked up among the nuns in England. Art seemed the most likely line to follow. There was an art school in Lahore, hitherto for natives only, and here I applied to be enrolled as a student. This was 1938, the year of Munich, and I was just approaching my sixteenth birthday.

Imagine the daughter of Lord and Lady Vere de Vere at that same period taking her place at a desk in the local elementary school! The division between the conquerors and the conquered in India was in social matters as real as that which in England cut off the nobility from the working class or as the Indians' own caste system. Had I not been frowned on as a little girl because I could 'speak Indian'? I imagine my stepmother also had raised some local eyebrows when she turned her domestic compound into a native clinic and performed there services normally only conducted by the specialists in that kind of activity – I mean the missionaries, whose standing in this respect was understood and accepted. It must have seemed altogether worse when it was known that I was to demean myself by sitting in the class alongside natives and accepting them as my teachers.

Mr Gupta, a Hindu, was the principal. He welcomed me delightedly as not only the first white person to grace his establishment, but also the first woman of any colour. For that first term I was everybody's darling among a group that included Hindus, Muslims, Christians, Buddhists and Sikhs, all more or less absorbed in the business of learning how to draw and paint, all more or less pleased to share the camaraderie of a delightfully heterogeneous set of human beings, aware that there was something modern and rather daring in our common feeling of being above the ancient taboos which had always kept the sexes apart and split men up into mutually hostile religious communities.

This was another paradise out of which I was to fall. I did not know it at the time, but this year of 1938 was a fateful one for India. After years of strife and haggling, the Indian Congress had extracted from the British the Government of India Act of 1935 and had gone on to win an overwhelming majority in the new elections held under the new constitution in 1937. Independence began to seem only a single step away, and it would be independence under a Government very largely in the hands of Hindus. The Muslims took alarm. Not the Westernised Muslim Maharajahs and their like, the rich element whose rights the British would guarantee by treaty, but a new kind of Muslim: the revolutionary, anti-Western, fundamentalist devotee of Islam.

Mr Mohammad Ali Jinnah, moved by hatred and fear of the Hindus, began to stir up the Muslim masses to demand the division of India into two nations, respectively Hindu and Muslim, and he found the task surprisingly easy. There is that within the spirit of Islam which detests Western liberalism and its fundamentally irreligious rationalism, its substitution of the will of the people for the will of Allah. Without knowing what we were doing we were providing a type in miniature of the very India which Mr Jinnah and his followers most bitterly resented, and we were doing so in Lahore, a town well within the frontier of what in a few years' time would be Muslim Pakistan.

Probably we should not have attracted much hostile attention had it not been for the arrival on the scene of blonde, blue-eyed, London-bred Dorothy Shooter, a born trouble-maker. She was the daughter of a leading Dockland trade-unionist and had been brought up a Marxist, taking in the notion of revolutionary struggle with her mother's milk. Then, coming to India – for what reason I never knew – she had become a devotee of Mahatma Gandhi. Setting aside her previous allegiances, or perhaps one should say transforming them, she had become a Hindu, taken to wearing the *tiki* on her forehead, and adopted the Hindu name of Ariga.

It was as Ariga that Mr Gupta introduced her to our group, de-lighted, poor innocent, to have another white woman among his students. He soon found out what a viper he was nursing in his bosom, for Ariga at once set out on a course which by the end of that school year was to destroy his decent and humane efforts to build a school across the divides of religious and political fanaticisms.

At the end of her first term she organised a students' union, re-cruiting its membership from the Hindu element and persuading those who joined to flaunt their political allegiance by wearing the little white, fore-and-aft style military caps adopted by the followers of Gandhi and called Candi-caps. She could not have stirred the latent fanaticism of the local Muslims more effectively had she been Mr Jinnah himself at his most vitriolic. Mr Gupta protested in vain. The quarrelling factions swept him aside, organising meetings and counter-meetings, entirely destroying our former interest in art, and making the college the catalyst of that explosive reaction which was to tear villages in half and set previously friendly people murdering one another over the length and breadth of the land.

Towards the end of the academic year the inevitable happened. The Muslim students at the college organised a demonstration to protest against all that Ariga had done with her students' union, against the college principal for allowing it, and by extension against the liberal, Westernised tolerance which permitted women and men to study together and took no account of the importance of religious difference. The local Muslims joined in, and soon there was a mass of excited people running amok in the compound, arming themselves with anything to hand, smashing windows, hurling stones, setting fire to bicycles and then, breaking the doors which had been locked against them, making a bonfire of books and furniture which threatened to set the whole premises ablaze.

Mr Gupta gathered those not involved into a top-floor studio which we made secure with chairs and desks, and there we cowered, listening to the banshee howls and concerted shouting of the mob outside and watching thick clouds of black smoke drift past the windows. The ordeal did not last long. Shortly, we heard the welcome sirens of fire engines and the whistles of the Police. Then we saw policemen with *lathis* clearing a path to the main block and thus to our beleaguered studio.

On Police advice the college was closed for what remained of the term. Ariga was put in prison. Poor Mr Gupta's experiment with women students came to a sad end.

Very shortly after that catastrophe a letter came from the Jinds inviting me to go with them to Kashmir. I could have cried for delight.

MICHAEL MULLER

In June 1929 my mother set sail for India to get married. My parents had known each other since early childhood in Cornwall, but she had never been to India before. My father, on the other hand, had been born in Mahablespur near Bombay, where his father was a professor at Elphinstone College. His mother, who died a few months after his birth, was the youngest child of an executive engineer in the Madras Public Works Department who had become its director shortly before his death in an accident. He had married a lady whose father was a mining engineer in Mysore. Her grandfather had been present in Wellington's army at Seringapatam. Therein lie my qualifications to be considered as a child of the Raj!

My father, having no mother, was brought up by aunts, largely in Cornwall. He was commissioned into the Royal Artillery and served briefly in France before the end of the First World War. The mid-twenties found him serving first with the Horse Artillery at Nowshera, and then transferring into the Frontier Force Mountain Artillery – at that time the only Indian Artillery. My parents were married in Coonoor in July 1929, where my great-grandmother had settled after the death of her husband, and then set up their first home in Kohat in the North West Frontier Province.

In the summer of 1930 my father went to Dehra Dun to undertake a course in animal transport, and my mother went to Murree to await her first child. That child was me, born in September in the British Military Hospital. They returned to Kohat, where I was duly baptised in the Frontier Force chapel, which was burnt down by tribesmen a couple of years later.

My father transferred in 1931 to the Indian Army (RIASC), Whitehall having decided to limit the time that Royal Artillery officers could spend with the Mountain Artillery. This was important, as it meant that returning to British service would reduce his pay and deprive him of an Indian Army pension. Government parsimony does

Michael Muller, who 'always wanted to be a Pathan', right, and with his parents, Rawalpindi, 1931. (Michael Muller)

not change! In consequence we moved to Rawalpindi, and spent the summer of 1932 in Kulu with Forest Service friends, of which I have some memories.

After home leave (and the birth of my first sister), we went to Dehra Dun (to the RIASC school), where my father was now an instructor in animal transport! Summer was spent in Mussoorie. I had acquired by this time a small grey pony called Rumpiaree, and I remember riding round the circuit in Mussoorie at top speed. We soon were posted to Meerut, where we lived in an old (pre-Mutiny) thatched bungalow. There was a famous family story of a cobra coming into the bathroom while my mother was in the galvanised tub which was the bath! I was not present, but remember the thick cotton sheets which were hung to do duty as a ceiling and to catch all the beetles and other small life that fell out of the thatch!

Other memories are largely of houses and dogs. We had a car, but horses and ponies were our normal form of local transport and recreation. The array of silver cups and spoons of showjumping and point-to-points that I still have bear witness to my father's favourite pastime. And of course I remember Shah Zaman. He was a Pathan from the Hazara district, and proud of it, and had been my father's

Michael Muller, a future civil engineer, inspects a local water supply near Dehra Dun, 1935. (Michael Muller)

servant before he was married, and he was our bearer until 1947. He was as much a part of our life and family as it was possible to be. Other servants came and went – they were mostly his relations or people from his village. He looked after us superbly – especially when my father was overseas during the War – and was my special friend. I still know a certain number of rude Urdu words thanks to him!

From Meerut we moved to Chakala, to which the RIASC school had been moved from Dehra Dun, In September 1934 we came home on RMS *Kaisar-i-Hind* and my father went to the Staff College. For three years we were in England – Camberley – while my father completed his course, and then in Ferring-on-Sea. In Camberley I remember the senior officer in charge of all the Indian Army student officers. He used to come to our house and draw excellent cartoon-type pictures for me in pencil. I knew him as Uncle Bill – the world knew him later as Field Marshal Lord Slim. The explanation for the latter is that my parents had found living in Camberley, and leading the sort of life expected of them, to be very expensive, so my father went back to living on his own to live frugally in Messes, and we took a cheap seaside cottage. I went to my first school in Ferring – a small prep school called Tudor Close. It is now a pub!

Michael Muller and Rumpiaree at the Simla Horse Show, 1939. (Michael Muller)

While on the subject of education, we were joined in 1933 by a lady schoolteacher who lived with us and moved wherever we went. She ran small schools in our houses – and I, of course, benefited as her one pupil with continuity of teaching! I could in consequence read, write and do arithmetic on my own by the time I was four. This was a marvellous grounding and – I suppose – kept me out of mischief!

In September 1937 family finances had recovered, and we set sail in the SS *Lancashire* and arrived eventually in Simla, where my father, as befitted a new graduate from the Staff College, was working in Army Headquarters. We stayed in Simla for a year, my father being on the skeleton staff left there when Army HQ went down to Delhi. Winter was quite an experience: snow of enormous depth everywhere, with the roads kept clear for horses and rickshaws. There were big parties for children at Christmas at Viceregal Lodge and in the mansion of the Governor of the Punjab. Four tennis courts at Blessington were opened up and flooded each night, so we went skating every morning – my mother broke her leg playing ice-hockey! Spring and summer saw us going out at weekends picnicking on beautiful flower-covered mountains – near Mashobra there was a hotel with the splendidly apt name of Wildflower Hall.

I read *Kim* about this time, and was fascinated to find the shop called Masters in the Mall which was Lurgan Sahib's shop in the book. Riding every day was not just a pleasure but a necessity, as horses became very difficult in the hills if not exercised. Long rides included going round Jacko or down to Annandale which was a drained lake where there was a racecourse. My pony used to go mad at the sight of a flat area to gallop on – however, she and I came third in the under-13 children's class in the Simla Horse Show – I was still seven.

In September we went down to Delhi. Father worked in the military secretariat in New Delhi, but we lived in quarters built in the grounds of Metcalfe House in Old Delhi. That was a great winter. We rode out every day after my father's work. He was a historian, and Delhi is all history. We went to all the seven cities, and on one memorable occasion all round the lot. I learned about every change of ruler and city, and saw their buildings. I could still do a decent job as a guide! We went out with the Imperial Delhi Hunt, hunting jackals. At eight I was at least 12 years younger than the next youngest hunt follower, and sometimes my father was unable to come. Providence and a remarkable pony saw me safely through. In early 1939 we were entered in the (last ever) Imperial Delhi Horse Show. I have a silver cup which says that I was the best child rider, all ages, and my pony won a highly commended citation. She actually earned them both.

In April we went back to Simla, and my younger sister was born in the Portman Nursing Home. It was to have been the last move for me in India, because I was eight and it was time to be sent home to prep school, England. However, events in Europe caused the cancellation of that plan, and indeed many other children came out to India rather than being sent home. It was, however, the end of our carefree existence. My father worked long hours and weekends and our picnics and outings around Simla were curtailed.

We went down again to Delhi in September, this time to a house in New Delhi, but were there a very short time as my father was posted as Chief Instructor to Chakala, where the RIASC school was being enlarged as fast as possible to fall in with the requirements of the War.

BARRY BRYSON

For a few months after we arrived in India my brother Peter and I attended a church school in Quetta. We cycled there and were given lunch from a tiffin carrier, small aluminium containers one above the other which slid on two handles. Our cook brought these from home by bicycle. Then in 1937 we were enrolled at Bishop Cotton's School, Simla. I went through the traumatic experience, aged seven-and-a-half, of being left by Mother in this huge, strange school, without saying goodbye (presumably on advice). It took several days to get over, sleeping in the matron's quarters. The school, founded in 1859 by Bishop Cotton, Bishop of Lahore, was run on English public-school lines, with senior prefects able to administer corporal punishment. We sang a long school anthem in Latin to the tune of the German national anthem. School turned out all right – the food was good, but never enough for hungry boys. Living was spartan, concrete-floored dormitories with iron beds with straw mattresses, which at first were great but by the end of nine months were very hard. Washbasins only had a cold tap and the boiler was lit on Saturday evenings for compulsory showers, whether needed or not. WCs had no doors, and one large block flushed every 20 minutes during free time to keep us moving along. Discipline was tough but fair – we were not allowed outside school boundaries without permission. Breaking this rule meant a certain caning. We had a church service every day and two to three on Sunday; but we were taught Indian history and could take Urdu as an alternative to French.

Probably because of the very long distances which had to be travelled, most boarding schools had a nine-month teaching period from mid-March to mid-December, with 10-day breaks in June and September, which system later an Army selection panel called 'a deprived childhood'. Those mothers who lived in India and could afford it came up to Simla hotels and took out their children for the 10 days. Others like us, in some years stayed at school but were allowed out each day. I believe our fees were paid by the North Western Railway, as Father was divisional mechanical engineer – but the extras were costly. For example, things like fountain pens to replace broken, mislaid, lost or stolen ones could be obtained on request, as could guava cheese, guava jelly and jam and toothpaste. Odol toothpaste gave a small gift in the carton so we asked for Odol almost daily until stopped! Tuck unfortunately was not available on demand. I have seen letters both home to Quetta and to my grandmother back in wartime Weymouth pleading for tuck to be sent to me – without response. Pocket money at a standard level seemed miserly, but it was usually spent by the evening of the Saturday it was handed out. A favourite purchase was a small tin of condensed milk – two opposite holes were punched open and the milk sucked out whilst lying in bed after 'lights out'.

Boys at Bishop Cotton's School came from mainly white, Anglican families in the Indian Civil Service, businesses or the services – particularly the Army – and a few Indian princes. At one time we had two Nepalese princes and they had an armed guard at night outside their dormitory. A number of boys had sisters or cousins at a sister school, Auckland House, near the Mall in Simla. We had a cousin, Greta, there.

The school had two music teachers who had been connected with the Viceroy's orchestra, and the school would borrow the orchestra for our annual Gilbert and Sullivan performances. Also we had a good choir, and my brother and I were in it. I don't remember any advantages of membership – just a lot of practice – but we were selected to sing at the wedding of Lady Anne Hope, the daughter of the current Viceroy, Lord Linlithgow, in Delhi in November 1939. We stayed in tents for five days in the gardens of the Viceregal Palace, right next to the swimming pool, of which we had sole use. We were given a conducted tour of the palace and had a tour of Delhi. The food – oh boy! The service was

Auckland House, Simla. (Robert Matthews)

memorable for its magnificent colour with maharajahs and rajahs and their families dressed in fine colourful clothes with jewels, and officers in morning dress or colourful dress uniform. All choristers were presented with a leather wallet with engraved card – soon lost, unfortunately.

Another year we sang the whole of Handel's *Messiah* at the Gaiety Theatre in Simla, with several public performances – one was recorded by All India Radio, but we were unable to buy a record. Following that, we gave a command performance of the 'Hallelujah Chorus' at Viceregal Lodge one evening in Simla.

After three months at Quetta we pleaded to remain at home but soon we were measured for new clothes and shoes, all of which were hand made. Slowly the boxes were filled. We each had a large, black tin trunk, a small one for tuck and other things and the large bed roll. This bed roll of canvas held all our bedding with pillows in a pocket one end. It was designed so that it could be unrolled on the floor or a bunk, used for the night and then rolled up again. It was standard kit for any traveller. After the first year we were despatched unaccompanied from Quetta to Simla, with some time spent at junctions. All along the North Western route, however, we were visited at each stop by the stationmaster to see that we were all right, and he no doubt reported back. Who transferred our luggage I don't know, but it got there. Then to Kalka to transfer to the narrow-gauge line up to Simla. The carriages were small with wooden, slatted seats. The train stopped at Barog for a meal and to allow an additional engine to be added to cope with the steep inclines ahead. The route had over 100 tunnels and if we opened the windows the dense smoke from the engines made us queasy.

The coming of the War in 1939 made almost no difference to our way of life. Certainly, fathers of some of our friends who were in the armed services saw active service and a few of our younger teachers enlisted, with some dying in service. Father enlisted in the Royal Electrical and Mechanical Engineers (REME) and mainly served in the Middle East. This meant that Mother and my younger brother

David had to leave our railway-owned home and for some months rented a flat in Simla, and we were able to spend each Sunday with her between church services at school. She was also able to come to school occasions like Speech Day. On other occasions she would bring us cakes from Wenger's or Davico's, two superb restaurants, so that we could share with friends whose mothers had similarly treated us – very important. Unfortunately, while they were in Simla our younger brother David caught dysentery and was critically ill in hospital, and the only treatment he seemed to get was doses of Epsom salts. After some weeks Mother elected to remove him from hospital back to the flat, and asked our cook who accompanied her from Quetta to go to the bazaar and buy the local herbs he would buy for his own children if they were similarly ill. This new treatment worked and he slowly recovered, but his doctor advised Mother for his future health to take him back to his place of birth, Quetta, where the water suited him. They moved into one of a number of bungalows allocated to officers' families in another part of Quetta.

We were privileged to live in Simla with its climate. We got up very early for PE before breakfast, and occasionally in hot weather we would get up even earlier and have one or two classes as well, which meant that there would be no classes between lunch and tea. We sometimes suffered from very long stretches of monsoon rain. All school buildings were connected by covered ways to cope with the heavy rains, and we were often lulled to sleep at night by what sounded like a waterfall on the tin roof of the dormitories. Sometimes, when we had a sunny day after a week or two of non-stop rain, the head boy would be asked to approach the headmaster for a day off, and usually we got it. Simla to me means hills covered in sweet-scented pines, especially when wet, with wind rustling through the trees and the constant noise of cicadas. We walked almost everywhere, only using rickshaws when there was a parent to pay for them. In any case there were no ranks of rickshaws near the school, which was isolated. Motor vehicles were forbidden in Simla, except for the few cars kept by the Governor or Viceroy.

Occasionally on a Sunday we would hire horses and gallop along a road to Wildflower Hall, with Mother going by rickshaw. There we would have a superb meal with unbelievable apple pie and cream. Other Sundays we would be treated to a lunch at Wenger's or Davico's, where I remember having a delicious meal of suckling pig. Their cream cakes were outstanding and such a treat. Food again.

Girls were nowhere around except once or twice a year we would have a dance and the girls from Auckland House would be invited to us and we would in return go there. If one was held during the monsoon we would roll up trousers, take shoes and socks off and walk barefoot the miles up to the Mall so we could arrive dry-legged. Coming back didn't matter. Who knows how to dance? – for weeks ahead we were coached, listening to a record up in one of the art rooms.

End of term was like 'demob' – days were marked off the calendar and at last we lined up in front of the school for our tickets and spending money. Over 100 coolies would descend on the school and have our tin trunks and bed rolls strapped to their backs ready to take them up to the station. These coolies worked remarkably hard – for example, two would carry an upright piano on their backs with sticks to steady their walking.

ROBERT MATTHEWS

My great-grandfather, William Arnold Matthews, arrived in India in about 1850, to seek his fortune with the East India Company. He became Deputy Collector of Revenue in the Punjab's Salt Range, a position he could only have obtained 'through influence'. An India Office letter to my grandfather, in 1938, admits this influence to have been a family connection with the Earl of Llandaff.

He sired two sons, one of whom was my grandfather. The tantalising thing is that, on his baptismal certificate, the space for his mother's name is left blank; but whoever his mother was, he was well looked after by his father. He went to Bishop Cotton's School in Simla, later joining the Punjab Secretariat as a clerk. He was to retire as Superintendent of the Secretariat. In 1920, on Founder's Day at his *alma mater*, the Lieutenant Governor of the Punjab invested him with the Imperial Service Order, for his 'sterling contribution to the success of the Delhi Durbar'. *Who's Who* for 1938 mentions that he won the Gold Medal in the all-India rifle-shooting competition three years in a row.

My grandfather's first wife died. His second was Henrietta Monteath, a Presbyterian missionary from Glasgow, and their only son, my father, Arnold Monteath Matthews, was born in Glasgow in 1900. He followed his father to Bishop Cotton's School, obtained his BA from the Punjab University and was then awarded a scholarship to Jesus College, Oxford. Here he obtained his MA and also his diploma in education. In 1925 he became Principal of the Sindh Madrassah, a prestigious Muslim school in Karachi, and in 1931 he joined the Viceroy of India's staff in New Delhi, with special duties concerning the affairs of the Indian princes.

He had, in the meantime, married my mother, Alys Belletti, grand-daughter on her paternal side of an Italian surveyor from Piedmont, appointed to the Everest expedition by George Everest himself. On her maternal side she descended from the ADC to the Governor of the Danish settlement at Tranquebar in south India, Just Jens Bech from Copenhagen.

I was born in Delhi in 1931, and one my earliest memories is of the peacocks strutting outside the Viceroy's House. We spent the winter in a house on the Viceroy's estate, but in the summer, in Simla, we lived at Auckland House.

My father attended the Third Round Table Conference in London in 1933, in company with the Indian princes, on whose behalf he was acting as advocate. It was there that he became concerned about what would become of the 'minorities' in India, specifically the domiciled Europeans and Anglo-Indians, if and when India gained independence. His long correspondence with Gandhi and others in the National Congress Party, including Muslim leaders, gives testimony as to how strongly he felt about the subject. Sadly, the postcards written to him in pencil by the Mahatma, who was in jail at the time, have long since been mislaid.

These activities were, however, wrongly construed to be a dangerous flirtation with the Indian Congress Party, and he was encouraged to resign his Government post. He took up teaching once more, at the Lawrence School, Lovedale, in the Nilgiris, then at Colonel Brown's School in Poona; finally he was appointed Professor of English at Forman Christian College, an American foundation, in Lahore, where he was to remain until 1939.

Early in that year there were the 'Quit India' riots at that college, and my father was thought, quite wrongly, to have been connected with them. He was, however, brought to trial by the Government on charges of sedition against the Crown, and in particular for incitement of those riots among the students. There followed a lengthy High Court case, in which he defended himself. As reported in the *Times of India*, his situation became something of a *cause célèbre*. But he was ultimately unsuccessful and was sentenced to nine months in Lahore Jail for sedition, under the Defence of India Act 1916.

Lady Willingdon Hospital, Lahore.

One of my most vivid memories is of seeing him taken away in a *tonga* by an embarrassed-looking Anglo-Indian inspector of Police, who sat beside him in the back seat. A constable sat rigidly upright in front, while the *tongawallah* flayed his thin horse to get it going on the metalled surface of the road. Sparks flew from its hooves as it tried to gain purchase, the wheels of the *tonga* creaked noisily in protest and, finally, the overburdened vehicle, groaning and swaying, headed off slowly down Abbott Road.

A few days later, one of my father's wealthy Hindu supporters, a Mr Naidu as I recall, offered my mother the use of his newly built art deco house in Gulbagh. Built on a bank of the canal serving Lahore, the magnificent white mansion came complete with a full complement of servants. Mr Naidu dismissed thought of payment, and said that we could live in his house for as long as we wished. We lived there in some style for a year, with meals being brought in daily from the Sunny Bank Hotel nearby.

7

The United Provinces
of Agra and Oudh

The United Provinces of Agra and Oudh achieved their final status under the British in 1902, when the new name of the United Provinces was introduced. The Governor had his seat at Lucknow, retreating to the hills at Naini Tal for the hot weather.

There was an immense variation in the physical conditions of the province, from the high Himalayas in the north, to the plateau of Central India in the south; and from the Punjab in the west to the rice lands of Bihar in the east. It was naturally well-watered by numerous rivers, fed by the melting snows, coming to join the Ganges; but also by one of the greatest irrigation works in the world, the Upper Ganges Canal. A new canal was opened in 1928, to carry the waters of the River Sarda to the ancient Kingdom of Oudh.

Its principal railway was the East Indian Railway, linking with the Great Indian Peninsular Railway at Allahabad, Agra and Cawnpore. Its industrial centre was at Cawnpore, where the great Elgin and Muir Cotton Mills were to be found, and where there were also woollen mills, tanneries and leather factories. Its export trade – which was considerable – was of agricultural produce, wheat, timber, cotton, sugar and molasses, for instance. There was a rum distillery at Shahjahanpur and breweries at Mussoorie and Naini Tal.

The population was 85 per cent Hindu, with the great sacred city of Benares at its heart. The principal language was Western Hindi, although Urdu (Hindustani) and Eastern Hindi were also spoken.

DOROTHY ALLEN

Our homes in India were always in the United Provinces – Mirzapur, Unao, Dehra Dun, Benares, Jaunpur, Baraich and Birpur.

My father was first of all a magistrate. Everyone in the ICS started like that, and later either went on to the executive side of the work and became a Collector and then a Commissioner, or became a Judge.

In one way, the life of a collector-commissioner was less exacting. He could get up early and do a great deal of his work before it was too hot, and then return for breakfast. In contrast, a judge had a set hour to arrive in court and had to be there all through the heat of the day, with only a brief interval back at the bungalow for lunch. I think a magistrate would only try civil cases; it was the district judge who tried criminal cases. It was fairly rare to have a jury; nearly always, the judge had to decide the verdict and pass sentence. I think court would end at about 4–4.30 p.m. and leave time for playing tennis or squash or going to the Club and having drinks, playing bridge etc. before returning to the bungalow for dinner, or just returning to the bungalow and relaxing.

After I returned to England for school, my father was also at Gonda, Fyzabad, Saharanpur and Agra, and later when I was grown up and spent five months in India he was the District Judge at Bareilly. He officiated on the High Court at Allahabad in 1931 and was offered a permanent seat on the High Court in 1933. He declined this owing to ill health and decided to retire. He had done his full 25 years' service in the ICS.

I do not think my father had any roots in India. A first cousin of my mother's, Carleton Moss King, was also a judge on the High Court at Allahabad. I think his father had also been in the ICS.

All houses in the plains were bungalows. I remember we twice had a house with stairs (quite unusual), once in Naini Tal and once in Mussoorie.

A bungalow always had a wide verandah around it. There were straw or cane blinds in front of the doors, I suppose to try to keep the sun out. Rooms all led out of one another. They were not linked by passages, as in England. The ceilings were two or three times as high as rooms in English houses. There was no electricity; lighting was by oil lamps (kerosene oil, I suppose similar to paraffin). High up, suspended down the ceiling of a room, there would be a *punkah*, and a rope from one end of it would go through the wall to the outside. A coolie would be sitting on the ground, holding the rope and pulling it to make the *punkah* flap backwards and forwards, the purpose being to cool the air in the room. If the coolie fell asleep in the heat, of course the *punkah* stopped. This could happen.

At times little lizards would drop down from the ceiling, and there were always insects about such as spiders, some quite big but not poisonous. We slept under mosquito nets erected around the bed. One never slept in complete darkness: there was always a little oil lamp burning in case one stepped out of bed on to a scorpion.

We saw a snake occasionally, but always out of doors, I think. I never saw a cobra. There was always a lot of dust about; the servants

The Judge's bungalow, Gonda. 'I must have been here, but only between about 18 months and two-and-a-half years old, and I scarcely remember it.' (Angela Allen)

would go dusting around, but it only stirred it up and then it settled down again. I think the windows in the rooms were always very high up in the walls.

The servants' quarters were separate, somewhere in the compound. The kitchen too was separate. I never saw the inside of a kitchen. Each bedroom had a bathroom leading out of it, with a tin tub (filled by the servants) and a commode.

My memories of the compound are that it was always huge. I do not remember much about the daily routine. My brother and I always seemed to be playing, either on the verandah or in the compound. We went riding on our little ponies, I think this must have been in the afternoons, and we also went on walks with Nanny.

We met other children, various families. I went to a dancing class in Naini Tal and met some there. At Baraich a girl a little older than I was (I was about six years old) used to turn up unannounced, and stay and play with us for ages. I am not sure if our mother and nanny appreciated this, but we enjoyed her visit immensely. She had what was called a 'chi chi accent' – a sort of sing-song accent that

Richard and Dorothy Allen in a *dandi* with their English nanny 'somewhere in the hills', about 1917. (Dorothy Allen)

Eurasians had (though she was not Eurasian). This intrigued us, and we used to imitate it; not to her face, of course!

When we were at Baraich, we were taken one day to some friends of our parents, to see 'panther and pussy'. This couple had a panther cub about the same size as their cat. It must have been very young, probably found in the jungle. Its mother may have been shot. My brother and I were fascinated. We heard later on that when the panther was older it was given to a zoo. It would not have been safe to keep a grown-up panther as a pet.

The games we played were largely games of 'pretend'. At Burpur we loved playing with water, and we were allowed to play with it once a week (Friday was water day) out on the verandah, and to get as wet as we liked. This was tremendous fun!

We had several servants: a bearer (not quite sure of his duties – he generally looked after everyone and sometimes dusted around, I think), a *khitmagar* (waited at table), a *khansama* (cook), a sweeper (the lowest caste, did manual jobs, emptying commodes etc. and also, strangely enough, fed the pets, dogs or cats). We also had a *syce* (groom), a very nice man, a *chowkidar* (watchman), who sat outside the bungalow at night to defend it. We had one or two *chaprassis*, who were messengers. There were no telephones in my childhood.

Richard and Dorothy Allen on their ponies, Saharanpur, 1918. (Dorothy Allen)

If you wanted to invite someone to a meal, you wrote a *chit* (a note) and a *chaprassi* would deliver it and bring back a reply.

During my father's junior years with the ICS, at the end of every hot weather, he was transferred to a different place in the plains. As he became more senior, he stayed longer in one place. All our train journeys in India seemed to take two days and two nights. I remember, after we had returned to England, when we were to travel somewhere, I asked, 'How many nights on the train?'!

When we were in our last bungalow in Mussoorie, now and again we used to go to a kind of park and take a picnic lunch. It seemed quite a long way, and I am not sure whether we walked all the way, or whether we (the children) were carried in *dandis*. A *dandi* was a kind of wooden structure, with two seats facing each other, and handles at each end. The Indians who carried them were called *jampanis*. When we went up to the hills from the plains, we would go as far as we could by train (probably to Dehra Dun) and then be carried the rest of the way in *dandis*.

I had sandfly fever when I was four years old. This was a disease allied to malaria, I think. Also, every now and again I used to have attacks of stomach pain and had to spend a few days in bed. Finally, this was diagnosed as appendicitis, and a little while after we returned to England I had my appendix removed. I was about eight-and-a-half years old.

It was my mother who taught me my first lessons when I was five years old, at Jaunpur. I had a copy book for writing and learned joined-up writing, not script. I had simple reading books, and took to reading quite well. I could read to myself at six years old, and the first books I read were *Little Black Sambo* and *Little Dekchi Head* (a *dekchi* was a saucepan with no handles). In Mussoorie I went to two day schools, a small one run by two sisters and the next year I went to a bigger school; both were day schools. At the first one we must have started arithmetic. I remember we had to learn all our tables, 2 times up to 12 times and we also learned the 16 times table, because there were 16 annas in a rupee.

I also started piano lessons with a private teacher, when I was seven years old. We had a Christmas camp every year, but when riding on an elephant I do not think we had a proper *howdah* – I do not remember one. I think we just sat on the middle of its back; perhaps we were clinging on to the rope on its spine. We always had a grown-up with us, our nanny or our mother or perhaps one of the servants. The *mahout* made the elephant kneel down so that we could climb on to it, and it had to kneel down again for us to descend. We enjoyed elephant rides, but it was something quite ordinary for us, just part of Christmas camp! Once when we were going along on an elephant in the jungle, we saw a buffalo calf tethered under a tree. It was the bait for a tiger, which would come by at night, and the person sitting up in the tree on a *machan* would shoot it. We knew why the calf was there, but I do not think it worried us – I may have felt a little sorry for the calf.

We had no car until the end of our time there. We went about in a trap called a *tum tum*. The pony was not like the small ones we

Elephants in the Allens' Christmas camp. (Angela Allen)

rode, but larger. My father got a motorbike and sidecar at Jaunpur, but we still used the pony and trap. It was not until we were at Birpur (our last place on the plains) that we had a car, a Ford, with very high clearance off the ground.

In November 1919 I was sent home for good. The ship was called the *Neuralia* and it was partly a troop ship. We left India from Bombay and came all the way by sea (instead of going across France from Marseille). The sea was rough in the Bay of Biscay. A young lady came with us on the voyage, her passage being paid by my parents. She was supposed to look after my brother and me. She was more interested in young men on board than in us, and sometimes we used to escape from her. We found a place somewhere inside the ship where you could stand on a bridge and look down at the engine room. This was a great interest, especially for my brother, who was five years old and I was eight. Our sister was 15 months.

We saw our first aeroplane at Suez. It was a small seaplane (I think) and flew quite low all round the ship. We disembarked at Plymouth and went by train to London (Waterloo Station) and were met by various unknown aunts.

This first parting was sad, but I think worse for my parents than for us. My brother and I and an English nanny were in a holiday home in a beautiful country house near Wantage, Berkshire. There were about five other children there. There was a resident governess who used to give the older ones lessons. Two girls from the neighbourhood came each day to join us for lessons. My sister (two years old) went back to India with our parents.

Later, we were in another holiday home at Broadstairs, Kent, where my brother and I went to a day school. Then, later still, we lived with an aunt (one of my mother's sisters) at Birchington, Kent. I went to a girls' day school and my brother to a boys' prep school.

When I was 13 years old I went to a girls' day school at Watford, Hertfordshire. My brother's public school was Oundle.

Our mother used to come home almost every year, from April to October, and our father came almost once in three years. Mother wrote to us every week and we wrote to our parents each week. Our father wrote now and again, too, and used to draw pictures for us. Our letters had to be at the main post office in London by Thursday to catch the mail to India. The letters went by train across France and were transferred to the P&O mail steamer at Marseille.

When our sister was eight years old, she stayed in England and came to the same boarding school where I was. Later, when I left school, she went to a day school at Chislehurst, Kent, where we were then living with another aunt and uncle.

I returned to India to Bareilly, United Provinces, for five months in October 1932, my father's last months in India before his retirement. It was mostly a social life for me. At different times I stayed on short visits, with various friends of my parents, at Allahabad, Lucknow, Moradabad (this was with an American couple and then two small boys whom I had got to know on board ship – the *Rawalpindi*). I also stayed a few days with friends of my parents at Delhi, and saw the 'new' Government building and part of Old Delhi. My parents and I stayed two days with friends at Agra, for me to visit the Taj Mahal, the Fort and Fatehpur Sikri.

ANN MITCHELL

My father was in the Indian Police in the United Provinces. He came out to India after leaving the Navy after the Great War in 1919.

My mother, Edna Evadne Mitchell, née Bion, was born in Simla in March 1901. The families of both her parents lived in Bihar. Her grandfather, born in 1819 in St Gallen, Switzerland, was a Lutheran missionary. Her grandmother's family were also missionaries. Her father was the youngest of a family of 11, so that when he left school there was no money to send him to university in England, so he was educated in India; he went to Sibpur Engineering College and subsequently joined the Irrigation Department in the United Provinces. When I was born, he was Chief Engineer of Canals, and was instrumental in the building of the Sarda Canal.

My mother attended infant school in Darjeeling, which was run by two of her father's sisters, Alice and Wilhemina Bion. She did not like this school as her aunts were very strict. Later she went to school in Cheltenham. After the War, she went back to India, to Naini Tal, where there were many young girls whom she knew. She took part in the life of the hill stations: rowing races and regattas on the lake and Gymkhanas on 'the flats' and also trekking and dancing at the Club or boathouse. She was married at the church of St John in the Wilderness in Naini in 1923, and the first years of marriage were spent in a small district, far from any town. My father worked very hard and was away from early in the morning. He came home for lunch and then went back to the office or Police *thana* till suppertime, and even then brought back files to work on. So it was a very lonely life, and one had to make one's own pastimes as best one could. My mother was very fond of animals and loved riding. She always had several dogs to keep her company, and it was not long before the local villagers were bringing her all kinds of injured or abandoned animals – baby squirrels which had fallen out of the thatch where their nests were, a baby blackbuck, and once a nilgai calf. He had to go to Lucknow Zoo when he got too big. Latterly, she ran the SPCA in Meerut from 1942 to 1945.

I was born in Saharanpur, where my father was stationed at the time. I do not of course remember anything, but photos show a great *tamasha* (show) with the Police and their superiors gathered round

Police Superintendent's House, Cawnpore. (Ann Mitchell)

the happy parents, who were laden with garlands of marigolds. The baby was held by the nurse and completely hidden in shawls. Later I enjoyed paddling in the water channels, which were opened three times a week to allow water from the canal to flow and water the garden. The villagers were allowed the same for their crops. There was also a well in the garden and my father's horse was trained to go round and round to work the Persian wheel.

Later, when we were in headquarters, in other words a town, friends were invited for birthday parties, or bonfire night. Our dog decided that fireworks or squibs were too dangerous and rushed to try and put them out with his paws. He was very annoyed at being restrained. For one birthday I was given a pony called Wendy, but it was discovered that she had killed her previous *syce*, so she found another home. Her successor was Silvia, a fat family pony who would stand up to a lot of attention from a child, but who was also a very good teacher. She was so quiet and reliable that I must have gone to sleep when I rode, because I always fell off as soon as she put her head down to graze. One day she bolted and, being an Indian pony, had a mouth like iron. I could not stop her, but I stuck on until she decided to stop. It was a salutary lesson, and I never fell off her again.

When I was four my grandparents, who had retired to England, came out for a visit, and we accompanied them when they went to see their old friends in the Irrigation Department. It was a treat to

'Our pre-mutiny bungalow in Meerut', 1934. (Michael Muller)

have other children to play with and to ride on the trucks which were used to build the new canal, and we ran all along the banks.

In the cold weather my father had to go to outlying villages to see if all was well and listen to the complaints and problems. This entailed camping for two months at least. Camping meant taking huge tents which had a sitting room and office, and bedroom tents with a section for the bath and thunder-box, tents for the dining room and cookhouse and of course the servants' tents. Everything had to be taken and my mother, who was used to years of such life, had an excellent 'bandobast' or arrangement. There were wooden boxes with partitions for all the cook's requirements: sugar, salt, flour, candles, kerosene for the lamps which were brought along too. All this was transported on bullock carts or sometimes camels, and when we had to move to another village the tents were struck early in the morning and went on ahead. My father went by car, taking any animals too small or unable to follow my mother and me on the horses. We also took two goats, as they provided milk, which the cow could not do if required to walk 10 miles or so.

At Christmas camp, friends often joined us, and we children had great fun climbing up to the top of the biggest tents and sliding down. The men would go out shooting to try and get a peafowl to replace the Christmas turkey, and wildfowl or pigeon for the pot. There was no electricity, so no fridge and consequently no fresh meat except what they could shoot. Sometimes we were lent an elephant and then we could accompany the guns. We occasionally saw a tiger slipping silently through the jungle, or a panther. They seemed to know that we were only after birds and they had nothing to fear.

On Christmas Day, all the Police from miles around would arrive to wish us a happy Christmas. They were accompanied by a band and mountains of fruit or sweetmeats. It was all very impressive for a small child.

We were always back in headquarters by the end of February, because it was getting too hot by two o'clock. The cold weather was really perfect: cold enough for a fire in the evening, but lovely and sunny and warm during the day.

I remember travelling from one camp to another with a friend from school: we were both on an elephant and I was trying to finishing embroidering a Christmas present for my mother as we rocked along in the sun.

When we were in Allahabad I had to go to dancing classes in the Club, and there were often big children's parties there, with a conjuror or some such amusement. At one of my own parties in the garden we had a chute which was very popular, everyone rushing to climb up again and getting too close to the one in front. The result was that I kicked out a small boy's front tooth with my shiny new shoes. Luckily it was only a milk tooth.

I also had a very beautiful Wendy House built in a big *neem* tree by one of the servants, and had great fun painting it with their help.

When in Lucknow I was often taken to the Residency and told all about the Mutiny in 1857. Being shown the actual ruins over which they flew the Union Jack made it all come alive for me.

When I was old enough, my mother gave me lessons, and later I had a governess. The first one was rather severe, but the next one was delightful, and we had marvellous times together when lessons were over. She invented all sorts of exciting things to do, such as re-enacting the Kipling jungle stories and being a *mahout* and riding on the rolled-up mattresses which had been prepared for our move up to the hills. Before we left we attended the Kumbh Mela in Allahabad, and saw a baby elephant of only a few months old. His mother did not seem to mind us playing with and patting him. He kept trying to climb up the pile of hay which had been put there for his mother, and was very strong for one so young.

Some time after that my mother took me home to England to boarding school. We travelled on the SS *Viceroy of India*, which was supposed to be the fastest liner at the time. In the Suez Canal she got her propellers tangled in the cables of a buoy, hit the bank and got stuck. It took several tugs to get her off, while all the other ships had to wait for the canal to be unblocked. It was very exciting to see the divers going down to untangle the propellers, but this episode ended our hopes of getting to England in record time.

ANGELA ALLEN

I remember practically nothing of my earliest years, as I was in England from three years old to six. But when I was six my parents took me back with them for 18 months before I joined my sister at boarding school. My life was much the same as she described, with early-morning pony rides and so on. But I had more animals: as well as my mother's cat I had a rabbit left by a missionary family when they returned to England, and a tea-planter gave me two pairs of pigeons. We had an ideal place to keep them, a sort of huge cage where they could be shut in until they forgot the way home. When we let them out one pair had not forgotten and flew back where they came from, but the others stayed and multiplied and became a flock. They would come and eat out of my hand.

When I left India they were left in the care of my father's former *syce*. When my father changed from horse to car the *syce* looked after the car and called himself Persotham Driver. Perhaps he did drive it (a Model T Ford), but I don't remember anyone but my father driving it. My father kept Persotham in his service throughout his time in India and paid him a small pension when he retired. I was impressed, because when Persotham died his son wrote to tell my father to stop the pension. I got regular news for years through Persotham of Anjala Miss Sahib's pigeons, though of course he didn't tell me what must have been the case: that they were also a useful source of food for him!

My parents were in Saharanpur when I was with them. The Judge's Bungalow was a very long building with a verandah running the full length of the back which gave on to tennis courts. It was reputed to be the longest verandah ever known! I don't remember any door in the house that closed, only gaps in the wall with a 'chick' hanging in front of them.

At the end of December 1996 my husband and I went to Saharanpur and with great difficulty found the district judge's bungalow. In my day there were only five or six houses in the area and all several miles from each other; now it is in the middle of a flourishing town of many thousands of inhabitants. The District Judge received us very kindly and seemed amused when I said that just over 70 years before it was my father who had had his position! I told him we used to put the beds out on the path in front of the bungalow when it was hot and that as I lay in bed I could hear the jackals howling at the bottom of the compound. He said, 'Come and see,' and took us out; the path was still there but only a bit of lawn and all the rest was built over. 'There are no jackals now.' There are electric fans in the bungalow now hanging from the ceiling but the little *punkah* windows high up on the wall are still there!

While I was in Saharanpur there was a case of hydrophobia (rabies) and someone had to go to the only place in India where you could be treated in those days, as there was then no vaccination.

Angela Allen feeding a pigeon in the garden of the Judge's bungalow, Saharanpur, 1925. (Angela Allen)

Everyone was supposed to destroy their dogs but one of our neighbours had a small pet dog that she kept and it didn't get the disease. The Collector had several outdoor dogs, red setters and golden labradors. These did get it. I remember seeing them shut up in their cage looking strange and foaming at the mouth. Of course, he shot them all, but they also had a red setter bitch that was the family pet, lived in the house and played with their boys, and I played with them and her. They kept her. I remember my mother being very worried (and I expect I was not allowed to go there till it was over). The bitch didn't get ill.

My memories of Christmas camp are of waking early on Christmas morning when it was just beginning to get light and seeing the ears of Pip and Wilfrid at the bottom of my bed, and crawling down without getting on the ground to pull them out. They were soft toys representing the dog and rabbit of a *Daily Mirror* cartoon. I already had Squeak the Penguin and very much wanted the other two. Then, later in the day there was a Christmas tree – of course, not a conifer, with lots of lights (candles I suppose) and shiny things on it.

One incident I always remember was of an elephant with people on it, all ready to go somewhere; it would not budge whatever they

above 'Me at a Christmas camp, aged six, 1924. I don't know where the camp was – some jungle in the UP not too far from Saharanpur.' (Angela Allen)

left 'Me and my father (Mr G.C. Allen, District Judge) in the garden of our bungalow, Saharanpur, 1925.' (Angela Allen) did to it, even lashing it with something sharp. Then the *mahout* got off and fetched a boy – about eight or ten years old – who climbed up on to the elephant with the help of its tail (probably the *mahout*'s son); then the elephant moved off quietly as requested!

I was very happy in India but I was very glad to come home and see my brother and sister again, though very sad not to be able to go back later. We, the children and parents, often talked and wrote in our letters about 'when we live in England', and made plans for that time, no doubt because of our longing to be all together. When I first went to boarding school, aged eight, I remember spending days and days mostly in tears, as my parents had gone back to India. I must have been an awful nuisance for my sister.

I think living in India when quite young has made it seem quite natural to me to mingle with people of different faiths – Muslim, Hindu, Christian – languages and skin colour, and think of them as just like ourselves. My father was for Independence but thought the Indians were not ready yet – that was when he retired in 1933. I can remember thinking when I was about 14 that I didn't see why we didn't let the Indians run their own country. I was sure that they were perfectly capable of it. I knew my father had had an Indian as his superior at one time.

GEORGE DUNBAR

I was born in Fathegarh during November 1915 of a Swiss/American mother and a Scottish father. Most of my schooling at various intervals between 1925 and 1934 inclusive was at Woodstock High School, Landour, Mussoorie. Woodstock was started in the 1850s by a small group of English ladies. Around the 1860s it was bought by, I think, the American Methodist Mission for the education of children of American missionaries. Somewhere along the line other American Missionary Societies joined in and it was opened up not only to Americans – though they were in the majority – but British and any other nationality including Indian. It was a co-educational, multi-racial, multi-national boarding high school. American students in the ninth and tenth standards followed the American curriculum, the rest worked for London matric.

My father, George Dunbar, was co-founder in 1889 with Albert Priestley, of Priestley & Co., Monumental Sculptors, Modellers and Founders, in Cawnpore. His principal claim to fame was in connection with two statues of Queen Victoria in Cawnpore. On the early death of his partners it was left to my father who, along with Priestley's wife, carried on the business, to complete the cutting of the Orcha granite pedestal for Thomas Brock's bronze statue of Queen Victoria, which in due course Father erected in Queen's Park, Cawnpore. It was unveiled in 1904. It was the first statue of the lady to be erected in India.

Just before his partner died in 1903, Priestley & Co. had been commissioned to model and cast a second statue of the Queen but in aluminium – it was believed to be the only statue ever made in this metal. My father finished the modelling, casting and supervised the erection of the effigy at Sursaya Ghat, Cawnpore. It was unveiled in 1907.

The business was closed down in 1912, following which my father joined the American Presbyterian Mission at Fathegarh. Here he built and started a large industrial school. It was at Fathegarh that he met and married my Swiss/American mother, who had come out from America to join the mission as a teacher. She died in America in 1919.

In 1930 George Senior married an American physician and surgeon of some renown. By then he had already been given the additional task of being the mission's 'master builder' responsible for the building of a large mission hospital in memory of those missionaries who had lost their lives during the Mutiny in and around Fathegarh. He was also responsible for the maintenance of all the extensive mission property in north India.

Due to the siting of the school in an industrially inactive part of the country, it became unviable and was closed down in 1932 and my father appointed to the post of treasurer of both the Punjab and United Provinces sections of the mission, with headquarters in Dehra Dun (winter) and Landour, Mussoorie (summer). He died in Dehra in 1945, five years after his retirement, having spent 56 years in India.

My stepmother, her amazing and hectic life the subject of a book I am in the process of writing, remained in India, mostly in Kashmir (next door to Rumer Godden), until 1950, when she returned to her native California where she died in 1976 at the age of 90.

Among her numerous mad exploits was riding a motorcycle and sidecar with an oversized American nurse as shotgun, from Ferozepore to Srinagar, not without a number of hair-raising events on the way. She was the first, if not the only, woman to undertake this journey on such a vehicle. This was in the early 1920s. Towards the end of the First World War she had been recruited into the Royal Army Medical Corps (RAMC) and given the rank of captain, probably the only American female to be commissioned into the British Army.

Nicknamed the 'crazy doctor', she could be seen riding around the country on her motorcycle clad in jodhpurs and khaki hacking jacket. Her medical and surgical experiences under some of the most primitive conditions were horrendous. Her work at the women's hospitals in Ferozepore and Ambala was legendary.

She was a compulsive traveller and had been all over the world. Her love of the outdoor, trekking and camping was manifest in her extensive travelling on horseback deep into Ladakh, along the Indus and Siok rivers, to say nothing of her extensive trips over North and Central India in a battered old Model T Ford. These wanderings took place mostly during the 1920s and 1930s.

She was to be called out of retirement in Kashmir by the Pakistan Government to help repair the battered and butchered bodies of women and children, the results of the slaughter following Partition, at the Women's Hospital in Lahore. Her final trip to Kashmir, by the old cart road, was made on the last mail bus to leave Rawalpindi; she was the only European on board. The bus was closely followed much of the way by marauding tribesmen at the start of the Pakistan/India dispute over Kashmir.

The missionary bungalows were situated in the huge Bhurpur Memorial Hospital compound, all that is except ours, which was clear of the hospital lands. Bhurpur itself was nothing more than a collection of three or four mud huts at the side of the road. The bungalows, as well as the hospital – a memorial to those missionaries and Indian Christians who lost their lives during the 1857 Mutiny at Fathegarh – were all built under the supervision of my father. They were of then modern design, constructed of red brick with flat roofs and having four or five large rooms. These high-ceilinged rooms each had tall doors leading out on to the verandahs which encircled the house. There were seldom any windows, only skylights high up in the walls. During the hot weather when the murderous Loo wind blew, during the daytime the house would be virtually sealed up and remain reasonably cool. The doors were opened at night. The rooms were sparsely furnished with rough shesham or mango-wood furniture. The floors were either of brick or hard mud. There were of course no such things as wall-to-wall carpeting – you were doing well if you possessed a large Indian-made cotton rug. There was no running water or water-borne sanitation. Baths were taken in large tin tubs, the water being heated in four-gallon kerosene tins on wood fires outside of the 'bathroom'. The water was carried in through the back door, which led directly out on to India, from the 'bathroom'. Father, who had lived a reasonably civilised life for many years in Cawnpore, had rigged up a system of pipes into which the 'menial' poured the water, making it unnecessary for him to enter the 'bathroom'. All water was drawn from wells near each bungalow by means of an earthenware pot and rope. Again, Father beat the system by ordering an amazing contraption from England which defies description, but which sat above the well: by turning a large wheel, water came out of a lion's mouth. Water for drinking was always boiled.

Electricity only came to Fathegarh, and then only to the hospital, the doctor's bungalow and, of course, to our bungalow, in 1926. The supporters of the hospital in the US provided the necessary funds for the purchase of an oil engine-driven generator at the hospital, which operated for five or six hours only each evening. The wiring of the bungalow and hospital was supported on porcelain cleats, a most hideous sight. On the night that the lights were first switched on in our bungalow, the old night watchman who slept on the front verandah was seen trying to blow out the light which took the form of a bare bulb in a sawn neck bracket attached to the wall above the door.

The earlier bungalows on the out-station of Rukha, the first mission station near Fathegarh, were of the pre-Mutiny type. Thick mud and plastered walls with very thick grass thatching, an ideal nesting-site but the haunt of snakes intent on getting some of the eggs. These bungalows were very similar to the Government and military bungalows and Government offices in the cantonments and Eurasian homes. They all dated back to the Mutiny, and many still showed signs of arson and looting, which took place during the rebellion.

The mission bungalows up in the hills were of a standard style. Solid wider stone walls, plastered inside and out and whitewashed. They were perched, rather precariously in many cases, on ledges cut out of the steep hillsides. They consisted of three or four medium-sized rooms – as sparsely furnished as those on the plains – a couple of bathrooms and a kitchen. The floors were cement, while the roofs were of galvanised corrugated sheets, the sound from which when it rained – and it did rain 'in them there hills' – was deafening. Mussoorie had had a public electricity supply from before the First World War. It also had a piped water supply. Considering the nature of the terrain and the long distances between the bungalows, the availability of these two services was quite incredible. There were, however, no WCs in any of the bungalows, except, of course, ours.

The mission out-stations I visited with my father when he went on inspections were scattered about within a radius of about 50 or

60 miles. Not far by today's reckoning, but to my tiny mind miles and miles. The most distant towns were reached by train – usually the night train. More frequently, however, the trips were accomplished in a day or even half a day. Though Father was the proud possessor of one of the earliest Model T Fords, he hated the thing and seldom used it, thus even the shortest journeys were undertaken by rail.

In 1918, my mother was taken very seriously ill. It was decided that she should return to America for treatment, taking me with her. Father no doubt thought that this would be a golden opportunity for me to start getting to know that I was not the 'monarch of all I surveyed' and to learn English, something else that I had flatly refused to do. I only spoke Hindustani.

After the farewell parties were over, the gold and silver ornaments donated by those heathens who had been converted to the 'faith' presented, Mother, Father and I set off on the long train journey to Colombo, two days after Christmas 1918. It was a journey marred by the heat, flies, dust and the atrocious behaviour of the *enfant terrible* who hurled abuse of the vilest nature from the carriage window at every passer-by on the stations we went through. At the end of the embarrassing few days for Father and Mother, she and I bade good-bye to Father, who was never to see his wife again, and boarded the liner *Navoro* bound for Yokohama out of Colombo.

A pale, tired face looking up at me from the crisp white sheets of a hospital bed is the only, now fading, memory I have of my mother, whose remains lie buried in Albuquerque, New Mexico. Her place was taken in my life by one of the missionary ladies, known to me as Auntie Jean. My memories of the few months I spent with Auntie Jean in California after my mother's death are sketchy. There were the days riding with the mailman on his cart, fighting with Barbra, Auntie Jean's youngest daughter, as we waited for Santa to come down the chimney, or gazing in overwhelming wonder at the huge glass-sided 'barn' beside Auntie's home, which was spoken of in hushed tones by her and other missionaries who came to visit as the 'house of the devil'. It was in fact a film studio.

Honolulu, Shanghai, Singapore, were all ports of call on the way back to India, but which meant nothing to me. All I can recall about the ship itself is its dark green hull and an officer in white standing at the bow as the vessel fought her way slowly up the muddy, garbage-strewn Hooghly River to tie up in Kidderpore Docks, Calcutta. I have no recollection of disembarking or the long train journey to Fatehpur, Auntie Jean's home some 800 miles from New Delhi.

Life with Auntie Jean and her large family was a happy one. We tiny tots romped and played in the bright winter sunshine of northern India. As much of our time as possible was spent in the servants' quarters playing with their ill-clad, snivelling 'untouchable' children, eating, with relish, the coarse bread and weak lentil soup they offered us from their own meagre portions. It always tasted so much nicer than the Indian food served daily at the table in the 'big house'.

As I recall, most American missionaries lived very frugally, and much of the food they ate was that as eaten by their flocks. However, their churches back home provided them with the latest automobile, more often than not a shiny black Model T Ford – while their friends and relations sent them large parcels of new clothes, toys for their numerous children and goodies galore at regular intervals. It always amazed me how they lived so close to their flocks and survived.

Auntie Jean in her turn would gather us up and off we would go to Mussoorie, considered the queen of the hill stations, 9000 feet above the burning hot plains and the one chosen by most of the American missionaries.

Just before we were due to return to Fatehpur for the long winter holidays, Auntie Jean's husband died after eating fly-smothered native food while trying to preach the gospel on the platform of a railway station. Auntie Jean returned to the US. I was taken down to Fathegarh to spend the winter with my father and once again came under the strict regime of Misri Lal. He was to have a profound effect on my life.

Misri Lal was a Bengali who had been employed by my mother on her arrival in India as her personal servant. On her marriage he remained with the family as head of the servants' hall with additional duties of supervising me on my arrival into the world. On my mother's death he remained with my father, over whom he took complete charge as he did over me when I came 'home' during the winter months. After Auntie Jean's departure I became a boarder at Woodstock during the long summer months.

While I do not appear to have suffered any ill effects of being with the hordes of American missionary children at Woodstock, I did however come very much under American influence and became addicted to pumpkin pie, ring doughnuts and their slovenly mode of dressing. I was, at first, very homesick. Not for my father, or Fathegarh, but for Auntie Jean.

The winter months I spent with my father at Fathegarh were, perhaps, among some of the happiest days of my early life. My father lacked the time, or apparent desire to control me with any more than the minimum of severity; that duty was left to Misri.

Each winter I was thrown into a world of starched linen, soup, fish, joint, pudding, finger-bowls and deserts each night for dinner, for which meal I was expected to be reasonably clean and smartly dressed. And I was, Misri saw to it.

At Christmas, Father really went to town in his efforts to show the Americans how to live: he invited the whole station and a few from further afield to dinner. I would help the servants, under Misri's supervision, bring out the leaves and elongate our massive mahogany dining table, which would be carefully laid with monogrammed cutlery, silver candelabra and silver bowls of flowers on a sparkling white damask cloth. The plumpest of the pet peacocks would be ritually slaughtered, an operation which I took an unhealthy delight in watching, and tins of expensive delicacies, purchased in small numbers over the year from Fortnum & Mason's Calcutta agents, would be opened. I would be dressed in one of my father's cut-down dinner jackets. A dozen or more liveried servants, hired for the occasion by Misri, where from Father never asked, and supervised by Misri, stood around the seated guests as though at a Viceregal banquet. Father always delighted in watching the Americans, their eyes popping out as they tried to discover which knife and fork they should use. There was of course no strong drink or smoking, in neither habit did he indulge.

I, however, longed for the platters of curry and rice which was all but thrown on to the missionary tables by near-naked menials. Father hated Indian food; I loved it. The only way I could satisfy my craving was to surreptitiously visit the servants' quarters and beg for a morsel from one of the women before my arch-enemy, Misri, would appear and chase me back into the bungalow.

Most of the puritanical American missionaries were very suspicious of my father and his, to them, strange British way of life. By his visits to that 'house of iniquity' the English Club, they were disgusted. He only joined to get away from 'some' of the missionaries and to be able to have a chat with his fellow Scots, officers with the Rajput Regiment garrisoned at Fathegarh, and to read *Punch*.

Earlier, my father had built for the mission, and managed, an industrial training school for Indian boys, in whose training he took a keen interest, in woodwork, blacksmithing, leather work, monumental stone-cutting, brick-making and laying and numerous other trades. I would frequently attach myself to one or another of these departments. These forays into the world of 'industry' stood me in good stead. I became acquainted with, but never master of, most of the trades and the use of the different tools even at my tender age, which was to stand me in good stead in later life. The friends I made with many of the boys enabled me to persuade them to 'skip school', at my instigation, and join me in adventures amongst the vast fields which surrounded the compound.

I was beginning to acquire a large collection of animals, amongst which was a pair of beautiful black bucks, which spent the days grazing over the 'lawns' of the huge compound which they made no attempt to leave. Each evening, as I returned from my drive, they would be waiting in front of the bungalow. The pony would not move past them until Father came out with three slices of bread, one for each animal.

The greatest jewel in the animal collection, which was ultimately to become father's favourite, though he baulked at accepting it in the first place as a present from a wealthy Indian landowner, was a three-year-old leopard. Moti, meaning Pearl, was a beautiful plump creature as tame as a kitten who wore a collar and chain. Occasionally I would take it into my head to terrorise the public and, strictly against instructions prohibiting me from being with the animal without one of the servants, usually my personal bearer, being present, I would take Moti and my pet mongrel dog Patch for a walk down the long driveway to the very busy dusty main road. Here the three of us would sit on a low wall, watching the kaleidoscope of colour which is India go by. The dog barked its head off, the 'cat' licked its paws and I shouted to add to the confusion when the passing travellers spotted the cat and panicked. There are no leopards in that part of India. Calm was not restored until Father came out of his office nearby and chased us off.

There was no running water and no electricity. One of my greatest pleasures in the evening was to accompany Misri, my arch-enemy, as he went round the house placing the shining, softly glowing oil lamps in their ornate wrought stands. Tinned delicacies such as fish, ham, beans, chocolates and toffees, their 'sell-by date' long since expired, were available from a couple of Indian stores in the bazaar. These luxuries were, however, beyond the means of the missionaries, with their large families, except at Thanksgiving and Christmas. They had to resort to making their own candies or risk buying Indian sweets from the open, fly-covered stalls of the sweetmeatwallahs.

I was lucky. I never experienced the blistering heat of the Loo wind thundering across the plains like a giant blowtorch. As a special treat, however, a day or two before I was due to return to Woodstock, I was allowed to help hang the massive *punkahs*, which would swing back and forth through the efforts of a sweating, near-naked native sitting on the verandah in the fierce heat tugging with a steady rhythm on a light rope which passed through a hole in the wall and attached to the *punkah* beam. The waving of the canvas skirt hanging from the waving beam created sufficient breeze, faint though it may have been, to cool the burning bodies of the *sahibs* sitting or slumbering below.

There were those most enjoyable occasions when Father had to visit some distant mission station which necessitated a long train journey on our small metre-gauge system. To get to the station with all the baggage it was necessary to hire a wooden box on wheels. There is just no English word to describe these hearse-like contraptions. In Hindustani they are called *thaka gharries* – hire vehicles.

With the aid of a couple of rupees Father always managed to get the one and only two-berth, second-class coupé compartment on the train. The current occupant would be ejected by the ticket collector on the pretext that his ticket was not valid to travel in such luxury.

The faithful Misri always travelled with us. Indeed, no matter how short the journey, his presence was essential. Who would obtain the tickets? Who would handle the baggage and pay the porters? Who would come to our compartment from his 'servant's compartment' at each station to ensure that all was well? Who would open the wicker tiffin basket bursting with tough, cold roast chicken, gooey grey bread, tinned butter and hard-boiled eggs? Then, of course, it was necessary for someone to take the teapot up to the engine to beg for some oily hot water.

On one of these trips, which was to last only the day, I insisted that we take one of my pet monkeys with us so that I could watch him annoy the public and snatch fruit off the trays of passing vendors going about their business on the station platform. Both Father and Misri objected. I won the day. Alas! Officialdom took a hand. The guard was adamant that the animal could not travel in our compartment but would have to ride with him in the guard's van. A couple of stations later the gentleman came running towards us, shouting as he did so, 'Mister, Mister. You must come and claim your monkey at once. He is eating His Majesty's mails.'

So the days of the winter holidays slipped by; I was more often than not in some kind of trouble – seldom very serious, I hasten to add, for most of the time. My relationship with the American missionaries was mixed. Some loved me, some, I have no doubt, hated that precocious, spoilt little English brat, while the remainder tolerated me. Father would not attend the mission church. This un-Christian act was not appreciated by the missionaries. The services were always in Hindustani, a language in which he never became, nor wanted to become, very proficient. On the first Sunday of each month he did, however, attend the Church of England Memorial Church in the cantonments. The service, during which Father sucked strong peppermints or slept alternately, was taken by the visiting regimental padre in English. No one from the Presbyterian missionaries ever attended the Memorial Church. That, no doubt, they would have considered to be a sin.

In 1927, the day came, which invariably it had to, for me to go to school in England before I became too American or Indianised, to be, hopefully, dehooliganised. Thus it was that my life in India came rapidly to an end as I watched the gap widen between the dock wall at Bombay and our ship *Britannia*. I was leaving what to me had been home for as long as I could remember. I was going to a foreign land.

Suddenly I had a burning desire to leap the gap and kiss Mother India farewell. I refrained; instead I turned my back on the scores of brown faces standing on the quay and crossed the deck to the other side of the ship. I watched – Father, Misri and even India forgotten – the two tugs huff, puff, pull and push *Britannia* into the lock. Gradually she sank lower and lower until the gates opened and the tugs dragged her out of the lock like a stubborn mule and pointed her head to the open sea. The tugs cast off their tows, turned, and with a cheeky blow of farewell of their whistles, scuttled off to re-enter the empty lock. *Britannia* was on her own.

DONALD HOWIE

I was born in Meerut at the end of September 1918. My father, a Staff Sergeant Instructor, originally in the Bedfordshire Regiment, had served through the campaign in Mesopotamia and had been mentioned in despatches. When I was born he was employed as Regimental Instructor to the Auxiliary Forces, India, for the North Western Railway. When he died very suddenly in Quetta in 1920, my mother was left with four young children, a girl of nine and three younger boys. We were accepted immediately, all four of us, by the Lawrence Royal Military School at Sanawar, in the Simla Hills. I went into the creche aged two and a half and finished up as head boy in 1937.

My mother undertook a teacher training course at Dowhill College, Kurseong, below Darjeeling and a long way from Sanawar. But they were extremely supportive and helpful to her in her traumatic aftermath arising out of my father's sudden demise. She was an unusual trainee student in being the mother of four children, and, being older than the normal trainee, was given kindly consideration. She was aided in her course of training by a grant to cover the two years of her course given by the Army authorities, who were also kind in arranging for her attachments to British Army units during the long Christmas vacations, thus enabling her to have the four of us children at home with her over the Christmas holidays.

She was allocated a married quarter and received all the rations and other benefits which the permanent regular families in the units received, so the Army was very much in the nature of a fairy godfather to her. God knows what would have become of her, and us, without the help of the Army. Their acceptance of the four of us as free boarders in Sanawar was wonderful, for we were provided with everything, free of charge to my mother.

The Lawrence Royal Military School in Sanawar was a wonderful school of great tradition. It was a school which catered for the sons and daughters of British serving personnel and accepted children from babyhood to mature adolescence. It was founded in 1847 by Sir Henry Lawrence, later to become famous for his defence of the Residency in Lucknow. Initially, his aim in founding the school in a good, bracing climate, 4000 feet above sea level in the Simla Hills, was to provide for the orphan and other children of soldiers serving or having served in India, 'an asylum from the debilitating effects of a tropical climate and the demoralising influence of barrack life'. They were to live in a healthy, moral atmosphere and receive a good, useful and, above all, a religious education.

Originally called the Lawrence Military Asylum, it was three miles from the hill station of Kasauli and about 50 miles from Simla, the British summer capital. In 1920, the title of the school was changed to Lawrence Royal Military School at the command of King George V, in recognition of the distinguished services rendered by the old boys of Sanawar in the War of 1914–18. The school's motto was 'Never give in', the famous last words of its founder.

In 1927 my mother undertook a year's specialist training course in domestic science in the UK, and in the following year became head of domestic science in the senior girls' department at Sanawar, so we were able to be as much together as a family could be under all the circumstances. There were 200 senior girls, 250 senior boys, 50 preparatory boys and 20 in the creche. My mother remained in that post until she retired in 1949. By that time the school was accepting children from any of the three services. Fees were charged to those parents who could afford them, but none were charged for orphan children.

Being a military establishment, bugle calls summoned the senior boys to their various activities. The girls and preparatory depart- ments were summoned by bells. Church parade, with colours, was held on Sunday, in the morning and after Evensong. The school colours were originally presented by Lord Dalhousie in 1853, but royal colours were given to the school by the then Prince of Wales, the future Duke of Windsor, in 1921, in the course of his official tour. These were shown to the public once a year in a Trooping of the Colour ceremony similar to that presented each year in London by the Brigade of Guards.

Under my first principal, the Rev. George Dunsford Barne, who had been at Clifton College, the school became one of the leading educational institutions in India. He introduced prefectorial and house systems, encouraged organised games, introduced the Cambridge examinations (Junior and Senior Cambridge, more or less equivalent to GCSEs and A levels today) and affiliated the school to London University. He left in 1932 to become Bishop of Lahore.

We were all extremely happy there, though I find it difficult to say why. Perhaps it was the timeless beauty of our surroundings, perhaps it was the sense of family that we all had, being up there, bonded together, for more than nine months at a time, our lives programmed for us, with abundant sport and great interhouse rivalries without any kind of bitterness. Whatever it was, a magnificent bond of friendship was built up which exists to this day.

SHIRLEY POCOCK

Our parents were Londoners. In 1919, as a Captain in the British Army, Father went to Cawnpore, where Mother later joined him. She nearly died when my sister was born, from medicine prescribed by the Army doctor. As Father couldn't see any prospect of promotion in peacetime he left the Army and went into business as a merchant, supplying raw cotton to the flourishing Cawnpore cotton mills.

My pre-war memories of Cawnpore are slight, as I left aged four-and-a-half. We had a house there from 1929, when it was first built, to after independence in 1947. It was rented from an Indian landlord and probably fairly typical of the bungalows of the period – wide verandahs, high ceilings with overhead ventilating windows, bedrooms each with a dressing room and bathroom and a back door allowing access for the *paniwallah* to bring in hot water for the bath. We had a drawing room with a grand piano and a dressing-up box. Everyone had to make their own amusements – my father had a good baritone voice and my mother, who couldn't read a note of music, was brilliant at ragtime, boogie-woogie and swing. The dining room was fairly large, as there were often dinner parties, for which the cook made miraculous things in his primitive kitchen in the cookhouse, which was connected to the house by a covered way. He was Goanese – they were considered the best cooks – and I can even now remember some amazing cakes he made for children's parties; one in particular was a ship at sea with a funnel and real steam (a tin with a live charcoal in it). The servants' quarters were quite separate from the house (left of photo) and accommodated not only the staff but their families. The garden eventually had a tennis court, fruit and shade trees and flowers in the colder weather. But I can just remember our children's parties with all the rented fairground things and the *gully-gully* man, who could conjure eggs and chickens from the most unlikely places.

Later on, the garden was used for my sister's wedding reception and the servants allowed to decorate the 'In' and 'Out' gates on the drive. This they did with garlands of the customary marigolds and two enormous banners reading 'God help the happy pair!'

I must have had an *ayah* but I don't remember her. But I do remember an Anglo-Indian nanny – perhaps because of the commotion she caused by running away with a soldier, Mother's ring and

Shirley Pocock (right) in the garden of their house in Cawnpore, lived in by her family from 1929 to 1947. (Shirley Pocock)

some bottles of Father's gin. My mother showed me the Victorian-style photograph she had sent with her CV – a sweet-faced girl with a dove perched on her upturned hand. I do hope that man was good to her, as marriage to a British soldier was probably the best she could hope for.

As was customary for European children, when she was seven a place was found for my sister at a school in England. On the voyage home she became ill with what the ship's doctor thought was malaria. She was visibly dying under his treatment, and my mother, who was travelling tourist class, literally climbed over the barrier into the first class on one of the games decks to beg the help of an IMS doctor whose name she had seen on the passenger list. Overriding medical etiquette, he examined my sister and diagnosed typhoid.

We were put ashore at Gravesend, and my sister went into an isolation hospital where we were not allowed to see her. She recovered, but was discharged without being warned that her weakened condition might cause damage to her spine. Consequently she always suffered back problems, which greatly affected her life.

My sister's illness was not uncommon, even in the 1940s. Typhoid was often spread by a carrier, who could remain perfectly well. My husband's grandfather was a doctor on the tea estates in Darjeeling and died of typhoid when he was just 26.

And so to school. Mother said she could hear my sister's scream long after she left her.

I joined my sister aged four and a half. I remember the dressing gown I wore when we caught the midnight train to Bombay and the seeds of the marigolds in my pockets long after the garlands had died. I remember, too, throwing my little white *topee* over the stern of the P&O liner as we sailed out of Bombay, and watching it disappear in the wake. This custom was followed by people leaving India for good; in fact, I came back with my sister 11 years later. My worst memory is of getting lost in this great ship. In various forms this is still a recurring nightmare.

My sister looked after me. Letters to and from India were sent every week, smothered in hugs and kisses. Mother kept every one of ours.

We went from one holiday home to another until an advertisement in *The Lady* resulted in a young curate and his wife giving us a home for many years for the Christmas and Easter holidays. Mother came home every year and we rented Le Chalet, a cottage in Devon, for the summer. Father came home when he could – once not for three years – but could only be with us for a month. As the days came closer to his departure it was dreadful for us all. We used to bury a 'treasure' in the hope of finding it the following year. Sadly, there was no year following 1938 – we never went back. Still buried somewhere is a small Oxo tin containing this message: 'We have been to the Grand Russian Ballet and stayed at the Palace Hotel, but we'd rather be here at Le Chalet, Mummy, Daddy, Shirley and Val.'

Our holiday homes were usually private family homes where they took in children for the school holidays (my mother always sent the money in advance in case they were too hard-up to feed us properly) and the magazine *The Lady* (which still flourishes) was a reliable and respectable go-between for advertisers, or a home might be recommended by friends whose children had been there.

DESMOND PAILTHORPE

Tuesday 16 May 1922 was a beautiful early summer day, and His Majesty's troopship *Neuralia* docked at Tilbury, looked resplendent in her new colours, brilliant white with a navy-blue band halfway down the hull running the length of the ship and a bright red line where the water lapped the side.

The quayside was a hive of activity with uniforms of the services prominent, a small batch of nurses watched as a battalion of the King's Own Yorkshire Light Infantry marched up the gangways, the long line of soldiers heavily laden with kitbags, packs and rifles. They seemed cheerful enough, excitement on the faces of the recruits, their white skins in contrast to some of the older sun-tanned soldiers, old hands who had seen it all before.

In the vast embarkation shed officers and their families were moving more sedately, guided to their cabins by a host of Lascar stewards. They would travel first class, the more senior would have cabins on the port side going out and no doubt have priority for the starboard side when they returned to England... hence the well-known term 'posh' – port out, starboard home.

A second gangway was being used by the families of warrant officers and senior sergeants, who would be located in second-class accommodation. Mary, the wife of Staff Sergeant H.N. Pailthorpe, Royal Horse Artillery, was helped up the steep gangway by her husband. They followed a young Lascar cabin boy down a flight of stairs and he opened the door of a two-berth cabin on the port side. There was ample cupboard space, a hand-basin and a couple of chairs. The cabin was light and airy; the porthole gave a good view of the quayside. The cabin boy grinned and said, 'This cabin no. 46, bathroom and toilet across passage, left hand ladies, right hand gentlemen, lunch for this cabin 12.30p.m. first sitting'.

At half past four, stewards marched the decks with bells. 'All visitors ashore please. All visitors ashore.' Promptly at five o'clock the ship's siren boomed, the vibration from the ship's engines increased, the gangways were lowered and lines cast off. As the gap between ship and quayside widened a military band on shore played 'Auld Lang Syne', and everyone cheered and waved. The ship was nudged out into the Thames by a couple of tugs, dwarfed by the ship they were shepherding. A few minutes later the pilot came aboard and *Neuralia* moved towards the mouth of the river under her own steam.

Social activity aboard ship was varied. Breakfast at eight was followed by deck games such as quoits and deck tennis, with coffee, tea and ice cream at eleven, then lunch, guessing how far the ship had sailed during the 24 hours till noon each day. Four or five miles each side of the Captain's estimate proved a good bet for Mary, who won two days running. More deck games, tea and sandwiches at four, a siesta, then dressing for dinner followed by dancing, tombola or boxing matches between the Army, Navy and Air Force personnel. The weather in the Mediterranean was particularly good. They enjoyed a short trip ashore in Cyprus and at Port Said before they entered the Suez Canal, with the De Lesseps memorial by the Egyptian shore.

Shortly after the ship passed Aden Mary sent for the doctor, and at three o'clock on the morning of 4 June 1922 I was born, a hefty eight pounds three ounces, the very first baby to be born on the troopship.

The Captain of the ship, accompanied by the Chaplain, visited my mother to congratulate her after breakfast, and the Chaplain gave my parents a temporary certificate of birth, telling them to register the birth as soon as they arrived at their military station.

This was Dehra Dun, in the United Provinces, where my birth was duly registered with the British Consul. The temporary birth certificate was mislaid and never found, and the Consul advised my parents to have me baptised; ever since then, my baptismal certificate has served me in good stead.

DONALD HOWIE

There were three other Lawrence schools founded in India, not founded by Sir Henry, but in his memorial. The nearest to Sanawar's set-up and traditions was the Lawrence Memorial Royal Military School, Lovedale, in the Nilgiri Hills in south India. I have never visited that school, but from what I've heard from people who have, I have the sneaking feeling – though as a Sanawarian I would never admit it – that Lovedale had the edge on us performance-wise. They had, of course, the advantage of learning from our experience! Their school motto was the same as ours, Henry Lawrence's dying words, 'Never give in', and it was the motto of the other two Lawrence schools as well. These were the Lawrence College at Ghora Gali, on the outskirts of the delightful hill station of Murree, *en route* to

Kashmir, and the Lawrence School at Mount Abu, in a more or less central position in India.

The Chelmsford Training College was only a small college where teachers for English-speaking schools were trained. When I was there the number of students, in both first and second years, was 24. The college was administered by the principal and his office staff, whose main function was the running of the school of some 400 pupils, boys and girls, in preparatory and senior departments. Teaching practices were easily catered for by virtue of having the normal school forms on the college doorstep. The course of training was for two years. Government grants enabled the students to attend the College. I am given to understand that the College closed down towards the end of the 1940s. It was opened circa 1926.

Before that date Sanawar 'housed' the teachers' training college. The change to Ghora Gali was because of lack of space on the hill top at Sanawar on which a new college could be built. One was envisaged, but was voted out, especially because Sanawar needed new school buildings to replace the old and outdated ones. The new buildings, called the Birdwood School, were opened by the Commander-in-Chief of India at that time, Field Marshal Birdwood, and they were built on the site where the old training college stood. Our principal at that time, 1926–27, was the Rev. G.D. Barne who, as a pupil at Clifton College, Bristol, was Birdwood's 'fag'. This was revealed by our 'Boss' when he came down on Founder's Day to be present at the annual prize-giving ceremony, and caused much amusement. Birdwood said, 'The least I can do to repay him for his services as my fag is to lay the foundation stone of his new education block' – which he did.

I seem to have forgotten to say that the college was opened by Lord Chelmsford, Viceroy from 1916 to 1921.

JOAN TOFT

I was born in Eastbourne on 26 July 1926. My parents were anxious that their children should be born in the UK, as they were afraid that the boys would be obliged to serve in the Indian Army. My father was a chartered accountant with the firm Price, Waterhouse, Peat & Co. I first went to India at six weeks of age. We were living in Cawnpore. I can remember the white bungalow with asters planted in the beds in front of the house – I remember vividly waiting for my father to return from the office each day. A furore was caused by my turning over a plant pot and finding a nest of young cobras underneath! I lived happily in India till the age of six, when I was left at school in England. This was the custom at that time, but it now seems a terrible thing to do to a child.

Our hot-weather holidays were spent in Mussoorie and I can remember my first ride on a pony, Bessie Bream. She, like all the mountain ponies, walked on the very edge of the paths winding round the hillsides. My sister Patricia was born when I was four, but as I was left in England two years later, I remember

Joan Toft and her *ayah* in the garden of their bungalow in Cawnpore, about 1928. (Joan Toft)

little of life with her. I do remember loving dearly my mother's cross-bred terrier Willie, and being desperately upset at losing his companionship.

My first boarding school was Chatfield at Westgate-on-Sea. I was there from six to ten, and was not very happy. At first my holidays were spent with one of my mother's sisters, Aunt Ada – she did her best and was very kind to me, but it was not a real family. When Patricia joined me we went to a children's holiday home – April Farm in Sussex. Again, the people running the home were kind, and I enjoyed the companionship of other children, the dogs and the freedom of the countryside.

When our parents came on leave they rented a house near to our school, to which we then went daily. I can remember one day walking to school with my father on the day he was returning to India. I was desperate, screaming inside, but he said, 'Don't cry,' and so I didn't. I walked away from him up the school path. I have often wished that I had cried and shouted so that he would have known how much I loved him and would miss him. I hope he did know.

DICK HINDMARSH

My great-grandfather was the first member of the family to work in India. He went out in the 1860s to work for the India Railways, though I am not sure in what capacity. Interestingly enough, there is an H.J.K. Hindmarsh mentioned as General Manager in *Bhowani Junction* by John Masters! My grandfather was born in India and became a doctor in Bihar, and was to be awarded the OBE. My father was born in Mozuffarpore in October 1892, later being commissioned into the First Kumaon Rifles. I myself was born in England but went out to India before I was a year old.

In Delhi we lived in a military cantonment, in a bungalow with a circular drive in front. In the summer my sister and I went up to Srinagar in Kashmir, where we attended a small school. I know that I had jaundice at some point and I remember being injected for rabies (in the stomach – most painful!), as my mother was very fond of dogs. We had several servants, but our favourite was our bearer Ali Din, who was more or less in charge of us and gave us pony rides etc. In the 1970s his son came to see me and my wife in England. He was the principal of a Teacher Training College in Pakistan. I shall never forget the kindness I received from Ali Din and all the Indians. I feel a great affinity with India, although I left it at the age of four-and-a-half. But the memories remain of that beautiful country: the smell of wood-smoke, marigolds and fly-flit in our bungalow in Delhi; the mournful-sounding shouts as we entered a station on the Bombay–Delhi sleeper; being made to dance (somewhat reluctantly!) in a hall above a shop in Connaught Place in Delhi; attending a military open day outside Delhi, carrying a miniature 'swagger-stick' of my father's regiment; driving home along the wide boulevard between India Gate and the Viceroy's House; stopping at a rest-house on the way to Kashmir and sleeping in a bed with brass knobs and eating custard creams; staying at my aunt's house on the coast near Bombay – a very tall, thin house; staying on a houseboat in the Dal Lake in Kashmir; a clear picture of the red-brick garrison church in Kashmir.

It is not a country that one can forget.

ROBIN MALLINSON

My mother was the sister of Sir Charles Carson KCIE OBE, who served in the ICS for 36 years. As a boy in 1936, I went with my mother to a major celebration in Gwalior, a Princely State not too far from Agra. My uncle was by now Finance Minister to the Maharajah. It must have been a wedding of the Maharajah or the equivalent of a coronation. The procession was unbelievable – medieval in concept. Scores of elephants, painted in many colours, caparisoned in rich embroidered hangings, surmounted by *howdahs* holding the state's aristocracy dripping with jewels. Smart state infantry in colourful uniforms, bands playing, cavalry on splendid horses. This was one state – what must the Delhi Durbar in 1911 have been like?

HEDI BRAUN

I was two when we arrived more or less penniless in Bombay from Vienna in 1938. Fortunately for us, my mother, a Montessori teacher, had worked in India a few years previously and she had kept in contact with a particular friend, who was married to an Indian politician. Immediately after the *Anschluss* my mother wrote to her saying that she thought we might have to leave our country. She answered with a cable and the news that a visa for her and her husband and child had been sent. She was offered a job at a newly opened Montessori school at Rajghat near Benares. My mother had to leave her parents behind in Vienna and we were not allowed to take any money with us. Our furniture, with my mother's precious piano, was packed up under the supervision of the SS and sent after us. We had transport to Bombay but no further, being told 'one can walk'. But my mother's friends sent 300 rupees to the ship so we didn't have to. When we arrived in Benares we were met and garlanded by some my mother's old pupils, a change from the hostilities of Vienna.

We were given a little bungalow in the school compound. I was the only European child in that school, a most beautiful building on the banks of the Ganges. We walked by the river every evening and I still use a fragment of one of the old temples, which I found there, as a paperweight.

But there was no work for my father, an engineer, in the holy city of Benares. He went to Calcutta and soon found work at Phillips, the Dutch firm. Our furniture, miraculously, arrived. We sold our dining-room suite to a Maharajah, which aided our survival. My mother practised her piano and, on one of her visits to Calcutta, auditioned at the radio station there, and this resulted in a contract.

Meanwhile the situation in Vienna had got worse. My mother's one wish was to get her parents and her other friends out of that hell. It was very difficult to get visas for them, but she did succeed, found some friends to guarantee it, and in 1939 my grandparents arrived in Calcutta, where they stayed with my father as there was no room for them at Rajghat.

I had been ill almost ever since I arrived in India, especially with malaria. My mother had to decide to give up her wonderful job but she found another, at The New School in Darjeeling, then just formed to receive European children evacuated from the War. We moved there, a place my mother has described as 'the most beautiful place on earth', in 1940 and stayed, with holidays in the plains, until 1947.

ZOE WILKINSON

My father was a manager of the Elgin Mills in Cawnpore, which is a big industrial city. Elgin Mills had been founded in 1864, and were contractors to the Government, manufacturing cloth for a range of uses from tents, towels, and khaki to dyed turban cloth. The mills were served by staff with lovely bungalows. It was a society where we looked after the whole community – every aspect of the mills. There were committees for all sorts of things. At the mill, my father did quite a lot with schools for the staff and the little hospital. He set up the Dairy, and he ran the RSPCA. He was chairman of the European Association, and at one time President of the Upper Indian Chamber of Commerce. And he was on the Parish Council. He wouldn't talk about it, but I knew that the local padre had the chance to send his wife to the Hills because someone had put more into the collection plate than might have been expected. Sometimes staff ran out of money and couldn't get back to England, and there were always committees to look after them.

It was my father's special treat to take me to the Mills on Sunday. I loved going with him, seeing all round. There was a big tank of fish, in particular. There was always this great contrast. You had Cawnpore and the Mills, all hot and dusty, and then the gardens, which were green and lovely. We would go to the Mills in his car, but otherwise we had a little 'tum-tum' and a pony, and we went for rides in that.

As a small girl, for the first eight years of my life I woke every morning to hear the hooters of the Elgin Mills calling the men to work. It was a glorious childhood. Sunshine and shadows, brilliant colours and endless horizons, multitudes of people, magic and mystery, strong scents and violent deaths, fabulous journeys and dreadful partings – oh, those partings! At eight came the trauma experienced by the great majority of the children born of English families working in India: boarding school in England. Grey skies, chilblains, doors that shut, tight formal clothes and aloneness.

Among our servants, Babu Lal (the chief bearer) had a pension fund, and by the time they left he had built a very nice house and was a member of the provincial Legislative Assembly for the Schedule Classes, as was my father for the Europeans. As an aside, they went off to the meetings of the Legislative in a car together, Burra Sahib and servant!

When I went back in 1970 and the servants came to garland me and the tears ran down their faces, I sensed that they wept for the lost security, the pleasant orderliness of the servants' compound, for the help with their children and the hope for the future, as much as for affection for me.

THEON WILKINSON

My father was fairly progressive in the British/Indian sense, in an industrial town rather like Birmingham, dealing with labour relations in a factory with Hindus and Muslims and all the political events going on outside. He was one of the leaders of the European community. He was in the United Provinces Legislative Assembly, so he met people like Nehru. He had extremely interesting contacts with the up-and-coming India, and knew that Independence was round the corner. He was also Director of The Pioneer, Lucknow. What he would tell me in his letters to me at school in England were really just the events in Cawnpore, and sometimes there would be a brief mention of the riots.

He was known to be unbiased in the handling of labour, which wasn't easy in those days. People were leaning one way or the other, and for people to recognise that you were genuinely objective was rare. In his factory, I think just before or at the beginning of the War, he opened a welfare department, which was a new departure for an Indian mill. It was to provide games facilities such as table tennis for the Indian staff and workers. I would go along too, and play table tennis with some of the Indian clerks. It was probably his initiative that put me in touch with those elements of India that I would otherwise have missed. He insisted on me learning Hindustani, and arranged for a *munshi* to give me regular lessons. Another contact with 'real' India was a holy man, *babuji*, who built a Hindu

above Mounted Police at the time of the riots in Cawnpore, 1939. (Ann Mitchell)

below Some of the damage caused by the Cawnpore riots in 1939. (Ann Mitchell)

temple without authority, right on the river's edge and close to our bungalow. Using his official contacts, my father managed to divert the PWD's access away from the temple. Later, when I was 15 or 16 and had tried to keep the monkeys away from our fruit garden by peppering them with pellets from my airgun, I accidentally killed a monkey. This was an unforgivable thing to do, and the servants were aghast. They sent for *babuji* and he gave me absolution, and cast the monkey into the Ganges. It could have been a nasty incident. When my son and I re-visited India 32 years later, the *babuji*, with whom Christmas cards had been regularly exchanged, met us in his full regalia and took us to his temple, and after garlanding us, placed a garland in the river in memory of my father.

My mother had grown up in Cawnpore and my father was based there, so they spent their entire life in just one or two bungalows in Cawnpore. As a result, the bearer, cook, *syce* and all the other servants with their families became much more integrated into the domestic establishment than they would have done if, like Service families, they had always been moving about from station to station. The White House, where we previously lived, was a typical old bungalow, built to ensure the minimum discomfort in the notoriously unpleasant hot weather, with its well-ventilated high-ceilinged rooms having top windows, surrounded on the shady side facing the river by a broad verandah.

The Wilkinsons' house in Cawnpore. (Theon Wilkinson)

It was approached by a curving drive between flower-beds and two palm trees, to an imposing porch with earthenware pots of blooming cinerarias and chrysanthemums (as I remember them), arranged in ranks one above the other on the sides of the steps. A 'chick' blind hung over the ever-open front doors with entry barred by a uniformed *chaprassi*, always present during the day. Once inside, there was a wide corridor with bedrooms leading off it, their doorway opened but heavily curtained, each with its own *ghusal-khana*, and at the far end of the bungalow a spacious sitting-room only used for entertaining guests, a dining room on one side leading to the pantry and path to the outside kitchen, on the other side my father's study, where he worked every evening, and a small room where we usually sat. Leading from these rooms was a broad curving verandah where we breakfasted, looking out over the river only a few yards away, and, if entertainment was required, there was a full size table-tennis table. On the side opposite to the pantry was a much smaller verandah where the *durzi* sat every day sewing, mending and copying the latest style of dress for the ladies. We were a small, self-contained community, with every need taken care of by one of the appropriate servants; the sweeper to bring our bathwater and take away the 'thunder-box' buckets, the *chowkidar* to prowl around the house at night to keep away thieves, the *chaprassi* at the door to take messages, the *syce*, the driver, the *malis* to tend the flowers and vegetables, plus the whole retinue of household servants.

Indian businessmen frequently called at our house to discuss commercial affairs, and at Christmas time a procession of them arrived to pay their respects, exchange compliments of the season and leave presents of fruit and cake. They always asked to see my mother and usually had some delightful but small presents for my sister and I. There was a clear understanding that valuable presents would be returned. These civilities never extended to meals such as invitations to dinner, as at that time there were social and religious obstacles in the way. We never saw their wives, and the only occasion they were permitted by their husbands to come out was to an annual *purdah* tea party arranged by my mother on our tennis court, closely screened, and that I witnessed in 1940 and 1941.

When I returned to India during the War I sensed a genuine feeling of friendship between my father and some of his Indian acquaintances. These were maintained after his retirement to England, and I kept in touch for a few years with one of their sons. Discrimination was not then such a politically loaded word as it has since become. All levels of society, British, Indian and Anglo-Indian (in the broadest sense of the word) discriminated between each other and within their own communities in different ways, and accepted it as the norm. There were Railway Clubs, Mill Clubs, Burra Sahibs Clubs, Hindu and Muslim exclusive gatherings. Life was lived without making an issue of seeking entry into each others' domain. My father belonged to the Cawnpore Burra Sahibs Club; my mother's family largely still resident in Cawnpore belonged to the Mills Club, and seldom did they meet, except for a Christmas party.

Discrimination existed on all sides and without making moral judgements it may be interesting to record a few examples. While at St Paul's School in Darjeeling, I made friends with a number of Anglo-Indian boys, one of whom invited me to his home among the railway community in Calcutta. When I returned the compliment by inviting him to Cawnpore I could sense some unease shown by my parents, but they did everything in their power to make him feel at home as one of the family. The discrimination came from the servants who were more than willing to put themselves out for the Chota Sahib, but were clearly not so disposed to my guest, as they showed in a number of small ways. As far as Clubs were concerned, I experienced no difficulty in taking him with me to the Cawnpore Club, and that was in 1941.

Only a few dramatic childhood incidents were burnt into my mind which remain within recall in my old age. Undergoing anti-rabies treatment in Kasauli after being licked by a mad dog in Cawnpore when 20 (or was it 30!) daily injections were put into my tummy while I was being held down by my poor mother. Being enveloped in a huge pink cloud of locusts on our way to the Hills. Walking to the Polo Ground below our hotel in Mussoorie and learning later that a leopard had been lurking nearby, and had taken a dog that very evening. Watching a noisy crowd form the corner of our garden and being squirted with coloured water from a Holi procession. And the sounds and smells in my deep subconscious; the beat of monsoon rain on a tin roof; the endless noisy calling of the crows, and the indescribable, unforgettable bazaar odours. I remember playing with the servants' children, always out-of-doors, and usually an Indian game such as kites, which we 'fought' with, cutting each other's kite-string with *manja* (fine thread rolled in ground glass). Great fun – I bought my kites 'home', but of course, there was too much wind. I can remember no games in England except those at school and organised indoor ones.

When my parents came home together (as they only did every three years), there were special holidays arranged and special family picnics to try and unite the clan of uncles, aunts, cousins, etc. My father was never seen in the routine of his work environment; he was always at our disposal and inclined to spoil us. When my parents retired after the War, I was then grown up, and enjoyed for the first time an English home, with my own room, my own furniture; a place to which I could invite my friends – it was at a time of great significance. But, at prep school in England, I always felt bound to return to India. I was just completing a necessary period of apprenticeship. Bits of India were always being brought home to me – a grain of rice with my name and a message from my parents on it; a seed pod with a hundred carved ivory elephants the size of a pin head inside; a weaver bird's nest; cotton seed and yarn through all its stages, and so on. I think this kind of education bred an early sense of independence and a kind of fly-on-the-wall objectivity; not quite belonging anywhere and able to look with detachment at Englishmen of all classes, and Indians of all castes and creeds.

My father undoubtedly loved India, and did what he could to improve the lives of everyone with whom he came into contact. He built bridges between Hindus and Muslims at his factory, he introduced a Welfare Centre for employees, and he organised the RSPCA locally to care for injured animals. Most of all, he enjoyed an excellent relationship with the Hindu holy man, whose temple he had saved from the progress of main drains. *Pujas* are still said for my father on each anniversary of his death.

JOHN JUDGE

My father, who was born in Derby in 1889, after private education went to sea in the Merchant Navy as a young deckhand. He arrived in India in about 1907, and then decided to leave the Merchant Navy and join the Indian Police. He was assigned to the Criminal Intelligence Department after suitable training, and was based mainly in Bombay and Delhi. In 1914, at the start of the First World War, he joined the Army and served as a Captain in the Intelligence Corps in Mesopotamia. After the War in 1919, he joined Raymond Grant Govan as a Partner to form a business venture – which started with the first bus service to Kulu, where the apples grow in the lovely Kulu valley.

Messrs Govan Bros, Ltd was incorporated in 1922, and expanded into several other commercial industries during the 1920s and 1930s, such as pioneering activities in hire-purchase business in Bombay, Delhi Flour Mills, Gwalior Sugar and Indian National Airlines, a small domestic airline using twin-engined Beechcraft aircraft. In 1932 the company built two Sugar Factories in the small Muslim state of Rampur. Rampur state is situated about 120 miles northeast of Delhi, on the Grand Trunk Road from Delhi to Calcutta. The sugar-cane fields in Rampur state were large and prolific, and Govan Bros built and ran a small narrow-gauge railway system for supplying the two sugar factories with sugar cane. My father was the Managing Agent in Rampur for the two sugar factories. Later, he enlarged the complex by building a distillery to use some of the by-products of the sugar. He needed to liaise closely with the Nawab and his ruling council, as the largest employer in the State.

My father met and married my mother in Bombay in 1926, she having travelled by sea from Sydney to visit her uncle, who was working in India. We lived in Delhi for the first four years of my life, and then moved to Rampur in 1932 when the two sugar factories were built. There were two homes in Rampur, the first a bungalow, one of several within the factory compound. The second was a 'burra bungalow' situated in a small residential area with about half an acre of grounds, surrounded by a high wall, separate servant quarters and a garage. The kitchen was a separate small building, where the *khansama* operated. At the back was a small field used by all the family for horse training, with a small set of jumps. We had a car and a driver, as well as a pony and trap. The large verandah surrounding the front half of the bungalow was useful for rollerskating, taking care not to disturb the resident *dhirzi*. Early morning horserides before breakfast was a normal routine.

Our journeys consisted mainly of the annual travel to a hill station for the hot summer months; in our case we had our own hut in Gulmarg in the Vale of Kashmir. My father usually remained behind in the plains, making occasional visits.

The great adventure was going shooting with my father, sitting on an elephant in the back of a *howdah*. The shooting was mainly for partridge and other game birds. Elephants were used because of the tall grasses and the danger of big game such as tigers and leopards.

Illnesses were minor: malaria was prevalent, but mosquito nets were standard. All drinking water was boiled and all fruit and vegetables washed in potassium permanganate – 'pinki pani'.

I have two younger sisters, one born in Delhi in 1930 and one born in England in 1933. Our friends were mainly other children of British and Dutch families, and Indian families of the managers of the Sugar Complex. The Dutch were employed as chemists in the sugar process. Occasionally, the children of the Nawab came to children's parties at our bungalow, where we played outdoor games in the garden such as hide and seek, French cricket, Twos and Threes and egg and spoon races, and for special birthday parties there would be elephant rides arranged by my father.

In 1933 my parents decided that I should advance my education by schooling in England. This meant a sea voyage with my parents and younger sister. We rented a house in Dorking, where my youngest sister was born. My first school was a pre-prep school called Oakleigh, near East Grinstead. It was co-ed, and I went there with my elder sister for about two terms. My next school was at Brambletye, in East Grinstead, where I started boarding at the age of eight. Meanwhile, my two parents and sister returned to India by sea (P&O or Orient Line). It was a good school, which remained located in East Grinstead until the outbreak of war in 1939. It was then evacuated to Lee Abbey in North Devon, and remained there for the duration of the War.

In the period of boarding, whilst my parents were away in India, I spent my holidays with friends of theirs in Penrith or Huddersfield, and once at a holiday home at Bexhill-on-Sea; all these arrangements were with children of my own age. As communications between England and India were slow (six weeks by sea), there could have been a sense of homesickness. However, it is difficult to recall one's feelings exactly – I have memories of many visitors, being taken out on Sundays for large meals, and being sent out large cases of mangoes, the other boys never having seen them, and curious about the various methods of eating them. The holiday home in Bexhill was better than expected, as there were other children there in the same situation as myself.

The Elgin Flour Mills Co. Ltd, Cawnpore.

8

The Central Provinces
and Bihar

Bihar and Orissa were incorporated as an administrative area in 1912. Bihar was almost entirely Hindu, although Gaya, its chief place of pilgrimage, had many associations with the Buddha. The great temple of Jagganath at Puri was, in fact, in Orissa.

Puri and Gopalpur were two of the seaside resorts of the Raj, both in Orissa, while the third, Waltair, was actually in the extreme north of the state of Madras. While there was a magnificent beach along almost the entire east coast of India, there was also a vicious undercurrent which rendered all swimming extremely dangerous, if not impossible, and minders were essential at all times.

The Great Bihar Earthquake took place in 1934, and was felt as far away as Darjeeling – where Government House had to be re-built – and Calcutta. One of the saddest casualties was the total destruction of the Government Research Centre at Pusa. Founded in 1905, it had done excellent work improving crops and agricultural methods, but perhaps its most lasting legacy was the two books by the Imperial Entomologist, Harold Maxwell-Lefroy. *Indian Insect Pests* (1906) and *Indian Insect Life* (1909) remain standard to this day.

Bihar had its own language, Bihari, while Oriya was the language of Orissa. Its railways were the East Indian, the Bengal and North

Western and the Bengal Nagpur. Nagpur was the seat of the Governor of the Central Provinces. In the hot weather, he went up to Pachmarhi, 3500 feet high. The Central Provinces, south west of Bihar, were largely an upland district, producing various crops other than rice, but it was particularly well-forested. Its principal manufacturing town was Jubbulpore, famous for the invention of snooker in one of its Army Messes, and for the handsome carpets produced in its gaol. But there was also a gun-carriage factory and large Government and railway workshops. It was served by the Indian Midland, the Great Indian Peninsular and the Bengal Nagpur Railways, and the languages were Western Hindi and Marathi.

BILL CHARLES

My family's roots in India took hold in the 1880s when my grandparents, Ernest and Elizabeth Charles, joined the Kurku and Central Indian Hill Mission, which had its Indian headquarters at Ellichpur, Berar, in the Central Provinces. Their English headquarters were at Arden, Bushey Heath in Hertfordshire. They established themselves at the Duni Mission Station, from where they administered the gospel and medical care to those in need. They were 60 miles from Burhanpur, on the Tapti river.

My father, his three sisters and brother were all born in India and went to schools in Panchgani and Ootacamund. On leaving school every one except my father went to university in England, joining the teaching and medical professions.

My grandfather met an untimely death as the result of an injury sustained while attempting to push a bullock cart from the flooded Tapti. It was the only form of transport other than horseback in that remote part of India at that time. The mission's circular leaflet number 114 of April 1918 had this to say:

Our brother Ernest Charles entered into the heavenly rest on Feb. 28th last, at Tembi, near Burhanpur, 28 miles from Duni. He has so long been a valued and faithful worker in the Mission, that one can hardly realise that he is not still with us. We know that all the friends of the Mission will grieve with us at the loss to the Mission, and will deeply sympathise with his widow and five children in the very sudden and unexpected bereavement.

Mr and Mrs Charles were the senior members of the Mission, having worked together in it from its earliest days. He had, on January 1st last, completed a quarter of a century of service as a missionary specially to the Kurkus, spending far the greater part of his time in the lonely station at Duni, which is not only in a remote part of the Melghat Jungle, but is for the greater part of the year cut off, owing to the swollen rivers, from the rest of the field.

There must be very few villages, for a long distance round, where Mr and Mrs Charles are not well known by these shy denizens of the forest, who are slow to trust themselves to strangers, but who had learned to trust Mr Charles and his devoted wife, coming to them constantly in all their troubles, and having profound belief in the simple drugs which were always at their disposal in Mrs Charles's store at Duni. Mr Charles has again and again been appealed to, to come with his gun when a man-eating tiger has been threatening the villages.

He had come so much into contact with them that he had a good knowledge of their language, and was able to help Miss Wardlaw-Ramsay, when she was translating the Gospels into Kurku.

Mr and Mrs Charles had started out early in February, with their two youngest children, so that Mrs Charles could take Dorothea back to school in Bombay, She was then to rejoin her husband for their usual spring tours among the Kurku villages.

It seems that, on their journey, they had been in danger of a serious accident more than once, owing to the river they had to cross, and it was a miracle that the driver was not killed. Mr Charles was trying to help with a rope on one of these occasions, and he told his wife he knew he had received some internal injury, as the animal lurched badly, and he felt severe pain at the time. They neither of them thought it was at all serious, however, and Mrs Charles went on to Bombay, leaving Benjamin with his father. He seemed rather better when she returned, but he gradually got weaker in the next ten days, and passed away on February 28th.

How thankful Mrs Charles was, when she looked back, that God had arranged it that her husband had reached the hospitable home of a friend, Mr Thomas, who did everything he could for his comfort, and who was able to help her bury him away in the jungle. What would she have done had she been by herself at Duni? But the Lord knew, and provided, and they laid him to rest there, wrapped in a simple shroud, like the Kurkus whom he loved, for it was impossible to make a coffin in that out-of-the-way place.

My grandmother remained with the mission and continued her work at Duni. My father, being the eldest son, decided to remain with her and was to establish himself on a cotton plantation in the neighbouring area. On a visit to England he met my mother. He returned to India, my mother following at a later date. They were married on her arrival in Bombay and proceeded to Duni to join my grandmother, and where they put the finishing touches to their bungalow, by now almost complete. Sixteen months later I was born, at the Sassoon Hospital in Poona.

I cannot remember much of Duni, but I have been told a great deal. The compound was fenced with bamboo to keep panthers, sambur and jackals out. My mother lost two or three of her dogs to panthers. On one occasion my father, like his father before him, was called out to hunt down a man-eating tiger which had been troubling a nearby village. Not content with a goat, it had run off with a small child. The tiger was hunted down and shot.

James Charles, father of Bill, with the man-eating tiger he had shot at the request of the local villagers. Duni, Berar, CP, June 1928. (Bill Charles)

Water was obtained from a well. Drinking water was boiled and cooled in earthen 'chatties'. Baths were taken in a tin bath, water having been heated in cans over a wood fire. Washing was done by the *dhobi*, in the nearby river. Lighting was by oil lamps. The mission bungalow was kept cool by the pulling *punkahs* – a large bamboo fan attached to ropes.

The only fresh meat to be had was when my father shot a sambur or other deer. The meat was always shared with the villagers. It was cut thinly and dried in the sun so as to keep for a few days.

We lived at Duni until my grandmother returned to England. The mission's circular leaflet number 159 of July 1929 recorded with the deepest regret that she had been 'so suddenly and unexpectedly been called Home', only a few days after she reached England in the spring.

The words of the Latin poet are very applicable to her: 'If thou seekest a monument, look around'. Duni is the place to see her life's work. There you have but to look around and on all hands you would see by the love of the people for her, how she had won their hearts, and how she had, through so many years, shown them that the love of Christ, whom she so truly served, meant a life given up to the needs of others in all their sufferings and difficulties. We at this distance are not fully able to gauge her work correctly, for the wild people, by whom she was surrounded nearly all her life in India, lived a life so unlike ours; and it is difficult for us too to realise how shut off and alone she was in the dangerous, wild jungle, which most Europeans shun because of its loneliness and terrible fevers. Here she lived a long life for God, and only eternity will reveal the harvest that has sprung from the seed she sowed, with her husband, the late Mr Charles, who died 11 years before her.

One of the older Christian women, speaking of Mrs Charles a few days ago said: 'The Kurkus looked upon her as a queen. But to the Christian community in the district she was "Mother" and to their children she was always "Nani" or "Grandmother".'

Just before she left Duni to go on furlough, a party of new missionaries paid her a visit in her jungle home. She was even then very frail and tired, and suffering from a bad leg, which had kept her low for many months. But she was so pleased at the visit, mentioning it as a cause for thankfulness in two or three letters afterwards.

Though glad to go home and see her daughters and friends, it cost her much to say 'goodbye' to her station and Indian Christians. The parting, too, from her son James and grandchild was no easy thing for her.

But once on the boat that was to take her to Europe she gave herself up to rest. A cheery letter, written on board, told how she was enjoying the voyage and fellowship with other missionaries who were travelling on the same ship. In concluding the letter, she wrote, 'I trust God will bring me back to India, unless He calls me hence.'

So it was a shock to all when the cable came to say she had been 'called hence', only a few days after her arrival in England. At first we thought it must have been the smallpox that was prevalent on the *Tuscania*, and for which she, with many others, had been inoculated on board. But her death certificate tells us she was carried off by an internal trouble.

Shortly after this my parents and I moved further south, to Bangalore, where my father took up fruit and dairy farming.

GLORIA HOLLINS

As I sit in my garden and look at my eucalyptus tree, 'snapshot' memories come flooding back of days in India, a land of contrasts, where beauty and squalor walked hand in hand with opulence and poverty, and Brahmin with beggar.

I was born in August 1927 in Jubbulpore, Central Provinces, a garrison town and railway junction, the only daughter with three older brothers of Albert and Agnes Hollins. My father commenced life in India with the Royal Artillery, but later joined the Great Indian Peninsular Railway. My parents married in 1909; my mother's father was also Army.

Early childhood days were spent mainly in the company of Ayah, who was my bodyguard and friend. Hindustani came more naturally than my mother tongue. Playmates were few, and we met on the *maidan* where our *ayah* took us for our daily walks. We had no electricity till I was ten, only oil or petrol lamps. No pasteurised milk in bottles was left on the doorstep; instead, the jingling cowbell announced the arrival of the *doodhwallah* and his buffalo, which was milked to quantity required. The milk had to be boiled, and the cream taken from the top made our butter. Cars were few, so our main form of transport was the bicycle, and we learned to ride one at an early age.

Jubbulpore in the summer had a temperature of 114 degrees Fahrenheit in the shade. In spite of thick *kus-kus tattis* made to fit the outer doors and doused frequently through the day with water, and the *punkahwallah* dozing in his outside shed rhythmically and monotonously pulling on a string to keep the indoor *punkahs* moving, there was little relief from the heat. May and June were the hottest of the summer: school days started at seven o'clock so we could be home by noon. I remember well how I hated and dreaded sleeping out of doors at the height of summer. The jackals howling and the sounds of rustling in the trees and bushes. A mosquito net was not much protection against the imaginary fears of a child. Winter months were the most pleasant – sunny cooler days, and often chilly enough to enjoy a fire in the evening.

At the age of eight, like so many other children in India, I was sent to boarding school. This was Hebron, Coonoor, in the Nilgiri Hills. Three nights' train journey and 10 months away from home each year. The parting from pets, home and parents was a wrench.

The train journey, however, was a camping adventure. We had a carriage to ourselves with its own toilet and washroom facilities. Very few train journeys in India were less than a night and most were more, so preparations for these was a military exercise. Compartments had to be booked and picnic hampers stocked with food for snacks *en route*. We did not 'travel light'. There would be a mountain of suitcases, school trunks and bedding rolls. These items all carefully counted and checked, usually my job, as the railway coolies put them on and took them off the train at every change.

Our destination in the Nilgiri Hills meant a zig-zag route. We left Jubbulpore 4 p.m. one day and arrived in Bombay the next morning. We then caught the train which crossed the continent to Madras. Yet another change and night three to Coimbatore and the last lap for the mountain railway to Coonoor. As the crow flies some 1500–2000 miles of travelling from home to school. To the background 'clickety clack' of the train we spent our time looking at the scene racing by. Small villages and small railway stations where the fast mail train did not stop. A parched landscape with patches of green, a native farmer ploughing his land and the women collecting water from a well. The journey was interrupted by stops at main stations, and as meal times approached this was where the dining-car bearer called at the carriages to take orders. At the next stop this was brought beautifully packed in a picnic-style basket with all the necessary accoutrements.

Coonoor and Ootacamund were reached by a short journey on the famous Swiss-designed, narrow-gauge railway. The train with engine at the rear, wound its way and climbed 8000 feet up the mountain range from the plains below, passing through magnificent scenery of waterfalls, forest and twisting roads. Hebron was a school founded for children of missionaries, and I was at the time one of the few exceptions. The school was perched on the hillside, built in terraces surrounded by tea bushes and eucalyptus trees. A temperate climate, an idyllic world. Days at school were regulated, with a time for leisure, compulsory games and study. There were short breaks between the school terms. In the May holiday of three weeks, we joined our parents, who also came up to the hills to get away from the heat of the summer. Apart from our main winter break at home from December to February, the other short holidays were spent at school. The War (1939–45) had little impact on our lives at school. We followed the main event as best we could. It was only when the Japanese invasion was threatened that we had a single air-raid practice. With its unseen wildlife, the jungle adjacent to the school was designated the shelter. In 1944 our senior Cambridge exam papers were written in pencil with carbon copies, there being every possibility that the originals would not reach their destination in England. Hebron was a haven from reality and the outside world.

HENRY BERRIFF

I was born in Simla in 1927. Simla is in the foothills of the Himalayas, so I'm biased in loving mountains. Although I eventually ended my schooldays in Simla at Bishop Cotton's School, the 1930 world slump destined my future. My father, Arthur Berriff, auctioned his stock in the clothing business – he had trained at E.P. Rose's, Bedford – and the family, my mother and father, my brother and two sisters and myself, moved to Jubbulpore.

Looking at the map of India and poking a pin in the centre of the 'V', you would be bound to hit Jubbulpore.

Our lifestyle changed completely. From mountains to plains, cool to hot. From deodar and pine forests, with snow in the winter and living beneath our shop in the centre of The Mall, we now lived in a hot, semi-detached bungalow with a large garden on three sides. There were ceiling fans in all the rooms – two bedrooms, lounge or drawing room and dining room. Houses were of brick with tiled roofs – two tiers of tiles separated by a row of skylight windows which could be opened by long ropes and a pulley. The houses differed in size according to the status of the staff employed to operate the Government's gun-carriage factory, and we lived on the factory estate.

The gun-carriage factory, through the eyes of a young boy, was a virtual fortress. The entire perimeter was surrounded by a high stone wall with barbed wire on top. In the wall at intervals were slots for rifle fire. It was vaguely reminiscent of what one imagined a French Foreign Legion fort would look like. In fact, from a security angle, with hillocks overlooking it, the site was most vulnerable, bearing in mind the snipers of the Khyber Pass.

An Army VIP remarked that it must have been some idiot that had had it built there. To overcome this weak point, small, square stone-walled redoubts were built on the top of each hill. They had strong metal doors with slots and on top, at opposite corners, square metal 'boxes' jutted out with rifle slots – even on the floor, for shooting downwards.

As Jubbulpore was a garrison town, with its strategic position, it always had an infantry regiment, signals and an artillery brigade – 15th Field Brigade, as I recollect, on the huge brass sign outside their HQ at the edge of the cantonment.

My life has been linked, albeit loosely, with the military. At the age of three I remember seeing, on the ridge at Simla, near the bandstand and with my *ayah* Surthia, the Gurkha Pipe Band in their kilts marching back and forth on this, one of the very few flat pieces of ground in Simla.

Then, with my many bouts of malaria in Jubbulpore, together with other minor illnesses, I was hospitalised in the local British Military Hospital. Whatever else, it was spick and span. Officious, but efficient, nurses, walking briskly, or pausing near your bed, with white starched uniforms and large white headdresses, matched the white sheets, always tucked tight round you to look neat against the blood-red blankets. Rows of black iron beds on either side of the ward. It was like kit inspection when Matron made her rounds. The white-uniformed orderlies, loaned from the local infantry regiment, would be bustling about, cleaning here, pushing packs of cards, chocolates etc. out of the way, and generally hiding any forbidden article.

These orderlies were my friends. They would play cards, teach me card tricks and keep me enthralled with their many tales of the Afghans on the North West Frontier. I suppose that this was an introduction to my liking Kipling's *Kim*. Rasmak, Landi-Kotal and Quetta – the hot punishment station – for they had been there, from the KOYLIs, the Welsh Borderers and other regiments, excluding the famous Bengal Lancers, who were only for house duty at the Governor's Residence, and this only very occasionally.

Although my father worked in an ordnance factory he was a civilian, in charge of stores. The factory – which was nothing like factories that I was to work in later in my life, as an engineering apprentice in Rugby, England – held a special appeal for me in the huge fire tank in its centre.

As the climate was so hot – up to 110 degrees Fahrenheit – the tank was adapted for the use of senior staff and their families as a swimming pool on weekends and holidays. It had low and high diving boards, a water chute, a raft and a round floating log on which one had to try and sit. This log featured in the pillow-bashing events in the annual gala held there. Coloured lights, bunting and the military band, playing light classics, Gilbert and Sullivan and popular tunes, added to the gaiety of the water sports, and gave one brief respite from the hot summer days.

My father liked swimming and would take us early on Sunday mornings to the factory tank. We had an Model A Ford. At the factory, the gates – huge metal doors with peep-holes – would be opened. After Father was okayed by the duty officer, in a meshed cage, we would pass on down the centre of a wide, tree-lined avenue with factory workshops on either side. Halfway down we'd turn left, past the fire station, to the tank. There were changing rooms, wooden structures open to the elements, with patterned floorboards where my lucky father often found money!

The factory estate was aloof from the rest of Jubbulpore and from the railway station, the GIPR, Great Indian Peninsular Railway: a dusty road for two miles gave way to the one and only tarred road. At the junction of these roads was a small, square, brick building known as the Octroy Post and the start of the factory estate. The road led to the factory gates, about two miles away, past a small *maidan* where *ayahs* would gather with their charges round swings, and a sand pit; past the large tiled houses with big gardens, tended by *malis*, belonging to the senior staff. The ribbon of tar went up and over between two hillocks named Burra and Chota Simla.

These hills were once peaks surrounded by water millions of years ago; the bones of a dinosaur had been found at the base of Chota Simla. The tar road continued, passing a small post office, other estate houses, past the cream-coloured walls of the Club, over a small concrete bridge, one of many bridges that straddled the wide-squared concrete storm drains that criss-crossed the estate.

It terminated at the huge, forbidding iron gates of the factory, reminiscent of a prison.

To the left side of these gates, and more familiar to the families, was the clinic. I remember baring my arms, queuing with mothers and children, to be scratched for a smallpox inoculation.

The Factory Club had many pleasant memories. It was mainly the meeting place for adults; children sometimes wormed their way in, accompanying parents, and were generally tolerated – provided they behaved themselves. The four *murram* – red soil – tennis courts, the billiard room and the large wooden sprung dance-floor, which doubled as a badminton court, supplied the sporting facilities. There was also a nine-hole golf course.

The flat-roofed Club building included, at the far left corner and approached from the outside, a shop for groceries, household articles and small two-anna tins of Nestlé's condensed milk, also Sharps' Toffee and packets-of-four Wrigley's chewing gum. Also on the ground floor were the bar, the billiard room and the reading room. Off the bar were the men's toilets. The women's toilets were at the other end, off the reading room. Wooden stairs led to a library and another reading room, also to a store room and a room often used for storing games equipment. There was another room where the food for big functions was prepared, and a verandah ran right round this floor, with wooden railings.

From the library a door opened on to a balcony overlooking the central dance-floor. At New Year's Eve dances, streamers and balloons would be thrown from there. A coir mat would be placed over a portion of the dance-floor when 'housie housie' and bridge evenings took place. Potato chips with tomato sauce would be carried round to each table by the bearers. The older children were allowed to join in all the games. There were also whist drives and the women had mah jong sessions on certain mornings.

I remember my mother rolling out endless amounts of pastry and filling them with curried mince for curry puffs; making trays and trays of shortbread; preparing sandwiches, mince pies etc. when she had been elected, by a committee of wives, to help with the catering for some big function. While all these drives, and other adult functions were in progress, the children would be left to their own devices outside.

In front of the Club was a old cannon (reminiscent of Kim's Zumzumar outside the Lahore Museum). This was usually our den for hide and seek. The vast grounds, with car and cycle sheds, the shop and various corners of the Club were ideal for this. There were also some outbuildings to the right of the Club entrance, which housed some servants, the Club stores and a bottling plant for sodas, lemonade and ice cream sodas. These bottles were much sought after when they broke, as they had a glass stopper excellent for marbles.

Christmas parties at the Club consisted of various athletic events for the families – the usual relay, flat and hurdle races. But beyond the perimeter hedge at the rear of the Club there was a *maidan* – a grassed, open area – up to the rail track that ran up to the factory. This space was used for hurdy-gurdys or tumbling boxes and roundabouts. However, the main attraction was a ride on the elephant – a docile, long-suffering creature, listening to the command of his *mahout*, humbly kneeling to let delighted kids climb up to the *howdah*.

I first went to school by *tonga*, which called for me and my two sisters, both older than myself, every morning, to take us some four miles, under a railway bridge. I was in the kindergarten, and both sisters were in the senior school. In the *tonga* I had to sit in front with the driver, who had a thin bamboo whip of knotted string. When performing, the horse's tail would go up, sometimes catching in parts of the *tonga*. In later years I used to cycle to school on a miniature Hercules cycle with inflated Dunlop tyres.

During the summer months we went very early to school – getting up when just light and finishing school at 1 p.m. Otherwise we remained until 4 p.m. When in the kindergarten I would have to walk across to the senior school for lunch. One of the verandahs outside the Standard 1 classroom had wooden benches and tables. The bearers brought our food on the cycles in tiffin-carriers – four tiers with charcoal in the bottom one. Our cook, Kunjilal, was most versatile in the culinary arts. We'd have potato chops, with vegetables; pancake rissoles, Irish and brown stews, but only occasionally curry with *chapattis* or rice. The flat potato cakes were my favourite.

Outside the barbed-wire fence of the school, vendors sold 'burra-ke-ball' – old ladies' hair, or, as we know it, candy floss. The vendor with brass bell would have a strap round his shoulder holding a modified paraffin tin with glass sides, in which was the fluffy pink stuff. Others sold 'armsuth', dried mango pulp like brown toffee. Others had Indian sweetmeats – 'tilly ludoos', sesame seeds in a toffee of brown sugar, 'chunna', from which Bombay mix is made, and many other tasty sweetmeats. Most of us were forbidden to buy these because of disease.

When waiting for the monsoons to break, the heat during the summer months was stifling. We had no fridges or air-conditioning. There was, however, an ice factory, where we could buy ice-blocks, covered in sawdust to preserve it. This could be used in insulated cooler boxes, or in ice cream pails for making ice cream. These pails were made of wood. The ice-cream mixture was in a cylindrical metal container which was gyrated in a quantity of ice. The handle to do this was geared to rotate the metal cylinder, which was on a bar fixed at the top of the wooden pail.

A form of air-conditioning was the use of *kus-kus tattis*. These were thick mats made of fibrous roots with a pleasant scent, fitted across the entrance of the front door. A perforated metal pipe, bunged at one end and fitted to a hosepipe the other, lay on the top, trickling water down the mat. Sometimes a table fan on the outside aided the flow of air. All other doors and windows would be closed and curtains drawn in efforts to keep cool. All rooms had ceiling fans which helped to circulate the cool air.

This method of air-conditioning was similar to keeping the compartments cool when travelling long distances by the five-feet-six-inch broad-gauge railways, which made a network across India. All shutters in the compartment would be closed, the two or three ceiling fans in protective wire cages would be on full blast, whilst in the centre of the compartment in a large metal container would be a huge block of ice ordered by telegram from the previous station. The telegraphic system was efficient.

With night temperatures up to 90 or 100 degrees Fahrenheit we would sleep outside. We had one set of beds outside and another set inside, in case it should rain. The *charpoys* – wooden frames strung with a net of rope or woven webbing – could be left overnight outside. Watching the stars, or cloud formations, at night, led to a kind of game. 'Look, that one is a face, with a hooked nose and double chin – looks like Mr So-and-so.' Those on the horizon could be mountains.

Sometimes we would hear the blood-curdling call of the jackals and see them stalking across the plain in the moonlight, or the hooting of owls or the 'tickt…tickt…churrah' of the nightjar. Or on a very bright moonlit night we occasionally heard the call of the 'did-you-do-it' plover. Termites had to be carefully considered. Nothing was left on the ground. The soles of slippers, newspapers, the covers of books, all could be taken in single night. Scorpions, or small krait snakes, could also cause concern.

With the coming of the monsoon, usually the beginning of July, there was change and relief. We kids would visit the *nullahs* or drains, on the other side of the main railtrack in the direction of Burn's Pottery, to see if we could find the small fish, said to be dropped by the clouds. We did find them, and scooped them up in butterfly nets. At this time of year, too, in sandy areas, would emerge from holes in the ground small sixpence-sized, bright red, velvet to the touch, 'lal-bootchies' or red spiders, all body with tiny legs. We collected them and kept them, with sand, in old, round cigarette tins.

There was no wireless for us in the early days of the 1930s, but we did have an HMV (His Master's Voice) wind-up gramophone. This would be taken out to picnics, to Pariate Tank, a huge reservoir a few miles out of town, or to one of the *jheels* or lakes, to entertain the women while the men were away shooting duck. A duck shoot often started before dawn, with 'guns' in place round the *jheel* to catch the first flight of the duck. The birds would be retrieved by men in their dugout canoes, which were normally used to plant and harvest 'singarahs' or water chestnuts.

Sometimes we would go in several cars to one of the government *dak* bungalows for the weekend. A popular one was Mandala. In the thick teak forests, away from the life of towns, it was wonderful to be walking, as silently as possible, behind my father, following up a red jungle fowl (father of the domestic chicken), or stalking a cheetah, or spotting deer; or listening, all quiet, for the rooting of a wild pig or for the cooing and whistle of a green pigeon in a fig tree. This as always held my attention. It is here that I felt as one with nature, raising one's thoughts to a higher plane.

Dak bungalows played an important part in our lives. Built in a more or less standard pattern, the Government had them dotted about the countryside for the convenience of travellers. They would be a square building with a bedroom either side of a central dining/drawing room, with bathrooms attached to the rear of the bedrooms. Basic furniture – wooden beds with four poles at the corners to support a frame for mosquito nets, and a dressing table. The bathroom would have a zinc tub in a recess in the cement floor. A wooden commode, a wooden table with enamel basin, water jug and soap dish. A short distance away would be the kitchen.

Once, when we arrived late at a *dak* bungalow, the *chowkidar* or caretaker, also the cook, was rather worried. 'Sahib,' he said, 'I have little food to cook for you – only some eggs which I can make you a curry.' This, with paratas, was one of the best curries I have ever tasted.

Another memorable meal, at Mandala *dak* bungalow, was a super stew that my father cooked from all the birds that had been shot. Green pigeon, a couple of ducks, a peafowl and the dove that I had shot myself with a pellet gun. This was a stew of all stews!

Moonlit nights were particularly attractive for a favourite circular drive through the jungle with a spotlight. After a hot, oppressive day it was a pleasurable respite to get away from it all in the cool of the night, with anxious anticipation for what the spotlight would reveal. 'Eyes! I see them! To the left of the big tree.' It could be a solitary *chinkara*, or four-horned antelope, a jackal, a *neilghai* or bluebull, or – sometimes – a tiger or leopard.

If one was lucky on these occasions, there were also ham sandwiches, a flask of coffee and a pail of ice cream. Bliss indeed! What else could one possibly wish for?

PAMELA HOPKINS

I was born in Jubbulpore in the United Provinces in 1932. My father was a junior Forest Officer in the Indian Forest Service (IFS). He had met and married my mother who had come out to India in the QAIMNS (Queen Alexandra's Institute of Military Nursing Sisters) to nurse at a military hospital in Secunderabad. My grandfather was in the ICS and my uncle was also in the Indian Forestry Service.

My first few years were spent in Jubbulpore until my father was transferred to Amraoti in the Central Provinces. His area was fairly extensive and, though we were based in Amraoti, most of the time my mother and I accompanied him on his tours. He travelled on foot – though I was carried by a forest guard for most of the time! Our belongings, plus cook and *ayah*, always preceded us in bullock carts. When we arrived at our camp the tent (enormous – like a marquee) would be ready, water for baths would be bubbling away in kerosene tins and the *khansama*, Louis, would have made us a meal. In time Government resthouses were built and then we managed the tours in relative comfort: my father eventually was able to buy a lorry – our only means of transport – so the journeys were quicker.

These were my earliest years – I was taught to read and write by my mother, but I was a very solitary child, so reading was a great pleasure.

After Amraoti we moved to a small hill station – Chikalda – used mainly by families escaping the hot weather on the plains. It was a small place but we had our first large bungalow and we were able to settle into a more permanent routine. I was able to have a pony which I remember riding fearlessly all over Chikalda, pursued by a panting *syce* who threatened to tell my father I would not just walk the pony as instructed but galloped it everywhere! There were lots of dogs by now and we always seemed to have an assortment of wild animals brought in by the locals who found them abandoned in the jungle. My father kept a small monkey, hated by us all but adored by him.

My time as a Forest Officer's daughter was immense fun: there was no schooling as such early on. I went now and then to the local convent and had 'lessons' with the French nuns. I recall very little of that, though I do still possess some of their beautifully embroidered linen. I had total freedom in Chikalda – I explored with my *ayah* or a *chaprassi* in the periods when I was the lone child. When the few other children arrived we explored together – we went on trips with my father to old colonial forts – to villages where panther or tigers were killing the cattle. We were even allowed to sit up with him over kills, though I do recall very vividly once sitting by a live offering – a bullock calf, a *boda* – and forcing my father to release it. Most live offerings were killed before my father was able to shoot the panther or tiger, and I was well aware of that fact, though I now understand why the life of one calf was less important than several heads of cattle to the local villagers.

Just before my seventh birthday we were transferred to Nagpur – civilisation! My father was made a Conservator of Forests so there was no more touring, living in tents, sitting up in *machans* over kills, no more Christmas Camps with visiting dignitaries, no more freedom to explore on my pony – no more pony, in fact, as he had to be left behind. However, life was good for me in Nagpur. We lived in a pleasant bungalow near the Club where there was a swimming pool. I knew several of the families who used to come up to Chikalda in the hot weather so I was able to continue my friendships with their children. There was a cinema, bazaars, a zoo, a lake where we kept a small sailing dinghy. We still had our dogs but Minnie, the monkey, had gone.

Proper schooling now loomed and I was sent to St Hilda's in Ootacamund. A most wonderful three-day journey there by train. Several children from Nagpur were accompanied by one parent and a bearer carrying our bedding rolls, food baskets and wash basins with leather covers. If we were lucky and missed the connection at Madras it meant an extra night, which we spent in the station waiting room. Exciting for us but, I dare say, a nightmare for the accompanying parent! From Madras we took the little hill train to Ooty and there to stay for two terms – just coming home for the Christmas holidays – except in 1942 when the Japanese invaded Singapore and we were hastily removed from school. Holidays spent at school were pleasant enough – Ooty had a lot to recommend it!

My parents were on UK leave in 1937 when my half-brother was left in boarding school. We were not able to leave India until 1947 to return to England in the grip of a very cold winter – rationing – a strange brother – a strange family, who thought we'd had it very easy in India during the War – no home and a mother who ended up her wartime years with a nervous breakdown. She had worked tirelessly with the Women's Voluntary Service and I had helped in the Junior Voluntary Service in the holidays, working on the Nagpur railway station with the soldiers going to and from Burma. Some terrible memories of the returning men.

PETER ROBB

I went through the Bihar earthquake, which occurred in 1934, possibly about a year after my father and family had sailed from Ceylon to take up the senior installation appointment at Budge Budge, some 15 miles south of Calcutta. In those days there was only one tarmacadamed road from the metropolis, as well as a well-used rail link.

In an earthquake you get an inkling that something atmospheric or climatic is about to happen. Either the earth goes unnaturally still, or animals stop barking or howling. Usually this occurs at the start of the monsoons. The morning of the earthquake there was this uneasy atmosphere about, and then there came the urgent tinkle of the telephone, from my father's office, with simple direct orders, which was to get everybody out of the house into the garden and stay there. The order from my father was relayed to my mother, and then to our cook, Abdul, so all of us went on to the front lawn, lying down with bodies spread-eagled, and each person positioned away from each other. The tremors were sickening, and felt rather like the up and down motion of tiny waves, with gusting, strengthening wind, raising all the dust from the dust-road which led from the offices to our home. The most worrying aspect was the effect on the River Hooghly and also of that on the tank farms, where leaks of petroleum products might occur. The river was made turbulent but the boats on it survived; the movements between our house (bungalow) and my father's office were conjectured to have swallowed up a goat and two kids, as well as the woman goatherd; they dropped into a fissure and were lost. It then closed inexorably. There was of course damage, but curiously none of it was serious, as most buildings survived. On his arrival in Bengal, my father had been made a District Magistrate (Voluntary 3rd class), and we did not see too much of him as he was out and about assessing and overseeing relief work. Inside our home pictures hung awry, the chandelier swayed and several things fell.

SHEILA WRIGHT-NEVILLE

Before we left India for home leave in England in 1935, my father was posted to a remote spot on the North West Frontier where wives and children were not considered to be safe. Since the posting was only for a few months, my mother and I went to stay with my mother's closest friend, Jean Finzel. Her husband, Hugh, owned a sugar-refining business in the state of Bihar. Their home at Pakri was surrounded by cane fields with a small-gauge railway looping through them. When the cane was cut it was piled on to flat cars drawn by a small steam engine with a shrill whistle, to be taken to the mill. The Finzels' son, Richard, and I were the same age and had become friends during several family meetings on holiday in Kashmir. Richard and I used to dare each other to jump over the rail lines in front of the engine, which brought gratifyingly loud curses from the engine-driver. I visited the mill where the sugar was produced and tasted the unrefined sticky brown sugar (*ghur*). Like the Indian children, we sucked the raw sugar juice out of cut pieces of cane. The Finzels' house was a show place: huge, with beautiful gardens, tennis courts and stables for the horses. But even surrounded by this luxury we still used the ever-present thunder-boxes. Pakri was a country place, but in India I never encountered indoor plumbing until living in Calcutta in the 1940s.

Our hosts led a lavish social life, with many dinner parties and fancy-dress dances. Tennis parties were held just as they were in England in the 1930s, with all the guests in white and tea, including tiny cucumber sandwiches and elaborate cakes, brought out into the

1934: Pakri in the State of Bihar. 'This was the home of the Finzel family, where my mother and I stayed for several months while Father was with his regiment in a North West Frontier post considered unsafe for women and children. When he returned, all three of us left for his six months' leave in England.' (Sheila Wright-Neville)

garden. While the ladies drank their tea the men drank something stronger. Jean Finzel was a fine horsewoman, and I have a photograph of her riding side-saddle. Hugh Finzel sold his business in 1936 and retired to England, where he bought an estate in Clavering village, near Saffron Walden in Essex.

above Travelling acrobats from the State of Nepal in front of the Finzels' house at Pakri. (Sheila Wright-Neville)

right 'Getting a ride (with the Mahout behind) on an elephant which was usually employed in the sugar-cane fields.' (Sheila Wright-Neville)

MICHAEL BRUCE

I was born in 1927 in Laheraserai, a district of Darbhanga in North Bihar, where my father was in the Indian Police. He had by great good fortune survived the Great War, as it was then called (many of his comrades didn't), winning an MC just a fortnight before the Armistice. He arrived in the Darbhanga District in 1924.

My mother had been a VAD nurse during that War, and was a fine player of the piano. Life in Bihar was frustrating for her, as the life of a piano, in those days before air-conditioning, was counted in months rather than years, voracious ants destroying the key pads and the woodwork.

One of my earliest memories is of the 1934 earthquake in Bihar, at Hazaribagh (the name means '1000 tigers', I believe). I remember the mango trees in the compound swaying about, and running barefoot – strictly forbidden, normally – into the compound from our Public Works Department (PWD) house. It was a very severe earthquake, more than 30,000 dead in a few minutes, and it would have been much more had it occurred at night.

Many stories arose around this earthquake. One was a message received, via the newly installed telegraph, by a Police officer from a point more than a hundred miles away over the flooded plain: 'Brother pursuing me with axe,' it said. 'Please advise.' Trained always to make an immediate, positive decision, the officer concerned, after due consideration, returned this decisive reply: 'Run as fast as you can. Coming Wednesday.'

Another was about a Police officer, doing his best with the chaos caused by the earthquake and surrounded by smoking ruins, being visited by a publicity-seeking politician from Calcutta, at least two hundred miles away. He came rushing up with a photographer, to ask, 'Oh my God, Sir, what has happened here?' To which the officer calmly replied, 'Well, Sir, we have this terrible problem here with mice.'

My father's war experience, in both Palestine and France, stood him in good stead when he arrived in Bihar to take up his appointment as a junior Police officer. He was given the following guidelines. Firstly, he would be almost useless for the first two years, until he had mastered the three languages most frequently used locally: Hindi, Urdu and Pushtu – the last-named for dealing with itinerant money-lenders from the North West Frontier – and, of course, the Sanskrit and Arabic scripts and usage of these languages on three levels: the cultured, the everyday and the bazaar. He was a linguist by nature, so this was no problem. Secondly, he should strictly follow these precepts: don't take money under the table (bribes); don't get involved with local women; don't get involved in local politics; always take a decision, on the spot and positive, and stick to it, particularly if it is a bad one; and, the most important one by far: keep your sense of humour!

The first guideline proved to be very true. Riots were usually communal – that is of a religious nature (Muslims vs Hindus). My father told me that his fluency in Hindi/Urdu came in handy on many occasions when, to defuse impending violence, he would stand on some raised platform (a table, perhaps), and bring forth a stream of naughty stories to set the crowd a-giggling, ending with, 'Oh yes, I forgot to say, there's a piece of paper here that says "Riot Act"... Now, you don't want to hear all that boring stuff, so why don't you go home – it must be mealtime.' If this had no effect, as a last resort he would ostentatiously bring forward the (usually) sole source of final persuasion: one military policeman, armed with a rifle.

In the late 1930s, having attained the rank of Superintendent and based in Patna, he sent a junior officer to Monghyr to investigate, and deal with if true, a report asserting that policemen on nightwatch were frequently asleep. This was indeed found to be true and was dealt with in the following manner: from every sleeper he removed one article of clothing or equipment – say, a boot, a belt or a *lathi* (standard issue stick) – and placed them on the desk of the sergeant in charge of the men. Result: an almost instantaneous solution to the problem, the uniform and other equipment being the most prized possessions of an Indian constable, and so to be guarded with the utmost care.

Our cook, Nabi, came from an aboriginal tribe from the jungles of South Bihar and as such he was black rather than brown. He was a natural genius as a cook, but my father, having taken him on as a servant in 1924, saw him develop from a scrawny supplicant seeking employment, with few family attachments, into a kind of bloated 'nabob' by the 1940s – he had his own establishment within our compound, several wives and many children and relatives, and he was lording it over the other servants. This included a very respectable Muslim *hajji* with a long beard, my father's most faithful aide over more than twenty years, who continued to write to him, through scribes in the bazaar, for years after my father retired, bitterly regretting the passing of the Raj. So Nabi had to go – and go he did, with his entire establishment, to be employed by incoming US communications troops, at two or three times the going rate for cooks at that time.

I clearly recall, on my first arrival in England at the age of six, at Tilbury, watching with astonishment the smoking chimneys, and asking whether the houses were all on fire. Communicating was a slight problem at first. While my mother had taught me to read English, talking was mainly done in Hindi with my *ayah*. So communicating with my granny was difficult.

Setting off on a tiger shoot in Bihar, mid-1930s. (Michael Bruce)

9

Bengal

The Presidency of Bengal was placed under a Lieutenant-Governor in 1854, although Government House in Calcutta dates from 1803. The Presidency reached its final size under the British in 1912. Its language was Bengali and, in 1936, 55 per cent of its population was Muslim and 43 per cent Hindu. Its capital was Calcutta, begun in the 1690s on the site of the village called Kalikata and sacred to Kali, the Goddess of Destruction and Retribution. There was a huge temple to her at Kalighat, and its river was the Hooghly.

Bengal stretched from its bay up into the foothills of the Himalayas to Darjeeling, 6800 feet high at the Railway Station, and the seat of the hot-weather Government. It was almost entirely agricultural, its special crop being jute, made from two plants native to Bengal. It was the sole world source, used for making ropes, sacking and other kinds of packaging. It had various uses in the world of shipping. There was some coal in Bengal, and tea was grown in the north, but rice was the main crop, grown on the huge alluvial plain, deltas of the Ganges and the Brahmaputra, where the monsoon never failed and where the principal problem was flooding.

Its railways were the Eastern Bengal Railway, with its terminus at Sealdah, in Calcutta, and the East Indian and Bengal Nagpur Railways, which left from Howrah.

ANONYMOUS

At the age of eight I left Burma and went to school in India, to St Joseph's College at North Point in Darjeeling. Darjeeling, now known throughout the world for its tea, was originally Dorjiling, 'Land of Thunderbolt', and in 1839 it belonged to the Rajah of Sikkim. A certain Colonel Lloyd, whose name endures in the Lloyd Botanical Garden, was appointed to sort out the deed of grant of land from the Rajah, but he mishandled it, advising the Government that it was a free gift. He omitted to say that a reciprocal gift was expected in return, and this, in fact, was never given. By the 1830s, sanatoria had been established at Simla, Landour, Mussoorie and Almora in the north, at Mahableshwar and Poona in the west, and at Ootacamund in the Nilgiris in the south. Darjeeling was recommended as a sanatorium, principally for British residents in Calcutta. In 1839 a team of Sappers and Miners, under a Lieutenant Gilmore, was sent to build a cart road up the hill. It was no more than a stony path, with a few huts as resting places on the way. Conditions for the labourers were so bad – they had no shelter either against the cold or the rain – that desertions were constant and the cost in lives and effort was great. Nevertheless, the work was completed within the year and it was a real engineering feat. The Eden Sanatorium, which is still there, was given the family name of the Governor-General of the time, Lord Auckland; and for many years the road above the cart road to Ghoom was called the Auckland Road.

The Darjeeling Railway, as it was originally called, which followed the cart road for much of the way, arrived in Darjeeling in 1881, another remarkable feat of engineering. It runs for 51 miles from Siliguri, in the plains, and is level for the first six miles. Then it begins to climb to Tindharia, at 19 miles and 2800 feet, by a series of zig-zags through cleverly designed reversing stations whereby the track rises 30 feet without forward travel. To reach Ghoom, at 47 miles and 7400 feet, it uses a number of loops to complete a circle and thus attain height in the shortest possible distance. There is one

above 'The Chunbatti loop on the Darjeeling Himalayan Railway was originally the third spiral, but such is the restless nature of the land that it has since become the first that is met by the up-train. The vegetation today does not allow it to be seen to full advantage, but this early photograph graphically shows the tortuous path that the train follows.' (From printed text accompanying photo, 1922)

right An engine of the Darjeeling Himalayan Railway.

below The great mountain of Kanchenjunga, seen across the cantonment of Katapahar, 7500 feet, above the town of Darjeeling. (Nicole Walby)

double loop which is sensational. From Ghoom the line runs down four miles to Darjeeling, 7100 feet high.

In 1922 the journey took five hours. One passed from tropical through temperate zones, through densely wooded forests and across valleys and ravines choked with luxuriant vegetation. Now and then there were glimpses of the plains below and then suddenly there is a panoramic view unrivalled in its grandeur. From Observatory Hill, Darjeeling, the view of Kanchenjunga presents the finest of its kind in the world. The peaks tower over the town and seem to annihilate the true distance, which is 45 miles.

The main schools at that time were St Paul's, for boys, and the Diocesan Girls' School, which were Church of England; the Loreto Convent and St Joseph's, which were Roman Catholic; and Mount Hermon, which was co-educational and Baptist. St Joseph's was founded by the Jesuits in 1888 and was run by them for about seventy years. It was then taken over by the Christian Brothers and its whole character changed.

It was called a college, rather than a school, because its tuition extended to the Intermediate Arts Examination of Calcutta University, covering the first two of the four years of study required for a Calcutta BA degree. A school only taught as far as Senior Cambridge exams, the equivalent of an English School Certificate in those days.

We had 20 Jesuit priests, four lay brothers and four lay male teachers Roman Catholics were given preference for admission, but there were non-Catholics in my class. The catchment area was chiefly Bengal – boys of European or Anglo-Indian parentage – but boys from other provinces, including Burma, were accepted. There were 20 boys from Burma in my time. The sons of nearby Rajahs and Maharajahs also went there.

I had two 'best' teachers. Father Bouvez, who was French, taught me at the ages of 13 and 14. He instilled in me an abiding love of history and nurtured in me what has proved to be a facility with languages. I have taken Latin, French, Hindi, Marathi, Gujerati, Sindhi, Russian and German in my stride. I owe him more than I can say. He gave us his all, quite unselfishly. As a Jesuit he had taken the vows of poverty, chastity and obedience, and owned nothing of his own, not even a watch or a fountain pen.

Father Laenen was Irish and he taught me at the ages of 15 and 16. He taught me what little English I know, to read, write and – especially – to speak it. He was fastidious about our diction and made us recite poetry. Both are buried in the North Point graveyard. RIP.

The Darjeeling school holidays lasted 10 weeks, from mid-December until the end of February, and then it was back to school in March for 42 weeks.

The family was now living in the British Military Hospital, Barrackpore, 17 miles north of Calcutta. My father was an assistant military surgeon. One day in February we went by train to Calcutta to renew my school kit at Hall and Anderson and Whiteway, Laidlaw, who were school outfitters. As a 'special treat' my sister and I were taken in the evening for a meal in Chinatown. The food was scrumptious and plentiful. The Chinese restaurant was welcoming. We were happy. Finally, ever so tired, we caught the last train home at midnight to Barrackpore.

The Indian Mutiny of 1857 began at Barrackpore. At the age of eight I was unaware of it. What I was aware of was the beautiful grounds of Government House, Barrackpore. They were open to the public. It was built in a curve of the Hooghly River to benefit from the evening breeze off the river. The Governor would spend time there to escape from the humidity of Calcutta.

The visit of the Prince of Wales to Calcutta in December 1922 was celebrated with a splendid fireworks display. We went to enjoy that. We saw nothing of the Prince; years later, I learned that there had been hostile demonstrations in Calcutta.

Back home, I remember learning to fly kites at the age of 11, and learning to ride my mother's bicycle by standing on the pedals – I was too small to sit on the saddle. And we watched our parents play tennis with friends. Soon it was time for school!

BLAKE PINNELL

My father, L.G. Pinnell, the son of a cabinet-maker, went to the City of London School. Having survived the First World War, he entered Balliol College, Oxford, with an open exhibition in classics. He decided to read modern history instead, because he felt that it was more relevant to real life, but he never obtained a degree; I suspect this was because he was anxious to start a career at a time when, as a demobilised Army officer, he had no particular qualifications. Evidently, the chance of joining the Indian Civil Service proved irresistible and so he sat the entrance exam, was accepted and arrived in India in 1920.

In the foreword to his privately published memoirs, *With the Sanction of the Government*, my father tells something of this process:

> I chose the title of the book for the following reason. As was the practice in those days, my father signed a 'Covenant' on entry to the Indian Civil Service. I have that Covenant with me: it is dated 26 October 1920, and countersigned by two members of the Council of India, Sahibzada Aflab Ahmed Khan and Sir Charles Arnold White. In paragraph 6, every new member of the Indian Civil Service covenanted with the Secretary of State –
>
> 'That he shall not at any time, directly or indirectly, ask, demand, accept, or receive any sum of money, or security for some money, or other valuable thing or service whatsoever, or any promise or engagement by way of present, gift or gratuity, from any person or persons with whom or on whose behalf he shall, on the part of the Government of India, have any dealings or transactions, business or concern whatsoever, or from any of the branches of the Government of India, he is or shall be restrained from demanding or receiving any sum of money or other valuable thing as a gift or present or under colour thereof.'

My father was mainly stationed in Bengal, and to begin with tended to live in remote areas of the country. In January 1924 he married my mother in Calcutta; she had come out to India for a visit from England. In the spring of 1925 they went back to England for home leave and I was born in a furnished house at St Leonard's-on-Sea on 28 August. My father had to return to India first, followed by my mother and me after Christmas, so India became my home when I was a few months old. For most of the next 18 years I lived in India, so that India, more than anywhere else, felt like home. However, within India we had no settled home, as my father was posted by the ICS from one place to another. In the first nine years of my life we lived at four or more widely separated places in Bengal: at Dacca, Calcutta, Rajshahi and Darjeeling. In Rajshahi my father was District Magistrate in 1930–32, and then Deputy Commissioner of Darjeeling in 1932–34.

The houses in which we lived were not our property, being government-owned or rented buildings, so my parents had no home that they could actually call their own. In the more remote districts our homes had no running water or electric light: water had to be fetched in kerosene tins from a well. Light was given by lamps which burnt kerosene. There were no electric fans, the air being kept cool by *punkahs*, which were like long pieces of carpet which were pulled to and fro while suspended from the ceiling. There were no hoovers and often no flush toilets.

All this meant that the household had to have servants for fetching and carrying, in addition to those who were employed in the kitchen and for cleaning and looking after the rooms; how many servants we had, I cannot remember, but home life would have been impossible without them, especially in the high Bengal temperatures.

My brother – born in Darjeeling in 1928 – and I kept fit in India and never had malaria or dysentery. We had an Indian nanny or *ayah* to look after us, as a result of which we did not see as much of our mother as a child would do in England. I remember practically nothing of our social life as young children, except that we were forbidden to go outside without wearing a solar *topee* or pith helmet. In Calcutta or Darjeeling there would have been plenty of other English families with children for us to play with, but in a remote provincial town there were perhaps only a handful of them, if any.

We must have learned to amuse ourselves. We did not go to school in India, but had an English governess who gave us lessons, no doubt with the emphasis on the three 'R's.

Martin and I talked in Hindustani to the Indian servants and probably spoke as much in that language as we did in English. No one gave us lessons in Hindustani: I suppose we learned it by listening. Whether what we said was strictly grammatical, I shall never know, but at least we communicated effectively. Later on, we learned that there was a brand of Hindustani known as 'Kitchen Hindi' which the *memsahib* or lady of the house used when speaking to her servants, and maybe we had picked up a bit of that.

MARTIN PINNELL

As my father tells in his book, he was at one stage in his career sent on assignment away from Government service, to act as Chief Manager of the Dacca Nawab Estate: he was working for the estates, and paid out of the income of the estates. At the end of his assignment, and before his return to Government service, an event occurred which caused him to write to the Commissioner of the Dacca Division:

Sir,

I have the honour to report that I was presented on 29th March by Nawab K. Habibullah and the proprietors of the 'BE' fund of the Dacca Nawab Estate with a gold cigarette case stated to be valued at not more than 300/- (Rupees three hundred).

In accordance with the Government Servants' Conduct rules I have the honour to report the facts for the orders of Government as to the disposal of the gift.

I have the honour to be, Sir, your most obedient servant, (signed) L.G. Pinnell Chief Manager

I have the memorandum, dated 18 April 1929, from the Under-Secretary to the Government of Bengal to the Commissioner of the Dacca Division:

Sir,

I am directed to say that the Government are pleased to permit Mr L.G. Pinnell, I.C.S., Chief Manager of the Dacca Nawab Estate, to retain the gold cigarette case presented to him by the proprietors of the B.E. fund of the Dacca Nawab Estate.

I am etc. H. Tufnell-Barrett Under Secy. to the Government of Bengal

I have the cigarette case; it has my father's initials on the outside, while inside are the words:

PRESENTED
WITH THE SANCTION OF GOVERNMENT
By NAWAB KWAJA HABIBULLA OF DACCA
AND THE HEIRS OF THE LATE
NAWAB SIR AHANSULLA BAHADUR G.C.S.I., K.C.I.E.
April 1929.

BLAKE PINNELL

One of my earliest memories is of the Bihar earthquake of 1934: we had been living in a camp in the Terai (the flat country in Bengal immediately south of the Himalayas) for a few months, when suddenly the ground shook and it became impossible to stand up. The violence of the earthquake destroyed or badly damaged many buildings in Darjeeling, including our own house, and we were fortunate not to have been there at the time. My own special loss was a record which I was playing on a child's gramophone at the moment when the earthquake happened. I remember that it had been playing a song called 'Forty-seven ginger-headed sailors', but the record was ruined by the vibrations. My father, of course, dashed off by car to Darjeeling to inspect the damage: in those days he drove a Baby Austin so as to cope with the ups and downs of the winding roads.

MARTIN PINNELL

I myself directly only remember a few things before leaving India at the age of nearly five. One of them was the Bihar earthquake of 1934: my father, as Deputy Commissioner of the Darjeeling district, was in camp in the plains below Darjeeling, at a place called Bagdogra – it was then undeveloped land on which one could pitch a dozen large Army tents to provide both office space for my father and for the District Inspector of Police, as well as living quarters for the two families, but it is now the site for both a military air base and a civil airport. One sunny day, my brother and I were out in the open playing with a toy gramophone, and I was playing my favourite record called 'The March of the Toy Tin Soldiers', when the needle suddenly slid across the record, scratching it severely. I don't remember any shaking of the ground: while the epicentre was a few hundred miles away, and some severe damage was done to houses in Darjeeling (including our family home), I only remember damaging my favourite record.

BLAKE PINNELL

My brother and I came home to England with my mother in 1934, and in 1936 we were put in a boarding school named Hurst Court, at Ore near Hastings. My mother then went back to India, so we spent our holidays with other children at various holiday homes: one at Shamley Green near Guildford and another near Farnborough.

The holiday homes were happy enough, and their use was un-avoidable, bearing in mind that it was not possible in those days to fly home to India for the school holidays; but I remember, in retro-spect, that it was another instance of a lack of a settled family home life which affected too many of the youngsters.

Having been fit in India, it was at Farnborough in 1937 that I became seriously ill. A severe pain in my knee led me to be taken to hospital where an operation was performed and I was encased in plaster from the waist down. The expected recovery was slow to materialise, so my mother came back to England by sea, my father following soon after by air. Fortunately a new drug had been developed; the drug was not yet on the market, but it was obtained for me and apparently saved my life.

My father had to return to India in 1938, but my mother stayed on to look after me during many months of recuperation: we lived in rented houses on the coast at Bexhill. I was initially in a wheelchair, but eventually learned to walk again; my morale was gradually restored, but I could not yet go back to school, so went to a tutor in Bexhill instead.

It was in August 1939 that my mother took me back to Calcutta to convalesce, leaving my brother at school in England: we arrived by boat in Bombay by chance on the day that war was declared.

In 1937–40 my father was Private Secretary to the Governor of Bengal, so we lived in Calcutta and Darjeeling. My brother had been left at school in England, but came out by ship in 1940 with three hundred other children.

My education continued firstly with a tutor at St Joseph's, the Jesuit College in Darjeeling; secondly with a brief spell at St Paul's School in Darjeeling; and then we shared a teacher with two or three other boys in Calcutta. But in 1940 a special school (The New School) was started in Calcutta and Darjeeling for the benefit of English children in Bengal.

STAR STAUNTON

My first recollection of life outside Lahore is of a Christmas journey on which Papa took me six months or so before I was packed off to do my first stint with the nuns in Paris.

Our hosts on this occasion were Professor and Mrs Roerich, who were in Darjeeling in the grand manner, sharing an elegant palace with their sons and daughter-in-law. I formed a mistaken impression of them then and kept it uncorrected until I began to ponder my childish memories and check them in the light of information available to me now. They told harrowing stories about the persecution of Jews in Russia, where they had previously lived, and about wicked atrocities suffered by their less fortunate relatives and friends. The word 'pogrom' in particular remained embedded in my memory, and I grew up with the notion of them fleeing by night before cruel and bloody Muscovites eager to do them harm. I thought they must have been very smart to bring away with them enough money to live in such luxury as they did.

Of course, I was quite wrong, and it interests me now to observe that an idea planted in one's mind in infancy like a seed can take on a life of its own and become quite a tree of fantasy. Professor Roerich, had I but known it, came of a very ancient Russian family and at the time I was his guest was already world famous as an archaeologist, artist, scientist and labourer for peace on earth. He had been head of two important art institutions under the Tsars and in association with the Russian impressario Diaghilev created the decor for a whole constellation of famous ballets including *The Rite of Spring* and the 'Polovtsian Dances' in *Prince Igor*. In America after the Bolshevik revolution he had vastly increased his reputation as a painter and founded many groups which later took the name of Roerich Societies, proclaiming his ideals of 'Peace, Beauty and Knowledge'. Then in 1923, when I was just one year old, he had come to India heading a three-year artistic/scientific expedition that had journeyed as far afield as Tibet, Mongolia, China, Turkestan, Altai and other remote places in central Asia, and by the time of our visit he had returned to India to settle there permanently. He was a man very highly thought of by Indians of all kinds. He may not, for all I know, have been *persona grata* with the Communist rulers of Russia, though they honoured him later on, but a refugee from anti-Semitic pogroms he certainly was not.

From my childhood visits to their house I remember not its architecture nor the wide views its windows commanded over the hills of the Himalayas, but the large, free-standing, wood-burning stoves. They must have been twice as tall as I and generated a glorious heat.

There were other house-guests at the time, a German and two English climbers who were planning, with the Professor's financial backing, to make an ascent of Mount Everest. The billiard room of the house must have been their operations room. I was allowed to clamber up on to the table and inspect at close quarters a huge clay model of the Everest range, with little flags and coloured pins to mark routes and camp sites. On smaller tables and benches, in fact on any available space in the room, were piled books, newspaper cuttings, sketches, maps and lists, which I was not allowed on any account to disturb as I wandered about, half-hearing the climbers' voluble and often heated discussions of the projected assault.

For this particular visit, however, a less ambitious expedition was in prospect, namely a journey in the dark on ponies to see the dawn of Christmas Day over Mount Everest from the top of a nearby prominence called Tiger Hill. This was the treat my father had planned for me to celebrate the fifth Christmas of my life in 1927.

So at four o'clock on Christmas morning, the land still bathed in moonlight, we mounted our ponies to begin the ascent. The early start was necessary as only at dawn would the mountain reveal itself in all its glory. Shortly after full light the atmosphere would thicken and cloud it in mist.

At the top of Tiger Hill we dismounted at the foot of a tower, similar in shape to a lighthouse, and climbed a steep internal spiral staircase, at the top of which we stepped out on to a railed balcony, the place of all places from which to see the coming spectacle. The silence was eerie. All eyes were focused on the starlit darkness before us as with bated breath we waited. Sagarmatha in Nepalese, meaning Head of the Earth; Cholmolung in Tibetan, meaning Mother of the Snows – Mount Everest was to show herself!

I wish I could continue, as I imagine what followed: dawn fingering the sky and mingling with that fading moonlight that still glints on the deodars below us. Slowly the spectral peaks becoming visible, towering high above us and piercing the very constellations. The dawn light stealing over the virgin snow. The mountains coming awake! Winds whispering in the deodars, breaking the unearthly silence that had prevailed till then. Then in one area of the sky appears a halo of light, which spreads and brightens, and in the midst, thrusting aside the veil of light, rises Everest, head and shoulders above her sisters. And so on!

Alas! I have culled all that from memories of books written by people who in their time have climbed that tower on Tiger Hill and been smitten by one of the most amazing spectacles the earth affords. I remember climbing the tower and coming out on top, and nothing more. Sleep must have overcome me. Descending the stairs, breakfasting somewhere near, remounting my pony and returning to my bed in the Roerich house – all has gone from me. Of the Head of the Earth and Mother of the Snows I have from that occasion no recollection at all.

What does that matter? I saw much of those mountains in the course of my childhood; later on, when I was nursing my newborn son Andrew in sight of them, I even tried to paint them. The picture hangs on the wall beside me at this moment. I found it among my husband's things after he died, and it moves me that he should have kept it all these years without my knowing.

For a few Christmases thereafter came Christmas presents from Professor and Mrs Roerich, which, of course, I acknowledged politely on each occasion. They were wonderful presents even to me, who at that time received so many. One was a 12-piece china doll's tea-set beautifully decorated with a floral design, another a toy sewing machine that actually worked. Our verandah tailor was highly amused by this object, and taught me how to use it. With him to guide me I spent many hours making dolls' clothes and have ever since been as nimble with the needle as the next woman. Wonderful presents indeed: the Roerichs certainly did things with style.

SHIRLEY ODLING

As children we lived in Kalimpong from 1926 to 1936 – 5000 feet up in the Himalayas in north east Bengal. Our parents had 17 gardeners and 9 indoor servants, including 2 *ayahs*. During bathtime all our clothes were thrown on the floor and picked up by the *ayah*, and were taken to the *dhobi* and returned next day, washed and ironed. Bath water was left in the bath and dealt with by servants. When I went to boarding school in England aged 10, I was hauled over the coals for leaving my clothes in the corner of the communal bathroom and

above The main school buildings of Dr Graham's Homes, Kalimpong, with the Memorial Chapel above. (Shirley Odling)

right 'The School, Kalimpong', June 1936. Back row, left–right: Miss Fern, Miss Kelly; middle row, left–right: David Coffey, 'Hari', Susan Burder; front row, left–right: Kathleen Killy, William Grice (four-and-half), Shirley Odling, John Murray, Timothy Tucker. 'David Coffey and Shirley Odling are both grandchildren of Dr Graham, founder of the Kalimpong Homes.' (Jane Grice)

for leaving the water in the bath: the next occupant was not amused. At the end of term, I used to pack my hot water bottle with the water in it, as I had never even emptied a hot water bottle.

In Kalimpong as children we went barefoot all the time – we didn't own any shoes – if there was an infrequent visit to Calcutta we had to have shoes, which we would discard pretty quickly on account of blisters, and would carry for the rest of the day.

My two sisters and I used to ride three miles to school at Dr Graham's Homes every day (in bare feet). The *syces* would wait at the Homes all day with the horses until we were ready to ride home at teatime. Besides us three girls, we had three boy cousins all living in the same house in Kalimpong, and we were a daunting gang for much better-behaved Calcutta children who came to stay in ones and twos in the hot weather. They wore hats and were pale, and we weren't very nice to many of them. One poor girl we pushed into a field of cows because we knew she was frightened of them – her sister helped us do it. One rather fat boy aged about six came to stay with a new bicycle – we had never seen a bicycle. I don't think he even got to ride it while he was staying with us: we took it over. Some of them must have hated us, and I am still full of remorse after sixty years. But the children who were a match to the gang were so admired. I suppose this is normal childish behaviour, but in rather more rugged surroundings with not a huge amount of white adult supervision.

I think it takes a lifetime to rub off the slightly rough edges to such a different, brilliant and happy colonial childhood. I have found it interesting that, of all the people I've met in my life since those days, the ones I have a particular affinity with are the people who lived their childhood abroad, either in Australia, New Zealand, South Africa or anywhere east of Suez. Maybe, as someone once said, they were 'British, but with the elastic gone'.

In 1944, aged 18, I returned to India (I had not seen my parents for five years) as a FANY and was stationed in Calcutta. One job was decoding newspapers from men dropped behind Japanese lines in Burma – SOE Calcutta in the War was so different to before the War, with thousands of troops milling about – Navy, Army and Air Force, with very few amenities – Kalimpong was a godsend, not only for me, but for hundreds of troops who went there for their leave.

I returned to India 47 years later – what a change I found. Perhaps one shouldn't go back after such a long break. The contrast is too stark.

Just another thought. It may seem strange to people in England, but as children in Kalimpong we went to everyone's funeral, and were very disappointed if we weren't able to go. It was a village and we knew everyone. The local people had processions through the bazaars which we joined in whether it was Buddhist, Hindu or whatever. Perhaps the Eastern attitude to death was so natural, and it must have had some effect on us.

JOHN BLANDY

I was born in 1927 in Calcutta, when my father was Collector in Barisal. I was delivered in a nursing home by Lieutenant Colonel Peter Gow, of the Indian Medical Service, who subsequently became my godfather.

On my father's side there were no roots in India: he was youngest of a family of 13, the son of a civil engineer. My father's background was in classics at Clifton and Balliol, where he read Sanskrit, and so it was natural to think of going to India. Many years later, when I asked him why he went out to India, he told me that it was for the adventure, and I think this was the truth. He was a natural sportsman and excelled in all ball games, he read voraciously and was, I think, a true romantic.

About 1914 he fell in love with the elder daughter of a Bengal jute merchant: she died of cholera within a year. After about five years he met her younger sister, then nursing in Calcutta, who in time became my mother. Her family had Indian connections going back to 1836 when her grandfather enlisted in the Bengal Army of the East India

Company: my maternal grandfather and my mother were born in Bengal. Her family had roots in India going back to the 1850s.

David Marshall, a carpet-weaver in Glasgow (I think), married Rebecca Shields. They had two sons, David Shields Marshall (b. 22 October 1827) and William Shields Marshall (b. 17 July 1830). These two brothers both went out to India and ended up marrying two sisters, Jane and Elizabeth Newbold, in 1858 and 1860 respectively.

David Shields Marshall, who was my great-grandfather, joined the Bengal Army of HEICS (Honourable East India Company Service) in 1852 and rose to the rank of Second-Class Permanent Conductor. He was transferred from Ferozepore to the Agra Magazine on 23 January 1868. My Uncle Bill use to tell me stories of him and how he showed him (Bill would be his grandson) his *tulwar* (Indian sabre) wound, and how he had fought at Chillianwallah when the elephants ran away. (I have no idea whether this was fact or fantasy.) He certainly served throughout the Mutiny.

I have before me as I write the draft of a rather sad supplication:

To Lieut Colonel A Walker, Superintendent,
  Small Arms Ammunition Factory, Dum Dum

This humble memorial of Hony Lieut and Assistant Commissary David Marshall, Head overseer, Store Department, Small Arms Ammunition Factory, Dum Dum.
Respectfully sheweth

That in accordance with para 8 of GGO No 514 of 1881 and OO No 13334E of the 19th Instant, he has been placed on the retired list, having served 36 years and 6 months, not including the boon of 2 years granted by GGO No 883 of 1859.

After a service of 35 years and 8 months he was promoted to be a first-class Warrant Officer. This position he only enjoyed for a period of 10 months, as a rule his predecessors, much to his detriment in way of promotion, enjoyed the position and pay of 1st class warrant officers for periods of from ten to fifteen years until the publication of GGO No 514 of 1881. Your memorialist always expected to reach the reward of his long and faithful service viz. the enjoyment for a term of years of the pay of a 1st class Warrant Officer and when no longer fit for duty that he could be retired on the highest pension that he could attain to which was that of a Deputy Commissary of Ordnance.

When a young lad he enlisted on the Streets of Glasgow for an unlimited period of Service. No man can give more than all the days of his appointed time upon earth to any Service. This he did and has kept his engagement. Starting in life, it was either an Indian Grave or a good pension. Having escaped death, he craves from the great liberal and just Indian Government the pension of a Deputy Commissary of Ordnance viz £216 per annum.

Two Warrant Officers about to be promoted to Deputy Commissary are about from 8 to 12 years junior to your memorialist, therefore they will be entitled to the highest pay and may enjoy the highest pay for a number of years.

Your memorialist craves most humbly that his case may be taken into consideration and be submitted to the Inspector General of Ordnance for favourable consideration and orders of Government with any such recommendation as his case may deem deserving of.

And your memorialist shall ever pray.

In the event, David Shields Marshall did get his pension and was able to retire to Glasgow, where he died on 4 May 1909. He had four sons and one daughter. The second son, David Edwin Marshall (b. 15 February 1869), married Mary Kathleen (Minnie) Lucas, daughter of Harry Lucas, a Hooghly pilot. Minnie, my grandmother, died in 1895 aged 22, shortly after giving birth to my mother, Dorothy Kathleen Marshall in Bera, Bengal, 21 August 1895.

In those days *jutewallahs* were rather towards the lower end of the social scale in Bengal, and my father's family, who were terribly 'Berkshire county', must have made my mother feel uncomfortable and done their best to put her down, especially since my father had married his deceased wife's sister – if his 12 siblings could not make him feel bad on the score of snobbery then they could try on the grounds of sin. You can imagine how riled the survivors were when she ultimately became entitled to be called 'Lady'!

I have one vivid memory, my first and almost my last of India in my first *avatar*. I would have been three and we were living in Darjeeling, and I recall riding in the Chowrasta in a saddle with a ring round it.

I think this is probably my first memory, and try as I can I remember nothing else of India in those days.

At the age of 5 my mother brought my sister Helen and me home on the *Modasa*. I have three images from that voyage: the first when I was in the bath and naughtily put my soapy foot between the side of the bath and the bulkhead. Engineers were summoned; I was very frightened, but in the end someone had the wit to use a simple manoeuvre and got me unstuck. The second memory is of being woken up at night and taken up on deck all sleepy to see Stromboli erupting. I can still remember it: the whole sky a brilliant red. The third image is of watching the crew doing a fire drill. One of the sailors put on a special kind of breathing apparatus that resembled an old-fashioned conical knight's helmet. It terrified me, and the frightful thing returned in my nightmares for years.

My sister and I were taken to a holiday home in Titchfield that was run by Canon and Mrs Morley. The vicarage is still there, beside a beautiful old church containing some tombs of the Wriothesleys, Earls of Southampton (in whose family Shakespeare served for a time to learn manners). Every Sunday the children went to church, and I can still remember how boring it all was, and how very frightened I was of the dead Wriothesleys. But I suppose the cadences of Tindall and Cranmer seeped in by a kind of osmosis. (How are the children of today ever to know good English prose?)

We were taught to read and write by a governess called Merry, who had the knack of making learning a delightful game. The parents of all the other children were in India or Africa in one or other of the services, and we grew up believing that this was entirely normal. I do not recall pining for either parent at this stage: I suppose I had seen little of either of them in India where we were looked after by *ayahs*. We wrote dutifully every week, and I can remember addressing letters to my father as 'Commissioner in Chittagong', thinking that it was tremendously important until corrected by a chum whose father was a 'Magistrate in Alipore', being assured that this was far more eminent. Maybe it was.

Looking back on those times, I think that the vicarage at Titchfield was well run. I cannot recall any cruelty or bullying. The canon himself was rather remote – but fathers were in those days. I do not recall him ever beating any of the children. It was really nothing like 'Baa-Baa Black Sheep'. My sister Helen was less happy: she was two years older and more sensitive than me. Helen hated cabbage, but was forced to eat it all up. However, she was allowed to borrow books from the Morley's library and got through everything Zane Grey ever wrote and all of Rafael Sabatini. However, I think Helen's unhappiness was probably quite serious, and was noticed by our Aunt Kitty (wife of my father's elder brother Lyster Blandy), and Kitty's report to India led in due time to therapeutic Christmases with the Harmsworths, and, in time, to our eventual liberation from the vicarage.

At the age of six I was sent to Edinburgh House, a prep school in Lee-on-Solent, and after a few trial weeks was left there as a boarder. On being abandoned by my mother I spent the first two or three hours crying in a cupboard, but having attracted sufficient attention and chocolate, recovered swiftly and thoroughly enjoyed the next six years. It was a very good school. Most of the boys were boarders: like me, their fathers were overseas, mostly in the Navy. As a result, it was common for a father's ship to be in Portsmouth and we were taken round as a treat. In this way I went over HMS *Warspite* three times, as well as *Hood*, *Nelson* and several submarines which determined me to be a submariner rather than an engine-driver.

My mother would come back for a brief leave every 18 months or so and embarrass me at the school sports. (In those days any parent, especially a rather striking and beautiful one, was a source of profound shame.) Twice my father came home for his leave, but in order to avoid paying income tax these holidays were spent in France or Belgium. He took us round endless *chateaux* and cathedrals, and held my sister and I spellbound by his charm and his endless stories. How I wish I had known him better.

In the holidays we were returned to the Morleys', until in 1936 my parents bought a small house in Lee-on-Solent and, acting on the advice of dear Aunt Kitty, we were liberated from the Morleys' and allowed to stay at home in the holidays, to be looked after by the 'maid' – Jacqueline – when my mother was out in India.

Looking back on those days I recall them as being very happy times. Jacqui was an extraordinary young woman: always unruffled and exceedingly kind. She had a devoted boyfriend, Arthur, who became my hero. He could make pea-shooters out of elderberry twigs, and told wonderful stories about the Navy, in which he subsequently served with considerable distinction a few years later. Lee-on-Solent was full of schoolfriends, so that we children were always in each others' houses and cared for very well, if unobtrusively.

The school itself was very happy and well run. It is customary to describe preparatory schools of those days as being hotbeds of buggery and beating. Our dormitory of four boys had been taking part on a hot summer's evening in a particularly bumpy pillow fight, forgetting that the headmaster's drawing room was beneath us, and ignorant that he was entertaining grown-ups. Justice was swift and condign – a single stroke of the cane – and it was never repeated. I remember all of the masters with great affection. With the wisdom of hindsight I do not think any of them were pederasts, and had there been any abuse someone must have mentioned it, and they did not.

ANN BURKINSHAW

My father went to Calcutta in 1921 aged 21. He joined Jessop & Co., which was the agent for Edgar Allen & Co. in Sheffield, where he had been apprenticed as a mechanical engineer. My mother was born in Murree in the Punjab in 1896 into an Army family. In 1914, she and her elder sister worked their passages to England, where they trained as nurses. My mother joined the Territorial Army Nursing Service and was posted to Egypt and Palestine. After the War she returned to India and joined the Lady Minto Nursing Service, and was posted to Calcutta. She met my father in Darjeeling and they married in Calcutta in 1927. My arrival on Boxing Day, 1928 was not popular with the doctor, Dr Brandon, as he had to miss the 2.30p.m. races!

Our first home was in Sunny Park Road in Ballygunge, but we moved to Alipore when I was about five. We lived in the downstairs flat of a two-storey, square-shaped house common in Calcutta. The compound was not large but encompassed a tennis court, garages and servants' quarters. At the gate was a small gatehouse for the *mali*. Before the War I remember a calling-card box at the entrance: I remember going with my mother to drop cards on one or two occasions. Flowers thrived in the garden: hollyhocks, dahlias, cosmos, cornflowers, salvia, sweet peas and above all cannas, which still bring Calcutta alive for me.

Our servants are vivid in my memory: my *ayah*, the bearer, who was an Ooriya from Bihar, the *khitmagar*, who was a Mohammedan, the *bovachi*, the *mali* and the sweeper. They all showed such loyalty and devotion without really asking much in return. We only knew

'Ayah and me in our garden, 7/2 Burdwan Road, Alipore. My *ayah* was Nepalese: we never knew her name, age or marital status, as she would never talk about her private life. She did not live in our compound, but, I think, in a "basti" nearby.' (Ann Burkinshaw)

about their families if someone was ill. Once a year each one went to his or her *mulluk*, their own village. They all humoured me shamefully, and there must have been times when they could cheerfully have murdered me! No one could have shown more devotion than my *ayah*, a diminutive, shy, stoical woman of unknown age from Nepal. Her patience with me was unbounded: I made her learn everything I was learning – the alphabet, sums, 'geogafy' (*sic*) and dancing. Only once did she complain to my mother: 'Memsahib, step-together-step-hop *curriga*, cartwheel, nay *curriga*!' She played games with me, took me to the park to play and slept by my bedside on the floor if my parents went out for the evening (the bearer would sleep on a mat in the hall outside my door). When I left to go to school in England in 1936 she gave me a silver-backed hairbrush with 'Ann' engraved on it, which must have cost her a small fortune. To my shame, the gift embarrassed me until I reached a more reasoning age. Although my mother had not asked her to join us again (she thought I would get impossibly spoilt) she was in the line-up of the servants who greeted me back in 1939! No one had the heart to send her away, and she stayed with me until she died when I was 14. She did not live on the premises, we did not know if she was married and had children, and I am not sure that we knew where she lived.

'My fifth birthday party, December 1933, in our garden, 7/2 Burdwan Road, Alipore. Our bearer (tall one, centre) was an Ooriya from Bihar. Taken by my father.' (Ann Burkinshaw)

My childhood days until 1936 I remember as joyous, exciting and full of incident (such as trying to cycle down the outside spiral staircase on my tricycle, and falling out of the car as my mother was driving into town).

I visited the New Market with its myriad vendors and big shops, like Whiteway, Laidlaw, Hall and Anderson and the Army and Navy Stores (which had a lovely toy department) and Thackers, Spink to buy books was always a highlight in my life. I went swimming at the Swimming Club next to Writers Buildings in the afternoons and my father joined us after work for his exercise. I also remember learning to ride my first bicycle and to play tennis in our compound; Saturday morning treats accompanying my father on his weekly inspection of the works in Dum Dum; late afternoon drives to the lakes just outside Calcutta and going with my mother to join Father after his round of golf at the Royal Calcutta Golf Club (where the club sandwiches were out of this world): such events were magic to me. Not so exciting was the annual visit of the corporation smallpox vaccinator, who petrified me. I would hide in the farthest corner of the flat, and when dragged back to him he would always say, 'Ebry year I come and ebry year you cry'! Likewise, visits to the dentist did not rate high in my enjoyment stakes and were a nightmare for my mother. I liked visiting Dr Brandon, but then he never did anything that hurt me!

Then there were visits to the hills in the hot weather. Darjeeling was our nearest hill station, but on one occasion only Mother and I went to Mussoorie to visit her mother and family. I still get a *frisson* when I recall the journey to Darjeeling. The train left Sealdah station in the evening: I remember battling through the crowds, keeping the *coolie* with our luggage in sight, the bearer making up our bunks, waving Father goodbye and settling down for the night – all exciting stuff for a child. Daybreak next morning heralded our arrival at Siliguri, with *coolies* fighting to take our luggage and then the search for a taxi. I think when I was very young my mother preferred two or three hours in a car rather than a whole day on the little train. The latter was an experience for later years. I was always fascinated by the hotel in Darjeeling, which was near the Chowrasta. There was a row of rooms – single storey and each room was divided into two: the front half was a sitting-cum-dining area like a railway compartment (Indian style), and the back half was the bedroom. Meals were served in your sitting room. I do not think there was a great deal to do in Darjeeling for children except going on pony rides and visits to the Botanical Gardens, where fortune tellers pestered us. But I do not remember ever being bored: maybe my mother was!

A major Calcutta joy for me was Peggy Godden's School of Dancing. I suppose I must have started going to dancing classes when I was four or five, about 1932–33, and I think that all of us would-be dancers, from three to twenty years old, worshipped Peggy (alias Rumer) Godden. The classes took place in a ground-floor room of a flat in the usual type of house with an upstairs and downstairs flat. Doors opened out on to the garden. My memory tells me the back of the room was rather dark: a lady – her name may have been Miss Muriel Cann – played the piano. Phyllis Bourillon, a lovely, plump, jolly person, used to illustrate the steps for us and help us to do them. We learned 'step-together-step-hop' and other basic steps for the very young, and then progressed to cartwheels, back-bends and gymnastic movements as well as the basic ballet steps when we were a bit older. I was there until I was seven or eight. The mothers sat round the edge of the room as far as I remember, watching their budding offspring.

The classes took place once a week. Ours, of course, was only one of many that Peggy Godden took. She taught from the very young to young adolescents, and the junior classes were mixed, boys and girls.

There was great excitement among us young dancers when we heard that Peggy Godden was to be married. Our class happened to take place on the very day, at the very time, that she walked up the aisle of St Paul's Cathedral in Calcutta. Phyllis Bourillon was in charge of us and had been given strict instructions that her pupils were not to attend the wedding. Our class began, but very soon

Phyllis could contain herself no longer. Her appeal to our mothers was successful and we all went off to the cathedral.

We were all seated in side pews facing the aisle – agog. I can see Peggy now, begin walking up the aisle and her look of horror, but I think amusement too, as she sighted her diminutive pupils gazing at her. And then, I think, we went back and finished our class! After Peggy was married, her sister Jon took over the dancing school and she was followed by their youngest sister, Rose.

The highlight – for us dancers – of each cold weather was the dancing show Peggy put on at the Empire, usually a cinema. The thrill of being on stage, backstage, and being dressed up was almost unbearable. One year, however, Peggy had, I think, broken her leg and had to direct operations from the side of the stage. I can see her all in white on her bed and feel the apprehension I had for her survival!

My schooling from the age of about five to seven was with an excellent lady called Miss Martin. To start with I joined one or two children in someone else's house for her lessons, but then she came to ours. She taught me alone for quite a time and then another child joined me. Lessons were in the garden in the cold weather and on the verandah in the hot weather. She gave me such a good grounding that I was ahead in the three 'R's when I went to my prep school in England.

My father had two leaves before I was eight. I remember little of either except a stay in a small hotel in Worthing where the seaweed smelt to high heaven. I do remember the voyages on the City Line ships which plied between Calcutta and Tilbury. I spent a great deal of my time when it was not rough in the 'box pani', my term for the canvas pool that was erected on one of the decks. It was very deep and therefore very exciting. Father Neptune always came aboard at some point during a children's party (my mother was very disappointed when I said I had seen him in the dining room!). The stewardess tending our cabin always had a busy time when it was rough: my mother was a terrible sailor and had to take to her bed, and I then had to be watched like a hawk. The voyage to England took six weeks. My father, not being very well-off in those days, chose this route because, receiving no leave pay, he had to find the cheapest way of spending his six months' leave. Three months of it were spent on the sea for a very reasonable price.

A vivid memory from the second of these voyages – on the return journey – was of the cyclone that hit us when the ship was just outside Madras harbour. We were buffeted back and forth – apparently the ship rolled over on each side as far as it could go, hovered whilst everyone on board held their breath, and then slowly came up again. I remember the noise of crockery and furniture crashing about and the weird atmosphere when one eventually emerged out of one's cabin.

We had spent that leave largely scouring the south coast of England for a suitable place to find a school, and I started at a prep school in Bexhill in 1936, when I was seven. My mother stayed with me for one term before returning to Calcutta, but I was perfectly happy being left and never remember feeling homesick, unfeeling

'The "box pani" – what I, as a child, called the swimming pool aboard a City Line boat – probably the *City of York*, probably in 1936. The "box pani" was just a canvas container filled with sea water. I'm on the right – photo taken by my father.' (Ann Burkinshaw)

child that I was! The holidays were obviously a problem to organise. I spent part of a summer holiday in a hotel in Bexhill, where the manageress and her sister were friends of my parents, and part in another summer with the headmaster and his wife in Towyn in Wales. The former was joy unbounded, the latter a bit intimidating until some Calcutta friends suddenly appeared for their holiday and took me with them. Discipline at my prep school was very strict, but I only remember once really resenting it. The teaching was excellent and my memories of those three years are, on the whole, very happy ones.

SHEILA FERGUSON

The first five years of my life were spent on a tea garden, Leesh River T.E., Pillans Hat P.O., Dooars, Bengal – situated in an area of north Bengal where the plains stretch out from the foothills of the Himalayas, and the hills could be seen from the bungalow. A bungalow on a tea garden was usually a two-storey building, sometimes with a thatched roof – but not many had that. This part of India was an overnight train journey from Calcutta, and about a three-and-a-half hour car journey from Darjeeling, our nearest hill station. The tea garden was situated between the Leesh and Guish rivers, and in the monsoon rivers had to be negotiated by tying two boats together with tough straw matting on supports on top, and the car was driven on to that and poled across to the other side. In the cold weather the river beds dried up and were easier to negotiate. However, the big river – the Teesta – never dried, and was very difficult to cross until a road bridge was built in the 1930s. This river had to be crossed to get to Darjeeling or to Siliguri, where the Calcutta mail train finished its journey.

In those early years, only managers of tea gardens were allowed to marry – so their wives and children had a fairly lonely life on the garden. There were usually two to three assistants on the gardens (one of whom was a qualified engineer), and their bungalows were slightly smaller than the manager's – but all were located not far from the factory, which was the central point of the tea garden.

Our bungalow had three bedrooms and three bathrooms. We had only cold running water, no hot, so that water was boiled up in kerosene tins and brought up by the *paniwallah* (water boy) when a bath was required. We had a dining room, a sitting room with an open fire which was lit in the cold weather, a verandah, and over the verandah a mosquito room – totally wire-meshed so that one could sit in these in the hot weather and monsoon, burning anti-mosquito coils and quite often wearing white hoods to try and prevent being bitten by mosquitos. All the bedrooms had mosquito nets which were put down at night and the room sprayed with Flit using a special spray gun.

We had a big garden front and back and at the bottom of the back garden was the cookhouse – when ready food was brought to the back verandah and kept warm in a hot cupboard – a cupboard lined with zinc or similar – with a small fire at the bottom resting on an iron grating, until dinner was called. No matter what time one ate – on a Club night it could be 1 a.m. – the food was always perfect. I think we also had a refrigerator on the back verandah which ran on kerosene – and there was a scullery there too.

Social life for my parents depended on some tennis parties in our front garden and Club life. All the planters would meet about twice a week at their nearest Clubs – the men would play polo and the ladies tennis. In the evening they would socialise and dance etc.

There was no luxury of air-conditioning – a lot of fans were pulled by boys to keep the air moving, and when electric fans were installed they depended on the factory running to keep going. As the factory closed down at midnight it could be rather hot at night! We had a small generator but this only helped the lights.

As a small child I spoke no English. My father said I could speak five Indian languages, but I remembered none of them when I returned to India during the Second World War. The idea of speaking English was to avoid picking up the sing-song local accent – or 'chi-chi' – particularly as I was a solitary child and played with the children of tea-garden workers in the 'lines' – one blonde head among the dark ones. I had an *ayah* to care for me and rode ponies from quite an early age, an interest that stayed with me for a long time.

top 'The "burra bungalow" at Leesh River Tea Estate, my childhood home. I am not sure who the people in front are.' (Sheila Ferguson)

above Cars crossing the River Teesta before the bridge was built (1920s and early 1930s). (Sheila Ferguson)

below 'Foot passengers crossing the River Teesta before the bridge was built.' (Sheila Ferguson)

Almost all of the men on the tea gardens belonged to the local territorial regiment – in our case the North Bengal Mounted Rifles, of which my father was Commanding Officer. HQ was Darjeeling but the highlight of the year was the annual camp at Jalpaiguri. I remember attending one or two, so wives and children must have been allowed to go along sometimes.

I can remember going down to the factory of an evening and watching the pluckers with their baskets coming in to have them weighed. They had worked all day picking their 'two leaves and a bud', and were paid according to weight. I sometimes watched the leaves drying out in the special drying shed, and then the smell of the fresh, dry tea. They were packed (in those days) in large chests ready to go off to Calcutta.

My father did a lot of his work on horseback – the easiest way to get around at about 6 a.m. Usually going to his office at the factory, he came home for breakfast at about 9 a.m., and was out again till 1 p.m., then he had lunch and an hour's siesta during the hottest part of the day – and back out again. Usually he came in for a cup of tea between 4 and 5 p.m., then did a final stint in the office in the evening, finishing at around 7 p.m. when possible.

Very occasionally the planters would have to organise a shoot – either because a rogue elephant was damaging crops or injuring workers, or because a man-eating tiger was around and had mauled a worker. Either of these types of animals would have to be destroyed.

Each garden had a dispensary and a small hospital – run by a Dr Babu, who was qualified more as a pharmacist than a doctor. There was also a police station on each garden, though I am not sure if they did very much.

We had pineapples, lychees and bananas and lots of vegetables in our back garden. Chickens were always bought alive – and the cook would wring their necks and pluck them before cooking, so they were always fresh.

Most of us suffered from malaria – my father had severe bouts of the illness even when on home leave – all he could do was swallow quinine and sweat it out – literally.

Leave in the UK was allowed every four years for six months. The sea voyage to and from India would take up over a month of their time. 'Local' annual leave was permitted, when a planter could go up to one of the hill stations – but mostly they only had a weekend break.

From photographs in my possession my family must have had home leave in 1927 and then in 1932. When I was nearly six years old I was taken home and left with a wonderful family in Dundee. There were three children in the family and they took in about seven of us

above The bridge over the River Teesta under construction, about 1936.

below Completed as the Coronation Bridge in 1937. 'It joined roads from the Dooars to Kalimpong and Siliguri on the other side.' (Sheila Ferguson)

from India, so that house was alive with noisy children – all happily settled. We all went to school in Dundee. During the holidays I would go and stay with my father's brother and his wife in Falkirk. They had no family, so it was like entering another world when I went to them.

My mother came home on interim leave to see me in 1934 and took me on holiday with her. We had a lot of fun. Sadly, though, it was the last time I was to see my wonderful mother – on her return home to India she developed pneumonia and died. I was eight years old and devastated, but the family I stayed with helped enormously.

It was not until I was older and married myself with young children that I realised how hard it must have been for parents to part with their children at such an early age.

The year after my mother's death, my father was given compassionate leave to come and see me – he also took me on holiday and on a cruise to Norway. Not long after his return to India he moved me from Dundee to Glasgow, nearer my grandmother – and a new school. That did not seem to work out very well, and in 1937 I was sent to boarding school in Sussex; I spent school holidays from then on with relatives in Falkirk. Friends at school kindly asked me out on *exeat* Sundays.

My father came home on leave again in 1939 and during that period he remarried – a lady much younger than himself. War was declared in September, and my father and stepmother returned to India.

JENNIFER BETTEN

In 1925 my father, Malcolm Betten, went out to the Darjeeling District to be a tea planter. Before he became the manager at Tukvar he worked in two parts of the district. His first posting was the Nagri Valley, where some gardens, including Chamong, lie on the Nepal border. In those days Nepal was a totally closed kingdom. He also spent time at Singla, an outpost of the large Tukvar estate where tea merged into a forest which reached the glistening silver sand and the

Teesta river's glacially cold, clear waters. The river separated India from Sikkim and the Tibetan border.

The two areas were different. Tukvar, 'close' to Darjeeling, was dominated by Kanchenjunga; the Nagri district was more in the foothills, had its own Club, chapel and tennis court. At Nagri, the planters met once a month for the whole day, everyone sitting at one table in the Clubhouse for a 'picnic' lunch. Managers, attended by bearers and *khitmagars*, ate five-course meals, assistants nibbled a sandwich! Many a story can be told of the ride home at the end of a long day, whisky breath mixing with the pony's sweat and the night's darkness, leopards prowling, a stony track and, in the cold weather, spiky pruned tea bushes at the side of the road.

My mother, Eva, joined Malcolm in November 1927. She has described a frightful two-hour ride, in a dress, from the railway station to Nagri. The pony was cold and hungry. As well as being lonely she was sent crazy by the cicadas. November was in the 'cold weather' days of sun. The monsoon was over and everyone relaxed, and tea was no longer produced. April, rain permitting, was the time of the 'first flush', which gave the most prolific harvest of the year as the days moved inexorably towards the monsoon.

My parents' first home was a bungalow close by the factory, surrounded by hills, tea and forest. As the factory assistant, Malcolm was called to work at three o'clock in the morning, possibly just as he was falling asleep from the previous day's work. Then came the monsoon, dripping water and Malcolm's legs dripping blood from his leech bites. The Dr Babu was a regular visitor to dress the new and freshly scratched ulcers.

An occasional game of bridge with the manager and monthly Club day, eight miles away, relieved the monotony. In the cold weather there were tennis parties and an annual camp from the volunteer Army of the NBMR (North Bengal Mounted Rifles). Once, Eva, firing a pistol for the first time, won the competition. Tea gardens were often border outposts, it was best that wives could protect themselves!

Estates were isolated and planters had to be self-sufficient. It was hot and dry in March, when land was often cleared by fires. Inevitably, some fires spread. One year, at Singla, a fire spread rapidly. The tinder-dry forest reached from the river, 1000 feet below, to the factory, the lines, labourers' houses with dry thatched roofs, and our wooden bungalow. Above us there was tea and another forest, also on fire. We were in the centre. There was no phoning for helicopter rescue! The fire breaks worked, I'm here today, but Malcolm, the typical planter, skilled at everything, was exhausted.

Promotion meant house-moving. When we moved from Singla every bit of furniture had to be carried on men's backs up the 5000 feet and 11 miles to Darjeeling. It was quite a palaver and most amusing watching the strongest porters fighting over the smallest and heaviest loads while leaving the lighter and large ones for the 'losers'!

Most planters were rained in during the monsoon, so pregnant women spent tedious weeks in Darjeeling waiting for the birth. The alternative was a personal midwife. Eva's arrived with denghi fever and very ill. Eva was busier when the children began to arrive and before they went to school in England she taught both my sisters, as she later taught me, the three 'R's.

And today I find that out of the blue a smell or sunset will trigger me back in time to British Sikkim and Darjeeling where mountains, on a giant's scale, require superlative descriptions. The sunset reds on Kanchenjunga's glistening snow is only bettered by the pinks of sunrise or the mystery of moonlight. Forty and ninety miles away respectively, Kanchenjunga and Everest, the world's third and highest mountains, set the spatial parameters. 'Tea garden' is, therefore, an apt name for an estate of several thousand acres.

Central to the state was Tukvar's bungalow and flower garden. Here the rich soil produced sweet peas, dahlias, arum lilies, frangipani, hibiscus and poinsettia, all prize blooms! In a moss-covered walnut tree, orchids flourished in a minuscule garden. Garden scents and sounds are evocative. A cockerel crowed in 'the lines' (labourers' houses), insects hummed and butterflies flitted. Within this idyllic setting I passed a somewhat lonely childhood. Dogs, cats, rabbits, a parrot and ponies were my main companions, with temporary guests including a barking deer. At night there were the eerie cries of the scavenging jackal packs, the warning cough of the hungry leopard and the perpetual cicadas. Night over, the working day was called by the great gong which summoned the labourer to pluck or husband the tea.

My personal memories are of a wonderful childhood, surrounded by tea. The hillsides were terraced, and during the onset of the cold weather the tea was pruned quite meticulously to give the maximum ground cover and leaf growth. Malcolm was proud of the lawn-like appearance of his tea. As well as the visual aspect, there are various scents associated with tea, from freshly picked leaf, always just the top two leaves and bud, to withered, rolled, fermented and then dried tea, each process producing its own scent. Finally the fragrant, black tea was packed into chests. As a homesick schoolgirl in England I wrote, 'I miss the smell of tea and so to make up for it I sometimes bury my nose in the tea here but it hasn't the same smell!'

SUSAN BURDER

As a young *sahib* working for Jardine Skinners, my father lived in Ballygunge Park, Calcutta, where my sister Caroline and I were born in the early 1930s. We lived in a white, colonial-style house, two storeys high, with wide verandahs and a flat roof surrounded by a balustrade. In the hot weather our parents would sometimes sleep on the roof under a canopy of stars and mosquito netting. The garden stretched down to a pond with ornamental ducks and a pair of flamingos, which enjoyed visiting the neighbours and had to be retrieved by a *mali* in a rickshaw.

A starched white nanny ruled us in the nursery, aided by Kanchi the *ayah*. We loved Kanchi. She had a daughter called Pooblums and she sang us to sleep with Indian lullabies, the words I remember to this day.

My father's personal bearer was a fine Sikh who wore a *puggri*, a luxuriant moustache and his beard neatly contained in a hairnet suspended from his ears. He slept on a mat outside my father's bedroom. Purroo, the Nepalese chauffeur, drove my father to work every morning in a Vauxhall with a dicky seat.

The day started early for my parents, with a ride before breakfast on the Maidan or out at Tollygunge at the weekend. My mother would then have a visit from the *bobbachee* to discuss the menus and sometimes unfathomable accounts from his forays into the bazaar; frequently there would be a mysterious entry for 'faggots'…

'Faggots! What for?'

'I forgets…'

In other ways, too, he was quite an artist: our favourite chocolate souffle would be elegantly piped in cream 'chaklak shuffle', but on one occasion he made his feelings clear with a disastrously tough steak and kidney pie on which pastry-trimming letters spelt 'Lady Burder'!

On the verandah the *dhirzi* sat cross-legged on the floor whirring away on his sewing machine, deftly gathering in the material with his toes. He could run up a fancy dress for a children's party, or copy the latest *Vogue* pattern for my mother, or indeed, turn a collar for the *sahib*.

Other members of the household, by no means large by Raj standards, were the ubiquitous sweeper – an 'untouchable', he wore a *dhoti* and seemed to walk bent double, permanently sweeping away with a handful of sticks; the *khitmagar* (he also groomed the dogs and prepared their food, presenting the bowls to my mother for her approval); Mulvi – a handsome Mohammedan with a wide smile, he wore a splendid turban with a cockade and a large silver brooch depicting the *sahib*'s crest pinned to his front; his assistant, the *chota bearer*, another Nepali, sat on the front doorsteps to answer calls and carry parcels, and there was a motley collection of the *bobbachee*'s relations making merry in the kitchen. As Indians love children I'm afraid the *missy-babas* were rather spoilt. Alas, all good things come to an end, and suddenly I found myself at the age of seven at boarding school in England and perching with alternate long-suffering grannies in the holidays.

PATRICIA TOFT

The first home that I remember was in Sunny Park, Ballygunge, Calcutta, although we had been living previously in Cawnpore, but I was too young then to remember anything about it.

My father was a chartered accountant and worked for Price Waterhouse Peat & Co. The offices were in Clive Buildings, but I don't remember the address.

In Sunny Park we lived in a first-floor flat, which consisted of a wide central staircase with what you might call a staircase running round it and all the rooms leading off. The first on the left was the dining room, with the kitchen leading off and with a separate outside staircase for the servants to come in and out. The next room, which was at right angles to the dining room was my playroom, which had a mosaic floor. This room led into the sitting room, which was, I think, L-shaped (there were doors to all the rooms leading on to the hallway, as well as intercommunicating doors). The next room was mine and my younger sister's bedroom, with its own bathroom, and this room led to my parents' room, also with its own bathroom. There was a large, wide driveway with garages and servants' quarters and a large walled garden where we had a swing, a big wooden Wendy House and hutches and runs for our guinea-pigs. I don't remember ever seeing the people who lived downstairs.

One afternoon my sister and I were having tea out in the garden, sitting at the table from the Wendy House. We sat either side of the table and there was a plate of bread and butter between us on the table. Suddenly there was a swooshing sound, and a kite swooped down, grabbed the bread and butter up in its talons and flew off, leaving chaos behind. My younger sister, then aged about two, cried, but I found it quite exciting – I was about five or six at the time.

During this period I remember the children's Christmas fancy-dress parties at the Saturday Club. Preparing for this event was enormously exciting. The *dhirzi* would come to the house with a book of pictures of all sorts of fancy dresses and we would look through them and then make the costumes from the picture – no paper patterns – and the result was always exquisite. I remember being in turn Little Bo Peep, a sunflower, a star fairy, a poppy and Snow White. The band for the party were always dressed up as different animals, and I particularly remember the giraffe.

The daily routine consisted of going to school in the mornings, which I enjoyed very much. We had lessons out of doors much of the time, sitting at a long table with some sort of canopy over to shield us from the sun. Then there was the mandatory 'rest' after lunch, and then going out to tea with friends or riding on the Maidan on a small pony (Sunny Park was very near the Ballygunge Maidan). There were visits to the Saturday Club swimming baths and dancing classes at the Peggy Godden (later Rumer Godden) School of Dancing. At this time my elder sister was in England in boarding school and I knew that soon it would be my turn to go. I had this awful anticipation of the impending separation and often had crying fits, which puzzled my mother, as she had no idea what I was crying about. The actual parting in England was awful. On the last day, when my parents were finally leaving my elder sister and me and going back to India with my younger sister, we had a day out with them. They had bought each of us a goodbye present which they hid in the hotel room, and we had to search for them. This was to try to lighten the situation. My present was a pink teddy bear. I will never forget the feelings of that day, and I can imagine what my mother went through. I did not see my parents again for two-and-a-half years.

The school my parents had chosen for us was good as boarding schools go in terms of looking after us and trying to keep us happy. I can remember playing rounders on the big green field, gardening and going for walks in crocodile. We used to be taken to a gymnasium, which I found rather terrifying, as we had to climb rope ladders and slide down ropes and go on a sort of swing, which consisted of a plank hung at each end with ropes. It would swing extremely high and was supposed to be a treat after having done all the other exercises, but I didn't like it at all and the instructor was a very fierce man who scared me; one didn't dare refuse to do anything he said.

On Sunday evenings in the winter we had to put on velvet dresses, take our sewing boxes and go the headmistress's drawing room, where she would sit and read us the *Just-So Stories* while we did our sewing.

During the holidays we usually went to a holiday home for children called April Farm, though for two Christmases we went to stay with our aunt, but only for a short time. April Farm was run by two ladies known as Auntie Bar and Auntie Jill. There were quite a few children there, including babies and toddlers, who were looked after by Norland nannies.

We schoolchildren had a governess to look after us. She used to take us for walks and we'd sit down in the wood and she would read *Jane Eyre* to us.

There were a lot of animals for us to play with and look after – ponies, dogs, a goat and chickens. We rode the ponies, fed the chickens, collected the eggs and broke the ice on their water bowls in winter. I remember one winter holiday when the house was completely snowed in and the gardener had to bring a ladder to put up against one of the bedroom windows for us to climb down and then we had to shovel snow away from the doors. I used to find it quite disturbing moving from school to holiday home, and equally disturbing going away from the holiday home back to school. In each case I got settled into the way of life and it was hard to readjust each time.

PAMELA ALBERT

Our next posting was Alipore Lines in Calcutta in 1934, where we were to stay for the next four years. We had been in the North West Frontier Province for so long that the very idea of coming into complete civilisation seemed like a wonderful dream. All the so-called life of the Raj – dances, garden parties – were going to begin again. For me, through the years, the big cities were a bore, for it was the countryside and the people of India I loved, the gentleness of its people never to be forgotten.

Alipore Lines was a large area that consisted of large homes, two floors for the officers and their families; an Officers' Mess-cum-Club; offices, stables, sergeants' and warrant officers' quarters and their Mess; sepoys' quarters; and in the centre a huge parade ground. The parade ground area was also used for all games: hockey, cricket, volleyball and polo.

We had a flat on the second floor with four bedrooms, sitting room, dining room, and a very large verandah. We also had, believe it or not, real lavatories with pull chains and all! It was a fascination for me to pull the chain often just to see the water gush up and then disappear! No thunder-boxes! It left quite an impression on a seven-year-old, and I can remember it as if it were yesterday. Two huge aviaries filled with exotic birds were built on the verandah, and there was a fish tank that held Japanese fantail gold fish. I liked the black ones best – they looked as if they were made of velvet.

We were happy to be there. The whole regiment had been transferred to Alipore, and so children I had not seen in a long time were all brought together. I think perhaps these were the happiest four years of my young life. There were wonderful home dinner parties. Hidden behind a large chair, I would watch the adults at play – throwing cushions at one another, stuffing the live goldfish down the ladies' dresses, and then off they would go to the Clubs (usually the Saturday Club, Firpo's or the Grand Hotel on Chowringee) to finish off the cheery evening. After the party had left our flat, and all was quiet, I would finish off the champagne left in the glasses. I just loved champagne, and do to this day. But, alas, this was not to last too long, as one night my mother had left her evening bag behind and, on returning to retrieve it, she caught me in the act. I was in the middle of the sitting room guzzling the left-over champagne, the empty glasses lines up in front of me. After that episode, the servants were not allowed to retire, no matter how late it got, until all the glasses were cleared away!

Life was a constant round of swimming parties at the Calcutta Swimming Club, the Saturday Club, children's parties at Belvedere (former home of the Viceroys), garden parties, the Royal Calcutta Turf Club events and especially the Saturday races. At such parties, the ladies wore beautiful hats and long dresses, the gentlemen attired in morning suits with top hats, regimental officers wore dress uniforms. Big, coloured tents offered refreshments of all kinds, and the ever-present regimental band would be playing. What a wonderful time to be growing up! Actually, I loathed getting dressed up for parties. I was happier to live in my jodhpurs, shorts or bathing suit. But rules were rules, and you were expected to conform no matter how much it hurt. I am really glad that my upbringing was so well-rounded, as it helped me to cope with every situation in life, usually landing with both feet firmly on the ground.

In the summer of 1938, trouble was again brewing on the North West Frontier and Afghanistan, and as a result part of the regiment was to be despatched to the border for the protection of India. My father, a line officer who was top of his field with firearms, especially the machine gun, was to be sent to the frontier and expected to be gone a year. He had just completed his examinations of a particularly difficult nature, with a higher standard Hindi in order to get his majority. He would now go to the frontier as a Major. My mother thought this would be an ideal opportunity to leave for England, and we were booked to leave Bombay on board the SS *Strathaird* in September 1938. By this time, things were becoming extremely unsettled in Europe and she wanted to go home before things got worse. The voyage was smooth until we reached Port Said, where we spent the day ashore. Shortly before the dinner gong for the first sitting, little lights appeared in the distance, hundreds of them – they were small boats accompanying a large and very beautiful barge. They were approaching the ship, and I ran quickly to the gang plank, which had been lowered towards the '*tamasha*' (goings-on). A very good-looking, well-dressed young man in a dark business suit walked up the gang plank accompanied by six or seven sheikhs, all smartly dressed in their Egyptian clothes. He stopped when he saw me, smiled and then said, 'How nice of you to come and meet me, and what is your name?' I told him my name was Pam and that I was going to England, and I asked if he was coming along too. 'Yes,' he replied, and in a flash was gone. We were to find out later that it was Prince Farouk of Egypt. A few days later a huge stuffed koala bear was delivered to our cabin for me, and a bunch of beautiful red roses for my mother. We never forgot that chance meeting. It was certainly a highlight of the voyage.

We arrived at Tilbury in the rain. We were met by my Uncle Claude and hurried to catch the boat train into London; we were to stay in Sidcup with my uncle, aunt and cousin Clive and a new cousin, Roy. It was to be a holiday that I was introduced to many 'firsts' in my life! The memories include an apple actually growing on a tree, which the family had left so that I could pick it off; Guy Fawkes night, with the children chanting 'Guy, Guy, stick him in the eye', as we carted wood in our little wagon to the bonfire. The story of Guy Fawkes is part of Britain's history, and how I recall the beautiful fireworks! I remember a real Christmas tree, not an artificial one, nor mango tree branches I was accustomed to; a visit to Selfridges where a giant Father Christmas opened and shut a window; snow and Christmas lights twinkling everywhere; the village school covered in snow, and the sweet shop next door with the most marvellous bulls-eye sweets! It was exciting and a whole new world to me.

HILARY VIRGO

Father was a manager in the Calcutta and Lucknow branches of the Imperial Bank of India. I have photographic records of being in Simla at the age of two, and later in Ooty, in both places the method of transport being either donkey or pony. Clearer memories of Calcutta, where we lived in those colonial-style houses with wide, porticoed verandahs. I had an *ayah* up to the age of three, when an English girl, Olive, became my nanny, though she was never called that. She was my companion, teacher, friend and of course I saw more of her than anyone else in the household. She taught me to read and count – long, narrow books – but at the age of four I was mad keen to go to kindergarten school, which I did at five. I also went to dance classes run by Peggy (Rumer) Godden, which I loved. We had an annual stage show – I believe the cinema was converted to a stage – and I have been a Briar Rose in a green tunic with a pink taffeta frill round the neck, Little Boy Blue in a satin Christopher Robin suit, and a cockerel. This was a magnificent costume, rich reds and greens with a coxcomb hat, but I longed to be the hen, who was a pretty little girl with a feathered tutu.

There were always plenty of other children to play with, some of whom I still count as friends. We loved dressing up and there were frequent fancy dress parties.

I also used to be taken to the grounds of the Victoria Memorial, where we played on the large slabs of marble which, as the building was on unstable ground, had not been added, though I believe they are all now in their rightful places. We also used to play in the cathedral grounds.

In the afternoons one had a rest on the bed. One day there was a rumbling sound like several lorries going past. Olive shot me out of bed and outside the house, staggering down swaying stairs. This was the earthquake that brought down the spire of the cathedral.

Then, one had to be vaccinated – scratched and inoculated and the place covered with a small plastic dome. Sometimes they 'took'; sometimes not.

When I was six we moved to Lucknow and a vivid picture remains of our first visit to the Bank House to a party given by the outgoing manager. The house had a Palladian quality and was surrounded by eucalyptus trees. The moon was full and we had brandy-snaps on the lawn. I also remember nights of pure terror when I thought lions were roaring in the garden, but it was only the bullocks in the compound. The house did have a ghost: I complained that someone (an Indian) was walking through my room when I was in bed, but he never turned up on the other side of the curtain where Olive was sitting.

The bathroom in the house had tin tubs and the water was brought in kerosene cans. There was a white bullock with blue holy beads round its neck which wandered around, mainly on the office side of the house. The bank was attached, and I used to enjoy going in to the big room filled with desks and people.

I used to play with two children in their garden, where they had one of the big double tents which were marvellous to climb up and slide down. The small boy, George, died fairly soon after we left, and I heard only later.

In the hot weather we went up to Naini Tal, and my mother would join us for short periods. I had my seventh birthday there. I used to ride round the lake. The journeys up to Naini were long and sick-making, but were compensated for by the hundreds of monkeys, with babies, swarming everywhere.

Early mornings in the hill stations had a wonderful smell – herby, crisp and cold. Occasionally one gets something similar in England, which brings it back vividly. I particularly disliked being carried in the sedan chairs on poles across the coolies' shoulders, and even at that age was embarrassed. But of course it was work and money for the men.

When I was seven, my mother, Olive, and I returned to England and I felt my world had ended when Olive said goodbye. It came as a great shock, but as we were all in Tunbridge Wells I continued to see her. Again, I longed to go to school, and joined a day school there until chickenpox curtailed that. We were living in the annexe of a hotel so it had to be kept fairly secret. My father joined us and I remember his excitement, and mine, at the Stop-Me-and-Buy-One ice cream cycle on the common! I had the same feeling again on my return to Calcutta, but this time it was coming out of an air-conditioned cinema to a hot, spicy night and buying an ice cream from the street vendor – there were no worries about hygiene. At eight I went to High Trees School near Horley, which catered for children such as me with parents abroad, and it became home. In the spring and summer holidays we went to Selsey, where there were bungalows made of railway carriages joined by a roof to make a living room. We slept in bunks and the windows had leather straps to open them.

My mother returned at intervals, and my father every two years. At Christmas I went to stay in Shropshire with my aunt. So family life was brief, but I still have close friends from those shared school holidays. We listened to Chamberlain's declaration of war from the radio perched on top of the lockers in the common room. My parents were still in England, so I spent the first Christmas of the War with them in Tunbridge Wells, where we again had private rooms in a hotel. They returned to India in the New Year and I went back to the fairly spartan life of school – windows were always open at night, whatever the weather – I was never really warm, and often frozen.

JAMES BENTHALL

My father was a partner and then director of the Bird/Heilgers Group in Calcutta, which was at that time owned by his elder brother. The group's main interests were in jute mills and jute trading, paper mills, coal mines, iron ore and limestone mining, engineering and refractory bricks, my father's early experiences having been in jute.

His grandfather, Edward, had been in the HEICS (Honourable East India Company Service), ending as a judge in Jessore before the Mutiny. Edward's eldest son, Clement, was born at sea while his parents were on their way back to India from leave. Clement was a captain in the Bengal Cavalry and saw active service during the Bhutan campaign. He died later at Allahabad. The earliest relative in India was a John Benthall, who was a merchant adventurer and silk merchant from 1618–28. He was in Surat briefly before going to the Persian Gulf. My mother's father was John Archibald Pringle, who was a mining engineer, working in the Kolar Goldfields when my mother was a child. His grandfather, David Pringle, and three brothers, were all in the HEICS about the middle of the nineteenth century.

My family was in England on leave in 1938, when I was four-and-a-half. I had early memories of gardens and people, but not much else, except a vivid memory of the sound of bombs or guns of the Spanish Civil War as we steamed past on our way back to India.

My father's principal home was 19B Raja Santosh Road, Alipore. Alipore was then on the outskirts of Calcutta, and was one of the more desirable areas in which to live. The house was a good example of a director's house in Calcutta, though much smaller than some. It was semi-detached, and of a typical layout, with a large central room on each of two floors, with smaller rooms at each end. It had a flat roof, on which my father grew plants in tubs, and they used to have dinner parties on the roof at certain times of the year, the servants having to carry all the food up several flights of stairs. As was often the case, the kitchen was across a back yard, and consisted of an earthen oven in a small, dark room. The conditions for cooking were pretty primitive, but cook performed miracles. In front of the house there was a decent garden, dominated by a large rain tree (*Enterolobium saman*) by the front gate. (Rain trees were a wonderful feature of Calcutta, but now, I believe, are mostly dead, owing to a drop in the water table.) The house was colour-washed a pale yellow, as were a great many.

The servants consisted of a cook, perhaps at times a boy to help the cook, a *khitmagar*, my father's bearer or personal servant, who looked after my father's clothes as well as serving at table, my mother's *ayah* to look after her clothes, a *masalchi* to wash up, a sweeper to clean the floors and to do any job which was beneath the caste or status of the other servants (such as taking stool samples by rickshaw to the laboratory whenever one had tummy troubles!), and a gardener, probably with a boy to help. There was also an office driver. In our case there was also, except for the first year or so, an English nanny, who even after several years spoke and understood virtually no Hindustani, but nevertheless had to be involved in the running of the household. My memories of this house at that time are few: whooping cough in the big central room upstairs, with ceiling fans going, mosquito nets over the beds, and whooping-cough injections for Richard and me (our first injections); a mud wasp which built its mud house on the wall of the house just by the front door (an early natural-history lesson); breakfast on the verandah, sometimes with our parents downstairs, otherwise with Nanny upstairs. The verandahs were large and airy, with bougainvillea flowering all round. One year a purple-rumped sunbird nested in the bougainvillea. Birthday parties were on the lawn with other children, watching either snake charmers, or a man with tame sparrows which performed tricks, such as picking small coins off people's foreheads and taking them back to their boss, who naturally pocketed them, and the inevitable monkeyman, with small monkeys dressed in skirts or trousers, dancing to a drum.

Early memories of Calcutta are mostly of Club life, such as the Saturday Club, where I learned to swim, diving in the children's section for large, red, rubber discs before I could swim on the surface, and of the railway stations, which must feature big in everyone's memories of India. There were also occasional trips to the zoo, and more often to the Agri-Horti, a pleasant large garden in Alipore with a serious research function, but to us a big area in which to run around, and to my father a real botanical interest. We were also taken for before-breakfast walks round the local villages beyond Alipore, where my father was studying the flora. (He later, partly as an occupation and relaxation while his family was in Darjeeling, wrote a book, *The Trees of Calcutta and its Neighbourhood*, which became the standard book on the subject.) Other early-morning excursions were river trips with my father to visit the jute mills. The business owned two steam launches, *Lilian* and *Ruth*, which were necessary to visit the mills on the far side of the Hooghly river, but which also saved a lot of time, if the tide was right, by avoiding the hot and tedious drive on the near side. River trips were always fun, and the steam launches, with awnings, were comfortable and cool. It was normal for the head-office *burra sahibs* to visit the mills before breakfast. After a walk around the mill, breakfast, and possibly a change of clothes, they then went on to do a full day in the office. Similarly, it was quite normal for men to get up for a round of golf before breakfast, going on to the office afterwards.

JEREMY LEMMON

My maternal grandfather, the son of a doctor in Leighton Buzzard, went out to India well before the turn of the century. After the proper period of youthful adventure (he became, among other things, a medical adviser in the retinue of Tsar Nicholas), he eventually settled, and, together with an American acquaintance, founded a mercantile company trading in goods medical and pharmaceutical; he always called himself a drugs merchant, though the title seems infelicitous now. He made a marriage, as if from a Kipling story, to a young widow whose husband had been killed while pig-sticking, and who already had a son of her own. I never knew this grandmother of mine, but an early photograph, by S.H. Dagg of Allahabad and Mussoorie, shows me a handsome lady with a determined chin and perhaps a hint of the 'Spanish' look of Kipling's Miss Castries. In 1896 my mother, the only child of this marriage, was born in Mussoorie; when she was old enough she was sent 'home', as convention required, to boarding school (in Bexhill), and later studied music in London.

My father's early life was very different. He came from Leeds, and was one of a family of 13 children. In the Great War he served as a sergeant of artillery, and emerged from it partially deaf and with a ruined thumb (it had been trapped in the breech of a field gun). In peacetime he went to India to find his fortune, joined the now-thriving company and soon rose to be managing director. My parents – to their friends they were Nimbu and Bossy – were married in St Paul's Cathedral in Calcutta and spent their honeymoon in a houseboat on the Hooghly. There were four children, of whom I was the third; we were born, to borrow Wilde's phrase, into the purple of commerce.

My father worked in Calcutta (his office was in Lal Bazaar), and we lived in comfortable Ballygunge, not far from the Maidan, that huge area of grass and trees in the middle of the crowded city. We were often taken to play there; there our dachshund Blitz was savaged by a monkey. Our house was large, square, white-plastered, set in a garden with a tennis court and zinnias and canna lilies tended by an incalculably ancient *mali*. A white marble staircase

'A picnic in or near Calcutta, 1927. I don't know who the photographer was. My father, Richard Dennis Lemmon ("Nimbu"), is on the extreme right. The lady majestically lying in the centre is my mother, Dorothy Constance Lemmon ("Bossy"). Kneeling behind and to the left of her, in shirt-sleeves, is my maternal grandfather. The little girl in front of him is my sister, Joan.' (Jeremy Lemmon)

led to the upper floor, which we occupied; at the turn of the stair, irresistible to a child's eye, stood an artificial tree with flowers made of quartz and coloured stones. A deep, covered verandah ran the full breadth of the house: there the daily traffic of family life chiefly flowed. We children played under the electric *punkahs* while my mother sat knitting or considering the latest prizes from Simon Artz of Port Said, the favourite emporium of sea-going *memsahibs*. Often the *dhirzi*, the tailor, would be sitting cross-legged in a corner, busily hemming sheets or making cool cotton pyjamas. Each day after work my father settled in a cane chair to smoke and watch the sky change colour, while a bearer brought to his glass-topped table a neat ham sandwich and a *chota peg* (a small whisky). Open archways, from which hung cages of canaries and bulbuls, led to the drawing room, a large and under-used room with a chequered marble floor and Persian rugs; the furniture, as I remember, was heavy mahogany, cane-backed in the colonial fashion, and in a corner was my mother's grand piano. On a hot afternoon the most popular place in the house was the cold room, a dressing room off my parents' bedroom; here the new device of air-conditioning (in the form of a bulky and clamorous structure fitted by the window) kept the air ice-cold. Leading into the dining room was a small inner hall, from the ceiling of which, during birthday parties, a bulging paper fish was suspended; at a given moment the excited children would beat it with sticks until it exploded in a shower of rice and tiny presents. The dining room was small, and almost filled by the octagonal table, which was said to have belonged to Warren Hastings. Of the kitchen I recall nothing – perhaps I wasn't allowed there – but I do remember, on guard at its entrance, the fridge, taller than I was and stocked with bottles of water. My father never liked Indian cookery – he preferred his food plain; the rest of us loved it, and our children's supper was often dahl and rice, or the little potato rissoles we called 'aloo chops'.

Behind the house was the godown, where the servants lived. I no longer remember them all (nor even how many there were);

but I think I can recall a stately head bearer, and two or three other bearers, all in smart white tunics, with striped cummerbunds and cockades in their turbans; there were the cook and his *masalchi* or assistant, the *jamadar* or sweeper, the *chowkidar* or watchman – there may have been many others. We loved visiting the godown, where we were petted and given delicious *barfi* to eat; but we were not allowed to take liberties. Once I impertinently tried out on a genial bearer known as Munshi my new discovery of a Hindustani insult. Almost at once I was summoned to my mother, who happened at that moment to be sitting on the lavatory; without moving from her majestic station she delivered her most stinging slap to my cheek; pain and humiliation made it improbable that I should misbehave in that way again. Of special importance in the household were the drivers; the car was a maroon Buick – my sister was born in it. The chief driver was Ghulam Rasul, a Muslim who retired after Independence to Pakistan, from where he wrote to my parents regularly and with wonderful affection: 'My joy knows no bounds while writing,' one letter runs,

> The reflection of the passed time in your service like movie picture is roaming before my eyes. You would be glad to hear my son Ghulam Mustafa has been blessed with a son. We are happy here and enjoying God's favour. All my family members are very desirous to be informed of your honour's family. I wish may God I see you once in life.

We were looked after by our Anglo-Indian nanny, Norine Bampton, who was as loving as she was loved. We also had an *ayah* called Lizzie, a diminutive and very dark Madrasi, with hair so long that, released from its usual tight bun, it flowed to beneath her heels. Lizzie could be bad-tempered, but she was also tender-hearted; from her I first heard the familiar lullaby, 'Nini, baba, nini, roti, makhan, chini...'. Our Calcutta life was happy, if unremarkable. There were visits to Firpo's for butterscotch ice cream (but all ice cream, even at Firpo's, was forbidden when there was a cholera scare); shopping trips to the Army and Navy Stores, Hall and Andersons, Whiteway, Laidlaw, or – special excitement – to the bazaar; Sundays at the

Swimming Club; picnics at the Golf Club, where at dusk we heard flying foxes bumping in the high branches (their droppings, we were warned, could scald the skin); we saw the Victoria Memorial painted black for wartime; and we went to a Viceregal party where long carpets were laid over the lawns for the children to play on. And of course there was the cinema: *Pinocchio* and *The Wizard of Oz* and *Coney Island* – for a time Betty Grable was my heroine.

The hot-weather months – in fact, the greater part of the year – we spent in the hills, in Kalimpong, then a small village. The nearest station, at Siliguri, was some 50 miles away, and it was necessary to drive by a sometimes terrifying road, narrow and broken by landslides; for part of the distance the ground on one side fell sharply away, in what was almost a precipice thick with teak trees, down to the gorge of the wicked River Teesta. We crossed the gorge once on foot (the car presumably took a longer route) by the kind of fragile bridge called, I think, a *jhula*, which swung sickeningly at every step. Most memorable was the occasion when a tiger emerged out of the forest and stopped on the road a few yards in front of our open car. It was a wonderful and frightening animal, and seemed then to be quite

'Dealing with a snake. In the background is St Alban's, our bungalow in Kalimpong.' (Jeremy Lemmon)

as big as a horse. The driver told us to keep quiet and still; the tiger stared at us for an interminable moment, and then, since we were of no account, it stepped quietly into the forest. We tore away, the driver shouting his warning of 'Bagh! Bagh!' to the villages as we passed.

In reminiscence, our time in Kalimpong seems the most magical part of my childhood, and the pictures it has left are vivid, though fragmentary. We rented a bungalow cosily called St Alban's, and from its low verandah we looked across the valley to rising hills and beyond them to Kanchenjunga and the great peaks. In the early morning you could sit over *chota hazri* and watch the peaks turn from crimson to pink to almost painful white as the sun rose. In the evening there were comfortable fires and paraffin lamps and the plopping sound of lizards falling from the low ceiling. In Kalimpong there was always something amazing to see: *bhoyitas* with bunched clothes and brass anklets often came to the village; devil-dancers from Tibet, with masks out of nightmare, once performed for us by firelight outside the bungalow. There were plenty of odd and delightful creatures, like the huge and beautiful moon-moths we saw on our walks, or the tame green lizards my sister kept in her sleeves; some were fascinating in a more sinister way: the ugly geckos we called blood-suckers, bird-eating spiders (I woke to the terror of seeing one roosting on my mosquito net), land-crabs, the occasional krait. And of course we had purely companionable pleasures too, like Bhansi Lal's shop, where the cream puffs were as light as air, and Sunday School, with the famous Aunty Mary, Lady Mary Scott: when we acted out the tale of the Prodigal Son, I experienced the glory of being cast as a husk-eating pig.

JOHN LANGLEY

My first real memories began after our transfer to Paksey, a railway colony about 150 miles north of Calcutta. This town was located on the main railway line running north to Darjeeling. As senior civil servants moved there from Calcutta before the monsoon struck in

May, the railway was considered one of the major communications links in India.

At Paksey the railway crosses the Ganges river via the Hardinge Bridge, which is about a mile and a quarter long. The problem was that the Ganges decided it did not want to stay under the bridge and had a great urge to move eight miles north. Father's job was to persuade it to stay and it was becoming rather a bore bringing it back, as well as being expensive. A special division was set up by the Indian Railways to construct guide *bunds* (banks) to contain the river. The engineer in charge of this operation was B.L. Harvey, with Father and Von Lindsay as his assistants. It was a tough project and the fact that their small team successfully accomplished the task was of considerable satisfaction to Father.

above Part of the Hardinge Bridge over the River Ganges, 123 miles north of Calcutta, 1935. (John Langley)

below Bungalows at Rajbari, 1931, *left*, and Paksey, 1935, *right*. (John Langley)

We had a very pleasant bungalow at Paksey. All houses, no matter how many storeys, were called bungalows. At Rajbari the bungalow had been a two-storey brick building with a fearsome-looking exterior. It had large arches supporting a roof over the open verandah with keystones at the centre of each arch. These were of different colour and material to the main brick of the facade. On either side of the arches were two circular holes that gave the appearance of a series of angry Mexican gods. By contrast, the Paksey bungalow was single-storey, with a pitched thatched roof and soft, mellow brick walls. It was set in a large, well-kept garden (called a compound), which helped to make it seem much cooler and more pleasant to live in.

One of the strongest memories that has remained with me from this period is of the thunderstorms. Spectacular storms were quite common in all parts of India, but on this occasion the memory remains because it affected us. It had been oppressively hot, which was the usual build-up for a storm, and at about 4p.m. it became pitch dark. When the first flash of lightning sizzled across the sky, Mother and I were in the lounge, and I was playing with the toy railway my 'Uncle' Mac had given me. Mother was always terrified of storms, but she tried very hard not to show it in case I became frightened. However, the crash of thunder that followed the first flash of lightning caught her by surprise, and at her involuntary yelp I joined her on the settee. Suddenly there was another flash, and almost instantly the thatched roof of the office was a sheet of flame. The speed with which the building burned was incredible, and it did not seem possible that anyone would have been able to get out in time.

Not unnaturally, Mother was very anxious, and it was with considerable relief that we greeted Father's entry about 15 minutes later. He was soaked to the skin but otherwise unharmed. He had actually left his office after the first flash of lightning, as he realised that we were in for a very severe storm and knew that Mother would not want to be left on her own. When the office was hit he turned back to make sure that everyone was safely out, which they were, and then returned home. Ever since that time I have had a dislike of violent storms and a great respect for their potential to do damage.

Another vivid memory from that period is of the earthquakes, and particularly the sound I associate with them. Earthquakes are quite common in certain parts of India, and many years later, when Father was transferred to Haflong in the Naga Hills, Assam, we would have minor tremors about every two weeks. But in Paksey they were rare. The year of the notorious Quetta earthquake was 1935, and tremors were felt far and wide throughout India. Our first intimation was the sound that resembled thousands of tin cans being rolled down a flight of concrete stairs. Then the ground started to undulate like a large swell at sea. The first tremor caught everyone off guard and my Nanny froze in terror. The safest thing to do when an earthquake occurs is to get outside in case the house collapses, which sometimes happens in severe shocks. At first I thought it was some new kind of game until I realised that Nanny was scared to death. Then I heard Mother yelling at us to get outside at once. By then the first (usually the most dangerous) tremor was subsiding, but once again we heard the sound of tin cans and still Nanny appeared incapable of movement. However, Mother arrived, her anger at Nanny overcoming her own fright, and she pushed both of us out into the garden just as the next wave rippled through and made us stumble and fall on the grass. This was followed shortly afterwards by the third and much weaker tremor, and then it was all over.

The house did not collapse, although there were a number of interesting and impressive cracks in the walls, especially over windows and doors, as well as in the concrete floor of the verandah. We were lucky – many others had homes that were destroyed, and in north-west India there was great loss of life, as not only did buildings collapse, but the earth opened up and swallowed people. The tin-can sound effect was caused by tremors moving across the steel bridge, causing it to dance and rattle. The sound was amplified by the river, leaving a vivid memory for a four-year-old.

Many years after the Paksey incident, when I was at school in Darjeeling, I experienced another memorable tremor. Darjeeling is not considered to be in the earthquake belt, so this was a pretty rare occurrence. I was a boarder at the school; our housemaster was a strange person by any standard, and I suspect he was unaware of the earthquake. Amongst his other peculiarities he liked music, which might have been a redeeming feature except that he had very strange tastes. He had a collection of classical records and played them late at night. Appropriately enough, on the night of the earthquake he had selected Debussy's scary 'Things that go Bump in the Night'. It was an odd experience listening to the music as we went up and down in our beds as the tremor rippled through the dormitory, accompanied by various objects falling off the walls and shelves and literally going bump in the night. By the time we realised it was a genuine earthquake and not the housemaster putting a touch more realism than usual into his entertainment package, it was too late to try and get out of the building. Fortunately, it was a minor quake, and little damage was done in Darjeeling.

Shortly after the earthquake incident, Nanny was released from service and I graduated to a bearer. Zahoor became my personal attendant and from then on accompanied me everywhere until I went to school in England. I think it was a good move for all of us, and I am sure Mother felt much safer in entrusting me to his care.

Although the majority of my time was spent either with Mother or Zahoor, there were a couple of families with whom we were friendly and who had children my age. Frank and Susie Smith lived at Saidpur, 200–300 miles north of us on the way to Darjeeling, and their son Paddy was a few months younger than I. He was also an only child and was in the same social position as I, in a very hierarchical environment. We did not have much chance to socialise with other children, and in Saidpur and Paksey there were not many white children of any age. It was not surprising that Paddy seemed nearer to being a brother than just a friend. When we got together we used to fight each other, hate each other and enjoy being together, and we hated it when we had to return home. We enjoyed exploring new things and always defended each other when attacked by other children or grown-ups. We have stayed good friends all through our adult life, even though we meet infrequently.

If Paddy was a brother, then Jennifer Goff was the nearest to being a sister. The Honourable Angela and 'G' (George) Goff were the other family. 'G' was 19 years older then Ange, and had been in the Army for many years before joining the railway. They had a romantic courtship of three weeks, and decided to get married. They had two children, Stephen and Jennifer. They were stationed in

left John Langley, right, and Paddy Smith at Rajbari, Bengal, in 1932. (John Langley)

below John Langley, right, with Jennifer and Stephen Goff and their minders at Gopalpur, 1934. (John Langley)

Paksey for part of the time we were there and, as with the Smiths, we often went on vacations together, sometimes to go to Darjeeling, but the more memorable ones were trips to the seaside. This was to a resort town, Gopalpur, south west of Puri, in Orissa, and on these trips the husbands were usually left behind. Gopalpur was famous for its sandy beaches, as well as being a fashionable resort town, and the swimming was excellent. However it was also dangerous because of the heavy surf and treacherous tides, and we were always escorted by fishermen, who were familiar with the vagaries of the sea, as well as acting as look-out for unwanted visitors such as shark and barracuda.

We had lots of fun together; we became excellent swimmers and quite good on horseback. We spent a lot of time in the local swimming pools as well as in the sea, so it was not surprising that we could swim almost as soon as we could walk. And on vacations to hill stations such as Shillong in Assam and Darjeeling we had plenty of practice in riding.

In Darjeeling, which is a hill station approximately 7000 feet up in the Himalayas, there was little for small children to do other than walk up and down mountains or ride the local ponies. For the adults there was a Gymkhana, which was a sort of social club-cum-skating arena and casino. It provided roller skating, tennis, swimming, putting and indoor games such as badminton and fives. On the social side it had cocktail bars, a restaurant, dancing, bridge rooms, billiards, mah jong and other similar activities. But none, with the exception of the swimming, appeared to be suitable for three-to-four-year-olds, so we were mounted on the hill ponies, each with a *syce* who ran alongside to make sure we did not fall off. This was a necessary precaution, because the animals were susceptible to being frightened and bolting on the narrow hill paths. In some places there would be a sheer drop of 500–600 feet, so the danger was real. Years later, when I was at school in Darjeeling we used to go riding quite often, and being very grown-up at 11 or 12, we would not require the services of the *syce*. On one such outing a pedestrian raised an umbrella just as I was going past, and the pony was so scared that it immediately bolted. This provided me with the most hair-raising and exhilarating ride of my life, and one that I have never forgotten. The pony was called Peter Pan and was well-known for its timidity, but less well-known was the fact that it had a mouth of iron. It was almost impossible for a 12-year-old to control it and it was one of the fastest ponies available for hire.

Due to considerable misuse during the war years, the ponies had developed mouths of iron ranging from soft iron to tempered steel. As far as I was concerned Peter Pan fell into the latter category, and nothing I could do seemed to have the slightest effect in reducing his speed. On the contrary, it just seemed to make him annoyed and start to go sideways across the path. Since this had even less appeal, as chasms began to appear, I let him have his head and ended up hanging on to his mane with my eyes closed and a grim determination that I would stay with him no matter how far we went. After about five miles of steady uphill galloping he became tired and slowed down. After a long pause for Peter Pan to get his breath back and for me to recover my nerve, we returned sedately to the stable, where I nonchalantly discussed my gallop as if it had been planned. But I also made sure that in the future I never again hired Peter Pan!

YOMA CROSFIELD

When my mother first arrived in India in mid-1933, she was thrilled to find that because my father was now the *burra sahib* (most senior man) as Branch Manager for the Burmah Oil Company in Chittagong, she was to be in charge of a very large house. Apart from the little house they had rented for the months after their marriage, it was my mother's first home of her own. But she was also, without a word of any of India's myriad languages, in charge of a cook, a cook's mate, a butler, a bearer, a *paniwallah* (who did the dishes), a *mali*, and a *durwan*. In her eighties she would only say she was 'rather intrigued' on the first morning when my father went to the office and she was left to cope with this household.

Beautiful though Chittagong was, to my mother's dismay, she found her life far more circumscribed than it had been in England. European women did not walk on the roads, let alone bicycle, nor, when she and my father got their own car, was she allowed to drive it. A driver took her everywhere. This was partly convenience, partly security. Although when my mother arrived the area was peaceful, toward the end of the 1930s terrorists began to create incidents in an effort to force the British to leave India. European men all carried revolvers, leaving them in rows on the mantlepiece at dinner parties. At the same time, the verandahs of the company bungalows were secured with chicken wire to prevent bombs being thrown into the houses. Life for Europeans was even more confined.

My mother found the social set dominated by the European staff of the Assam–Bengal Railway and their wives. This was 1933, but only a very few years earlier the junior wives had been forced to take it in turn every morning to lace up the corsets of the previous most senior wife. The current senior wife called on my mother to give her advice on running a household. Initially awed, my mother was soon covertly amused because her domestic-science training had already taught her so much that the redoubtable lady had to offer. This lady had three menus for dinner, and everybody knew that she chose which one to serve according to the rank of her guests.

My mother at once became active in the Girl Guides. Initially she supervised groups of English-speaking Guides, in which Hindu and Muslim girls participated side by side – a situation hard to imagine today. Communal enmity was far less strong at that time, and my mother found it more remarkable that the girls had never been allowed to run before they came to her meetings. After a hesitant beginning, they were soon running freely. This episode demonstrated another dimension to my mother's rationale for Guiding – improving the health of girls who were frequently shut away from outdoor exercise and any contact other than their family.

Life in Chittagong was not all Guiding, however. My mother found that there were convent-trained women who made beautiful embroideries but had no outlet for what they produced because they were *feringhees*, strangers, of mixed race descended from sailors visiting the port. As such, they were unacceptable to either the English or the Indian community and were almost destitute despite their talents. My mother, with a friend, collected orders for their work, provided the materials and even the designs, and had the women come to her house every week to show off and sell the results on the wide verandah. The European community in Chittagong was not enthusiastic about her efforts, and her successor stopped the practice.

My father played on the BOC cricket team and my mother, well trained by her own father, kept score for the matches. One Sunday afternoon when she was keeping score at a table on which the players had, as usual, put their revolvers for safekeeping, two armed terrorists attacked the gathering. The players dashed for their guns. My mother took cover behind a tree. The attack ended when one of the cricket players brought down the leading terrorist with a rugger tackle, breaking his own wrist in the process. The second was beaten to death with wrenches by the Indian drivers of the Europeans' cars. My mother did not comment on this when she told us the story, but the violence between Indians reflected the fact that they were deeply divided on the subject of the British role in their country. The drivers who killed the terrorist could have had any number of motives, from fear of their jobs or loyalty to those who paid them, to dislike of an intruder from another caste or tribe or way of thinking.

My mother could not escape taking part in the Club life of the Europeans in Chittagong, spending hours by the Club pool, in the bar, on the tennis courts, even playing bridge. She appreciated the tennis for exercise and eventually felt that playing bridge saved her mind during her years in the East, but she regarded coffees and teas, with their attendant gossip, as a waste of time. Busy with the Guides, she never had any patience with some of her fellow BOC wives, who made no effort to do anything useful or to get to know any Indians.

CARL HIGGINSON

I was born in November 1935 in Andal, West Bengal, India, the third of five children born to Charles Higginson and Dorothy McCready.

My grandfather, Edward Hugh Higginson, was an Englishman born on the ship that brought his parents to India. When they returned to England, he did not come with them. He was in his teens and decided to make his own way. He worked for the Bengal Nagpur Railway. At 24 years of age he married Stella Elsie Doyle, an Anglo-Indian, aged 14 years. They had six children; my father was their fourth child. Stella Doyle's grandfather was Martin Doyle, an Irishman from Kilkenny. He was a private in the 105th Regiment of Foot.

My grandfather William Cecil McCready married Sarah Henrietta Burnett. They had five children. My mother was the eldest. Little is known of my grandfather's parents. His father and older brother made life difficult for him. When his mother died he left home and went to sea. He was 15 years old. He never saw them again, even though they all lived in Calcutta.

My father worked for the East India Railway. He started as a cleaner, then became a second fireman, fireman, shunter, and then a driver: first of goods (freight), then of passengers, starting with the slower and smaller trains and progressing to the larger, faster express trains over a longer distance. The top drivers were the mail drivers. Only the best got to that level. My father was one of those men.

Railway people lived in railway quarters, also known as the railway colony. When you were employed by the railway, you also got somewhere to live, and as you worked your way through the grades you got better quarters. The railway colony was divided into two sections, loco quarters and traffic quarters. The traffic quarters were usually near the station. They were occupied by people who worked on the station – the stationmaster, ticket collectors etc. The loco quarters were by the running shed, referred to as the 'shed'. This is where the locomotives were kept and maintained and prepared for work.

Each driver was allocated a locomotive. He and his crew of two, a fireman and a second fireman (jack) took care of it. They booked the repairs and checked that they were done, and that all was in order. They were the only people to use the engine. When major repairs were done the driver and crew would take the locomotive on a test-run and put it through its paces. On these occasions my father would take one of us with him, and we enjoyed it. It was a fairly long run lasting a few hours.

In the colony there was the Railway Institute. This was a place of entertainment and relaxation for the employees and their families. Some even had a cinema, reading room, library, swimming pool, billiard room, bar, tennis courts and sports ground. There was also a small hospital and dispensary and a doctor. Employees were looked after very well.

The Dancing Class at St Patrick's High School, Asansol, 1937. (Carl Higginson)

There was also the railway school. All of us started our education there. They were very good schools, properly run, with a headteacher and full staff. We went there until we were about ten years old. After that out parents sent us to fee-paying schools, sometimes as boarders. It was a sacrifice our parents made to give us a decent education.

A railwayman's life was a hard one, with long hours and difficult conditions. When he was promoted, he had to move where the vacancy was, so a lot of moving was involved. The East India Railway mainline was from Howrah in Calcutta to Delhi, over 1000 miles away, so transfers could involve moving long distances.

Although there were difficult times in the early years, life was still good. We usually managed to employ two servants, a cook and a sweeper, which made life easier for my mother. The kitchen was away from the house, and by the kitchen were the servants' quarters: when you had servants you also gave them somewhere to live. Besides paying your servants, you also helped them when they were ill or had any problems. The sweeper was an 'untouchable', the lowest in the Hindu caste system. He or she did all the dirtiest jobs.

We were transferred from Andal to Asansol in 1939, shortly after the start of the Second World War. We were still in West Bengal, not very far from Burma, so we saw soldiers of many nationalities in the area. As children, it was an exciting time for us. I was still at the railway school, but my two older brothers went to the local public school, St Patrick's High School, until the armed forces took it over and used it as a hospital.

JANE GRICE

I was born at 3, Penn Road, Alipore, Calcutta, but I only remember the house from photographs. It was large and grand with large lawns and loads of pot plants and probably owned by the chemical company of which my father was a director. My father married my mother in England, but she had also been born in India, as had my maternal grandmother and her parents; so I had an inborn feeling for the country, which is hard to explain to people who weren't born there. My grandmother had a house in Store Road and as she was widowed early she kept this on and spent six months in Calcutta and six months in Surrey for much of her life. My mother experienced boarding-school life in England away from her parents from the age of eleven. Up until that time she had a string of English governesses who taught her little. She didn't go away to school earlier because, being born in 1910, she was in India for the First World War, as my brother and I were for the duration of the Second World War. The house I remember was in Ballygunge, Circular Road, where we moved after a 'home' leave in 1939.

As I was only three-and-a-half years old, I remember little of this leave. Three months were spent in Leamington Spa with paternal grandparents and a stiff white nanny called Nanny Paxton. I had my tonsils out during this time. Three months were spent with my maternal grandmother in Epsom – where she lived permanently – and another stiff white nanny called Fox. The only significant thing I remember about this was trying on masks, as I had to wear a Mickey Mouse one and was absolutely terrified. This was the leave where we left my brother, aged seven, at prep school, and returned to India without him. My memories of the actual voyage are hazy, but we travelled on one of the P&O 'Strath' ships. There were many; The *Strathmore*, *Strathnaver*, *Strathallan*, *Stratheden* and *Strathaird*. I had a collection of souvenir sailor dolls, a legacy of all our collective sea voyages. These little dolls were made of blue plush material and they had cute little smiley faces; they had little white collars, and sailor hats with the name of the ship on the hatbands. I wonder where they are now – I'm sure they would fetch a fortune on the *Antiques Roadshow*! We returned to Penn Road for the cold weather from November to February, and then I was packed off to Rathlyn Hall, a small boarding school in Darjeeling for white children run by a man called Bruce with a wooden leg. The uniform was grey and maroon. When I returned to India many years later, the school still existed but was renamed Bethany Hall. The uniform was still grey and maroon, but the children were all shades of brown.

SHIRLEY ODLING

My grandfather Odling went to India aged twenty-five in about 1895 with two other pioneers. They planted a tea garden from scratch in Assam and called it AMD – it was very successful, is still going strong. After twenty-five years on the tea estate, he returned to London aged fifty. He then married and had four children, one of them being my father, Norman Odling. He died aged ninety, having lived two completely different lives. So both my parents had Indian connections.

My grandfather Graham arrived in Kalimpong, 4800 feet up in the Himalayas, as a Scots missionary in 1889, with his wife Katharine. For the first few years in Kalimpong he did the usual missionary work, but then he became very worried about the plight of the Anglo-Indian child in India. In those days, India was no place for white women, and European society was mainly made up of men. In the circumstances, a large mixed population grew up, with its attendant complications. Many of the men sailed back to England leaving these children of mixed blood abandoned, and this was particularly so in the tea gardens near Kalimpong. He had

Weaving at the Arts and Crafts Centre of the Kalimpong Homes, about 1938. (Shirley Odling)

a vision of a home for these children in Kalimpong, leased a bare hillside above the town, and started building his first cottage, for six needy children. In 30 years there were six hundred children there, and with his enthusiasm for the home and school he had the gift of inspiring many benefactors, who made it possible to build many more cottages, and also a central school with all the amenities a large school required. In 2002 there were 1200 children at the homes – his vision a hundred years before became a reality. In the meantime, my grandmother was busy with various projects in Kalimpong – as well as having six children she started what she called The Lace School, and taught local women how to make lace. This eventually ended up as the Kalimpong Arts and Crafts, which my parents ran for twenty-five years. Every kind of craft was taught to local people – carpentry, weaving, carpet-making, hard-block printing, handbag-making, embroidery, etc. These products were sold all over India, and at Liberty's in London.

Although the buildings were destroyed by fire twenty years ago, the local people who learned their crafts there now have shops in the Kalimpong bazaar selling goods they learned how to make at the Kalimpong Arts and Crafts many years before.

AURIOL GURNER

I left India at two years of age, when my eldest sister was seven, but I have no memories of this. From 1929 to 1931 I lived with a nanny and two elder sisters in accommodation provided within a boys' prep school where the headmaster's wife was a friend of Mother's. Happy memories. In September 1929, I was sent to boarding school – the Preparatory Department of St Monica's School in Kingswood, Surrey – with my sister Lynette, who was kept behind, ill, for a short period. My memories of this time are full of confusion and unhappiness. I greatly missed Nanny, with whom I had shared a bedroom, and who had sung me to sleep every night. I was the youngest pupil then, next to my sister, and had no school uniform.

I had to wear button-up gaiters, and generally seemed to be always at the back. The school allotted a sort of nursemaid to my sister and I, and I remained at this school until summer 1939, by which time I was totally conditioned to it and happy.

Having no relatives with whom to spend the holidays, we were initially sent to a holiday home in the New Forest. Children from 10–18 years of age were accepted, and riding and various activities were provided. My eldest sister entered happily into the life, I think, but Lynette and I were actively unhappy. As I remember it, we were totally at the mercy of older children, and neglected by the adults. Memories are of being frightened by animals and children, of waking up from a nightmare crying and being eventually comforted by Lynette, and of hiding for long periods in a deep window seat with a curtain pulled across, together with Lynette. We were taken away after my 11-year-old (eldest) sister suffered a fractured skull after falling from a pony while riding unsupervised. My aunt came back from London and my mother came back for a period from India. By then, my aunt had found us a new home for the holidays in a large rectory where the rector and his wife had daughters of the same age. Starting out with dread and apprehension, we rapidly became totally happy there, and those days are still among my happiest memories, even now. My father got home leave every four years, but my mother – and this was unusual – always came home in between his leaves. Although I failed to recognise her on her first return, she never again seemed strange to me: when she was coming home we could barely contain our excitement, and when she left we felt despair.

HAZEL INNES

At the age of 14 months, my twin brother, Geoff, and I were taken out by my mother to join our father in Dum Dum, just outside Calcutta. Daddy worked as a Sales Assistant with the Gramophone Company at Dum Dum, and we lived in a bungalow adjoining the factory and offices. The company was well-known for the famous

HMV (His Master's Voice) records it manufactured and sold, as well as for its electric and portable gramophones, or 'phonographs', as the original machines were dubbed in the US. The Gramophone Company's Head Office was based in Hayes, Middlesex in Britain, and its Indian factory in Dum Dum proved to be a huge success, with the Indian population taking to the twin wonders of gramophone and record with enthusiasm.

We had an *ayah* – a beautiful girl from Southern India whom we grew to love dearly. She had trouble with my name and never managed to pronounce 'Hazel', which she transcribed into 'Oozoo' or 'Oozoo-Baba'. I must have been a bit of a pain for the poor girl, as I never liked the dresses she picked out for me to wear, and she'd rush off to my mother crying 'Oozoo-Baba, naughty Baba Mem Sahib', when I'd had a particularly bad tantrum. My brother was far less trouble, and watched stoically as I went through my routine.

One of my most vivid memories is of the standpipe and tap in the lovely garden. We would watch as various people came to fill their *chattis* (earthenware pots) or pails from the tap. Seizing our moment, we would allow our shadows to pass over the receptacle and

'Posh Picnic' near Dum Dum, about 1934. Hazel Innes, extreme left, behind her father, her brother Geoffrey, back to camera, and their mother, to the right of the *ayah*, with unknown friends beyond. (Hazel Innes)

giggle delightedly as the unfortunate owner would throw the water away, contaminated as it was with our shadows, and have to start all over again. Little horrors.

The New Market or, to give it its correct title, the Hogg Market in Calcutta was a favourite haunt of my mother and her friends, and we were taken there regularly. However, much as I enjoyed our trips to the Market, this was not a pleasant experience for my brother. The sight of all those bloody carcasses suspended from the butchers' hooks while our mother bargained invariably made him retch. But he cheered up when we visited the other stalls, and later we would imitate the importunate cries of the owners as they tried to entice us with 'Neduls, cottons, ladeez is-stockings, over here, Mem Sahib...'

On one memorable occasion Colin, a five-year-old friend and next-door neighbour, was with us. His mother handed him a coathanger to hold while she tried on a jacket at a stall full of ladieswear. Colin hung on to it without thinking and suddenly discovered it in his hand half-an-hour later when his mother was at another stall trying on yet another jacket. He made our day when he looked at the hanger and said, 'Coo, bloody look what I've got!' and received a clout for his blasphemy. We were delighted, not having the courage to use such a naughty word ourselves.

Colin and his older brother, Ian, lived in the next bungalow to us. These were Gramophone Company bungalows and I would suppose we would call them semi-detached today. But in those days they were 'joined-on', in our parlance. The boys' father was a colleague of our father's, and both would go through the little wooden door at one end of the garden into the Gramophone Company offices adjoining. Soon, we went back to England, to spend three years with a family friend while Ma and Pa did another tour of duty.

10

Assam and Burma

Assam became a province of its own in 1912, with a Governor resident at Shillong, 4900 feet up in the Khasi Hills. It consisted of two valleys, those of the Brahmaputra and the Surma, and is known the world over for its tea. The tea-bush *Camellia viridis* is native to Upper Assam, and it began to be cultivated commercially as early as 1825. It has six varieties, four of them from Assam, and is the preferred sort on account of its leaves being larger than those of, for instance, *Camellia bohea*, a Chinese plant. 'Assam indigenous', as it was called, would grow up to 2000 feet in that latitude; above that they were generally bushes from China.

Rice and timber were the other products of Assam. There was a small coalfield at Ledo and a small oilfield at Digboi. Its language was Assamese, though Bengali was widely spoken, and its railways were the Assam Bengal and the Dibru-Sadiya.

Assam was separated from Burma by a range of mountains rising to 10,000 feet, running from north-east to south-west, and known variously as the Patkai Hills, the Naga Hills, the Manipur Hills, the Lushai Hills, the Chin Hills and the Arakan. Burma had long been an independent kingdom, but it was annexed by the British after three wars, in 1826, 1852 and 1885. It was then, rather tactlessly, made into a province of India, an ancient enemy, becoming independent of it in 1937, and of Britain in 1948.

It was a singularly beautiful country, with the wide valley of the Irrawaddy between various hills, entirely Buddhist and with two principal languages, Burmese and Shangale. In the 1930s it became one of the richest countries in South East Asia, its exports being rice and teak, precious stones, silver, and, to an extent, oil. The Governor had his seat in Rangoon, moving to Maymyo in the hot weather, and the British commercial presence consisted of the Bombay Burmah Trading Co. and the Burmah Oil Company. The Burma Railways and the Irrawaddy Flotilla Company attended to the transport, and it was administered by the Indian Civil Service.

RUBY HADLEY

My father was a chief accountant for the Burmah Oil Company, working in Rangoon when I was born there in 1921. In that same year Burmah bought the Assam Oil Company and my father was transferred there after a home leave in 1923. It consisted of just one oilfield at Digboi at the extreme north-eastern corner of Assam with distant views of both Burma and Tibet. One could travel all the way by rail, changing several times.

Our home was a wooden bungalow on stilts on a hill – each bungalow had its own hill! There was no electricity, no running water, and for coolness there were enormous bamboo *punkahs* the length of each room and verandah, the cord from the *punkah* going through a hole in the floor to where an elderly relative of one of the servants would pull it. For servants my parents had a cook, *paniwallah*, butler, bearers, sweeper, two *malis* and an *ayah* for the baby (me). We had oil lamps and drinking water was boiled. Water bearers came twice a day. The bathrooms were under each bedroom and were really just godowns with tin tubs in. I remember one day being bathed by my *ayah* when there was an awful noise: all the bungalows had corrugated iron roofs and it sounded as if the roof was being pounded in. The *ayah* bundled me up in bath towels and ran upstairs to see what was going on, shrieking for my mother. The source of the noise was a freak hailstorm – and I clearly remember my mother and father running around the garden picking up these hailstones which were the size of billiard balls, my mother with a tape measure shouting for Daddy to come and look, she'd found an even bigger one than the last one!

There were very few other children, but I do remember that the General Manager at that time was called McAllister, and his son Ronald and I would be taken in the afternoons to the Club pool to swim and play by our *ayah*s. But I left shortly after my sixth birthday to go back to boarding school in Edinburgh.

STAR STAUNTON

'Name her Star,' said my mother as she took my tiny, prematurely born body into her arms. 'She will soon be one.' It was November 1922.

That seems a good point at which to begin the story of my unusual childhood. She meant that I was not long for this world, and in the circumstances well might she have thought so. She had just given birth to me in some sort of clearing in the middle of the Assamese jungle where, although she was seven months pregnant with her first child, she had gone tiger-shooting with my father. Typical of my father that he should have let her accompany him. He was cool and indifferent to all his womenfolk, but passionately devoted to shooting tigers. He told me once that my mother herself was an excellent shot and had insisted on coming with him for the sport. I can imagine him telling her that she was a fool but raising no objection. He was like that.

So there was this hunting party thrown into confusion by my unheralded arrival. No sanitation, no hygiene, water from the hole, male servants, male hunters, my father and, fortunately for me, my foster-mother during infancy. 'Name her Star,' said my mother. 'She will soon be one.' Then she died.

It was a squalid and agonising death, and my father understandably was reluctant to talk about it. So I know little about the event except the details I have set down, including the one sentence that gave me my name. I wonder where my mother had picked up that fancy about dying babies becoming stars in the sky. At least she died on a joke.

I believe she was beautiful. 'Your beautiful mother,' the Carmelite nuns would say when I stayed with them in Paris. She was French, a Montgomery descended from the Montgomery who accidentally killed a king of France at sword-play – or so I was told – and, presumably, a Roman Catholic. Her family disowned her when she married my father, a divorcee and non-Catholic, and my only contact with them was when some Montgomery cousins at the convent took me home for an afternoon visit to their grand house overlooking the Jardin du Luxembourg, I suppose to satisfy their parents' curiosity. Evidently I did not pass muster, for the invitation was not repeated, and thereafter the girls, who had been friendly enough before, turned up their noses when they saw me.

I do not even know how my mother and father met, whether it was in Paris or French Indo-China. I have no photograph of her. By the time I was old enough to develop a serious curiosity about her, my father had married again and I had a stepmother, and neither my father nor she were given to discussing family matters with me. Mother gave me a life and a name, and there an end. Whoever and whatever she was, let her rest in peace.

The family home at that time was in Cawnpore. Thither I was hastened and put into hospital and there in baptism (Church of England style, not Roman Catholic!) I was duly christened Star.

That I arrived there at all must have been due to the *ayah*, whose upbringing in Nepal probably fitted her to cope with the crises of my birth better than a Western woman would have done. She would know how to cobble together a layette from my dead mother's clothes and how to feed me with a rag dipped in condensed milk suitably diluted. She would be the one to find and hire the Bhutanese wet-nurse who nourished me once we came again within reach of human habitation. Bless her! She had a shrewish tongue and never demonstrated any affection towards me, which both she and her employer would have considered out of place, but I have no doubt that I owe my survival to her.

TIMOTHY O'BRIEN

I was born in March 1929 in Shillong, in the Welsh Mission Hospital. My father's regiment at that time was the 2nd Battalion of the 8th Gurkha Rifles, but he ended up as Director of Military Intelligence, India, towards the end of the War. As a child I was dressed in a miniature version of the regiment's khaki uniform. So my shorts were creased at the sides and not back and front and I had three material tabs and buckles at the waist to keep them up and to grip a shirt with shoulder straps. Got up like this, I would try to halt detachments of riflemen on the open road, but they politely filed round me without breaking step. I had a Khasi *ayah* called Ibon, who knitted me a scarf, which I didn't lose until the free and easy 1960s. My memories of my time in India are few, as I had my fourth birthday on the boat, SS *Rajputana* (which was lost in the War), coming home. I recall red and grey skies and water-filled ruts, and the river steamers of the Brahmaputra at night, five decks lit up better than wedding cakes and brass thresholds to the cabins, stoutly appointed in teak. But I was offered magnificent hearsay, since I was put in the care of my mother's mother and father near Tavistock in Devon. My grandfather had retired in 1931 as Deputy Commissioner ICS for the Chin and Lushai Hills, after signing my birth certificate and walking 20 miles to see his first grandchild. They were enough to make me feel in touch with India. They took the *Statesman* by mail from Calcutta, and had boxed tea sent to them directly from a shipper in Darjeeling, and my picture of India and its relation to 'home' was partly painted by the story of their courtship and marriage.

My grandfather was born in 1881 and my grandmother in 1883. Both families were Wykehamists, and my grandfather was four years in the cricket eleven and a star. He fell in love with my grandmother – a sister of a boy at school – when she was 'in the schoolroom'. Naturally, neither family saw any value in a hasty marriage between a 19-year-old and a 17-year-old, so Stephen Mackenzie left Margaret Freeman behind and sailed to India to begin life in the ICS. Three years later Margaret was put in the care of a randomly selected married couple on a steamer to Calcutta. After six weeks they arrived and Stephen met them. They drove to the Anglican cathedral and, in a side chapel, the marriage was witnessed by the married couple, who went on their way immediately after the service was over. Together again for an hour or so after a three-year separation, the newly weds faced each other and my grandfather said, 'What shall we do this afternoon? Shall we go to the races?' However, in those early days, I think my grandmother was much moved by the beauties of her new world, as the wife of the sub-divisional officer in Narayanganj and later in the Assam Hills. She said she learned to ignore the leeches on treks with her husband and to empty the blood out of her boots in the evenings.

So it went on for me in Middlemoor on the edge of Dartmoor. A brigadier general would show me the bloodstain still on the knife of a murderer he had long ago brought to justice. My grandfather's younger brother, Sir Duncan Mackenzie, was resident in Hyderabad, Deccan; two of my uncles were soldiers in India. Both my mother's sisters married in Assam. My mother and father were in Shillong, and later in Quetta, during an earthquake. My father's right arm had been amputated in 1931 as a result of wounds sustained in Mesopotamia in 1915, when he was 17 years old, and he was something of a much-decorated mascot.

He was detached in Waziristan and was there with a detachment of Gurkhas in the wilderness – few huts, a wireless post, a flight of Gloster Gladiators. One day he arranged for his *havildar major* to go up for a short flight and afterwards he walked him back to the lines. The *havildar major* said, 'Sahib, the mind of man is a wonderful thing. Men may speak unseen over great distances and fly above the earth in machines, but it was only last year that we thought to put the Company colours on the kitbags!'

So from 1933 until, I suppose, 1942, I felt very connected to India and seemed to live among people with Indian memories and imperial convictions and to sustain an education largely fitted to make me a cadet for an imperial role. How quickly all that dissolved!

LAURENCE FLEMING

I too was born in the Welsh Mission Hospital in Shillong, exactly six months after Timothy O'Brien. My father was then acting General Manager of the Assam Oil Company in Digboi. But on my birth certificate, which was signed by Timothy's grandfather, the hospital is still called Dr Robert's Hospital.

I was quite old before it occurred to me that a Welsh Mission was rather unusual; indeed, I sometimes wonder, now, if there was another anywhere. But the system in British India was simple: the Anglicans missioned the plains, while the non-conformists were given the hills. So, for instance, the Church of Scotland was active in Sikkim and the surrounding hills and the Welsh Baptists were given the Khasi Hills, where Shillong was situated. The Protestant missionaries were not, in fact, very successful. Their principal triumphs were in areas where there had been no previous religion, such as the Khasi Hills in Assam and the Kachin and Karen Hills in Burma. These were converted by the Baptists and, of course, by the Roman Catholics, who seem to have been a law unto themselves, getting in everywhere and even keeping their own records.

So my first nanny was a Roman Catholic Khasi lady called Berilla. The Khasis are a matriarchal tribe living only in their own hills, a fertile, rolling bastion rising to 6500 feet, with the Brahmaputra Valley on the north and the Surma Valley on the south. Property descends through the youngest daughter. Of Berilla's family I know nothing.

ASSAM AND BURMA 387

She was with us for many years, until after my sister was born, but then she married a British soldier and went to live at Andover.

I was the first of the Assam Oil children to be born in India. Before that the expectant mothers went 'home' to give birth, partly because there were no very favourable facilities locally, and partly because they were not sure that the child would have full British nationality. But Dr Roberts founded his hospital in 1921 and it is certainly still there today, though probably under another name.

All the houses in Shillong were of light construction, wood and plaster and with corrugated-iron roofs, thatched or with wooden tiles, and of one storey only. This was a rule made after the great

Laurence Fleming in front of the 'burra bungalow' at Digboi, early 1934, and on a picnic near Digboi, with Bukhta and The Car in the background, 1934.
(Laurence Fleming)

earthquake of 1897, in which every house made of brick or stone collapsed, with great loss of life. The British community was having a cricket match and were therefore all outside, their only casualty being a man unwell and in bed at home. The town was consequently very spread out, surrounded by grass-covered, pine-clad hills and with an artificial lake at its centre. Sir Joseph Hooker, the great Victorian botanist, considered the flora of the Khasi Hills to be the richest in India. Shillong was, however, only 36 miles from Cherrapunji, then considered to be 'the wettest place in the world', having an average annual rainfall of 426 inches.

I do not, of course, remember this delightful place. By the end of the following year, we were living on the Burmese oilfields at Yenangyaung. I know that to get there we travelled by train to Prome and then by launch to the landing at Nyaunghla. I know that we went up into the hills in the hot weather, to stay at Kalaw, and that, by the end of 1933, we were living in Rangoon. But, at the beginning of the next year, my father was returned to Digboi as General Manager and he was to be there for the following ten years.

We sailed, via Akyab, from Rangoon to Chittagong, and were there given a private coach which was attached to any mail train that happened to be going in the right direction. I have a faint recollection of this, but my earliest memories are of Digboi, going round The Field in the evenings with my father in an open car driven by Bukhta; of a group of strange objects called the 'boiler battery' – which looked like very early steam engines without wheels; and of going to a neighbouring tea garden to see my sister, who had been born in the doctor's bungalow there. I had a swing made, I imagine, in the refinery, with cast-iron posts, a solid wooden seat and iron 'ropes', which made a wonderful grinding noise as you went higher and higher. Every morning I was woken by the sound of burnt toast being scraped, as my nursery was very near the cookhouse.

It could not last, of course, and it didn't. I began my education 'at home' at the age of six; but every Sunday I wrote a letter to 'Digboi P.O., Upper Assam', and hoped that I would one day go back there.

MARION ALEXANDER

In north-east India, in the province of Assam, was a small, thatched bungalow, where I was born, in the foothills of a mountain range on the border of Bhutan. Here my father was manager of a tea estate with an outlying smaller garden some few miles away.

A larger, more modern bungalow was built in the mid-1930s as the garden 'expanded', with surrounding jungle reclaimed and planted with more tea.

New ideas, developed from past experiences, were used and, with the help of local labour, it soon became an ideal home. The position, ideally situated on a small plateau, enjoyed the benefits of cooling winds and magnificent views.

The open-plan building had three bedrooms and built-in mosquito netting cages, eliminating the daily preparation and removal, night and morning, of cotton nets enclosing the beds.

A verandah, again with wire netting, jutted out from the building ensuring plenty of circulating air and no unwelcome spiders and snakes.

Marion Alexander with her Khasi *ayah* on the verandah of the old bungalow, 1934. (Marion Alexander)

above Corramore Tea Estate. Pruning the tea bushes on the plateau behind the new bungalow, about 1000 feet high. (Marion Alexander)

below 'Families walking down main road to allotments leased by the company for rice growing. On left, factory building at foot of plateau on which tea was grown; the picked tea transferred mainly by ropeway in large baskets. On arrival at a lower ground level it was then spread out on large shelves to dry. After grading and cutting leaves, it was packed and dispatched to Tangla Railhead for Calcutta. In the background lie the Bhutan hills rising eventually to 7700 feet on the right of the picture. High snow-covered Himalayan mountains could be seen on fine days to the left of the picture. A small group of market stalls was situated at the road-side behind the photographs. This market was visited also by Bhutias who had their own routes to and from other areas.' (Marion Alexander).

opposite top A children's tea party on an Assam tea garden, about 1935. (Marion Alexander)

opposite bottom A small wedding group visiting the tea-garden manager at his new bungalow after the ceremony, about 1937. (Marion Alexander)

A lounge, dining room, small kitchen, office and godown (store-room), and a visitors' wing completed the layout. The main cook-house at the rear was reached by a covered walkway. The fair-sized compound, fenced off where possible, and a cattle trap on the driveway preventing estate workers' animals from devouring the plants, allowed the cultivation of many attractive flowers, fruit and vegetables.

The proximity of the jungle prompted the need for constant alert-ness. Troublesome elephants and tigers were quickly reported and necessary steps were taken to provide safety for all.

A small number of staff looked after one's daily needs and the running of the household. A *dhobi* collected the laundry and dealt with it in the local river – to everyone's satisfaction, on the whole! How the ironing was done was a mystery. In the garden there was a small hospital run by the Dr Babu, who also attended to our ailments. An English doctor was on call for the more serious problems which needed perhaps hospitalisation in Shillong or elsewhere. Indians who were house/family servants also became good and caring friends to their young charges. This link was reciprocated.

The weekly gathering at the Club, about 20 miles distant, provided the main contact with other families in the district. The rain in many cases dictated the visits from the more remote gardens, as the sudden absence of bridges or dry river beds was a serious drawback.

Club afternoons enabled adults to pursue sporting interests such as tennis, polo (before the War), bridge and billiards. Christmas and New Year called for greater celebrations, with visits occasionally from touring padres.

Returning late at night along deserted jungle roads, one often saw, in the headlights, animals hunting their prey. I don't remember my father ever carrying a gun in the car, though others never went without one. The driver always accompanied us on these trips.

When the tea was ready for plucking, I remember, as many workers as possible made their way to the designated area in the early morning and, working all day, some mothers carrying young babies, filled baskets which were then weighed, tallied and put into larger containers to be hooked on to a ropeway for delivery across a steep chasm to one of the factory buildings at ground level, returning empty uphill for the next load. This method may have been used in other hilly tea gardens, but I don't remember seeing it elsewhere.

The next process – drying – in which the green leaf was laid out on large areas of hessian racks in open-air sheds, took quite a long time, until the leaves were sufficiently dried, when big rotating machinery further dried, cut and then graded the tea.

Finally, packed in wooden tea-chests, it was despatched by lorry, then train, to the Calcutta tea market.

ANONYMOUS

My ancestor Jean-Antoine was born in the Haute Savoie in 1733. In 1757 he sailed from Marseille to Pondicherry to trade as a merchant. In the Seven Years' War (1756–63) the English and the French were fighting in India and so, when the English sacked Pondicherry, in 1761 and again in 1778, he fled to Travancore, an independent native state in the south of India, where he was very successful. His son Maurice was born in Tellicherry in 1772, served in the secretariat of the Rajah of Travancore and died in 1830.

His son Jean, his name now anglicised to John, served in the French Merchant Navy, and his tombstone can still be seen in the family vault at Trivandrum. He died aged 46, in 1852. His son Richard, 1844–1900, was superintendent of Customs in Travancore, at Alleppey, and his son, Basil Richard (1885–1944), was my father.

My father served as an assistant surgeon in the Indian Army for 33 years from 1911. He was on active service for five years in Mesopotamia, 1916–21, and for one more year on the North West Frontier of India in 1935. I still have the five medals that he was awarded. I was born in 1913 in Burma, while my father was serving at the British Military Hospital in Maymyo.

Maymyo is 3500 feet above sea level and lies 40 miles east of Mandalay. It was chosen in 1886 by Colonel James May of the 5th Bengal Infantry and established as a hill station for British soldiers.

The name Maymyo means the village of May: 'myo' means village in Burmese. The railway from Mandalay to Lashio was opened in 1900 and completed in 1903 the 181 miles to Lashio. It is possible to visit the Goktek Viaduct, which is 83 miles from

Mandalay. By road it takes two hours from Maymyo to this wonderful steel trestle bridge, 2260 feet long, built 320 feet high with a great cavern around it.

The bridge was erected in 1901 by an American company. It is worthwhile descending the 900 feet by a good path to the cavern through which the river flows under the two bridges, i.e. the natural limestone bridge and the viaduct built on it.

I was six years old in 1919 when a party of us visited, or rather picnicked there. In our party were friends of the driver and the guard, who stopped the train specially for us to alight, and on its return in the evening stopped again to pick us up. It was not a scheduled stop at all. It is good to have friends in the right places at the appropriate time. I remember scrambling down this deep ravine and finding an enormous concrete block into which one of the huge trestles of the bridge was planted. From there we looked up at this mass of steel girders and trees and mist and clouds, and listened to the roar of the water of the river rushing through the gorge.

I was born in the British Military Hospital, Maymyo, when my father was an assistant surgeon. We lived in a bungalow near the hospital. The Government provided the hospital, the staff quarters and the barracks in the Maymyo cantonment, built apart from the native city. The railway station was south of us, and so were the Club and golf course and Botanical Gardens. The Forest Department had constructed several 'rides' for its officers to reach otherwise inaccessible forest on horseback.

My first school was the Roman Catholic convent. Another director's son and I were taken to school in the hospital 'ambulance'. This was an iron-wheeled cart drawn by two bullocks. The seat rests could be folded down flat to carry two stretcher-carried soldiers.

My second school was the Church of England St Michael's School. My father was sent on active service to Mesopotamia from 1916 to 1921, and my mother and my sister and I stayed on as paying guests with a Mrs Baxter, whose daughter was a teacher in the Church of England school just across the road. This caused my mother much soul-searching – she was, I believe, a devout Roman Catholic.

I remember this as a happy boyhood. My father 'had gone to the War and he wore uniforms'. My mother told me how she and I were walking with my sister in her pram when we met this pleasant young man 'in uniform' and I asked 'Are you my father?' My 26-year-old mother blushed in confusion!

My father came back 'from the War' in July 1921, a complete stranger but handsome and strong and with such comforting arms. Oh yes, I remember that.

NANCY LLOYD

My father was in the ICS (Indian Civil Service), which in the days of the British Raj was the Government of India. My father served almost entirely in Burma which, until 1937, was a province of India. He was a Deputy Commissioner in Toungoo and also Akyab (Arakan) and later was Commissioner in Taunggyi, in the Shan States; otherwise he was in the secretariat in Rangoon. He became Financial Commissioner and finally Finance Member. The whole secretariat moved up to the hills, Maymyo, twice a year in the hot weather. I was born in Maymyo. It was a beautiful hill station, with rolling hills, quite unlike the mountainous Simla or Darjeeling in India.

In those days English children were not kept out in the East after the age of about four, but were left at home in England. So for that reason I have very few memories of life in Burma as a little child. I was very pampered, with an English nanny and an Indian *ayah*, but I saw plenty of my parents, and every evening we used to drive out round the lakes in Rangoon and watch the lights on the beautiful golden pagoda, which dominates Rangoon, spring into being.

All the houses in Rangoon were built of wood, with wide verandahs all round to keep out the heat. There was no air-conditioning, no refrigerators and no electric fans. One of my earliest memories is of my mother calling out to wake the *punkahwallah*, who would be sitting outside in the garden pulling the rope that flapped the *punkah* back and forth. I also vividly remember lying in bed, looking up through the mosquito net at the many lizards on the ceiling. They have sort of suction pads on their feet, so they did not often fall. Mosquitoes were, as now, a trial, as were ants, and the legs of all the food cabinets were set in tins of disinfectant to stop the ants invading the food. Food was kept cold in a zinc-lined chest, with huge chunks of ice brought from the bazaar. Most of the food was purchased daily in the bazaar by the cook. There was no frozen food, though quite a lot of canned stuff.

I played a good deal with other English children in the gardens of our homes or at the Club, always carefully supervised by our nannies, I am sure.

As I was left in England from the age of about five, joining my older sisters and meeting them for the first time, I have very few other memories of childhood in Burma, and certainly at that young age I did no lessons or schoolwork.

After my childhood and schooldays in England, I returned to Burma in October 1936, shortly before my eighteenth birthday, with my parents and second sister (my eldest sister was now married and living in England). We travelled by sea to Bombay by the P&O line, and crossed India from Bombay to Calcutta by train. This was long and very hot journey, 36 hours if I remember rightly. After a night or two in Calcutta, we crossed the Bay of Bengal by a smaller steamer. My father was by then a senior member of the Government, being Finance Member, and was due to retire the following April after Burma had ceased to be a province of India and was to become a separate country in its own right on 1 April 1937. After a day or two in Rangoon we travelled by train up to Maymyo, a very pleasant hill station in the Shan States, about 450 miles north of Rangoon, which became the seat of Government during the hot season and again towards the end of the monsoon in October. It was a marvellous change for someone who had been a schoolgirl only three months before, with endless fun – golf, tennis, riding and swimming, and of course dancing through the night. Maymyo was also a military station, and there was no shortage of charming and attractive young officers to escort us in all these amusements. Those forest officers who worked long months at a time in the jungle supervising the timberwork, the extraction of the huge teak logs, would also come into Maymyo for a couple of weeks of relaxation in a bit of civilisation and they too would join in the fun and social life.

When we returned to Rangoon in November, we enjoyed the same round of parties and games in an equally frivolous and cheerful way. I accompanied my parents to various more serious meetings and displays, but I don't think I took much interest in the way the country was run and its politics. We took part in concerts and little shows, and it was in a performance of a Gilbert and Sullivan opera that I first met my future husband. He was a pianist and I played the violin, so we did lots of music together, evading my mother's rule of us girls never going to a bachelor 'chummery' unless there was a married couple present, by pleading shyness at playing music with other people listening!

There were many servants to take care of the household. They were mostly Indian, as the Burmese are not so efficient or so hard working. The cook, who did all the marketing at dawn, was Mugh, that is from Chittagong in India, and he produced wonderful food from the sketchiest of kitchens. The Mughs were mostly trained by the French in days gone by, so the standard was high, and I remember the most elegant puddings. But I don't remember that we had many dishes of Oriental flavour, except the frequent Sunday lunchtime curries.

H.C.G. BROWN

I was born in Rangoon in 1918, my Cornish father at that time being captain of a sailing ship which was wrecked in a cyclone off Calcutta. He then joined the Port Commissioners as a harbourmaster, ultimately becoming the Deputy Conservator or Chief Executive of the port. My Irish mother had been a governess in China and met my father when he was Chief Officer of a B.I. ship plying between Shanghai and Calcutta and she was returning to the UK. After a stormy altercation over a chow dog owned by my father, which she considered unkempt, they were married in Calcutta.

Europeans in the East, by and large, tried to create a 'little Britain' around them, with the result that, in Rangoon, there was little social contact with Burmese or Indians. The principal Clubs were strictly European and there was no doubt as to who were the rulers and who the ruled. Much has been written about the Indian caste system but there was also a definite pecking order amongst Europeans, which has not been sufficiently documented. My family, during my childhood, was certainly not regarded as from the 'top drawer' to which belonged the Civil Service, or 'heaven-born', as they were known. Heads and senior executives of firms were tolerated but tended to be regarded as *boxwallahs*. There was a great deal of snobbery, and a European who married into the country was regarded as somebody who had 'gone native' and was, therefore, beyond the pale.

We lived not in a fine house in the leafy environs of Rangoon, but in a flat on top of a huge block on Strand Road. Unlike my sister and brother, who came later, I did not have an *ayah* or nanny, and when, years afterwards, I asked why, I was told that no one was prepared to stay with me. It seems that I was a 'difficult' boy with a pathological hatred of any authority other than that of my father and mother.

My earliest memories, when I was about six years old, are of playing on the waterfront with Indian, Burmese and half-caste *chokras* completely unsupervised. The Rangoon River, crammed with shipping and lighters, was, and is, a dangerous watercourse: tides and undercurrents are strong. On one occasion, finding a sampan beached in the glutinous mud, we boys pushed it out into the stream and jumped aboard. The current took hold, whereupon all the boys, except me and one smaller than I, dived overboard and swam ashore. I couldn't swim, and the little fellow began to cry. There were no oars in the sampan, so I took up the floorboards and with these paddled towards the shore, which we reached some way downstream. We had to watch out for snakes, which abounded in the river and the mud.

I also remember long walks through Chinatown, wearing a green shirt and a home-made bow slung over my shoulder, my head filled with the exploits of Robin Hood, with whom I closely identified. The Police sent reports to my father of sighting me alone in particularly unsalubrious areas of Rangoon but I can't remember anyone getting excited about it or being punished. Nor was I punished for pinching the bicycle of an Anglo-Indian resident of a downstairs flat and riding it all over Rangoon, my right leg between the crossbar and the pedals.

I can remember the Maidan where the big Sikh policemen practised tug-o'-war. Twelve of these stalwarts on one end of the rope and double that number of locals on the other seemed unfair to me, so I joined the Sikhs and helped pull them to victory. An additional excitement was finding a man hanging by the neck, very definitely dead, on one of the trees nearby. I avoided the naked *fakirs* sitting trance-like about the Maidan; they scared me.

Nearby was Dr Crowe's Gardens, where most European children congregated with their *ayahs* and nannies. I occasionally visited the place but was made to feel unwanted, presumably because I was *ayah*less. I conceived a great dislike for these guardians, and things came to a head one morning. I had been taken to the cinema the previous day and seen a film called *The Mask of Zorro* in which Douglas Fairbanks as a masked master-swordsman left his mark on his enemies by cutting a Z on their cheeks. Temporarily forgetting Robin Hood, I became Zorro, procured two bamboo sticks with sharpened ends and challenged the boys in the gardens to mortal combat. This was too much for the assembled *ayahs*, who rose in a body and chased me away. Furious, I returned home, grabbed a carving knife and returned to the gardens. This time it was the *ayahs* who were put to flight. Repercussions followed, and my father put his foot down:

I was sent to a large Baptist Mission school at which I was the only European boy. When I was not at school, I was to report to the office of the harbourmasters, where I was assigned a seat in my father's boat with my own special miniature oar. The *kalassis*, all fine seamen, taught me to row and kept a close eye on me when we stood by the buoys to moor the ships. It was all very exciting, and my love of the sea and ships was born.

At school, meantime, I was having a difficult time, until I tackled the main Anglo-Burmese bully and won my first fight. I was so pleased with myself that I told the schoolmistress all about it. I was deflated by her comment that I had come to school to learn, not to fight.

Then I was taken ill, and not just the odd fever or 'touch of the sun', which were common enough. My parents swore that it was the result of the stuff I used to eat at school – curry and rice, of which I was very fond, and nuts and sweetmeats filched from vendors at the school gates. But I knew better. I hated papaya and said so when it appeared on the table. My father said I should eat some. No one else did, fortunately. That night I began vomiting and worse, and my distraught mother plied me with brandy and castor oil alternately until the doctor arrived. I was immediately removed to the isolation hospital with cholera. There is little doubt that the cause was a cut papaya from the ice-box. My father and the taxi driver who took me were also impounded for several days, much to their fury. Cholera in those days, before antibiotics, was a sure killer, and it was some time before I was in a position to prove it to be otherwise. My having been so near death persuaded my father that the time had come for me to go home for my education and, hopefully, training, and to stay there.

The voyage home I remember well, especially going through the Red Sea. I thought it would be a good joke to sneak into the saloon, crank up all the portholes and throw the crank overboard. Unfortunately, no one else saw the joke, and I kept very quiet indeed amidst the furore which followed. Tiffin was not a very successful meal that day, as it took some time to manufacture another crank.

My father looked pretty hard at me but nothing was said. There was also an episode when a boy of about my age was bullying my sister. My father spoke to the boy's father but only got the advice from him that 'boys will be boys, you know'. My father instructed me to keep an eye on the boy and, if he worried my sister again, to punch him on the nose. Only too pleased to employ my energies productively, I did just that. When the boy's father complained to mine, he was given the same advice, that boys would indeed be boys. My sister was not bullied again.

In Norfolk, I missed the sights and smells of Rangoon, but I could picture them without difficulty: the marvellous evening skies full of kites doing battle, their strings having been marinaded in rice water to produce a razor quality. I lost several fine kites in such battles, so my father built me a six-foot giant of light canvas on stout bamboos with thick, strong twine instead of the usual fine string. This we flew at a great height, and watched while lesser kites challenged, became entangled and capitulated. When we hauled it down we had several kites attached, making up for the ones I had lost. I remembered the smells of *ngapi* (dried fish) and durian fruit which, once smelt, could never be forgotten, such was their pungency, as they were trundled along the road in carts drawn by coolies; the buzz of crickets and cicadas, the calls of lizards (particularly the *tuck-too*) and, in the monsoon, the croaks of frogs which filled the night with sound; and the everlasting whine of mosquitos. I called to mind the vast thunderings of the monsoon and the cataracts of rain which washed away your prickly heat, giving blessed relief from scratching; the festivals of water and of light; the golden pagodas and the *poongyis* in their saffron robes gliding along with their black, lacquer begging bowls held out before them; the Boat Club where I nearly drowned, having walked off the end of a boat jetty whilst watching a flight of wild geese passing overhead (a boatman, hearing my splashes, dragged me out by the hair as I was going down for the third time but I was consoled with a fine lime juice and soda and marvellous chips); the occasion when I fed ginger biscuits to the crows from the verandah, to be rewarded with a smacked bottom from my father, awakened by the noise from his siesta; and my incarceration in a store room where I found tins of cigarettes and whiled away the time learning to smoke.

FAY FOUCAR

In 1925 we moved from Moulmein in south Burma to Rangoon, the capital, where my father joined a law firm. My brother, Tony, was born there in 1926. We lived in one of the Gymkhana Club houses, of which there were three in a row with gardens backing on to the Club grounds. It was an old, two-storey, wooden house with stone floors downstairs. It had a porch, a large open hall with rooms opening off – my father's study, a small sitting room, a bedroom with bathroom and the dining room at the far end. Upstairs was the same plan with an open verandah over the porch, an open hall which was our main living room, with bedrooms, each with its own bathroom opening off it, and my father had a dressing room. We had a large compound (garden) with a tennis court in front, the cookhouse and servants' quarters at the back. We had electricity and a well in the garden with a heavy, child-proof cover, but no running water in the house. Bathrooms were equipped with tin tubs and thunder-boxes and large stone jars (called *pegu* jars) like those used by the forty thieves of *Arabian Nights* fame, for the cold water. Bath water was heated in kerosene tins on charcoal and carried up the back stairs. The cooking was also done on charcoal, meals being brought to us via a covered way between the cookhouse and the pantry. In the pantry was a wooden ice-box, lined with zinc, and a wooden meat safe which stood in tins filled with kerosene to keep it free from ants and cockroaches.

We had Indian servants, Madrassis. The cook went very early each morning to the bazaar to buy us fresh food. He would lay it all out on the kitchen table for my mother to inspect. My mother knew he was making a profit and he knew that she knew it, so it was kept within reasonable bounds. The head servant was the butler, in charge of the others. He waited at table, brought the tea and drinks, laid out my father's clothes, cleaned the silver and generally supervised all activities in the household. He wore a white uniform and a turban. The *paniwallah*, literally 'water man', kept the water jars full, heated up and carried up the bath water, washed up, cleaned the shoes and was, in fact, the general 'dogsbody'. The sweeper not only swept and polished and washed the floors, he also looked after the loos; he had all the menial jobs. The *mali* looked after the garden and, at night, we had a *durwan* or nightwatchman – in India he would have been called a *chowkidar*. We had an Indian Christian *ayah* called Antony. Sharing the same name as my brother, she had a great affinity with him. Her job was to look after us, wash and iron our clothes and take us out for walks. She also attended to us at meals and slept in our bedroom. She was later replaced by a Karen nanny.

For the car, we had a Burmese driver, Maung Ba In. He wore traditional dress, a gaily coloured *lungyi*, a short, dark jacket and a coloured, silk *gaung baung* round the top of his head. He was most particular about his and the car's appearance. Not only was he a good driver, but he was also an excellent mechanic. He came to my father in 1922 and stayed until my father had to leave Burma in 1942 when the Japanese invaded, incidentally saving both our lives when he drove at full speed through a ring of fire. When my father returned in 1946 he returned and remained with my father until his retirement in 1951.

The servants and their families lived in the servants' quarters. There were always lots of children and we knew them all, but I can't remember them ever being a nuisance. They always seemed to be quiet and unobtrusive. The number of servants makes it appear we were affluent, but in fact this was the minimum number for a normal European household. The servants' wages were small but adequate, food being cheap and plentiful and their housing free. We were giving work to several families, and it was a very happy household.

Our first meal of the day was milk and biscuits, then when it was still cool we would go for a walk, meet our friends in each others' gardens or houses if it was raining. My father would be working in his study but we all met for tiffin which we ate together *en famille*. My father would then go to his office and my mother went shopping while we played indoors or in the garden. We had to wear *topees* in the sun, hats made of cork and well blanched to keep them white.

In the heat of the day Nanny had time off, and we would lie on my mother's bed and she would read to us. During the monsoon, there were terrific thunderstorms, the lightning dancing along the wires which held the mosquito nets. It would be so dark that we would sometimes switch on the bedside light and my mother would make shadow animals on the opposite wall with her hands. Somebody must have kept a toucan because he often visited us in the afternoons. He was very black and glossy with an enormous orange bill; he looked very handsome and wise, perched on top of the wardrobe.

After our rest, we washed, put on clean clothes and watched Nanny getting ready to go out. She would wear a clean, white *ayngyi* (a sort of blouse) and a *lungyi*, and we were fascinated to see her build up her hair with switches until it looked like a child's sandcastle, into which she would insert flowers: hibiscus, jasmine, frangipani and other flowers from the garden. We were very proud of her, she looked so pretty.

Then Ba In would take us to the park on the Royal Lakes, a beautiful spot. We and Nanny would meet our friends. We would walk round the park and chase each other, one favourite game was to roll down the steep, grassy slopes. We would arrive back at the entrance in time to be picked up and taken home. While we waited, we made use of the bronze statue of Queen Victoria, the Queen Empress, standing on its marble plinth of steps, daring each other to jump from a higher and higher step. Then we would go home for tea, my father having returned from office. Often there would be a tennis party for the grown-ups or they would go to the Club to play there. We children attended many parties, birthday and others, from which we would return laden with balloons, sweets and presents. Supper, bath and bed followed. We enjoyed watching our parents dressing for dinner, always a black tie for my father and pretty evening dresses for my mother – there was much entertaining. When my brother was very little, Ayah would croon to him and pat him to sleep. We always slept under mosquito nets, carefully tucked under our mattresses.

Little, pale brown lizards (*chik-chaks*) ran about all over the walls and ceiling catching flies and mosquitos, sometimes leaving their wagging tails behind in their hurry. Their tails always grew again, we were assured. Outside, under the eaves, lived a large *tuck-too*, so called because of the noise it made. A very large lizard of fearsome aspect, it ate cockroaches, insects and baby birds if it could get them; it was said that if it got on your arm you had to induce it off, as its suction pads were such as to be irremovable. Nonetheless, they were regarded as a lucky charm. In the evening, the flying foxes (fruit bats) would awaken us as they left their roost in a tree in the garden, flying in a vast swarm to find a tree with ripe fruit. Occasionally, one would get lost and land in our bedroom, and there was great excitement as my father caught it between two tennis rackets and put it out of the window.

Every morning early, the *doodhwallah* would bring his cow and milk her while my mother watched to make sure no water was added and that it was boiled. Once a week, the *dhobi* appeared bringing the clean washing back in a large bundle, and go off with all the soiled clothes, a careful list being made of everything he took.

There were no ready-made children's clothes in the shops. Our outgrown clothes were given to the servants or to the orphanage while a verandah *dhirzi* came to the house to tailor us new ones. He would arrive in a rickshaw with his sewing machine. My mother would give him the materials and tell him what she wanted. He would measure us and cut out on the floor and then spread out a sheet and sit on it, cross-legged behind his machine and stitch away. He made little shirts with button-on shorts for my brother and little dresses for me.

He would also do any mending required. But my party dresses were made for me by my mother.

Sometimes, my mother would take us shopping with her. The first call, after dropping off my father at his office, was to the ice factory to collect a large block for the ice-box – this was a daily routine. We also collected soda water in bottles and filled a large jar with drinking water from the ever-flowing tap outside the factory. There was always a queue for this, but Ba In simply ignored this and we did not have to wait if Mother was in the car. Rangoon was blessed with purest-water artesian wells so we did not have the usual performance of having to boil and filter for drinking as usually occurs in the Tropics. Imported food like bacon and cheese we bought at the cold stores; also chocolates and chocolate biscuits, luxuries we enjoyed, being allowed one piece of chocolate each day after tiffin. Our last call was to the Japanese toy shop, full of brightly coloured and ingenious toys. I usually had something for my dolls' house and Tony would take a small animal or mechanical toy.

One tiffin time, when Tony was very small, he was in his high chair and Ayah was helping to feed him when he broke wind loudly. 'Tony,' my mother exclaimed, horrified. 'It wasn't me,' Tony replied, 'it was Ayah,' as he carried on feeding himself. Ayah pulled her sari across her face, collapsing in giggles, while the butler had to leave the room hurriedly. European children, especially boys, could get away with anything.

The servants called us 'Missy-baba' and 'Tony-baba', our parents being 'Sahib' and 'Memsahib' (except for Ba In, for whom they were 'Thakin' and 'Thakinma'). Not surprisingly, we used many Hindustani words including nursery ones such as 'ninny' for sleep, 'num num' for food, 'doodhi' for milk and 'soo soo' for spending a penny.

With many of my friends, I went to kindergarten run by an English governess who had come out with some friends of my parents to teach their children. Tony was still too young for this experience.

Because of the prevalence of rabies we were not allowed to keep a dog, but we had cats, rabbits and budgies. I had a kitten of my own whom I loved dearly, dressing her up and wheeling her round in my doll's pram.

Under the porch we had a sand pit which kept us happy for hours. We also had the usual soft toys and dolls while Tony had a pedal car. I had a magnificent dolls' house presented to me by a grateful client of my father's. It was very large, the walls and roof all opening easily: it was lovely to play with it. When I went home to school, it was given to Bishop Strachan's Orphanage, which my mother visited regularly.

One hot afternoon over a weekend, we were all together upstairs in the sitting room when my parents had an argument. My father stalked off to his study. Some time later, two shots rang out and my mother leapt to her feet crying, 'Oh God, he's shot himself!' She was wrong, of course. My father appeared from their bedroom carrying his revolver. One of the servants had spotted a snake coiled up under the thunder-box in my parents' bathroom and reported it to my father. He had loaded his revolver, gone up the back stairs and shot the cobra. The sweeper cleaned it away and it was given to some Chinese workmen who were mending the roof. Stir-fried snake being a great delicacy, they were delighted. The argument, whatever it was, was forgotten.

Looking out of the window next day, we saw the cobra's mate. The pair had obviously been living in the garden but luckily we had never come across them. The servants went looking for it but we never saw it again. We did, however, see scorpions, spiders, huge centipedes and ants of all kinds. There were flying ants which shed their shiny wings, big black soldier ants about an inch long, tiny red ants which bit madly and enormous cockroaches. The garden was full of noisy crows and cheeky mynah birds in pairs and little tree rats which looked like chipmunks. At night, there was the cacophony of crickets and lizards, their chorus being swollen during the monsoons by the croaking of frogs.

Occasionally, on Sundays we went to the zoo. In beautiful surroundings the Rangoon Zoo had a good selection of animals and birds, well kept and very popular. At the gate we bought nuts for the monkeys, wrapped in paper cones. Despite instructions to us not to eat them, I am afraid the monkeys didn't get many. Riding in the elephant cart and feeding the elephant with bananas afterwards was a great treat, and the *camera obscura*, which brought us views of the zoo from all angles, we thought pure magic.

One of the Rangoon monasteries, or Phongyi Chaungs, on top of a hill, had a sacred fish tank and a vast statue of the Reclining Buddha. We had to climb up what seemed to be hundreds of steps to get to it and the *phongyis* in their orange robes always seemed pleased to see us. We weren't interested in the tank, which appeared dark and sinister. We had come to see the Buddha. Cunningly constructed, like the pagodas themselves, of bricks overlaid with plaster and painted, this huge effigy lay on its side, propped on its elbow, feet together, smiling serenely. Before him were flickering candles and offerings of rice, fruit and flowers. His big toe was the size of a man's head. We stood and marvelled. Sadly, he was destroyed in the War.

My parents belonged to several Clubs. They sometimes took us to the Boat Club on the Royal Lakes. It was built over the lake. We would sit on the verandah upstairs and below, the boats were stored. We watched people taking them out, sculls, rowing boats and punts. Our interest was in fresh lime juice (*nimbu pani*) and chips with tomato sauce.

My mother used to ride at the Country Club which was some distance out of Rangoon. We enjoyed the drive there and especially the toasted bacon sandwiches. My father was president of the Gymkhana Club one year, where he and my mother sometimes won the mixed doubles at tennis. The Military Police Band occasionally played there of an evening, very smart in their white uniforms and *topees*. I was fascinated by their marching and counter-marching back and forth across the rugger pitch, which was floodlit for the occasion.

On Sundays we would often take a picnic lunch and drive out to the Big Lakes. There we found an old, wooden bungalow complete with punt which we children paddled about in when we were not swimming. It was a lovely spot and there always seemed to be a cool breeze.

To drive into town from our house, we had to pass Rangoon Jail. A grim wall, some 15 feet high painted grey with whitewashed bricks placed loosely on top, surrounded it. One year there was a serious jailbreak. When my father went to his office he left his loaded revolver with my mother. The house was kept shut and we were not allowed to play in the garden. One afternoon, when the servants had gone off duty, there was a suspicious noise downstairs. My mother stationed herself at the top of the stairs with the revolver at the ready. It proved a false alarm, but it was a nasty moment.

Sometimes, if I awoke in the night, I would run into my parents' room, untuck their mosquito net and climb into their bed. One night, as I arrived, a naked man came in through the window, crossed to the dressing table and picked up my mother's silver brushes. I screamed, he dropped everything, rushed to the window and jumped straight out. Mother woke instantly; it took Father somewhat longer but it took an age to rouse the *durwan*.

One very hot, still night in 1930 we had just got into bed when all the ornaments and glasses on the dressing table started to tinkle, then rattle. There was a very loud rumble and our beds careered across the room towards the window, the fan smashed against the ceiling and all the lights went out. Our parents rushed in to make sure we were all right. This was the great Pegu Earthquake which devastated the town of Pegu, which was about 50 miles north east of Rangoon, but did not affect Rangoon too badly. Our old house stood up surprisingly well, though some bits of the roof and eaves fell off.

In the hot weather every year, my father would take a house in Kalaw in the Shan Hills to give us a break from the heat. My mother would go ahead, by train, taking us, Nanny and the butler, and my father would drive up later. It was an adventure to sleep the night on the train. At the stations there was great activity, people selling food and drinks, everyone shouting at the top of their voices, *coolies* carrying mountains of baggage, people getting off and on. When we awoke in the morning we were at the foot of the hill section. A second steam engine was attached to the rear of the train, and, slowly and laboriously, with much noisy puffing, we would zig-zag up the steep incline. It became cooler and fresher as we progressed. On one occasion, during the climb, my mother's straw hat, which was on the rack, blew out of the window and sailed down the hill. Without hesitation, the butler, who had been sitting on the floor, opened the door and jumped out after it. My brother, fearing that the butler would be left behind, burst into tears and cried for the train to stop. The butler, meantime, retrieved the hat and simply climbed straight up the slope, well in time to meet the train on its next 'zag', much to everyone's relief.

Kalaw was a heaven, smelling of pine trees and wood smoke. We lost our prickly heat, we collected fir cones on our morning walks and watched them burn as we sat around a real fire in the evenings.

The Burmese have a water festival every year just before the onset of the monsoon. It is a time of great rejoicing, everyone throwing water over everyone else. The little boys in the street especially enjoy themselves. My parents were not so keen on it, keeping the windows of the car tight closed, but Tony and I thought it great fun watching grown-ups behaving as we'd like to behave ourselves.

A client of my father asked us to visit his shop to celebrate Diwali, the Hindu Festival of Lights. He sold mirrors and glassware, and he had decorated the place with strings of coloured electric lights. The effect was to produce a veritable Aladdin's cave, the reflections sparkling like jewels. We were offered Indian sweetmeats covered in real silver foil, glasses of raspberryade and green ice cream sodas all adding to the colour of the festivities.

The time came when we had to return to England when my parents took home leave. Of the voyage I remember the Egyptian *gully-gully* man, a wonderful conjuror whose main trick was to produce little, live fluffy yellow chicks from many places – from his sleeve, his hat, our ears and noses. Real magic! At Port Sudan we viewed the colourful fish and jellyfish through a glass-bottomed boat. I was unhappy at leaving Burma and my kitten behind.

After their leave, my parents returned to Burma and we had to go to school. Together we were left in a small private boarding school in January. I was nine and Tony was six. It was a most unhappy time. Without our parents for the first time in our lives, we felt abandoned and unloved in spite of knowing that we had grandparents and aunts to stay with in the holidays who were kindness itself.

The school had no central heating, only upright stoves in the classrooms. We felt the cold badly, the food was dreary, the other children appeared unfriendly and we had to wear ugly, scratchy uniforms. Lessons we could cope with, but games like hockey were quite alien. We missed being the centre of attention and having the household apparently revolving around us. We were in a dormitory with six other children, and for many nights I cried myself to sleep. But we gradually got used to the conditions, made friends and began to enjoy school and to look forward to holidays.

STAR STAUNTON

Since I spent my infancy in India, India was home for me, the place of the familiar and predictable. The exotic, exciting, and also deadly and dangerous, country for me was Burma, where I spent with my father the Christmases that followed respectively my ninth and tenth birthdays, in 1931 and 1932.

My childish memories cannot distinguish between Rangoon and Mandalay, or the smaller places we visited. They only see three kinds of scene, each very different from the others and awaking a different emotional response: first, the towns, thronged with people; second, the dark and frightening jungle among the hills; third, the peace and security of the Buddhist lamasery into which I stumbled half-dead on that occasion when the jungle let me go, of which more later.

On my first visit it was the Burma of the towns whose acquaintance I made. I heard the different tones of a language quite distinct in kind from the languages which I had been absorbing in India; I marked the bright colours of the skirts from waist to feet, which seemed to be worn by both sexes, and the white blouses buttoned with gold or red, blue or green jewels, the brilliant sandals, the parasols, the flowers in the hair, the jewelled combs. It was evidently the people that attracted me, especially the men, who always seemed to be strolling about with nothing to do except to be admired, and admire them I did. To me they were attractive creatures from another world almost, although I suppose most of them spent their days in dusty offices as clerks or small functionaries. Burma was not in those days a land of great riches. I understand that the same is true today.

I remember one room in a house I must have entered for some purpose or other. It surprised me by its emptiness, and yet made on my childish sensibility an impression of great solemnity. There must have been only two or three pieces of furniture, but pieces that were beautifully made and exquisitely related to the dimensions of the room. Why this room stands out so clearly in memory, apart from its aesthetic appeal, I cannot say.

Such is the jumbled but favourable generalisation of Burmese town life that I have carried with me from childhood. It is enriched for me by a set of vivid images of the particular time which I was on one occasion allowed to accompany my *amah* to the burial wake of an uncle of hers. Amah was the Burmese word for *ayah*, and on that holiday in Burma my father had hired an *amah* to replace my own *ayah*, who was then on leave. Could Missy-baba come with her to the wake? Why not? It would be good for her education. And off we went.

As we entered the road where the dead relative had lived we found a dance in progress. Huge and terrifying masked dancers swayed to and fro: they were, of course, men on stilts. Up and down they went -in front of the house, grotesque and menacing, to the accompaniment of loud drumming and shouting and the continual explosion of firecrackers. I was not really frightened, for the sensation of alarm was a pleasant one, though I held hard on to Amah's hand. She told me these were devils, but not to worry, they would soon be driven away. Sure enough, from round a corner appeared white-faced creatures, also gigantic, dressed in flowing white and red robes, pink-cheeked and red-lipped, with bells on ankles and wrists, manifestly 'goodies' come to attack the 'baddies'. A stilt dance followed, in the course of which the devils were gradually forced to give ground before the jingling bells and low whistling of their adversaries. Then away they all went, and the fascinated crowd that had gathered to watch them disappeared – except those who, like my *amah* and I, were privileged to go inside and pay our respects to the corpse.

Amah led me through the entrance, up some stairs to the second floor, and into a room in the centre of which was a long trestle table laden with food and flowers. At the end of the table, seated in a fine carved chair, dressed in his best clothes and wearing a smiling face-mask, sat the dead man himself. Amah said, 'Bow to your host and wish him a happy death day'. This I did without any sense of embarrassment, the action seemed so right and natural. Then the whole family sat on cushions around the table and fell to feasting with all the gaiety of an Irish wake, though with greater sobriety. It would have been bad form to show sorrow or shed tears and so spoil what everyone wanted to be a 'happy death day'.

During the feasting some men took our host as he was in his chair and carried him up to the flat roof where, I believe, his clothes were solemnly burned. I was privately concerned that they should not also burn the chair, which was beautiful. But from that day to this I have never been afraid to look on death.

Amah's background was Buddhist, but with an open-hearted tolerance of other people's manner of conducting themselves in matters of religion, that contrasted, I fancy, with the Christian norm. She had absorbed some knowledge of Christianity and took me to attend a nativity party given at the local Christian mission school. She proved to know almost as much about the Christian story as I myself had learned at that stage of my life, in spite of the time I had spent at the convent.

A large crowd was already seated on the lawns surrounding the mission house. As usual, the Burmese were gorgeously dressed, making the Europeans, both men and women, seem drab by comparison. We sat there singing carols in Burmese and English and eating our picnics for a matter of hours, and then at midnight rose and formed a procession, each of us holding a paper lantern or candle, and wended our way to the place where the 'stable' was set out in a kind of tableau. Flanking the stable were children of all ages, Burmese, Europeans, Eurasians, light skins and dark, and darker still, cheek by jowl singing 'Away in a Manger'. In the stable itself, with Joseph beside her, lay a young Burmese Mary cuddling a real-life Christ-child, a real-life ox and ass in attendance, and a few chickens picking in the straw. I have attended a number of such nativity celebrations here in England, but never one that took such powerful hold of my imagination.

Now for two other aspects of Burma which still haunt my imagination with impressions that are vague and dreamlike, though they are related to the most dangerous moment of my life, except the very beginning. I mean the jungle and the lamasery, the sinister and the peaceful. I know that my memory of the details must be unreliable and owe something to invention and fantasy, for what happened was frightening and disturbing in the extreme and left me, I imagine, too dazed and bewildered to retain an accurate notion of what had befallen me. I will set down fantasy and fact together, trying as best I may to distinguish between them, though I am conscious all the time that fantasy can be as important to my self-understanding as what actually happened. Both have long since been digested into the living stuff of which my personal self is constructed.

My tenth birthday had passed. Our Christmas jaunt that year was a visit to a friend of my father whom I was allowed to call Uncle Dick, a well-known and highly reputed zoologist. I came across his name not long ago among the descriptive notes attached to one of the cages at Edinburgh Zoo. He was on safari among the hill country that stretches endlessly from the eastern edge of the valley in which Mandalay stands and rises higher and higher towards the Chinese frontier. His quest on this occasion was for butterflies and moths.

In those days, I believe, the last considerable station in this direction was a place called Maymyo, for I remember that the journey from then on was on horseback and that some days passed before we arrived at Uncle Dick's encampment. This was an open space surrounded by thickish scrub and taller trees with a number of square stockades made of strong pallisading, and near the middle a group of low, khaki tents. There was also a high mesh enclosure to which I gave a wide berth because it housed the captured insects, and I never liked creepy-crawly creatures. A path of sorts had brought us to the enclosure which, apart from a number of scarcely visible tracks, seemed to be a dead end. The next day Uncle Dick conducted my father and me along one of these tracks to show us where he had captured his specimens. He warned me that I must never go out of the camp alone because the area was very dangerous, as indeed it proved to be, and I should never have been there. The *ayah* was on hand, of course, to attend to my needs, but so had she been when my mother died. That fatality might have warned my father of the lack of wisdom of bringing a vulnerable female into a spot so wild and remote, but he was apt to do what he wanted, expecting circumstances to support him, which they usually did – even, in the end, on this occasion.

They told me afterwards that it was on Christmas Eve that I lost myself in the jungle. My recollection is that Uncle Dick had given me a tiger cub as a Christmas present, a beautiful friendly creature no bigger than a cat and quite harmless. I called him Rollo and we romped together all over the clearing that evening. I forgot Uncle Dick's repeated injunction never to go out of sight of the tents and, indeed, in my bliss, forgot everything but Rollo. Gradually we played our games further and further away from the clearing until he completely disappeared. I called him but he did not come and, in utter dejection, I gave up and set off back for the camp.

But where was the camp? I realised that I was both lost and in danger and it has always seemed interesting to me that, at that dreadful moment, I was more afraid of my father's rebuke than in any dread of natural danger.

What did occur was that I was found next day by some of the very primitive inhabitants of that locality and taken by them to their camp. I remember coming to myself and seeing a brown toothless female face looking down at me as I lay, pinioned, to a kind of stretcher. I was loosed and stood up on painful feet, to pass several nights in a little tent of skins stretched over hoops of bamboo. After some days – I never decided how many – the toothless female, who must have been their chieftain, gave me over into the hands of a few men and we set off together into the jungle. Our joint expedition came to an end when my sharp-eared escorts heard the sound of a bell and vanished almost on the instant.

Following the sound of the bell, through broken and scrubby terrain, I found myself in front of a great iron gateway covered with jangling wind-bells and I realised that I had come to a Buddhist lamasery. In Burma the main gate is never the point of entry, being put there only to deceive devils, the real entry being elsewhere and less obvious, but I wonder if I knew this at the time? However, the lamasery was real enough. A Buddhist monk took my hand and led me into a high, long room and before long a voice behind me said, in Urdu, 'I am glad that you have returned, daughter.'

It was the abbot of the lamasery, towering high above me, my ideal of the handsome Burmese male, but with a loftiness of expression, an air of dignity and command, which I revered on sight. I believe I just fainted at his feet.

The abbot told me he had heard of my disappearance and, on my arrival, had at once sent a brother to the nearest telephone, which was at a mission station, to inform my father. I remember that they cut my hair very close, but am not sure why. I remember being given a bowl for a chamber-pot, with water in a jar and a yellow cloth instead of lavatory paper. I remember the arrival of a lady from the American mission – a large lady with a loud voice – who put a rough vest on me that hurt my blistered skin abominably and had to be removed. And I remember being sent for to see my father, who had come to fetch me, and walking with some trepidation into the room where he was awaiting me.

But he was kind and concerned, took note of my thinness and my bald head but otherwise behaved as if nothing of great importance had happened. I am sure he was pleased that I had turned up, but he never said, as the abbot had done – 'I am glad that you have returned, daughter.' Similarly he was polite but unimpressed when, at our departure, the abbot promised that the bells would ring to remind us of the prayers that would speed us on our way.

Jumbled and distorted as my recollections of that Christmas are, I still find them moving and even disturbing, as though they had sunk down into my subconscious and become a dream.

BETTY PAKENHAM-WALSH

My childhood was idyllic. A simple life spent moving from district to district in Burma with my father, who was Sessions Judge. These upheavals were not upsetting, as a retinue of Burmese and Indian servants moved with the family, so routines continued without much change.

In the 1930s there was no electricity up country. 'Tilly' lamps were used, and tin tubs provided baths, the water being heated outside in old Kerosene tins over a wood fire. I can still smell the smoke from these tins when hot water was poured into the tub by the *paniwallah*. Cold water was kept in the bathroom in a large clay pot called a pegu jar.

The climate could be very hot and sticky. Early-morning exercise was important for everybody. For me and my brother John, breakfast followed on the verandah – then lessons with a governess until

from top to bottom

'Our house in Mandalay, about 1930.' (Betty Pakenham-Walsh)

'My parents in their first car in Burma, 1924.' (Betty Pakenham-Walsh).

Betty, Meryl, John and Timothy (left to right) paddling in the Irrawaddy 'when the Seymours came to stay with us'. Around 1932. (Betty Pakenham-Walsh)

The Ava Bridge across the Irrawaddy, 'three more spans still to be built'. Early 1930s. (Betty Pakenham-Walsh).

mid-morning. I played a lot with my dolls; one broke its china head. My mother packed it in a shoe box and posted it to the Dolls' Hospital in London. Six months later it returned, complete with a new china head. As it had travelled both ways by sea (five weeks each way), it was a wonderful day for me, aged seven.

An outbreak of plague in the district of Sagaing caused the medical officer to ask if John and I would come and have the necessary injections done in the bazaar on a platform, to encourage the villagers to come forward. The syringe was very large and filled with thick yellow fluid. When pumped into the arm it came up like a tennis ball, but with a morning off from lessons it was accepted stoically.

When Burma achieved its Independence from India in 1937 my father's job transferred to the Punjab, but both my brother and I were at school in England by then.

HELEN MCLAREN

I was born on the 10 July 1926 at 7A Fytche Road, Rangoon, Burma, and christened Catherine Helen Seton McLaren. My father and mother were Alexander and Catherine McLaren, and my father came to Rangoon after the First World War and joined Stuart Smith and Allen. He was a Chartered Accountant.

I'm afraid I can't remember very much about the first few years, though when I was about four years old we spent a year out at Mingaladon Golf Club, where my father was Secretary, but he still drove into the office every day. I can remember the peacocks we had in our garden. Beautiful birds, but so very noisy. That was the time when my father started me playing golf, and I also had my own caddy! My father was a very good golfer, and I think he was keen for me to start learning at the young age of four. My mother told me about the occasion when they got word that there was a possibility of me being kidnapped! Plans were made that I was to be taken to the halfway house at the ninth hole on the golf course. However, nothing happened, which was just as well, as my mother would not allow my father to load his revolver. Bullets were kept in the dressing table drawer, while Father sat up all night at the other end of the room!!

Our next home was 11 Churchill Avenue, and I have quite a few memories of living there. I had a very attractive Burmese nanny called Ma Shwe, which translated means 'Miss Gold'. She used to wear her hair coiled quite high on her head, and then had flowers hanging down the side. She also wore very colourful *lungyis* and silk *anghis*, which are jackets. I did speak Burmese and Hindustani quite fluently, but sadly do not remember very much any more.

Other memories: the night when a wild cat was caught in the cupboard under the stairs caused great excitement. Also, lying in bed and watching a snake eating all the baby birds that were in a nest near my window. Help didn't come in time to save the birds. Maung Thet and Maung Hala were our house boys, and then we had a cook and a *mali* who looked after the garden, and of course there was Ma

7a Fytche Road,
Rangoon.
(Helen McLaren)

11 Churchill Avenue,
Rangoon.
(Helen McLaren).

Shwe. We also had a driver called Po Soo, who was half-Burmese and half-Chinese, a nightwatchman, and a man who looked after the water pumps that enabled us to have running water for the house.

I went back to Scotland twice. Usually I went in one of the Bibby Boats (the shipping line that went from Rangoon to Liverpool), and, if I remember correctly, called in at Colombo (Ceylon). The other port of call was Port Sudan, where we went out in the glass-bottomed boats and saw the many coloured fish and, of course, coral. Sadly, I don't think that exists any more. Next was Port Said, which had the famous *gully-gully* men who magically produced masses of baby chickens from every pocket. Also, you were able to eat delicious Turkish Delight, some of it made in the shape of mice with string tails.

My second boat trip was when I went home to school. I spent about seven years at the McLaren High School in Callander, Scotland. I had a guardian – a Miss Clark – who looked after girls whose parents were overseas. I saw my parents once in that time, when they came home for six months' leave.

DENNIS POWELL

Holy Innocents' Day 1931 saw my birth at the District Hospital in Toungoo. Fortunately for all concerned, I was not christened Innocent. My father, Edwin Valentine Murray Powell (always known as Val) was District Locomotive Officer for the Burma Railways and stationed at Toungoo. As such he was responsible for all the locomotives in the district, providing all the engine power that the traffic department might need, and ensuring that it was in good repair and up to the requirements of the job.

My childhood recollections really begin (with one or two minor exceptions) with our time at MyitNgè, when my father was firstly DCWS (District Carriage and Wagon Superintendent) and then DYC. DYC stood for DeputY Carriage and Wagon Superintendent, who was one of two deputy heads of the locomotive, carriage and wagon department of the Burma Railways – the other was DYL. As DYC, my father was the *burra sahib* in MyitNgè, which consisted almost entirely of the carriage and wagon worlds, the labour to man it, and the housing to accommodate that labour and its families.

When Father was still DCWS I was about four-and-a-half or five years old, and still in the care of an Indian *ayah*. I can remember nothing of Ayah but, when Father became DYC (though not as a consequence of it!), it became obvious that I was too much of a handful for a woman to handle, and my parents engaged a young Pathan lad of about 15 years old, Mulkh-i-Amman, to watch over me. His job was very largely to see that I did not fall into the local irrigation canals, in which we fished with more enthusiasm than worthwhile results.

They were 'golden days' indeed. MyitNgè was 10 miles from Mandalay, but otherwise in the back of beyond. I think we roamed very widely in the hot dustiness of Burma's dry zone. I suppose there might have been risks to me, but I was never aware of any, and all the world seemed to be friends. There was excitement too. The time we located a wild bees' nest in the tamarind tree beside the DYC's bungalow (two storey, of course) and got some oily rag on the end of a bamboo to smoke the bees out. The honey was thin and brown and so very fragrant! With Mulkh-i-Amman I learned to be rather more fluent in Urdu than I was in English, indeed, I can remember dreaming in Urdu; I also had a smattering of Pushtu. Being, like so many children, an insufferable brat, I was given to correcting my mother and father when they spoke Hindustani. It is a measure of the Indianisation of the Government of Burma that Europeans learned Hindi or Urdu rather than the language of the country. I enjoyed my childhood with Mulkh-i-Amman but, in retrospect, I see it as a pity that I did not have as close contact with a Burmese youth.

Father's home leave of 1938 found me renewing acquaintance with my two sisters, Nancie and Daphne, who had been at school in England since my father's last leave. It was on our disembarkation from the Bibby ship MV *Shropshire* at Plymouth that young Dennis, entering the hotel dining room for breakfast, saw daffodils in the vases on the table and announced, 'Hmm, orchids, I presume?' An elderly gent at an adjacent table nearly had a seizure, but I hadn't seen daffodils before, whereas I was moderately familiar with orchids.

When Father and Mother returned to Burma in spring 1939 I stayed behind to start my schooling. These days, with the speed of jet aircraft to shrink time and distance, it is very hard to remember the parting which was accepted as being so much a part of life. Indeed, my own mother had been separated from her parents for something like seven years; when her father was due for home leave, the First World War had broken out and he was unable to take it for four years. When at last they were reunited Mother had two baby sisters she had never seen! And her mother felt quite unable to tell her the facts of life, after such a long absence. One of the unusual aspects of my parents' courtship was that they read Marie Stopes's book together – in 1920!

One consequence for me of my separation was that, from being fluent in Urdu, I lost all trace of it. I never recovered it, even when back in the East later. I have no conscious memory of it, but I suspect that at the home-school I was at, the use of any language other than English was strongly discouraged for disciplinary reasons, if for no other. It would not have done to have had children carrying on conversations which the staff could not monitor, would it?

Appendix of Authors

PAMELA ALBERT: Born London 1927, only child of Lt. Col. Edward Francis Albert, 7th Rajput Regiment, and his wife Lydian Gladys Ross Perri. Hallett War School, Naini Tal. Married. 2s 1d.

MARION ALEXANDER: Born Kerkeria, Assam 1929, only child of Gordon and Margaret Alexander, Corramore Tea Estate. The New School, Calcutta and Darjeeling. Whincroft Girls' School, Crowborough, Sussex. Women's Royal Naval Service. Nursing 1978–83. Married. 2d.

ANGELA ALLEN: Born Mussoorie 1918, younger daughter of Guy Oldfield Allen, ICS, and his wife Barbara Egerton. Corran School, Watford. Kinnaird Park School, Watford. Saint Anne's College, Oxford. Teacher of German and French. Full-time with Moral Re-Armament Movement, now known as Initiatives of Change. Married. 2s.

DOROTHY ALLEN: Born Mirzapur UP 1911, elder sister of above. Studied piano at Howard-Jones School of Music, London. Worked as a photographer throughout Second World War. Private piano teacher. Married.

ROBERT C. ALTER: Born Srinagar, Kashmir 1926, Son of Reverend D. Emmet Alter, and his wife Martha Payne Alter, Missionaries under United Presbyterian Church. Woodstock School, Mussoorie, both as pupil and as Principal, 1968–78. Church Administrator and Social Worker. Married.

BEATRICE BAKER: Born Kodaikanal 1916, daughter of George Alexander Baker, Owner/Planter Travancore, and his wife Maud Jessie Hooper. Malvern Girls' College. Royal Academy of Dramatic Art. Women's Auxiliary Air Force. Married. 3s.

ROBERT BAKER: Born Kodaikanal 1913, brother of above. King's School, Canterbury. War service in Army. Married.

DOROTHY MARGARET BAKER: Born Ootacamund 1928, elder daughter of Frederick Charles Baker, Customs and Excise, Madras, and his second wife Phyllis May Holton. Bishop Cotton's Girls' High School, Bangalore. London School of Economics BSc (Econ). University of London Institute of Education Graduate Teacher's Certificate 1968 and Diploma in Sociology 1970. Teacher, Secretary and Civil Servant. Married. 1s 1d.

JESSICA MAY BAKER: Born Madras 1930, younger sister of above, Bishop Cotton's Girls' High School, Bangalore. BA (Open University) 1975. Worked for Shell for nearly forty years. Now does voluntary work with Citizens' Advice Bureau and Mediation. Single.

PHILIP BANHAM: Born Poona 1922, son of William John Banham, Indian Police, and his wife Winifred Roberta Waller. Cathedral School, Bombay. Chelmsford College, Ghora Gali. Emergency Commission Indian Army Ordinance Corps. School Master. Married. 2s 1d.

PATRICIA BANHAM: Born Poona 1923, sister of above. St Mary's High School, Poona. Barnes High School, Deolali. VAD Nursing Sister 8th Army North Africa and Palestine. Married. 4ch.

JAMES BENTHALL: Born Calcutta 1933, younger twin son of Sir Paul Benthall KBE, The Bird/Heilgers Group, Calcutta, and his wife Mary Lucy. The New School, Darjeeling. Eton College, Berkshire. Magdalene College, Cambridge. Bird/Heilgers Group, Calcutta. Prep. School Teacher. Married. 1s 1d.

HENRY BERRIFF: Born Simla 1927, elder son of Arthur Berriff, of Alan Henry & Co. The Mall, Simla, later Stores Manager at the Gun Carriage Factory in Jubbulpore and the Railway Repair Shops, and his second wife Elfriede Davison. Christ Church School, Jubbulpore. Bishop Cotton's School, Simla. Apprenticed to The British Thompson-Houston Company, Rugby. Director Cameraman with the Central African Film Unit, Salisbury, Rhodesia. Southern Rhodesian Engineers. Owner of Bridge Film Productions, Salisbury, Rhodesia. Single.

JENNIFER BETTEN: Born Darjeeling 1934, third daughter of Malcolm Betten, tea planter with Williamson and Magor, and his wife Eva. Singamari School, Darjeeling. Author of *In the Shade of Kanchenjunga* (BACSA). Married. 5ch.

JANE BIRKMYRE: Born Calcutta 1929, daughter of Sir Henry Birkmyre, Bart., Chairman and Managing Director, Birkmyre Brothers, Calcutta, Member Bengal Legislative Assembly 1935–44, and his wife, Doris Gertrude Austen Smith (daughter of Colonel Austen Smith, CIE), Assistant Red Cross Commissioner for Military Hospital Welfare, India and Burma, Kaisar-I-Hind Silver Medal. St David's School, Englefield Green. The New School, Calcutta. Singamari, Darjeeling. Evendine Court Domestic Science College, Malvern. Secretary at War Office, London. Married life in Kenya. Married. 2d.

JOHN BLANDY: Professor, CBE, MA, DM, MCh, FRCS, FACS, Hon. FRCSI, born Calcutta 1927, son of Sir Nicolas Blandy, KCIE, CSI, ICS, Governor-elect of Assam, and his wife Dorothy Kathleen Marshall. The New School, Darjeeling. Clifton College, Bristol. Balliol College, Oxford. Consultant Surgeon. Emeritus Professor of Urology, University of London. Hon. Fellow, Royal College of Surgeons, Ireland. Past Vice-President, Royal College of Surgeons. Past President British Association of Urological Surgeons, and much more. Married. 4d.

NANETTE BOYCE: Born Mussoorie 1928, eldest daughter of Brigadier Thomas Walker Boyce, OBE, MC, MM, 14th Punjabi Regiment, and his wife

Heather Baxter. The New School, Darjeeling. MI5 in London and Singapore. Married. 1s 1d.

LORNA BRADBURY: Born Nagpur 1924, daughter of Herbert Edgar Bradbury (born Bellary 1886), Superintendent, Post & Telegraphs, and his wife Daisy Beryl Harvey Johnson. Bishop Cotton School, Nagpur. St Mary's Training College, Poona. School Teacher at Baldwin Girls' School, Bangalore. Married. 1s 2d.

JOAN BRAGG: Born Rawalpindi 1927, elder daughter of Lt. Col. H.V. Bragg, 3rd/9th Jat Regiment, and his wife Bessie Pinkerton. Sheikh Bagh School, Srinagar. Presentation Convent, Srinagar. Teacher of Art and Languages. Married. 2ch.

BOB BRAGG: Born Norwood 1930, brother of above. Sheikh Bagh School, Srinagar. Bedford School. Birkbeck College, London, BSC, MA. RAF pilot. Married twice. 4ch.

HEDI BRAUN: Born Vienna 1936, daughter of Rudolph M. Braun, Engineer, and his wife Elise (Lisl) Herbratschek, Concert Pianist. The New School, Darjeeling. Barnard College and Columbia University, New York. Teacher of Musical Theory at Hunter and Mannes Colleges, US. Married. 1s.

PETER BROADBENT: Born Bournemouth 1933, son of Col. R.B. Broadbent, Bombay Pioneers and Rajputana Rifles, and his wife Jean Thorburn. The New School, Darjeeling and eight others. Royal Naval College, Dartmouth. Captain Royal Navy. OBE 1982. Registrar Institute of Landscape Architects. Married. 1s 1d.

H.C.G. BROWN CBE DSC: Born Rangoon 1918, son of H.C.G. Brown, Deputy Conservator of Port of Rangoon, and his wife Matilda Mann. Hammond's School, Swaffham, Norfolk. Choral Scholar, King's College, Cambridge (Boxing Blue). Director, Burmah Oil Trading Ltd. DSC 1945, CBE 1966. Married.

MICHAEL BRUCE: Born Laheraserai, Dharbanga District, North Bihar 1927, son of Harold Easton Bruce, MC, Deputy Inspector General, Indian Police, and his wife Aileen Fitzgerald. Oratory School, Woodcote. Hallett War School, Naini Tal. Exeter College, Oxford. Lieut. Royal Artillery 1948–50. Director Reinsurance Brokers, London and Vice President, New York. Underwriting Member of Lloyds. Now Freelance Translator, Member of Institute of Translators and Interpreting. Married. 3s 1d.

BARRY BRYSON: Born Weymouth 1929, younger son of Andrew Bryson and his wife Kathleen. Stepson of Reginald Wallace Thom MBE, Divisional Mechanical Engineer North Western Railway, Quetta, Baluchistan. Bishop Cotton's School, Simla. National Service in RASC. Company Secretary. Married. 3d 2s.

SUSAN BURDER: Born Calcutta 1931, elder daughter of Lt. Col. Sir John Burder, Member of Council of State 1943, President Bengal and Associated Chambers of Commerce, India 1943, President Imperial Bank of India 1947, and his wife Betty Bailey. The New School, Calcutta and Darjeeling. PNEU course at Dr Graham's Homes, Kalimpong. St James's, West Malvern. Married. 1s 3d.

CAROLINE BURDER: Born Calcutta 1933, younger daughter of Sir John and Lady Burder, Jardine Skinner & Co. PNEU course at Dr Graham's Homes, Kalimpong. St James's, West Malvern. Married. 1s 1d.

ANN BURKINSHAW: Born Calcutta 1928, only child of Dick Burkinshaw, Jessop & Co., and his wife Kathleen Grimley. The New School, Calcutta and Darjeeling. St Anne's College, Oxford. Her Majesty's Overseas Civil Service, Tanganyika. Foreign and Colonial Office, London. British Oxygen Company Group, London. Married.

ERNEST YOUNG CAMPBELL: Born Sialkot 1917, second son of James Garfield Campbell, and his wife Mabel Young, Missionaries under United Presbyterian Church. Woodstock School, Mussoorie. Wooster College, Ohio. Representative in India of United Presbyterian Church of America. Director of Relief and Rehabilitation in Vietnam. International Church in Bangkok, Thailand. Flood Relief Organisation, Punjab. Conducted Study of Bengal Refugees. Church of North India. Married. 2s 1d.

DONALD CATTO: Born Quetta 1921, son of Major Herbert Catto, Royal Indian Army Service Corps, and his wife. Infants Boarding School, Murree. Bishop Cotton's Day School, Bangalore. Lawrence Schools at Lovedale and Ghora Gali. Commissioned into Indian Army. Served in Burma, Captain 17th Indian Division, later as Major, 23rd Indian Division. Transferred to British Army in 1947, serving mostly overseas. Retired Major. Married. 1s.

BILL CHARLES: Born Poona 1928, son of James Meadows Charles, Sergeant in British Army, 1914–18, later Planter, fruit and dairy Farmer, and his wife, Ethel Gladys Smith. Breeks Memorial School, Ootacamund. Took over father's plantation until 1948. Thomas Cook Financial Services. Married. 2s.

YOMA CROSFIELD: Born Broadstairs 1936, only child of Leonard Crosfield, Burmah and Assam Oil Companies, and his wife Margaret Daniell, Chair of Training, Girl Guides, All-India. The New School, Darjeeling. Effingham House, Sussex. Lady Margaret Hall, Oxford. Editor, Academic Research Assistant, Writer. Divorced. 2d.

ISABEL DAVIDSON: Born Glasgow 1936, only child of John Davidson, Drilling Engineer with Burmah and Assam Oil Companies, and his wife Agnes Calder. Ida Villa, Darjeeling. Laurel Bank School, Glasgow. Glasgow and West of Scotland College of Domestic Science. Institutional Management Association

Course in hotel management and catering. Assistant Caterer Royal Victoria Hospital for Children, London. Part-time Fashion Consultant. Married. 2s 1d.

GEORGE DUNBAR: Born India 1915.

SHEILA FERGUSON: Born Darjeeling 1926, daughter of Lt. Col. Robert Ferguson, Northern Bengal Mounted Rifles, Tea Planter in Dooars 1909–1944, and his wife. Battle Abbey, Sussex. The New School, Darjeeling. Married. 1s 1d.

DAN FERRIS: Born Calcutta 1940, son of Edward Ferris, East India Railway Company, and his wife Iris, Commissioner for Training in Bengal, Bharat Scouts and Guides. St Paul's School, Darjeeling. Highgate School, London. Trinity College, Cambridge. Principal of Language School. Married.

JANE FLEMING: Born Chabua, Assam 1935, daughter of William Fleming CIE, General Manager, The Assam Oil Company Limited, and his wife Jean Lennox Hastings. The New School, Darjeeling. Headington School, Oxford. Royal Academy of Dramatic Art. BBC Production Assistant. Children's Television Recruitment Assistant, BBC. Office Manager, Janssen Pharmaceutical Company Ltd. Divorced. 1s 1d.

LAURENCE FLEMING: Born Shillong 1929, brother of above. The New School, Calcutta and Darjeeling. Repton School, Derbyshire. National Service RAF. St Catharine's College, Cambridge. Author, Artist, Garden Designer. Single.

FAY FOUCAR: Born Moulmein, Burma 1923, daughter of E. C. V Foucar, Barrister-at-law, author of several books on Burma and of the official history of the First Burma Campaign in 1942. Father and two brothers started a timber business in Burma in the 1880s. Private school in Rottingdean. Roedean. Married. 2d.

ADRIAN FRITH: Born Wellington, Coonoor 1928, son of Lt. Col. John Frith, Indian Army, The Baluch Regiment, and his wife Erica Bovey. Winchester College, Hampshire. National Service in Military Police. Queens' College, Cambridge. Bombay Burmah Trading Co., Singapore. Craigmyle Company Ltd, London. Married. 1d.

PATRICK GIBSON: Born Walton-on-Thames 1928, son of Edward Leslie Gibson, The Bombay Burmah Trading Co., and his wife Charlotte Noreen Fuller-Good. Uplands School, Heathfield, Sussex. Highlands School, Kaban Djahe, Sumatra. Hallett War School, Naini Tal. Highgate School, London. 47 years in the Chemical Industry. Author of *Childhood Lost*. Married. 2s 2d.

ELSPET GRAY: Born Inverness 1929, daughter of James MacGregor-Gray, Lloyds Bank, and his wife Elspet Eleanor Morrison. Actress. Married. 2d 2s.

JANE GRICE: Born Calcutta 1935, daughter of William Henry Grice, Managing Director ICI (India) Ltd, Commanding Officer Calcutta Light Horse, and his wife Doris May Walsh. The New School, Darjeeling. St Felix School, Southwold. Ordrey Fleming School of Speech Therapy. Speech Therapist. Married twice. 2s 2d.

JOAN GRIMLEY: Born London 1930, elder daughter of Lt. Col. Harry Bridgeman Grimley MBE (Military), Royal Indian Army Service Corps, and his wife Margaret Elsie Grimley, Pianist. Loreto Convent, Simla. Secretarial Course at Brighton Technical College. Diocesan Office, Lahore. Peabody Trust, Secretary to Director, then Admin Officer. Single.

AURIOL GURNER: Born Calcutta 1927, third daughter of Sir Walter Gurner CSI ICS and his wife Phyllis Mills Carver. Southall, Surrey. Westonbirt, Gloucestershire. The New School, Calcutta and Darjeeling. Garnell College of Education, Roehampton. Lecturer, Further Education, Open University (BA Hons), Teacher of Secretarial Subjects in Technical Colleges. Married. 2d.

LYNETTE GURNER: Born London 1925, elder sister of above. St Monica's, Surrey. Westonbirt, Gloucestershire. The New School, Calcutta and Darjeeling. Garnell College of Education, Roehampton. Lecturer, Further Education, Open University (BA Hons). Married. 2s.

EVELYN ROSE HADLEY: Born Edinburgh 1934, second daughter of Owen Hadley, Chief Accountant Burmah Oil Company, and his wife Effie Richardson. Married.

RUBY HADLEY: Born Rangoon 1921, eldest daughter of Owen Hadley, sister of above. Married. 3d.

BRIAN PETER HASKINS: Born Lewisham 1933, only child of John Begley Haskins, Chief Engineer Oudh & Tirhout and Bengal Nagpur Railways, and his wife Joan Mary Lilley, a professional nurse. Woodstock School, Landour. Portora, Northern Ireland. Loughborough College. Chief Engineer for British Waterways. Married. 1s 1d.

CLARE HAYNES: Born Cork 1921, third daughter of Major Edward John Haynes, IEME (Indian Electrical and Mechanical Engineers) Indian Army, and his wife Marjorie Denning. Convent of Jesus and Mary, Murree. Red Cross VAD 1944–46. Married. 1d.

ANN HENRY: Born Bushey Heath 1925, eldest child of Brigadier T.R. Henry CBE, 8th Punjab Regiment, and his wife Dora Dalton. Uplands School, St Leonard's-on-Sea. Presentation Convent, Srinagar. Hallett War School, Naini Tal. Radio Mechanic in Woman's Auxiliary Corps (India). Trained as Nurse at St Thomas's Hospital, London. Married. 3d.

ROBIN HERBERT CBE: Born London 1934, son of Sir John Herbert GCIE Governor of Bengal, and his wife Lady Mary Fox-Strangways. Singamari,

Darjeeling. Eton College, Berkshire. Royal Horse Guards. Christ Church, Oxford. Chairman, Leopold Joseph Holdings PLC. President and Chairman of Council, Royal Horticultural Society. Divorced. 2s 2d.

CARL HIGGINSON: Born Andal, Bengal 1935, third son of Charles Higginson, Mail Driver on East India and Northern Railways, and his wife Dorothy McCready. Railway Schools at Asansol, Bengal, and Dhanbad, Bihar. St Patrick's High School, Asansol. Girls' High School, Cawnpore. Storeman at Energen Food Limited. Fitter/Machinist (Engineering) at Babcock Wire Equipment Limited. Married twice. 2s 1d.

DICK HINDMARSH: Born Lyme Regis, 1931, son of Lt. Col. J.H.L. Hindmarsh and his wife Phyllis Palmer, National Service in Royal Artillery. University of London. Teacher of English and Physical Education. Examiner in English for University of Cambridge Board. Married.

FRANK HIPPMAN: Born Aldershot 1923, son of Sergeant W. Hippman MM, Royal Fusiliers, and his wife Chrissie Leedham. Lawrence School, Mount Abu. Apprentice RAF Cranwell 1939. Fleet Air Arm 1942–44. Commissioning Course 1956. Flight Lieutenant 1959. Retired from RAF 1978. Technical writer, retired. Married. 3s.

GLORIA HOLLINS: Born Jubbulpore 1927, daughter of Albert G. Hollins, The Great Indian Peninsular Railway, and his wife, Agnes Kenny (born Rangoon 1894). Hebron High School, Coonoor. Lawrence School, Lovedale. Hebron again. Nurse. General Training, St Mary's Paddington. Midwifery at Shoreham-by-Sea and Epsom. Norfolk General Hospital, Ontario. St John's Hospital, Lewisham. Single.

PAMELA HOPKINS: Born Jubbulpore 1932, daughter of Alan Hopkins, Indian Forestry Service, and his wife. St Hilda's, Ootacamund. After marriage, lived mostly in Ghana. Married. 3s.

DONALD FERGUSON HOWIE: Born Meerut 1918, younger son of Staff Sergeant Charles Thomas Howie, the Bedfordshire Regiment, later Regimental Instructor to the Auxiliary Forces, India for the North Western Railway, and his wife Ethel Muriel. Lawrence Royal Military School, Sanawar, Simla Hills. Chelmsford Training College for European Teachers, Ghora Gali, Murree. War Service in Indian Army Ordinance Corps. Royal Army Educational Corps until 1964. Retired Major, later School Teacher. Married. 1s 1d.

HAZEL INNES: Born Ickenham 1930, daughter of Norman Innes, The Gramophone Company, India and London, Lt. Col. Indian Engineers (Emergency Commissioned Officer) and his wife, Daisy Phillips. Mount Hermon School, Darjeeling. Author of *Under the Old School Topee* (BACSA 1990 and 1995). Married.

ELIZABETH IRELAND: Born Scone, Perthshire 1914, only child of John Ireland, Manager, Confectionery Department, East India Distilleries and Sugar Factories, Nellikuppam, Madras, and his wife Bell McGibbon McCormick. Prep School at Coonoor. St Hilda's, Ootacamund. Adcote School, Shrewsbury. Secretarial Training in Glasgow. Finally Secretary to General Manager, Director of Redpath, Dorman, Long Limited, Glasgow. Single.

LAVENDER JAMIESON: Born Edinburgh 1914, younger daughter of Henry William Jamieson, Chief Auditor, Great Indian Peninsular Railway, and his wife Lorna Grieve. School Matron. Red Cross in Belgium. Single.

BARBARA ANN JARDINE: Born Peshawar NWFP 1925, eldest daughter of Lionel Jardine ICS, serving in Lucknow, Peshawar, Dik, Kashmir, Central Provinces and Baroda, and his wife Marjorie. Sherfield School, Simla. Sophia College, Bombay. Married. 2d.

JOHN JUDGE: Born Sydney 1928, eldest son of 'Mick' Judge CIE, MD of Govan Bros Ltd., Delhi & Rampur UP. Sheikh Bagh School, Srinagar. Aitchison College, Lahore. Bradfield College, Berkshire. Royal Navy 1946-83, followed by several civilian jobs. Married. 1d 2s.

DESMOND KELLY MD FRCP FRCPsych: Born Loilem, Shan States 1934. Son of Lt. Col. Norman Kelly OBE, Burma Frontier Service and his wife Betty Megarry. Hallett War School, Naini Tal. King's School, Canterbury. Visiting Professor University College, London. Medical Director, The Priory Hospital, Roehampton. Married. 2s.

MAEVE KELLY: Born Loilem, Shan States, 1933, sister of above. Hallett War School, Naini Tal. Felixstowe College, Suffolk. Journalist and Registered Nurse. Divorced. 4s 2d.

NETTIE LAMONT: Born Glasgow 1926, eldest daughter of Donald Lamont MBE, Shipping Engineer with Simons & Co. Clydeside, and his wife Jane Beattie Wilson. Hebron High School, Coonoor, Women's Auxiliary Corps (India). Domestic Science at Orchard Road College, Edinburgh. Married. 2d.

JOHN LANGLEY: Born Calcutta 1931, only child of Horace Vernon Langley, Eastern Bengal and Assam Bengal Railways, and his wife Mary Audrey Clark. The New School, Calcutta and Darjeeling. Convent, Haflong. Gresham's School, Holt, Norfolk. Royal Naval Air Service. Bournemouth School of Art. School of Architecture, Oxford. Architect. Fellow of Royal Architectural Institute of Canada. Received an Award for his restoration of the Old Masters Galleries in Ontario Art Gallery, Toronto. In Canada since 1957. Married 1s 1d.

JONATHAN LAWLEY: Born Murree 1936, eldest son of Wilfred Lawley OBE, Indian Service of Engineers and his wife Elizabeth Lowis. Sheikh Bagh,

Srinagar. Whitestone School, Bulawayo. Rhodes University, Grahamstown. St John's College, Cambridge. Colonial Service in Africa 1960–69, in business in Africa 1969–94. Africa Director of British Executive Service Overseas 1994–2000. PhD City University 1996. Director The Royal African Society 2000–2003. Married 1s 2d.

ELIZABETH LEIGH: Born Preston 1939, eldest child of Cecil Leigh, Agent, Imperial Bank of India and his wife Eve Ashcroft. Acton Reynold School, Shropshire. Women's Royal Naval Service, Admiralty and Gibraltar. Communications/Secretary, Foreign and Commonwealth Office, Delhi, Budapest, Lagos and Washington D.C. Lived in Canada for six years after marriage. Married.

JEREMY LEMMON: Born Calcutta 1935, third child of Richard Dennis Lemmon, Merchant, and his wife Dorothy Constance Harris. Hilltop School, Kalimpong. Northaw, Kent. Harrow School, Middlesex. Christ Church, Oxford. Head of English at Harrow School for 25 years, Author of several books on the Shakespearian Theatre. Single.

JOHN LETHBRIDGE: Born Leeds 1926, eldest son of Montagu Lethbridge ICS, and his wife Ann Christian. Hebron School, Coonoor. The New School, Calcutta and Darjeeling. Royal Military College, Dehra Dun. Commissioned into Royal Engineers, attached Bengal Sappers and Miners. Trinity College, Cambridge. Chartered Accountant. Married. 1s 1d.

NANCY LLOYD: Born 1918, youngest daughter of Sir Idwal Lloyd ICS and his wife. Teaching Diploma ARCM, teacher of the violin for over twenty years. Married.

RUTH LUCAS: Born Bolton 1917, daughter of Frederick Lucas, Captain Indian Army Royal Engineers and Chief Engineer, Carnatic Mill, Perhambur, Madras, and his wife Sarah Anne Caldwell. St Hilda's, Ootacamund. Adcote School, near Shrewsbury. Skerry's College, Liverpool. Secretary, Ministry of Transport. Teacher of Shorthand, Post Office, London. Village Sub-Post Master. Married. 1s 1d.

JONQUIL MALLINSON: Born Jubbulpore 1930, elder daughter of Lt. Col. Ernest (Simon) Mallinson, 17th Dogra Regiment, Indian Army, and his wife Flora (Pat) Carson. St Joan's School, Srinagar. Rosemead, Littlehampton. Married into Colonial Police Service, living in Kenya, Uganda and Sarawak. Married. 3d.

ORIOLE MALLINSON: Born Srinagar, 1932, younger sister of above and niece of Miss Muriel Mallinson MBE CMS, Principal Sheikh Bagh School for Girls, Srinagar. St Joan's School, Srinagar. Hereford House, Ilfracombe. Limura Girls School, Nairobi. Married life in Bihar, Tanzania and Kenya. Married. 1s.

ROBIN MALLINSON: Born Srinagar (on a houseboat) 1928, elder brother of above and nephew of Sir Charles Carson KCIE OBE ICS, Finance Minister in Gwalior. Breeks Memorial School, Ootacamund. Fettes College, Edinburgh. University College, Oxford (Hockey Blue). National Service in Royal Artillery, 2nd Lieut. serving in Kenya. Chartered Accountant and Finance Director, Alcan Aluminium (Latin America). Married. 4s.

ANN MARINDIN: Born London 1934, elder daughter of F.J. Marindin, Burmah-Shell, and his wife Marcia Gordon Firebrace. St Hilda's, Ootacamund. Married. 1s 1d.

ROBERT MATTHEWS: Born Delhi 1931, second son of Arnold Monteath Matthews, Professor of English at Forman Christian College, Lahore, and his wife Alys Belletti. Lawrence College, Ghora Gali. Managing Director, Deutsche Extrakt Kaffee UK Ltd. Married twice. 3d.

PATRICIA McCOY: Born Bangalore 1928, only child of Captain William James McCoy, Queen Victoria's Own Madras Sappers and Miners, and his wife Florence Brake. Bishop Cotton's Girls' High School, Bangalore. Secretary to Builders Merchant. Married. 1d 1s.

HELEN McLAREN: Born Rangoon 1926, only daughter of Alexander McLaren, Head of A.F. Ferguson & Company, Lahore, and his wife Catherine Mitchell. McLaren High, Callander, Scotland. Mrs Ancrum's School for Young Ladies, Gulmarg, Kashmir and Lahore. Married. 2s 1d.

MOLLY MILNE: Born Rangoon 1927, eldest child of Eric Ivan Milne, Traffic Manager, Burma Railways, and his wife Doris Ransford. Pinewood, Crowborough, Sussex. BBA School, Rangoon. Hallett War School, Naini Tal. Eastbourne School of Domestic Science. Married twice. 2s 2d.

ANN MITCHELL: Born Saharanpur UP 1928, daughter of Harold Mitchell CIE, Indian Police, Deputy Inspector General, Allahabad, and his wife Edna Evadne Bion. Woodstock School, Landour. Council of Europe, Strasbourg. Married. 2s 1d.

MICHAEL MULLER: Born Murree 1930, son of Colonel Hugo Muller, Indian Army, and his wife Veronica Buck. Sheikh Bagh Preparatory School, Srinagar. Wellington College, Berkshire. Jesus College, Cambridge. Consulting Engineer. MA FR Eng FICE. Married. 2d 1s.

MALCOLM MURPHY: Born Madras 1920, son of Joe Murphy, Senior Chargeman, Madras and Southern Mahratta Railway, and Company Sergeant Major Auxiliary Force (India), and his wife Louise Magee. St Mary's European High School, Madras. War Service in Wiltshire Regiment and Indian Army Corps of Clerks. Served on North West Frontier and with Chindits, Burma. International Computers Limited (India), Bombay. Married. 1s.

SHIRLEY ODLING: Born Kalimpong 1926, third daughter of Norman Odling, Architect, and his wife Bunty Graham, daughter of Dr Graham of the Homes. Educated at the Homes, Battle Abbey, Sussex and Sherborne School for Girls, Dorset. Joined Field Artillery Nursing Yeomanry 1944 in UK and returned to India. Married. 2s 1d.

TIMOTHY O'BRIEN: Born Shillong 1929, elder son of Captain Brian Palliser Tighe O'Brien, 2nd Battalion 8th Gurkha Rifles, and his wife Elinor Laura Mackenzie. Wellington College, Berkshire. Corpus Christi, Cambridge. Stage Designer. Married.

IAN O'LEARY: Born Oxford 1927, son of Michael George O'Leary MBE, Lieut. Colonel 8/2 Punjab Regiment, and his wife Daphne Sylvia Osmaston. Hallett War School, Naini Tal. Royal Indian Military College, Dehra Dun. Commissioned into Royal Indian Engineers. Service in Burma and Singapore. Managed a trading company in Nigeria. Pilot's licence in UK. Various employment in USA. Married.

TONY ORCHARD: Born Mombasa, Kenya 1926, elder son of G.L. Orchard, Burmah-Shell Oil Company, and his wife Dorothy Watkins. The New School, Calcutta and Darjeeling. Hilton College, Natal, South Africa. University of London. Director, European New Products Development, Quaker-Europe Oats Company. Married. 2s.

GILLIAN OWERS: Born London 1927, only child of Bernard Charles Owers, Sinclair, Murray of Calcutta, and his wife Millicent Ellacott Pethick. The New School, Calcutta and Darjeeling. School of Art, Calcutta. Ruskin School of Drawing and Fine Art, Oxford. Sculptor and Arts Instructor. Divorced. 4ch.

DESMOND PAILTHORPE: Born at Sea 1922. Retired Major. Lives Lancashire.

BLAKE PINNELL: Born St Leonard's-on-Sea 1925, elder son of L.G. Pinnell CIE ICS, District Commissioner for Chittagong, and his wife Margaret Coxwell. Hurst Court School, Ore, Sussex. The New School, Calcutta and Darjeeling. University of Cape Town, South Africa. Balliol College, Oxford. Economist with Finance Corporation IBM (United Kingdom) and Pilkington Brothers. Married. 1s 1d.

MARTIN PINNELL: Born Darjeeling 1928, younger brother of above. The New School, Calcutta and Darjeeling. Balliol College, Oxford. Computer Systems Engineer. Married. 3d.

SHIRLEY POCOCK: Born Cawnpore 1925, younger daughter of Major S.R. Pocock CBE MC, The Leinster Regiment, The Machine Gun Corps and The Welch Regiment, and his wife Florence Albin. Hallet War School, Naini Tal. Sophia College, Bombay. Associated Advertising Agencies, Simla. Married.

DENNIS POWELL: Born Toungoo 1931, son of Valentine Murray Powell, Chief Operating Superintendent, Burma Railways, and his wife Kathleen Kendall. Bishop Cotton's School, Simla. Felsted School, Essex. Royal Engineers. Data Analyst with Welding Institute.

ANNE PROWSE: Born Ootacamund 1935, elder daughter of Dr Arthur Skardon (Keith) Prowse, Medical Director, The Assam Oil Company, and his wife Joan Willoughby Grant. The New School, Darjeeling. St Hilda's, Ootacamund. Effingham Hall School, Bexhill. Uplyme Domestic Science College. Nursing training Middlesex Hospital, London. Ward Sister to 1961. Married. 1s.

BETTY PAKENHAM-WALSH: Born Rangoon 1926, daughter of Wilfrid Pakenham-Walsh, ICS, and his wife Gwen Elliott. Uplands, Heathfield, Sussex. Tormead, Guildford, Surrey. Mrs Ancrum's Class in Lahore and Gulmarg. Women's Royal Naval Service 1944–46 at Bletchley Park, decoding. Motor Transport Section, Royal Naval Air Direction Centre, Haverfordwest. Married. 2s.

JOHN PAKENHAM-WALSH CB QC: Born Rangoon 1928, younger brother of above. Bradfield College, Berkshire. University College, Oxford. Barrister. Crown Counsel, Hong Kong 1953–57. Parliamentary Counsel, Nigeria 1958–61. Home Office 1961–87. Standing Counsel to General Synod of Church of England 1988–2000. Married. 1s 4d.

PATRICIA RAYNES: Born Rangoon 1932, elder daughter of Charles Raynes, MC King's Police Medal, Deputy Inspector General, Burma Police, and his wife Doreen Heenan. Hallett War School, Naini Tal. Uganda Electricity Board, Kampala. Part-time Secretary at Bracknell College. Married. 2s.

PETER ROBB: Born Ceylon 1927, son of James Alexander Robb, General Manager of ESSO, Ceylon and Bengal, and his wife Dorothy Louisa Bicknell. The New School, Calcutta and Darjeeling. King William College, Isle of Man. National Benzole, Shell and BP. Married. 2s 2d.

RONALD RULE: Born Singapore 1918, son of Malcolm Rule, Operator and Accountant with the Eastern Extension Telegraph Company in Batavia, Singapore and Penang, and his wife Margaret Fitzpatrick. Bishop Cotton's School, Bangalore. Breeks Memorial School, Ootacamund. Deal School, Kent. War Service with the Buffs. British Malayan Administration, Singapore Magistrate. Shell Group from 1949. Married. 3ch.

THELMA SMART: Born Jhansi 1929, daughter of Major J.W. Smart, Royal Army Ordinance Corps, and his wife Leah Mary Carvalho. Convent of Jesus and Mary, Murree. St Mary's Convent, Naini Tal. Married twice, 2d 5s.

LYNETTE SMITH: Born Madura 1931, daughter of Charles Harry Smith (High School, Baldwin's, Bangalore), Special Grade Driver, South Indian Railway, Madura, and his wife Hilda May Cuxton, Steno-Typist at A. &F. Harvey Mills, Madura. St John's Vestry High School, Trichinopoly. London Chamber of Commerce, Madras. Diploma of Short Stories and Creative Writing, Melbourne, Australia. IBM Data Processing, Australia. Private Secretary, Australian Federal Government, Perth, Western Australia. Married twice. 1s 1d.

PADDY SMITH: Born Calcutta 1931, son of Francis Arthur Smith MBE CEng FIMechE, Chief Mechanical Engineer, Bengal and Assam Railway, and his wife Lilian Evelyn. Loreto Convent, Darjeeling. St Paul's School, Darjeeling. Campbell College, Northern Ireland. Naval Architect. Married.

HAZEL SQUIRE: Born Lahore 1928, eldest daughter of Sir Giles Squire, Indian Political Service and future Ambassador to Afghanistan, and his wife Irene Arnold, teacher at a Muslim Girls' School in Hyderabad. Headington School, Oxford. Royal College of Music. Worked with Moral Re-Armament Movement. Married. 2s.

KRISTIN SQUIRE: Born Mount Abu 1930, second daughter of Sir Giles Squire, younger sister of above. Auckland House School, Simla. Badminton School, Bristol. King's College of Household and Social Science, London. Degree in Social Science. Worked in many countries with Moral Re-Armament Movement. Bred and showed Haflinger Ponies. Married.

STAR STAUNTON: Born Assam Jungle, 1922, only child of Major Staunton and his first wife. Convent in Belgium. Married. ch.

BEULAH STIDSTON: Born Lahore 1933, only child of Dr Dudley Stidston, North Western Railway and Major Indian Army, and his wife Elizabeth Violet Brown-James. St Mary's School, Poona. Moved to New Zealand 1948. Chartered Accountant, New Zealand. Company Accountant, Australia. Judged Australian Cattle Dogs at Crufts, 2002. Married twice.

PATRICK HUGH STEVENAGE: Born Bangalore 1922, younger son of Emanuel Anthony Stevenage, Captain, Senior Assistant Surgeon, Indian Medical Department, and his wife Helena Augusta Rylands. Loyola College, Madras. MA (Econ). Fellow of Association of Certified and Corporate Accountants. Senior Finance Officer, British Railways Board. Author of *A Railway Family in India* (BACSA). Married twice. 2s 2d.

DAVID MICHAEL THOM: Born Quetta 1938, son of Reginald Wallace Thom MBE, Divisional Mechanical Engineer, North Western Railway, and his second wife Kathleen. Half-brother to Barry Bryson. Presentation Convent, Rawalpindi. Karachi Grammar School. Hardeys School, Dorchester. Heles School, Exeter. National Service RAF. Architectural Consultant. Married. 4s 1d.

GRETA THOM: Born Rawalpindi 1930, daughter of Francis Thom, Assistant Mechanical Engineer, North Western Railway, and his wife Audrey Grassby. Auckland House School, Simla. Property Negotiator. Church Organist. Musical Director of a Gilbert and Sullivan Society. Divorced. 2s 1d.

VALERIE THURLEY: Born Bangalore 1934, daughter of S.J. Thurley OBE, Principal of Lawrence College, Ghora Gali, and his wife Doreen McLeish Game. Lawrence College, Ghora Gali. Married. 1s 5d.

LAVENDER TODD: Born Quetta 1926, younger daughter of Sir Herbert Todd KCIE ICS, Resident for the Madras States 1943, Resident for the Eastern States 1944 (later Chief Representative, Iraq Petroleum Company, Baghdad), and his wife Nancy, second daughter of Col. A.F. Pullen, Commanding Officer, Royal Artillery, Rangoon (awarded the Kaisar-i-Hind Gold Medal and the Red Crescent for her work in the Second World War). Godolphin School, Salisbury. 'Sherfield', Delhi and Simla. Women's Auxiliary Service (Burma) 1943. Married. 1s 1d.

JOAN TOFT: Born Eastbourne 1926, eldest daughter of Walter Toft, Senior Partner, Price, Waterhouse, Peat & Company, Calcutta, and his wife Kathleen Kearney. Chartwell, Westgate-on-Sea. St Bridget's, Bexhill. The New School, Calcutta and Darjeeling. Teacher's Training Course at Bishop Sutton School, Alresford, Hampshire. Later ran her own Riding School, first at Alresford, then at Fordingbridge. Single.

PATRICIA TOFT: Born Cowley, Middlesex 1930, second daughter of Walter Toft, sister of above. The New School, Darjeeling. Nazareth Convent, Ootacamund. Wessex School of Dancing, Bournemouth. International Ballet School, London. Ballet Teacher. Aromatherapist. Married. 1s 3d.

SALLY TOFT: Born Cowley, Middlesex 1934, youngest daughter of Walter Toft, sister of above. The New School, Darjeeling. Lowther College, Abergele. London College of Secretaries. Secretary to Bishop Trevor Huddlestone. Married. 1s 1d.

MARK TULLY: Born Calcutta 1935, eldest son of William Tully, CBE, Gillanders, Arbuthnot, Calcutta, and his wife Patience Betts. The New School, Darjeeling. Marlborough College, Wiltshire. The Royal Dragoon Guards. Trinity Hall, Cambridge. Joined BBC in 1964 and became their Chief of Bureau in New Delhi. Author, Journalist and Broadcaster. Knighted 2002. Married. 2s 2d.

ROY ELMO DE VANDRE: Born Sibi, Baluchistan 1926, son of Frederick Charles Valentine Downes, Loco-Foreman North Western Railway, and his wife Janet Maude Stringer. Lawrence College, Ghora Gali. St Anthony's High School, Lahore. Chelmsford College. Commissioned into Indian Army, 10th Gurkha Rifles. Transferred to British Army Sherwood Forresters. Wounded in

Korea. Colonial Police, Kenya and Uganda. Later Dunlop and British Leyland. Married. 2s 8d.

BETSY VICKERS: Born Windsor 1927, daughter of O. Lionel Vickers, Methodist Missionary Society, and his wife Bertha Isabella Aitken. Hebron High School, Coonoor. Edgehill College, Bideford. Hebron again. Worked as a Secretary in The Gambia, then for the World Wildlife Fund as a volunteer for 15 years. Married.

HILARY VIRGO: Born Calcutta 1927, only child of Sidney Virgo, Bank Manager with Imperial Bank of India, and his wife Rita Hay. High Trees School, Horley. The New School, Calcutta and Darjeeling. Bournemouth School of Art. Central School of Art, London. Painter, Theatre Costume Designer. Fellow of Guild of Glass Engravers. Single.

NICOLE WALBY: Born Antwerp 1926, elder daughter of Herbert Walby DSO MC Croix-de-Guerre, Manager of Jenson & Nicholson Ltd (paints, varnishes etc) Calcutta, and his wife Marie Magdeleine Ville. The New School, Darjeeling. Slade School of Art, London. Ecole des Beaux Arts, Paris. Worked in a textile studio in Paris. Art Teacher in London. Married. 2s 1d.

THEON WILKINSON MBE: Born Cawnpore 1924, son of Harold Arthur Wilkinson CBE, Managing Director of Begg, Sutherland & Company Ltd (Agents for Cotton, Electricity, Sugar etc) and his wife Ruby Georgina Butterworth. Radley College, Abingdon. St Paul's School, Darjeeling. Captain, 3rd Gurkhas. Worcester College, Oxford. District Commissioner, Kenya. Personnel Management, various organisations. Founder of BACSA 1976. MBE 1986. Married. 1s.

ZOE WILKINSON MBE: Born Cawnpore 1922, sister of above. Wycombe Abbey, Bucks. MBE 1958 for work in India at the United Kingdom Citizens Association School (now Shieling House), a community enterprise. Author of *Traders and Nabobs: The British in Cawnpore 1765–1857* and *Boxwallahs: The British in Cawnpore 1857–1901*. Married. 2s 1d.

FRANCES WINDRAM: Born Holywood, Co. Down 1929, Daughter of Major William Windram, Royal Inniskillings, and his wife Jessie Hadland. Hebron School, Coonoor. Wellesley School, Naini Tal. Hallet War School, Naini Tal. Women's Royal Naval Service 1949–66. Married. 1s.

SHEILA WRIGHT-NEVILLE: Born London 1927, elder daughter of Col. V.R. Wright-Neville, 5th/2nd Punjab Regiment, and his wife, Gwenneth Northe. The Old Vicarage School, Richmond, Surrey. The New School, Calcutta and Darjeeling. Secretarial College, London. Managed an antiquarian bookshop with international mailing list. Human Resources Officer with Provincial Government. Married. 1s 1d.